Socialism:
What Went Wrong?

Socialism:
What Went Wrong?

An Inquiry into the Theoretical and
Historical Sources of the Socialist Crisis

Irwin Silber

Pluto  Press
LONDON • BOULDER, COLORADO

First published 1994 by Pluto Press
345 Archway Road, London N6 5AA, England
5500 Central Avenue, Boulder, Colorado 80301, USA

98 97 96 95 94
7 6 5 4 3 2 1

British Library Cataloguing in Publication Data
is available from the British Library

Library of Congress Cataloging in Publication Data
    Silber, Irwin, 1925–
    Socialism—what went wrong? : an inquiry into the theoretical and
historical sources of the socialist crisis / by Irwin Silber.
    295pp. 22cm.
    Includes bibliographical references
    ISBN 0–7453–0715–9 (hardback)
    1. Socialism—History. 2. Communism—History. 3. Post-communism.
I. Title. II. Title: Socialism.
HX36.S545   1994
335'.009—dc20   94–18170
                                                                      CIP
    ISBN 0 7453 0715 9 hardback

Designed and produced for Pluto Press by
Chase Production Services, Chipping Norton, OX7 5QR, England
Printed in the EC by TJ Press, Padstow

Contents

DEDICATION

To my grandson Benjamin Silber Hutchins who, for me, personifies those chapters which remain to be written.

Preface

Since meaningful communication requires a common language, let me make clear at the outset how certain ideologically charged words and phrases are used in this book.

The use of the terms socialism and socialist in the text do not constitute a value judgment. They refer to the idea of socialism, the movement for socialism and societies which have generally been considered 'socialist'. The term 'actually existing socialism' is not (despite the quotation marks) a sarcasm; in fact, while obviously containing an implicit irony, the phrase itself was coined by Soviet Marxist-Leninists and was widely used by the Communist Party of the Soviet Union (CPSU) and its supporters in polemics with those who postulated a model of socialism significantly different from the system developed in the Soviet Union. Its point was that various alternatives to the Soviet-derived model existed only in the minds of their advocates, while 'actual socialism' existed in the real world.

Marxism-Leninism refers to the theoretical construct which emerged in the Soviet Union after Lenin's death; this incorporated Stalin's theories of 'socialist construction' and subsequent theories developed by the CPSU and accepted by the constituent parties of the Third International and its successor, the International Communist Movement. Other ideological claims on Marxism-Leninism are referred to by more specific appellations – Trotskyism, Maoism, and so on.

When capitalized, the International Communist Movement refers to the formal organizational structure of the pro-Soviet Communist Parties. In lower case, the international communist movement is a more generic term referring to the general movement for communism.

Emphases in quotations are always in the original unless otherwise indicated.

The text contains a handful of frequently used acronyms: CPSU for Communist Party of the Soviet Union; CPUSA for Communist Party of the US; NEP for the New Economic Policy; RSDLP for the Russian Social Democratic Labor Party. See also the bibliography at the end of this volume for acronyms used to refer to a number of frequently cited books and periodicals in the footnotes.

Aside from the printed sources referred to in the text, this book is informed by the experiences of a lifetime in the socialist cause. From 1941 to 1958 I was an active member of the Young Communist League and then the Communist Party in the US. In those years I was a section organizer in the party's Cultural Division, a writer for the *Daily Worker*, and the organizer/producer of a number of large-scale Communist Party meetings and celebrations. From 1951 to 1967, I was the editor of the magazine *Sing Out!* which – in addition to publishing folk songs and leftwing political songs – ran a booking agency for blacklisted artists and organized the popular 'hootenannies' of the 1950s.

In the late 1960s, I became the Cultural Editor and subsequently Executive Editor of the *Guardian* for a period of eleven years. From the early 1970s until roughly 1987 I was an active figure in various attempts to organize what I thought would be an alternative to the CPUSA. Since 1990 I have been an editor of *Crossroads* magazine. Particularly important in these experiences were not only discussions and debates related to the questions and issues considered in these pages, but a prolonged firsthand encounter with the principles of Marxism and Marxism-Leninism on both a theoretical and a practical basis.

This work is also informed by extended visits to several Communist countries – in particular, Cuba, China, Vietnam and the Soviet Union – providing me the opportunity to engage in lengthy dialogues on theory and politics with a number of prominent scholars, intellectuals, artists and party officials.

Of particular importance was a six-week trip to the Soviet Union in 1989 at a time of flourishing society-wide debate concerning the socialist experience and the problems of Marxist-Leninist theory. By that time I had developed a concept and outline for a book I then called *Gorbachev's Revolution in Marxism* which gradually evolved into this volume.

It was during that trip that I first had the opportunity to exchange views with scholars, journalists and political figures whose entire lives had been spent in a socialist society and who were grappling with the crisis of socialism in personal as well as theoretical terms. Among those whose thinking particularly enriched my own were: Vladimir Amelin (Professor at the Moscow Higher Party School); Professor Solomon Gililov (Institute of Social Sciences attached to the Central Committee of the CPSU); Siim Kallas (Chairman, Estonia Trade Union Council; People's Deputy of the USSR); Alexander Kabokov (novelist and journalist at *Moscow News*); Boris Kagarlitsky (important figure in the socialist opposition); Viktor Kisselov (historian, Institute of Economics of the World Socialist System); Alexander Koltakchan (staff member for two People's Deputies; Afghanistan veteran); Viktor Krivotorov (Institute for Foreign Economic Relations); Boris Kurashvili (Institute of State and Law); Sergei Kurginyan (theater director); Valeri Kuvakin (Chair, History of Russian Philosophy, Moscow State University); Julia Latynina (sociologist); Valentina Levina (Editorial Board, *Social Sciences Today*); Xenia Malo (sociologist); Vladimir Posner; Alexander Prokhanov (Editor-in-Chief *Soviet Literature*; prominent nationalist); William Smirnov (Vice-President, Soviet Political Science Association); Yuri Zamoshkin (US-Canada Institute). These identifications reflect the positions they held at the time of our meeting in 1989.

In addition, Fred Weir, then the Moscow correspondent for the *Canadian Tribune*, and his wife Masha, who comes from a distinguished Armenian revolutionary family, were enormously helpful in facilitating my work in the Soviet Union. So too was Natasha Perova, then the English Language editor of *Soviet Literature*, who rendered invaluable assistance in tracking down many of the people I interviewed, arranging for meetings and, in a number of cases, acting as translator for our conversations.

Likewise helpful were Arkady Kudrya of the Novosty Press Agency; Risto Reppo (Moscow correspondent for a Finnish left newspaper); Malik Rozykulov of Radio Tashkent; Irakli Aneli, a leading architect and city planner in Tblisi; Walter Ojakaar who hosted a popular jazz program in Tallinn; and my old friend William Mandel of Berkeley, who shared with me the names and phone numbers of his extensive contacts in the Soviet Union.

A number of friends – Muhammad Ahmad, Ralph Beitel, Max Elbaum, David Engelstein, Elizabeth Martinez, Rob Prince and Herman and Julia Schwendinger – read the manuscript at various stages and offered me their criticisms and suggestions.

Some of the material in this book appeared in less elaborated form in the pages of the newspapers, *Frontline* and the *Guardian* and in *Crossroads* magazine. The general dialogue promoted in *Crossroads* on the socialist crisis has been extremely useful in helping to shape my own ideas – as have the lively discussions I have participated in along with my fellow editors of that periodical.

The interaction with and encouragement offered by my dear friend Carolyn Mugar has been especially valuable.

Finally, thanks to my wife, Barbara Dane, who wanted me to write this book and then had to abide its demands for nearly five years – but mostly for being who she is.

Irwin Silber,
Oakland, California
March 1994.

Introduction

History does not forgive a large-scale political movement such as ours a wrong perception of reality or the advancement of false slogans.

Amath Dansokho, General Secretary of the Central Committee of the Party of Independence and Labor of Senegal.[1]

A work of this kind requires of the author a forthright statement of purpose. Mine can be simply put. Convinced that the world has not heard the last of the socialist project, I believe it is now incumbent on those of us who worked for and devoted our lives to the socialist cause to undertake a rigorous – I would say merciless – analysis of why the first extended attempt to build a socialist society failed. Such an inquiry, in my view, is the indispensable initial step toward rejuvenating the socialist movement and making it a political force in the world once again.

While such a goal and the assumptions behind it situate this undertaking as a conversation among socialists, it should nevertheless be of interest to others beside the veterans of the socialist cause. For better or worse, socialism and the philosophy behind it have been a powerful influence in the world for almost 150 years. Understanding its history, its theoretical disputes and sectarian quarrels, its achievements and its failures is, therefore, a challenge that may well make this colloquy worth listening in on even by those who do not identify with its purposes.

The Socialist Crisis

Plumbing the depths and complexities of the socialist crisis is not an easy task. Many on the left simply want to put the painful events of the last few years behind them and focus instead on more immediate political enterprises. Others are understandably fearful of a discussion that might lend credence to the surge of capitalist triumphalism presently sweeping the ruling classes of the existing order. For some – reflecting the ingrained habits of a lifetime, to say nothing of decades of Marxism-Leninism's dogmatic overload – the prospect of braving a relatively uncharted world is too unsettling to consider. Nor can one simply overlook the inertia of career considerations in trying to understand why many old communist leaders refuse to confront the depths of the calamity which has overtaken this once-powerful movement.

Nevertheless, facts must be faced. 'Actually existing socialism' and the alternative world system it supposedly represented are gone. Its flagship and mainstay – the Soviet Union – has disintegrated into a host of contending countries and an even larger array of autonomy-seeking nationalities and regions.

Swept away in largely bloodless revolutions their ruling Communist Parties could no longer hold back, Moscow's socialist dependencies in Eastern Europe have likewise been removed from history and are now reeling off into a variety of scenarios for reestablishing capitalism. Those socialist countries whose communist regimes continue to hold power are, in varying degrees, turning more and more to capitalist enterprise and private property relations in order to survive. Without exception, those Third World countries whose 'non-capitalist paths of development' put them in the orbit of the world socialist system have also abandoned that always dubious but now totally untenable and fruitless course. And that construct of Communist Parties nominally united in a single International Communist Movement has likewise fallen apart, most of its constituent organizations themselves rendered futile by their own internal divisions.

The once-powerful mass Communist Parties of Italy, France, Japan and Spain are likewise testament to the socialist crisis as they too have suffered an erosion of their social base. Their only successes – as in Italy – have come about to the extent that they have departed significantly from their ideological histories. In the United States, socialism is so marginal to both intellectual discourse and the real motion of politics as to be virtually irrelevant. The most troubling development of all, perhaps, is that socialism has lost credibility with the one force in contemporary society for whom it was supposed to be its natural magnet – the working class.

The socialist movement and the socialist idea are also in a state of disarray. None of the politically powerful European socialist parties have succeeded in moving their own countries closer to socialism, even when they have taken power in the parliamentary sense. If anything, they have lost considerable credibility even in their natural working-class base as their programs and policies of social reform have been unable to survive the vicissitudes of capitalism's cyclical ups and downs.

These dramatic events and the accompanying disarray of the political forces associated with Soviet socialism have altered the world's political map in ways that were unimaginable a decade ago. No one can safely predict what new socio-economic arrangements will replace 'actually existing socialism'. But one thing seems certain. The model of socialism developed in the Soviet Union and subsequently imposed on the 'socialist camp' has no future. Inevitably, the passing of 'actually existing socialism' has also undermined Marxism-Leninism, the theoretical construct which rationalized this system and became its ideological touchstone. One would have to sever completely the relationship between theory and practice to conclude otherwise.

The challenge we socialists face is not so much to determine whether an obituary is called for – historical circumstance has already performed that rite – as to undertake a postmortem. For without an understanding of why the first significant challenge to capitalist world hegemony collapsed, socialism will remain vulnerable to the very cancers which finally overwhelmed the Soviet-style socialist model and the Marxist-Leninist theoretical system which exalted it.

The obvious question is: what went wrong? With no small measure of justification, the communist movement has traditionally attributed the difficulties of 'actually existing socialism' to the machinations of the West. But in time it became increasingly clear that just as the 'Soviet menace' was used to sustain and expand a mammoth military establishment in the US, so the specter of the CIA and an ever-scheming and hostile world imperialist system was used to fuel a culture of political repression in the Soviet Union and to explain away every flaw in what was otherwise deemed to be a near-perfect system. Such alibis no longer ring true. Today it is fairly obvious that a pattern of decay and stagnation had effectively undermined the system's economy and political institutions long before Mikhail Gorbachev openly acknowledged socialism's true state of affairs.

That the communist regimes of Eastern Europe should fall apart when it became apparent that Soviet troops were not about to rescue them should not be surprising. Although the socialism imposed by Stalin and reinforced by subsequent Soviet governments had brought about many improvements in people's lives, these systems never had a popular political base. Their governing parties always depended on Moscow's approval and, ultimately, its military might.

But the Soviet Union had had its own revolution and had managed despite the staggering human costs of Stalin's authoritarian rule – to transform a vast semi-feudal empire into a modern superpower in less than 50 years. In the course of a single decade (1930–40), it had achieved a level of industrialization which brought it within hailing distance of the most developed capitalist countries. Where pre-revolutionary Russia had been brought to its knees in World War I, Soviet armies played the main role in defeating Hitler's juggernaut in World War II. And, popular prejudices to the contrary, Soviet socialism had dramatically improved the conditions of life for the vast majority. But that system too collapsed. It did not fall to an invading army, nor was it consumed in a bloody civil war. Nevertheless, it disintegrated so rapidly and with such little warning that the world was left breathless even as it struggled to grasp the full historical consequences of the debacle. How is this to be explained?

For those who see the capitalist social and political order as the final fulfillment of historical possibility, the question is not at all perplexing. They have long argued that socialism is an inherently unsound system and that its vision of social cooperation for the social good will never work because it cannot motivate people in the way that private gain can. Naturally, they now feel vindicated. And even those of us who continue to subscribe to the socialist idea must acknowledge that in so far as this thesis assumes that the Soviet system was the prototype of socialism, it cannot be lightly dismissed.

Inevitably, the search for answers to this dilemma invokes feelings of trepidation in those who continue to believe that, whatever one calls it, a more equitable social order than capitalism is both necessary and possible. Have we been wrong in holding to this belief? Is the world destined never to go beyond the morass of privilege for the few and want for the many, present throughout recorded history but seemingly brought to new heights of inequity in the capitalist era? This challenge confronts not only those who believed that 'actually existing socialism' was the harbinger of humanity's future, but even those who never considered the Soviet system socialist in the first place.

In this light, the more particular aim behind this inquiry is to put to rest once and for all the dubious legacy of anachronistic theoretical doctrine which – in its hyphenation of Marxism and Leninism – became the sacred text of the only kind of socialism the world has heretofore seen. For I am convinced that socialism will not become a politically relevant vision once again unless its advocates can free themselves from the twin shadows of the Soviet prototype and its Marxist-Leninist hagiography.

Still, while Marxism-Leninism now enjoys little credibility in socialist ranks, it will not be so easy to dislodge. For a perspective of fundamental social change cannot develop in an ideological vacuum. And in the absence of a credible alternative, the assumptions of the past will continue to hover over the socialist movement.

Even in the midst of their theory's ruins, some number of apparently unfazed Marxist-Leninists continue to hold out for their old-time religion, arguing that with a reassertion of traditional ideological authority, the axioms of yesteryear will once again demonstrate their validity. Arguing that the old Soviet model encompasses the fundamental characteristics of a new socialist order, they are sure that the Soviet debacle was brought on by the 'opportunist' – if not conspiratorial – machinations of Mikhail Gorbachev and other pseudo-reformers who had been enlisted in the cause of capitalist restoration.

Others argue that a presumably healthy Marxist-Leninist baby can still be rescued from the murky bathwater in which, they acknowledge, it has been immersed. Still others fear that tampering with – let alone renouncing – Marxism-Leninism will lead to the abandonment of socialism. But the greatest danger to the socialist cause, by far, is that its proponents will remain locked into a mode of thinking which has clearly reached an impasse.

The challenge facing those of us who find both capitalist triumphalism and Marxist-Leninist dogmatism unacceptable is no small one.

We may believe that capitalist celebrations of the death of socialism are presumptuous, but the fact remains that, historically speaking, the Soviet collapse undermines the claim that socialism has been 'verified'. That assertion no longer has substance. As was the case prior to 1917, Marx's historical paradigm in which socialism is seen as the scientifically decreed next stage of human development after capitalism is, once again, only a theory; and socialism itself still remains to be invented. As a result, tens of millions who might otherwise be enlisted in the socialist cause are more likely than ever to dismiss socialism as an unrealizable dream.

Nor is there any reason to believe that the failed concepts of the past will solve the present socialist crisis or provide the ideological underpinning for a politics capable of reawakening the socialist vision and changing the world.

Of course, the present discourse in the socialist movement did not begin when the Berlin Wall came down and communist regimes began falling in Eastern Europe in 1989. Some socialists have had a critique of long standing, going back not only to the days of Stalin but to Lenin as well. For many, disenchantment began in 1939 with the Nazi-Soviet pact, or in 1956 with Khrushchev's secret speech exposing Stalin's crimes. For others, it was the Soviet invasion of Czechoslovakia in 1968. The rise of Solidarity in Poland was another turning point highlighting socialism's lack of a popular base in the very countries where it supposedly existed. And it is safe to say that all of us were provoked by the dramatic changes in the Soviet Union in the course of Mikhail Gorbachev's star-crossed attempt to overhaul a society whose economic stagnation was closely and inexorably linked to its mechanisms of political repression and its climate of intellectual suffocation.

However, this colloquy is also based on the historic failure of every trend in socialism: not only the Marxism-Leninism which constituted Stalin's theoretical legacy to his successors in both the Soviet Union and the International Communist Movement, but the failure of any to transform the socialist vision into a demonstrably viable alternative to capitalism.

Still, the disintegration of the 'socialist camp' and the discrediting of the Soviet socialist model does not guarantee eternal life to capitalism. On the contrary: I remain convinced that, as with all previous modes of production, that system too will reach its terminus. For, despite a remarkable history in which it drastically altered the terms and conditions of human existence, capitalism continues to evidence deep-seated system-threatening contradictions. Its revolutions in science and technology have brought the planet to the point where its unsupervised economic activities now threaten human existence, even while its enormous economic and political power can frustrate efforts to check its destructive potential. Likewise, capitalism's inner logic constantly drives it toward an ever-deepening chasm between huge individual wealth for a relative handful and abject misery for hundreds of millions. So far, capitalism has managed to survive these crises and even use them to fine-tune itself. But the human cost has been staggering, a condition made the more bitter as it becomes clear that capitalism itself has brought into being the material basis for a society in which all human beings have the possibility for secure and rewarding lives.

We can expect, therefore, that the conflicting pulls between capitalism's inherent rapaciousness and popular discontent with the limited share of the collectively produced social product available for people's needs will intensify. Under these conditions, the yearning for an alternative social order will again appear and take a political form. It is this reality – not Marxism nor any variant thereof – which gives rise to the search for an alternative. And that search will become a potent political force no matter what the present generation of socialists does.

In that sense, the reappearance of a viable socialist movement (or movements) is not dependent solely or even mainly on the subjective activities of those who have come through the socialist experience. We can contribute to that inevitable renewal by passing on the insights – positive as well as negative – to be derived from our common history. But movements to replace capitalism with a more equitable (and, yes – despite the Soviet debacle – a more efficient) social arrangement are sure to be a permanent feature of the world's political landscape so long as capitalism rules.

But Was It Socialism?

I am not unaware of the fact that many who consider themselves socialists will take exception to the title of this book. Some argue that there wasn't anything fundamentally wrong with 'actually existing socialism'. If you believe there was, declares US Communist Party head Gus Hall, 'You are limited to the concept that the crisis is caused by the systemic flaws in socialism.' [2] (It seems to have escaped Hall's notice that his equation of the recently existing socialism of the Soviet Union with some quintessential model of a socialist system actually reinforces the idea that there is something inherently unsound in socialism.) Others hold that it wasn't socialism that failed but something else; and that dignifying the old system by referring to it as such is a disservice to 'true' socialism. Both these approaches, it seems to me, underestimate the depths of the socialist crisis.

The first, by asserting that a genuinely new and more progressive mode of production can be undermined so readily simply by policy errors and human weakness, flies in the face of a materialist analysis of history. Attributing an epoch-shaking event such as the collapse of a supposedly 'irreversible' new mode of production to the corruption or plotting of a handful of individuals would seem to be of a piece with the contention that the emperor's new clothes, however elusive to the eye, were still at the cutting edge of high fashion; a tribute to the power of faith, perhaps, but hardly a serious social observation.

Long before Gorbachev broke the news that the Soviet system was in an advanced state of torpor, all but the most blissfully optimistic of the Marxist-Leninist faithful could see that its planned economy was far from problem-free and that it was obviously not a paragon of democracy. The obligatory ideological conformity of its public life was unappealing to the outside world and, what was worse, suffocating to the intellectual and artistic initiative of its own people; nor did the heatedly denied charges of anti-semitism and national chauvinism seem to be without foundation. Certainly the crude suppression of views contrary to those of the ruling Communist Parties and the repeated use of Soviet armed might to keep Eastern European communist governments in power strongly suggested that 'actually existing socialism' might not have the boundless popular support those governments claimed.

On the other hand, those who would deny the failed system even the term socialist are undertaking the dubious task of rewriting history. Of course, no one likes to be associated with a loser. But socialism, after all, is not only a social system; it is also a movement. That movement – at least one section of it – directed a revolution which it called socialist and then established a new country called a Union of Soviet Socialist Republics, even when those who designated it as such were aware of the fact that theirs was not yet a fully socialist society in an economic sense. Lenin pledged to build socialism in the new country and to render assistance to the socialist revolution elsewhere. And the system built by Stalin had many features usually associated with socialism – particularly the centrally planned and directed economy and the abolition of private property. Finally, the USSR was generally referred to as a socialist country and much of the world accepted this as a legitimate descriptive term.

It also strikes me that there is something Plato-like in the intimation that socialism in some idealized state is already known and that it is now up to humanity to match reality to this ideal. Belief in or search for a socialist blueprint is the certain road to political futility or, what is worse, one more attempt to impose a preconception of future society on history. If a viable socialism is ever to appear, its form will be realized in the course of tackling the practical problems of constructing not only a more just but a more efficient society.

In the detachment that can only come with distance, history may well conclude that the Soviet-style system was not simply a false start but an elaborate ideological cover for some kind of hybrid that was neither capitalist nor socialist. For the moment, however, socialists – even those who were sharply critical of 'actually existing socialism' and have legitimate reason to feel that recent events have vindicated their views – must take responsibility for what has been propounded in our name. Otherwise we run the risk of fulfilling the historic dictum (if I may slightly amend Santayana) that those who do not understand the past may be condemned to recreate it.

The Ideological Component

Assuming therefore that the Soviet system represented at least a failed attempt to build socialism, it is still essential that we determine the sources of that failure. With this in mind, I find myself returning again and again to Marxism – the theoretical framework which was credited with guiding the Bolshevik seizure of power in Russia in 1917, the construction of socialism in the Soviet Union and subsequently the development of a world socialist system. An analysis of that theory as it evolved from Marx and Engels through the particular historical continuity represented by Lenin, Stalin, Brezhnev and the Soviet-sponsored International Communist Movement is the substance of this book.

In focusing on the ideological component of the socialist crisis, I do not mean to suggest that an analysis of Marxist theory will, by itself, show what went wrong. But theory – and not simply as a statement of ideological principles – has played a most important practical role in the socialist tradition.

Marx and Engels, critical of the unrealistic utopianism characteristic of nineteenth-century socialism, sought to bring scientific principles into the class struggle and their projected new social order. Similarly, Lenin's theoretical writings are principally concerned with making realistic assessments of the state of capitalism and providing a foundation for consciously directed practical political activity. But the main thrust of this examination is directed at the theoretical construct developed after Lenin's death: Marxism-Leninism.

Nominally a synthesis of the main conceptions developed by Marx and Lenin, Marxism-Leninism came into being principally as a function of Stalin's attempt to legitimize his claim to power. But under Stalin's tutelage, Marxism was transformed into a crude and highly schematic doctrine shorn of the scientific rigor, crucial qualifications, shadings and nuances characteristic of Marx's own work. Similarly, its embrace of Leninism was highly selective, taking many of Lenin's ideas out of their historical context and gliding over others which ran counter to Stalin's own views.

Used to justify Stalin's policies – in particular, his conception of socialism – Marxism-Leninism became over time not so much the theory which guided the Soviet socialist project as its idealized reflection and ultimate ideological authority. No change could take place in the societies of 'actually existing socialism' without reference to one of its texts; nor could one aspire to positions of trust and privilege without proclaiming adherence to its principles. Marxism-Leninism provided the sole theoretical framework for public discourse in politics, history, science and the arts. Whatever the communists accomplished was attributed to it; whatever mistakes or setbacks occurred were due to departures from its precepts.

Here it may be useful to recall Boris Ponomarev, a name to be reckoned with in the pre-Gorbachev years. A member of the Soviet Communist Party's Politburo and its foremost theoretician, Ponomarev was the arch-defender of the Leninist faith and the ideological scourge of the international communist movement. His ubiquitous commentaries were hailed as the last word in Marxist-Leninist theory and dutifully repeated and paraphrased throughout the communist world. If Marxism-Leninism can be said to have had one voice more official than any other, it would be Ponomarev's. Thus spake the Soviet Zarathustra in 1980:

> Everything the Soviet Union and the fraternal countries have achieved would have been inconceivable without the Marxist-Leninist revolutionary theory. There is no other theory confirmed by the practice of many decades for refashioning the world in the interests of the working people and for the building of socialism ... The socialist countries are free of economic crises, inflation, unemployment, and other vices of capitalism. All this was achieved on the road charted by Marxism-Leninism .... To assert that Marxism-Leninism has grown outdated is to assert the invalidity of the general principles underlying the organization of the economic and all other aspects of the life of socialist society .... Marxist-Leninist theory is an integral teaching 'closed' to alien and unscientific concepts and views. Not one basic premise, not one essential part can be eliminated from it without departing from the objective truth. Conversely, not one alien concept or principle may be added to it without destroying its integrity and scientific nature.[3]

Those of us whose political activity and intellectual outlook were influenced by Marxism-Leninism cannot help but cringe when we recall such Orwellian commentaries today. But one cannot fully grasp the significance of Marxism-Leninism's passing without understanding the overweening function it performed back in the days when 'actually existing socialism' actually existed.

Of course, the collapse of the Soviet Union and its 'world socialist system' has rendered the vast body of such ideological extravagance embarrassingly moot. But socialists will not be able to learn from this experience by simply closing the book on this chapter in human history; or by attributing the Soviet debacle to such ready-to-hand targets as Stalin's reign of terror, Gorbachev's 'betrayal' of socialist principles, or the machinations of the Central Intelligence Agency.

To be sure, it would be unfair and historically unjustifiable to reduce

Marxism-Leninism to the worst of its self-parodies. Few theories have played such a significant role in world history. Entire societies were transformed, peoples uprooted and wars fought in its name. Even its numerous doctrinal disputes and bitter schisms often had a profound impact on the course of events.

At its best, Marxism-Leninism was an ideological touchstone for movements, organizations and individuals who worked tirelessly and heroically for social justice. Its martyrs often fought for noble causes. Many of its theoretical insights helped uncover otherwise hidden or obscure social realities – even while falling short of that ponderous law-governed universality which its adherents constantly claimed. And for all the hubris implied in their vision, the best of those who called themselves Marxist-Leninists believed that they were instruments of a historical momentum which would one day bring to life humanity's most cherished dreams of peace and justice.

Yet Marxism-Leninism's dark side can no longer be dismissed as unfortunate excesses in the service of good intentions, let alone historical progress; especially since at some point it became an ideology for justifying, reinforcing and perpetuating a system whose claims to historical progress had become dubious. The omnipresent terror and dishonesty which became indispensable building blocks of that system are no longer debatable.

Likewise, the discrepancy between Marxism-Leninism's claims to science and its religious character generated a sub-culture which fostered scripturalism, intellectual intolerance, utopianism, voluntarism and political sectarianism. One need only recall the pronouncements of its high priests in the not so distant past to be forcefully reminded of the extent to which Marxism-Leninism's ideological enforcers had become the intellectual heirs of the Spanish Inquisition.

Still, we cannot restrict our critique to Stalin and his Marxism-Leninism. The socialist movement has been indelibly stamped by the work of Marx, Engels and Lenin, and their ideas also require reevaluation. Such a review requires that we look once again at the offerings of others – both in the Marxist tradition and outside it – whose views were long considered beyond the pale of acceptable Marxist-Leninist discourse. (I am thinking here particularly of such disparate and contrary figures as Kautsky, Luxemburg, Bukharin and Trotsky, among others, many of whose arguments will resonate in light of the Soviet failure.)

In short, I believe that in order to investigate the sources of the socialist collapse thoroughly, we will have to work through and reevaluate the entire Marxist paradigm, trying to determine what parts of it may remain valid, where it may have been accurate in its time, where it suffered from unrealistic expectations and assessments, and where it opened the door to those concepts which, in practice, turned out to be disastrously mistaken.

It will already be obvious that in taking up this quest, I entertain neither the hope nor the illusion that such a review will demonstrate the viability of the socialist prototype which emerged in the Soviet Union and subsequently became the frame of reference for the other countries of the 'socialist camp'. Far from it. I believe the Soviet system was built not only on sand but on terror – both physical and ideological. And while its downfall has undoubtedly imposed a heavy price on those who lived under it and on the socialist movement itself, in the long run the socialist cause will be the better for its demise.

Rather, I have endeavored to situate the various theoretical questions addressed in both a historical and political context. Unfortunately, although most Marxist theory arose out of practical realities, it has not always been formulated or perceived that way. The works of both Marx and Lenin – to cite the two most prominent figures in the particular theoretical continuity being addressed here – are replete with examples of sweeping generalizations and absolute certainties which not only have proven unwarranted but which have encouraged far too many of their followers to do likewise.

The result has been that depressing tendency toward iconography which became one of the less salubrious characteristics of 'actually existing socialism' and the international communist movement. It is to be hoped that by reminding ourselves of the circumstances which gave rise to various Marxist theories and recalling the political purposes they were designed to serve, we will be able to shatter the mystique of Marxism and, thereby, better understand it. This is the goal of the first chapter, 'Political Anatomy of a Doctrine', which attempts so to situate Marxism, Leninism and Marxism-Leninism.

Clearly it is not possible to take up every theoretical question in the Marxist legacy. Rather, I have focused on those propositions which, it seems to me, have been the most determinate of the attempt to bring about socialist revolution and actually to build socialist societies. Those are an appraisal (in Chapter 2) of the assessment – by Marx as well as Lenin – that capitalism is a historically outmoded and moribund system and that the objective conditions for its demise are ripe; the theory and practice of the vanguard party (Chapter 3); the transition from capitalism to socialism (Chapter 4); and the legacy of world revolution (Chapters 7 and 8).

Chapter 5 examines the main economic features of the Soviet socialist model, while Chapter 6 takes up the dictatorship of the proletariat both as a theoretical construct and as the political, social and ideological structures and practices of 'actually existing socialism'. The concluding chapter explores the political wreckage and theoretical vacuum left in the wake of the socialist collapse, discussing such questions as socialism's future (does it have one?), the state of the Marxist paradigm, the validity (or otherwise) of Marxism and Marxism-Leninism, and some thoughts on the nature of a socialist political agenda in the twenty-first Century.

1 Political Anatomy of a Doctrine: From Marxism to Leninism to Marxism-Leninism

You've been a good old wagon, honey, but you done broke down!
Old Blues.

Few ideological systems have had such a profound impact on world history as the one whose line of continuity stretches from Marxism to Leninism to Marxism-Leninism. In the name of that construct revolutions were fought, old social orders were toppled, new economic systems established. Communists in the world's largest country took power and set out to build an unprecedented socialist society on the strength of what they believed were the scientific principles that theory had uncovered. Marxism-Leninism provided the ideological foundation for an international communist movement dedicated to a coordinated, consciously directed struggle to bring down capitalism everywhere in the world. While falling considerably short of that goal, communism – fueled by Marxist-Leninist theory – became a powerful political force. The specter which had once haunted Europe now cast a long shadow across the rest of the world as communist-led revolutions challenged the domain of capitalism in Asia, Africa, Latin America and even outer space.

In 1980, Soviet Communist Party leader Leonid Brezhnev would attribute these extraordinary developments of the previous six decades largely to the insightful character of that ideology:

> We Communists believe – and not only believe, we know – that the eighties will be years of fresh successes in building communism. They will be the years of consolidation and development of world socialism .... Our optimism stems from a sound theoretical and methodological basis – Marxism-Leninism, the time-tested doctrine standing for the revolutionary transformation of the world. [1]

But even as Brezhnev was celebrating Marxism-Leninism's anticipated successes, the entire edifice of 'actually existing socialism' of which the Soviet Union was the international center was already experiencing those disjunctures between its claimed achievements and reality which would culminate with such devastating consequences as that same decade came to an end.

Therefore, one cannot uncover the sources of the debacle which has removed the once-powerful 'socialist bloc' and its associated International Communist Movement from the world stage without examining Marxism-Leninism. (There are other claimants to the Marxist-Leninist legacy, but since these are, by and large, departures from the 'official' Marxism-Leninism of the CPSU, they are referred to here by the variant with which they have been mostly identified, that is, Trotskyism, Maoism and so on.)

Socialism as an idea is not, of course, exclusive to the configuration which culminated in Marxism-Leninism. Most socialists acknowledge Marx and Engels as seminal contributors to the socialist idea. Yet a considerable number explicitly reject Leninist theory and even more disdain Marxism-Leninism. Many of these critiques will now have to be considered anew in light of recent events, as will earlier attempts to revise Marxism itself. But to begin the process, we must place Marxism-Leninism in the context of its nominal forbears – Marx and Lenin.

Marxism

Marxism is, in many respects, the ungrateful offspring of nineteenth-century capitalism. Both Marx and Engels came out of the more privileged sectors of nineteenth-century German society. Marx's father was a successful lawyer wealthy enough to enroll him in the Law Faculty at the University of Bonn and subsequently at the University of Berlin, where he quickly came under the influence of the teachings of Hegelian philosophy. His wife, Jenny von Westphalen, was the daughter of Baron von Westphalen, a somewhat enlightened member of the German aristocracy who took the young Marx under his wing and introduced him to the ideas of the French utopian socialist Saint-Simon.

Marx's famed associate, Friedrich Engels, was the son of a successful German textile manufacturer who also had a branch of his business in Manchester, England. From 1850 to 1870 Engels managed the Manchester factory, accumulating sufficient wealth to support Marx and, subsequently, to retire and devote the rest of his life to communist political and theoretical work.

However ironic the contrast between their individual circumstances and subsequent beliefs, it was not unusual in those post-Enlightenment years for young scions of the advantaged classes to be advocates of the most advanced ideas of their time. (There is an interesting parallel here with Lenin, who also was born into what today would be considered a comfortable middle-class existence and whose political life was likewise shaped by a pending bourgeois-democratic revolution in Russia.)

Impelled by the rising bourgeoisie's need to replace the privileges of inherited rank with the power of capital, the great Enlightenment of the eighteenth century had generated an intellectual climate characterized by an abiding belief in rationalism, science and natural law. Deism, agnosticism and even atheism were challenging traditional religious beliefs in a personalized God who directed worldly affairs. Throughout Europe, Marx's contemporaries feasted on both the ideas and inherent dramas of the American and French Revolutions.

Nowhere was this more the case than in Germany where, despite an already advanced capitalism, the political order was still in the hands of the old Prussian aristocracy. But a society in which there is a disjuncture between economic and political power cannot long endure. Capitalism in particular needs a social structure freed from the hierarchy of rigid class stratification based principally on birth. Nor can it long comfortably exist with the social values and ideological reflections of an outmoded and non-productive class. As a result, the German bourgeoisie – the real driving force of society – found itself increasingly hampered in its efforts to utilize the political machinery of the state to expand capitalism further.

Typically, the ideological harbingers of that already overdue bourgeois-democratic revolution were to be found in the universities, the one place where abstract ideas and principles could be most easily entertained and where young minds were the least calcified by traditional thinking. The dominating figure in German intellectual life of that period was Georg Wilhelm Friedrich Hegel, whose philosophical framework was deeply rooted in historical development and whose credo was that history is 'progress in the consciousness of freedom'. Although Hegel himself supported Prussian rule politically, his philosophy – based on the view that consciousness determines being – was in harmony with the needs of a rising capitalist class which firmly believed in the ability of men (both literally and generically) to shape their own destinies.

Marx and Engels were deeply influenced by Hegelian thought and – like many other German university students of the 1830s – translated it into political activity. They joined a group called the Young Hegelians who argued a radical interpretation of Hegel's ideas, to protest the Junker system and its restrictions on individual liberty.

Of particular importance in shaping Marx's own philosophical method and study of history was Hegel's work on dialectics. While Marx was philosophically opposed to the idealist underpinnings of Hegel's view of the world, he felt that Hegel's dialectical method had opened valuable new territory in the realm of philosophy:

My dialectic method is not only different from the Hegelian, but is its direct opposite. To Hegel, the life-process of the human brain, i.e., the process of thinking, which, under the name of 'the Idea' he even transforms into an independent subject, is the demiurgos of the real world, and the real world is only the external, phenomenal form of 'the Idea.' With me, on the contrary, the ideal is nothing else than the material world reflected by the human mind and translated into thought .... [But] the mystification which the dialectic suffers in Hegel's hands by no means prevents him from being the first to present its general form of working in a comprehensive and conscious manner. With him it is standing on its head. It must be turned right side up again if you would discover the rational kernel within the mystical shell.' [2]

While still in school and afterwards Marx began to experience those unpleasant encounters with the authorities which lasted his lifetime. Blocked from a university position because of his opinions, Marx became the editor of *Rheinische Zeitung*, an influential liberal newspaper supported by Rhenish industrialists. But largely because of his articles on economics, the government shut the paper down and Marx went into semi-voluntary and ultimately permanent exile.

Marx and Engels were also the progeny of capitalism in a broader sense. They came to maturity as the entire world was being riveted and revolutionized by the awesome power the still relatively young system had placed in the once-disdained bourgeois class. Marx was barely 30 and Engels only 28 when they wrote:

The bourgeoisie, historically, has played a most revolutionary part .... It has been the first to show what man's activity can bring about. It has accomplished wonders far surpassing Egyptian pyramids, Roman aqueducts and Gothic cathedrals; it has conducted expeditions that put in the shade all former exoduses of nations and crusades .... Constant revolutionizing of production, uninterrupted disturbance of all social conditions, everlasting uncertainty and agitation distinguish the bourgeois epoch from all earlier ones. All fixed, fast-frozen relations, with their train of ancient and venerable prejudices and opinions are swept away, all new-formed ones become antiquated before they can ossify .... Man is at last compelled to face with sober senses his real conditions of life and his relations with his kind .... The bourgeoisie, during its rule of scarce one hundred years, has created more massive and more colossal productive forces than have all preceding generations together. Subjection of Nature's forces to man, machinery, application of chemistry to industry and agriculture, steam-navigation, railways, electric telegraphs, clearing of whole continents for cultivation, canalization of rivers, whole populations conjured out of the ground – what earlier century had even a presentiment that such productive forces slumbered in the lap of social labor? [3]

How was this phenomenon to be explained?

Here is where Marx began to carve out that unique niche which places him among the great thinkers of history. For while most of his contemporaries tended to explain historical development as the consequence of God's will, the realization of ideal principles or the result of ideas seemingly generated in the human mind, Marx inverted the process. These very explanations, he argued, were themselves the product – not the cause – of human activity. (Unflinchingly, Marx would have been the first to admit that his own materialist view of the world grew out of a society in which science, industry and the ledger book were clearly the prime movers.) In this sense, capitalism enabled Marx to develop what may be his most lasting theoretical achievement – historical materialism. This was subsequently summarized by Engels:

> The materialist conception of history starts from the principle that production, and with production the exchange of its products, is the basis of every social order; that in every society which has appeared in history the distribution of the products, and with it the division of the society into classes or estates, is determined by what is produced and how it is produced, and how the product is exchanged. According to this conception, the ultimate causes of all social changes and political revolutions are to be sought, not in the minds of men, in their increasing insight into eternal justice and truth, but in changes in the mode of production and exchange; they are to be sought not in the philosophy but in the economics of the period. [4]

Within this framework, Marx saw changes in the forces of production – new and improved instruments of labor, transportation, communication, storage and so on, and new scientific knowledge in such fields as chemistry and physics – as the trigger setting off change through a society's economy and, indeed, in society as a whole. From the cotton gin to the steam engine to the iron smelter – and, one may add in our own time, the computer, the nuclear reactor, the fax machine and bio-technology – capitalism has validated this proposition again and again, expanding its productive capacity many times over.

Marx was also keenly aware of capitalism's other side: its periodic, devastating financial crises with their resulting waste of human lives, productive forces and finished products; its wars; its transformation of once largely peasant populations into depressed armies of proletarians with no means of survival other than selling their labor power, thereby becoming commodities themselves; and its inevitable tendency toward the concentration of capital into fewer and fewer hands.

But Marx did not simply decry the inherent brutalities and injustices of this social arrangement. Capitalism was clearly too powerful and productive a system to be undone or significantly modified by appeals to abstract moral principles, let alone the nobler sentiments of the capitalists. Individual capitalists might avow humane and moral sentiments, but they could not consistently act on such sentiments without being overwhelmed by more ruthless competitors. Thus the great bourgeois-democratic principle of separation of church and state – a major advance in the struggle against feudalism – is, at the same time, a reflection of that other capitalist principle that considerations of morality and religion have little bearing when it comes to business.

And so Marx was led to two other areas of investigation: the analysis of capitalism's own inner logic; and the consideration of alternatives to it. From this point of view, Marx's choice of England as his permanent residence-in-exile (in 1849) was fortuitous and probably deliberate. There, where the industrial revolution had begun 100 years before reaching the continent, capitalism flourished in its most developed form. Britannia ruled not only the waves but the world capitalist economy. (The two, of course, were inseparable.) Its manufacture was the most advanced, its trade the most extensive of any country in the world. The pound sterling was the currency of international commerce and the Bank of England its greatest and most powerful repository. Likewise, the British working class was the most developed in the world and the furthest along in trade union organization.

From England, too, had come the most significant investigations into the workings of capitalism – in particular the work of Adam Smith and David Ricardo. Long before Marx, British political economy had identified the labor theory of value and class struggle as features of capitalist economics. Marx built on much of this earlier work and then formulated a theoretical construct on the nature of capitalism that became a school of its own (Marxian economics) which has had a profound and lasting impact on all studies of capitalism.

It is far beyond the scope of this undertaking to summarize – let alone reproduce – the sum of Marx's analysis of capitalism. There is an enormous literature devoted to this subject at the heart of which still stand Marx's own studies – especially his most extensive work, *Capital*. Here it will be enough simply to note several points which made his insights unique.

First, while many others developed definitions of capitalism which included most of its obvious features, it was Marx who situated it as *a mode of production* tied to a definite stage in the development of the forces of production and, therefore, to a definite historical period. Capitalism presupposed the existence of a social surplus significantly larger than that needed for the reproduction of the laboring force and a life of luxury for the rulers. Although the initial accumulations of capital which helped launch capitalism as a system often came through outright aggrandizement – expropriation of the peasants from the land, seizure of the wealth of primitive peoples and so on – over the long run it was the fact of the social surplus which made possible the continued reproduction and expansion of capital.

Second, Marx identified the *relations of production* which gave capitalism its unique character. This was the fact that capitalists owned the *means of production* while those who worked for them, owning nothing of value (other than personal possessions), were obliged to sell the only economic asset they had – their labor power.

Third, Marx solved the enigma of capitalist profit. Classic political economy had recognized that human labor was the source of the value of all produced commodities, and that over time the price of a commodity would reflect its value. But if this were the case, where did profit come from? Some economists attributed profit to the entrepreneur's own expended labor, but since the profit went to far more use than producing a luxurious life for the capitalists this left unanswered the source of the expansion of capital. Marx's discovery was the theory of *surplus value;* that is, the value produced by labor power over and above that needed to reproduce itself. Although produced by labor, this surplus went to the owner of the means of production and was the principal source of the growth and accumulation of capital which is the underpinning of capitalist expansion.

Marx also identified capitalism's internal contradictions, which, he predicted, were ultimately unresolvable. He saw capitalism's anarchy of production as the source of its periodic and apparently intensifying cyclical crises. He also saw the contradiction between the growing socialization of production and the increasing concentration of ownership in private hands as a fundamental source of the system's future destabilization. Moreover, Marx identified an inherent tendency toward parasitism among the owners of capital as they became further and further removed from the processes of production and anticipated a tendency toward monopoly which, he believed, would ultimately retard the continuing development of the system's productive forces.

The ideas of socialism pre-dated Marx by at least two centuries. Even as modern capitalism was beginning to take its first self-confident steps toward world domination, conceptions of alternative social arrangements also began to appear – usually drawing their inspiration from the self-proclaimed ideals of bourgeois-democratic revolutions. A radical movement known as the Diggers whose ideas had much in common with later socialist thought emerged as far back as the English Civil War (1642–49). Similarly, the egalitarian principles espoused by the French Revolution and the fact that this upheaval drew masses of early proletarians into its ranks inspired François Babeuf, whose Conspiracy of Equals was committed to fighting for a socialistic program. (This movement came to an end on the guillotine when the conspiracy was uncovered and Babeuf and his main associates were executed.)

France and England were also the sites of that early nineteenth-century phenomenon which has come to be known (thanks largely to Marx and Engels) as 'utopian socialism'. Appalled by the glaring inequities and cruelties of capitalism, a number of French and British intellectuals began trying to construct ideal social orders based on logic, science and the attempt fully to implement bourgeois-democratic principles. Chief among these were the Comte de Saint-Simon, Charlies Fourier and Robert Owen. Despite some significant differences, all had in common, as Gareth Jones puts it, a 'focus on the moral-ideological sphere as the determining basis of all other aspects of human behavior.' [5] Saint-Simon and, later, Fourier devoted themselves principally to the spread of their ideas, which found their most receptive audience among university students and intellectuals. Owen, on the other hand, tried to construct ideal socialist communities which would serve as a model for others to follow. None connected their efforts to the early economic and political movements then beginning to emerge in the working class.

Independently of the utopians, socialism was beginning to emerge spontaneously in workers' movements. The most notable of these were the English Chartists of the 1830s and 1840s, whose political goals went beyond the alleviation of immediate conditions to include broader ideas of democracy and equality in the social order as a whole.

It was during Marx's one-year exile in France that his intellectual embrace of socialism began. There he had his first extended encounters with the various socialist groups then existing in France and also with the early French trade unions. Over the next several years, in addition to pursuing their theoretical projects, Marx and Engels increasingly became involved in political activity, eventually joining the Communist League, an organization of German emigré workers headquartered in London. In 1847 the League commissioned Marx and Engels to draft a statement of principles that would represent its broad outlook. It was this statement that became *The Communist Manifesto*. (It was, perhaps, both appropriate and ironic that *The Communist Manifesto* should appear in 1848, the year in which bourgeois-democratic revolutions swept across Europe.)

The Communist Manifesto is a landmark in the history of socialism because (a) it is the first elaborated statement on the development of capitalism incorporating Marx's historical materialist paradigm; and (b) it is the first significant attempt to situate socialism politically by linking it to a particular class – the proletariat.

In making his leap to socialism, Marx's materialism forced him to reject the various strains of utopian socialism which basically appealed to the good sense and better instincts of those who then managed society. None of the utopians seriously considered the possibility that the working class – a generally uneducated, uncultured lot with apparently little desire for anything but an alleviation of their worst conditions – could possibly be the bearers of their ideal society. But Marx concluded that no other force in contemporary society could play that role and that these objects of history were on the verge of becoming powerful historical actors in their own right; that, in fact, capitalism – out of its own compulsions – would train them, educate them, set favorable conditions for lifting them out of the hopeless stupor which was a common condition of their lives.

Marx was not the only one who saw the workers as the bearers of a new society, however. One of the most influential figures of that time was Pierre-Joseph Proudhon, the progenitor of modern anarchism, who declared that 'the abolition of exploitation of man by man and the abolition of government are one and the same thing.' Proudhon advocated a new system based on the voluntary organization of self-governing producers linked in a form of economic federalism. Marx's critique of Proudhon's views for not being rooted in the real world (see *The Poverty of Philosophy*) was the first in a long series of debates that became characteristic of the socialist movement over the decades.

Marx's emphasis on the role of the working class itself reflected his understanding that fundamental changes in the power and property relations between the principal classes in any society did not occur automatically as a result of changes in the productive forces. On the contrary: those in power whose positions were threatened by these changes resisted with every means at their disposal. Social revolution, therefore, is an indispensable part of the historical process. But, said Marx, it could only succeed to the extent that the class or classes striving for power reflected the strength of the newly revolutionized productive forces. In that case, however, they were bound ultimately to prevail.

While Marx's identification of the working class as the foundation and leading force of the struggle to overthrow capitalism and embark on socialism marked a turning point in the evolution of the socialist movement, neither he nor Engels spent any appreciable time or intellectual energy in trying to elaborate a conception of what socialist society would look like. The most important theoretical breakthrough Marx made on this issue was to draw out an entirely new perspective on socialism as a 'transitional' society between capitalism and communism – a society which inevitably would have aspects of both. (This point is discussed at greater length in Chapter 4.)

Beyond that, Marx insisted throughout his life that socialism would emerge by way of a historical process which would be based, first of all, on the intrinsic laws of capitalist development, and that any attempt to draw up a blueprint (or even a definition) for it in advance was itself a futile and idealist exercise. The main exception to this approach was Marx's *Critique of the Gotha Program* which took issue with some of the conceptions of a future socialist society advanced at a unity congress that brought together the two main branches of the German workers' movement and launched what would become the German Social Democratic Party.

The knowledgeable reader will note that this (exceedingly) broad summary has followed the outline of Lenin's well-known *Three Sources and Three Component Parts of Marxism* in which he identifies philosophy, political economy and socialism as the main categories of Marx's thought. Since, on closer examination, it can be seen that virtually all of Marx's work can be subsumed into one of these categories, I have found it a useful method.

Unfortunately, the elevation of Marx's writings to the rarefied status of an 'ism' has obscured the rather obvious (but no less profound) distinction to be made between these categories; that is, between analysis based on historical phenomena and predictions which, by their very nature, must be conjectural.

Marx's philosophical work, being rooted in history, remains a compelling methodology which is far more complex than the simplistic economic determinism generally characteristic of shorthand Marxism. Nevertheless, because of its emphasis on economics it remains significantly one-sided. Other enormously important and complex questions – race, nationality, sexual orientation, the environmental consequences of economic activity – are barely considered, if at all. Some attention was paid to gender-related issues (especially in Engels' *Origin of the Family, Private Property and the State*), but this is clearly an underdeveloped area of investigation. Ideological matters are considered at greater length, but with insufficient attention to their relative autonomy within the broader Marxist historical framework.

None of this is said to diminish the significance of what Marx and Engels achieved. The insights of historical materialism were indeed earth-shaking and provide an extremely useful foundation for investigations into other areas.

A more serious dilemma is posed by the impact of capitalism's revolutionary advances in science, technology and production on Marx's basic historical paradigm. For historical materialism is founded on the assumption of the virtues of limitless progress in human domination of nature and the inexhaustibility of productive resources. Perhaps with the evolution of a planned society and further scientific progress, those concepts – appropriately modified – will retain their validity. At the moment, however, some of the precepts on which historical materialism is based cannot simply be viewed as the certainties many of us once assumed they were.

Marx's investigation into capitalist political economy is rightly considered his principal theoretical accomplishment. It was in this area that he was able to shed new light on the formation and workings of capitalism, in the process demonstrating the worth of historical materialism as a method of scientific inquiry. Nevertheless, it is readily apparent that Marx's analysis, however perceptive regarding nineteenth-century capitalism, is not an adequate basis for analyzing world capitalism as it approaches the millennium. Twentieth-century capitalism has produced an array of new productive forces even more startling and more consequential than the wonders celebrated in *The Communist Manifesto*. As a result, one cannot hope to understand the dynamics of contemporary capitalism simply within the framework offered by *Capital*.

Such phenomena as the enhanced role of the state, the shrinking size and role of the proletariat in production, the full globalization of the capitalist economy, and the transformations in production resulting from the revolutions in biotechnology, computer science, nuclear energy and the like have brought capitalism to a qualitatively new stage of development. (Indeed, contemporary capitalism is *several* stages removed from the model Marx unraveled.) Just as modern biological science, while honoring Darwin for his pioneering work, could not function on the basis of the insights provided in *The Origin of the Species*, so modern political economy – while acknowledging its debt to Marx – clearly must go far beyond the insights to be found in *Capital*.

Marxism's most problematic category is its theoretical speculations on socialism. These are principally Marx's concept of a connected and more or less continuous world proletarian revolution and some extremely broad suppositions on the political forms and economic structures of a future socialist society. (The former is discussed at some length in Chapter 7, while the latter is taken up as a point of reference in the chapters dealing with socialism and the dictatorship of the proletariat.) Since these speculations are based principally on the world as it was in the last half of the nineteenth century – or, to be more precise, on Marx's assessments of that world – their usefulness to socialist thinking today is, to say the least, highly dubious.

Unfortunately, the attachment of that pernicious 'ism' has tended to cast all of Marx's work as an indivisible whole. Lenin implied as much in his *Three Component Parts* and – as noted earlier – the apostles of a latterday Marxism-Leninism made it a principle from which one deviated at the risk of heresy:

> Marxist-Leninist theory is an integral teaching 'closed' to alien and unscientific concepts and views. This teaching (is)...cast from a single piece of steel, and not one basic premise, not one essential part can be eliminated from it without departing from the objective truth.[6]

Perhaps that unintended and ironic epitaph for Marxism-Leninism will at long last enable the socialist movement to appreciate Marx's famous declaration that he was not a Marxist not simply as an example of modesty but for the formidable intellectual warning Marx meant it to be.

Leninism

Leninism is the Marxism of the epoch of imperialism and proletarian revolutions, of the downfall of colonialism and the triumph of national liberation movements, of the epoch of transition from capitalism to socialism and communist construction.[7]

In the period immediately following Marx's death in 1883, socialism began to develop a significant working-class base. Social Democratic Parties, spurred by the growth of trade unions, appeared in much of Western and Central Europe. But over time, as both the unions and their parties grew in numbers, their socialism increasingly became a program for reform within the capitalist framework. The unions, organized principally along craft lines, established themselves as bargaining agents for the skilled workers who made up their membership, while the Social Democratic Parties depicted themselves as the political representatives of the working class as a whole in the electoral arena. A number of these parties gained a foothold in their respective parliaments and, in some cases, even assumed cabinet positions. Pointedly eschewing all extra-legal – let alone revolutionary – activity, they became permanent fixtures in the capitalist political structure, their principal function being to represent the immediate interests of unionized workers within the prevailing social arrangement.

Thus, while the upsurge in trade unionism was a major advance in the self-organization of the working class, it also had the effect – largely unforeseen by Marx – of diverting the workers from the socialist cause. For while large numbers of unskilled and semi-skilled workers – in effect, the proletarian core of the working class – may have been ideologically inclined toward socialism, they lacked organization and leadership.

This phenomenon found its chief theoretical reflection in the work of Eduard Bernstein. An early member of the German Social Democratic Workers Party, Bernstein became a close friend of Engels, who ultimately made him his literary executor. Armed with these Marxist credentials, Bernstein gradually adopted an 'evolutionary' (as opposed to revolutionary) approach to socialism, arguing that socialism would appear as the result of a continuous accumulation of social and economic reforms within capitalism. Declaring that social democracy was already 'a democratic, socialistic party of reform', he urged social democrats to declare themselves openly as such and to shun the revolutionary side of their legacy. But Bernstein and others like him did not so much hold back or divert the workers' movement as reflect the relatively privileged position of its best organized and most economically secure sector.

(The situation in the US was even more extreme. There the trade unions, under the leadership of the American Federation of Labor [AFL] and Samuel Gompers, adopted a narrowly economistic strategy which rejected independent trade union politics and concentrated on advancing the interests of the skilled craft workers who made up the bulk of union members at the time. Although the most important socialist figures of the period – Eugene Debs, Big Bill Haywood and others – came out of union struggles, socialism and trade unionism were pretty much on distinct and frequently antagonistic trajectories.)

To the extent that revolution was brewing anywhere, it was in those countries where the remnants of feudalism were still a powerful force retarding capitalist development. Of these, no country was more teeming with revolutionary ferment and possibilities than Russia. The last major European country not to have undergone a bourgeois-democratic revolution, the land of the czars was increasingly wracked by the classic contradiction between a rapidly growing capitalist economy and an anachronistic feudal-based autocratic state. It was no accident, therefore, that the next major upsurge in the revolutionary side of Marxism took place in that country and was largely articulated through the figure of Lenin.

Although Marx had predicted that the most industrially developed of the capitalist countries would be the site of the impending socialist revolution, the maturation of the revolution in backward Russia was not the surprise it is sometimes made out to be. For Marx and Engels had carefully distinguished between those countries most ripe for socialism and those countries where revolution might break out. In 1848 they had declared:

> The Communists turn their attention chiefly to Germany, because that country is on the eve of a bourgeois revolution ... and because the bourgeois revolution in Germany will be but the prelude to an immediately following proletarian revolution.[8]

In his last years Marx began to look at Russia from a similar perspective. It was not that he and Engels expected a socialist revolution in Russia but they thought that even a bourgeois-democratic revolution in that country might well be the catalyst which would trigger proletarian revolution elsewhere in Europe.

This was the caldron out of which Leninism emerged. For it was in the course of grappling with the theoretical and practical challenges of the impending revolution in Russia that Lenin was forced to confront Marxism not as a sacred text but as a source of living ideas whose relevance to the Russian struggle would have to be tested and, where necessary, modified or rejected. As a result, Lenin's theoretical work is imbued with a passion, an urgency and a political incisiveness inseparable from the fact that in czarist Russia revolution was a practical question.

Impelled by the revolutionary nature of the times and a family history of opposition to czarism (his elder brother had been implicated in a plot to kill the czar and was subsequently executed), Lenin had been drawn to Marxism through the efforts of the first generation of Russian Marxists, particularly the writings of Georgi Plekhanov, considered the 'father of Russian Marxism'.

Like many others influenced by Plekhanov, Lenin was dissatisfied with the main revolutionary currents in late nineteenth-century Russia. While the bourgeois current sought to eliminate all anachronistic restrictions on the development of capitalism, Lenin believed that its commitment to a democratic republic was questionable. Its goal – to break the hold of the landed aristocracy on the state and to establish the bourgeoisie's own political authority – did not necessarily include removal of the czar or the establishment of a genuinely popular government. On the contrary: Lenin was convinced that in the Russian circumstance, the bourgeoisie would never advance beyond the extension of democracy to itself. Rather, given the existence of an already active and growing trade union movement, it would inevitably seek an accommodation with the czarist authority in order to restrict the power of both the workers and the great majority of poor and middle peasants whose interests ran counter to its own. If this could be accomplished by making the czar a constitutional monarch responsive to the bourgeoisie's interests and views, it would be more than satisfied.

Nevertheless, Lenin urged the Russian working class to support the already gestating bourgeois-democratic revolution because 'In countries like Russia, the working class suffers not so much from capitalism as from the insufficient development of capitalism.' It was only the fullest flowering of capitalism, he argued, that would enable the proletariat to grow and become a political force in its own right.[9] Within this framework, he said, the mission of the working class would be to push the revolution to fulfill its own declared democratic objectives.

A seemingly more 'radical' trend, made up of various political representatives of the peasantry, envisioned a post-czarist society based largely on an egalitarian peasant model. But Lenin had even less confidence in the prospects for a revolution whose alternative to czarism was a peasant-based 'socialism' which he considered both a contradiction in terms and a futile attempt to reverse or hold back the growth of capitalism. The peasantry – especially its poor and middle strata – could play a revolutionary role, he believed, but not so long as it was mired in the illusion that its own primitive mode of production could provide the foundation for a new system.

Nor did Lenin believe that Russia, with its small proletariat, an economy still dominated by small-scale agriculture and still awaiting both an industrial and cultural revolution, had as yet the material basis for socialism.

Given these frustrating prospects, Lenin developed a major theoretical alteration in traditional Marxist thinking. In the specific conditions of Russia, he argued, the working class could take power provided it did so in a revolutionary alliance with the peasantry, whose principal political objective was land reform. Those peasants – and these were the vast majority – who were either landless or had plots so small that they could barely eke out a subsistence existence, could be won to an alliance with the working class if the latter pledged itself to a redistribution of land that would enable them to generate agricultural surpluses for the market.

But while a worker-peasant alliance might succeed in coming to power in Russia, it still could not advance beyond capitalism since the peasantry, comprising roughly three-fourths of the Russian population, was inherently capitalist. Nevertheless, the victory of this alliance might still advance the socialist cause if the revolutionary spirit it unleashed were to become contagious and spill over into those countries where there already were mass working-class movements and where the level of development of society's productive forces was advanced enough to provide sufficient basis for a socialist economy.

Should the working class actually take power in several of the major capitalist countries – a possibility Lenin believed more and more likely with the outbreak of world war in 1914 – then Russia under the rule of a worker-peasant alliance itself had the possibility of becoming socialist. For in the context of a presumed economic integration with and aid from the socialist states in Europe, all the conditions which made it unlikely that socialism could come to Russia on its own would be overcome.

This perspective inevitably brought a whole series of ancillary questions to the fore, chief among them the role of what Lenin called 'the conscious element', that is, the revolutionary organization which would guide and direct this process. Lenin's solution to this problem was his 'party of a new type', a disciplined, ideologically cohesive, highly centralized, clandestine vanguard organization which would be the proletariat's own 'advanced detachment' in the broader revolutionary process. Such a party bore no resemblance to the largely educational organizations typical of the First International or to the largely electoral and legalistic socialist parties of the Second. (The 'vanguard party' concept is examined at length in Chapter 3.)

Even Lenin's writings on broader international issues were inspired and shaped – at least in part – by the demands of the Russian Revolution. For once the possibility of socialism in Russia was linked to the success of socialist revolutions elsewhere, the general state of world capitalism and the prospects for its overthrow became compelling questions for the Russian Revolution as well.

Thus, Lenin's critique of Bernstein took shape as he encountered 'Bernsteinism' – in particular the 'economists' against whom he polemicized against in *What Is To Be Done?* (1902) – in the internal struggles of the Russian revolutionary movement. This was also the case with Lenin's analysis of *Imperialism* (1916), which was principally provoked by the impact of World War I on socialist politics. His conclusion – that capitalism had entered upon its final, 'moribund' stage – is totally bound up with his view that proletarian revolution in the major capitalist countries had become a timely and practical question. Seeing that war-weariness was playing a galvanizing role in the rapidly ripening Russian Revolution, Lenin believed that the mass slaughter of the war might likewise trigger revolutions elsewhere in

Europe. But when a number of Social Democratic Parties supported their own governments in the war, he attributed this 'betrayal' of the socialist cause to the 'opportunism' of a 'labor aristocracy' bought off by the 'super-profits' derived from the exploitation of colonial labor and resources. (See, in addition to *Imperialism*, *The Proletarian Revolution and the Renegade Kautsky*.)

In the same vein, sensing that the outbreak of the Russian Revolution in February 1917 had opened up realistic prospects for the Bolsheviks to come to power, Lenin turned his attention to questions of revolutionary violence, bourgeois democracy and the dictatorship of the proletariat. Thus we have the remarkable anomaly of Lenin writing his major theoretical work on the topic, *State and Revolution*, in the summer of 1917 at the precise moment when the Bolsheviks were positioning themselves to take power.

This phenomenon contributed significantly to Lenin's perspective on colonialism. Previously, Marxists had attached little significance to the anti-colonial struggle, generally seeing the emancipation of the colonies as a *consequence* of the triumph of socialism in the 'mother' countries. Lenin posed a new role for oppressed peoples and nations as an integral part of world proletarian revolution. But that revolution, he believed, would have to be consciously organized and directed by an international vanguard party. This was the theoretical basis for the founding of the Comintern.

Finally, Lenin declared, the appearance of the first working-class state and the beginning of the epoch of the new social order signified the onset of capitalism's 'general crisis', which would henceforth be characterized by the shrinking of capitalism's realm and the growth of a world socialist economy.

In short, what ultimately became the main tenets of Leninism emerged in response to a historically concrete set of *political* circumstances and was shaped in the intense polemics with other socialist-minded and revolutionary forces over strategy and tactics.

Still, it is doubtful that an ism would have been added to Lenin's name were it not for the Bolsheviks' success in seizing, holding and consolidating power. Here was a 'verification' which none of Lenin's opponents in the fierce polemical battles of the previous two decades could claim. Prior to the cataclysmic impact of the Bolshevik Revolution on socialist thought, 'Leninism' was usually used pejoratively to suggest a body of thought which was attempting to introduce alien, ultra-left and undemocratic concepts into Marxism. After 1917, however, and especially after the establishment of the Comintern in 1920, its adherents confidently proclaimed Leninism as the one true Marxism and the only revolutionary alternative to social democracy.

But, as with Marxism, the term tended both to clarify and mystify. On the one hand, just as Marxism connoted a new, distinct and enormously influential trend in socialism, so Leninism likewise signified a new, distinct and enormously influential trend in Marxism. On the other, the identification of both trends with particular individuals tended to canonize all their work as equally valid 'sacred texts'.

And, as the Bolsheviks set out to use their revolutionary bastion in Russia to push forward the mission of world revolution, the temptation to universalize Lenin's theoretical work became irresistible. It was a problem that would be magnified a thousand-fold when the subsequent incarnation of Marxism-Leninism became an exclusive ideology guiding and implementing state power.

Stalin and the Canonization of Leninism as Marxism-Leninism

Viewed literally, Marxism-Leninism would appear to be a synthesis of the main theses developed by the two men whose names have thereby been elevated to the dizzying heights of communist ideological authority. In fact Marxism-Leninism is, in the first place, the product of the fierce power struggle which unfolded in the highest reaches of the CPSU after Lenin's death. For with no single figure Lenin's obvious political successor, each of the main contenders – Trotsky, Stalin and Bukharin – sought power by laying claim to the Leninist mantle.[10]

Of these, Stalin was clearly the most skillful; considering his lack of theoretical talents, he had to be. Less than three months after Lenin's death, this shadowy eminence who had previously given almost no inkling of a theoretical turn of mind arranged to deliver a series of lectures at Sverdlov University in Moscow. Called 'The Foundations of Leninism', the enterprise was vintage Stalin. The talks were an artful exposition of that tendentious doctrinairism which would thereafter be the hallmark of Marxist-Leninist exposition. Not coincidentally, the lectures were dedicated to the 'Lenin Enrollment', a mass recruitment to the party which significantly strengthened Stalin's political base. 'Foundations of Leninism' not only enabled Stalin to establish himself as the party's ultimate ideological authority; it became, in effect, Marxism-Leninism's birth announcement, what one champion would subsequently call 'the most concise statement extant of twentieth-century Marxist-Leninist theory'.[11]

But if 'Foundations' was Marxism-Leninism's baptism, a further elaboration two years later served as the doctrine's canonization. For it was then, in an article called 'Concerning Questions of Leninism', that Stalin made adherence to the principles of Leninism he had earlier elaborated into an obligatory article of faith:

> Is not Leninism the generalization of the experience of the revolutionary movement of *all* countries? Are not the fundamentals of the theory and tactics of Leninism suitable, are they not obligatory, for the proletarian parties of *all* countries? [12]

While this reification of Lenin became an enduring characteristic of the new ideology, Marxism-Leninism also incorporated a number of propositions reflecting subsequent political decisions made by the CPSU under Stalin's leadership. For the most part, these borrowed from the letter – but hardly the spirit – of Lenin's writings. Some simply wrenched citations from Lenin out of context. But in one crucial area – what came to be known as the basic principles of 'socialist construction' – Stalin ventured into the realm of theory on his own. These included the theory of socialism in one country, the historical rupture with capitalism (concentrated in the 'Great Turn' of 1929) and the elaboration of the 'laws' of socialism reflecting the economic and political structures which became the hallmarks of the Soviet system.

Stalin's innovations were hardly his alone. Nor were they foisted on a reluctant party. However much terror may have produced the ideological conformity of the later years of Stalin's rule, the burden of the political evidence indicates that in his battles first with Trotsky and then with Bukharin, Stalin's views enjoyed greater support in the party leadership than did those of his opponents. As Soviet philosopher Alexander Tsipko would note six decades later, 'Stalin's thinking and his idea of socialism were typical for Marxists of that time'.[13]

In weighing Stalin's role in the shaping of Marxism-Leninism, however, one must look beyond the various theoretical propositions which – for better or worse – he initiated. For just as Stalin introduced the methods of the witch-hunt into communist political practice, so too did he shape Marxism-Leninism in the spirit of the Inquisition. Marx, imbued with the spirit of science, constantly struggled for precision and nuance, invariably lacing his assertions with critical qualifications. Lenin, the master of strategy and tactics, assiduously monitored his conclusions through the prism of changing conditions, thereby maximizing the art of political flexibility. But Stalin's tendency, especially in theoretical matters, was toward absolutes – a trait he seems to have shared with his arch-nemesis, Trotsky. Absent from his simplistic assertions of Marxist principles is any semblance of an inquiring disposition. For Stalin, Marxism-Leninism – and his own role as its ultimate arbiter – helped establish the party's infallibility through 'science'. Not surprisingly, the climate thus generated was inevitably reproduced throughout the communist movement in the relationships between party leaders and the party mass, and likewise between the party and the people.

But while Stalin is clearly the historical figure who most graphically embodies the ideological and political totalitarianism which came to characterize the Soviet system, he was at least as much the instrument of a broader historical process as its progenitor. For what has become known as 'Stalinism' was itself the reflection and consequence of the class dynamics operative in Russia at the onset of Soviet power. A dozen years after the Bolsheviks came to power, Russia was still a country dominated by small-scale agriculture and, therefore, with a largely backward peasantry who comprised the vast majority of the population. Its proletariat, in whose name the revolution had been won, was extremely small and, for the most part, only one generation removed from the countryside.

Lenin attempted to deal with this dilemma through the worker-peasant alliance which would, for a long period of time, supervise and guide a mixed economy containing both capitalist and socialist elements. The demographics aside, Lenin believed that the working class – as the more 'progressive' of the two – would play the leading role. But with the Communist Party replacing the working class as the real source of power in the country and claiming – in the name of the working class – the right to uncontested rule, conditions that would subsequently abet the exclusive concentration (and abuse) of power in the party's hands were established as a political norm.

Under these circumstances, Stalin's attempt to force history into a preconceived mold – that is, trying to 'construct' socialism without the material basis which such an undertaking would have required – could only proceed by relying on totalitarian methods and the exaltations of ideological zealotry. Thus while capitalism grew up and flourished under the ideological patronage of both theocratic and secular states and has been administered by believers and non-believers alike, 'actually existing socialism' came to be characterized by an exclusivist, state-enforced ideology.

Since Marxism-Leninism was the only permissible ideology, the determination and interpretation of its principles became the exclusive domain of communist hierarchies who exercised absolute control over the state, economic life and civil society. In turn, Marxism-Leninism provided these ruling groups with the theoretical justification for their power, holding that the construction of socialism and the march to communism can only be achieved under the leadership of a Marxist-Leninist party in a one-party state.

Ever since, one of the party's main compulsions has been to buttress its own ideological authority. In a social sense, this is the source of the schematic version of Marxist philosophy Stalin brought into Marxism-Leninism. His most ambitious effort in this regard was an article written for the notorious *History of the CPSU (Short Course)* and subsequently issued as a separate pamphlet called *Dialectical and Historical Materialism.* Here Stalin describes dialectical materialism as the Marxist view of the natural world, from which he concludes that:

> Historical materialism is the extension of the principles of dialectical materialism to the study of social life ... to the study of society and its history.[14]

This statement would certainly have come as quite a surprise to Marx, who had little use for philosophical proclamations of a comprehensive world view explaining all natural as well as social phenomena. Indeed, the very term 'dialectical materialism' is nowhere to be found in the body of Marx's work, but seems rather to have been the brain-child of Plekhanov, who first used it in 1894.[15] But even Plekhanov did not venture Stalin's remarkable claim that historical materialism is an 'extension' of dialectical materialism – a view which found its theoretical counterpart in the Social Darwinism so beloved by conservative theorists. Contrary to Stalin, historical materialism was not derived from an a priori philosophical construct but principally from Marx's study of society. For it was only in studying the history of previously existing societies – and hardly all of them at that – that Marx arrived at those insights concerning the ultimately determining roles of the productive forces, the relations of production and the class struggle which comprise the principle theoretical building blocks of his outlook.

The practical consequences of Stalin's inversion undoubtedly help explain the importance he attached to this otherwise unlikely venture into philosophy. For his argument culminates in what amounts to a 'scientific' justification for the authoritarian and voluntarist course embodied in the 'socialist' system he devised – the administrative-command economy, the 'leading' role of the party in a one-party state, and a 'dictatorship of the proletariat' in which all dissent would be suppressed and all political opponents and critics characterized as 'objective' enemies of the working class:

> If the world is knowable and our knowledge of the laws of development of nature is authentic knowledge, having the validity of objective truth, it follows that social life, the development of society, is also knowable, and that the data of science regarding the laws of development of society are authentic data having the validity of objective truths. Hence the science of the history of society, despite all the complexity of the phenomena of social life, can become as precise a science as, let us say, biology, and capable of making use of the laws of society for practical purposes.[16]

Lenin would have been taken aback by Stalin's essentially metaphysical view of Marxism. Rejecting the idea of 'Marx's theory as some universally compulsory scheme of history, as anything more than an explanation of a particular social-economic formation', he declared, 'The Marxists unreservedly borrow from Marx's theory only its invaluable methods, without which an elucidation of social relations is impossible.' [17]

Stalin's Marxism-Leninism, by contrast, accorded its high priests ideological authority over all questions of law, politics, religion, art and philosophy. (It even supported the 'scientific' authority of the political state over biology when the two came into conflict in the notorious Lysenko case.)[18] In short, under Stalin, Marxism-Leninism became not only a complete and closed world outlook to which all under its authority could be held accountable, but also a prescription for the voluntaristic reordering of society.

Stalin also added to Marxism-Leninism an assessment of the state of the world after World War II which became the underpinning of the International Communist Movement for the next 35 years. The emergence of a 'socialist camp,' he said, signified: 'the disintegration of the single all-embracing world market ... [which] has had the effect of further deepening the general crisis of the world capitalist system'.[19]

Predicting that a fast pace of industrial development by the socialist countries would soon leave them 'in no need of imports from capitalist countries', Stalin concluded that:

> The sphere of exploitation of the world's resources by the major capitalist countries (U.S., Britain, France) will not expand, but contract; their opportunities for sale in the world market will deteriorate, and their industries will be operating more and more below capacity. That, in fact, is what is meant by the deepening of the general crisis of the world capitalist system in connection with the disintegration of the world market.[20]

Stalin also revived the earlier thesis – shelved by the wartime alliance with the West – that inter-imperialist rivalry would once again operate as the driving force in the capitalist world. Criticizing those who held 'that the contradictions between the socialist camp and the capitalist camp are more acute than the contradictions among the capitalist countries,' he argued that 'Capitalist Britain and, after her, capitalist France, will be compelled in the end to break from the embrace of the U.S. and enter into conflict with it in order to secure an independent position and, of course, high profits.' [21]

Suffice it to say that history has not dealt kindly with these assessments and predictions. Even as they were being trumpeted as theoretical breakthroughs in Marxist theory, world capitalism was embarking on one of the longest periods of expansion in its history. And while relations between the major capitalist countries were hardly tension-free, war between them remained a remote prospect. There was, in fact, much more tension – at times taking a military form – in the 'socialist camp', as witness Hungary in 1956, Czechoslovakia in 1968, Poland in the early 1980s and the Sino-Soviet conflict from the late 1950s onward. And while the socialist countries may have managed to 'secede' from the world capitalist market, it was they – rather than the capitalist countries – who had their development constricted as a result.

In 1929, as Stalin was cementing his grip on the Soviet Communist Party, the Second All-Union Conference of Marxist-Leninist Scientific Research Institutions adopted a resolution 'On Contemporary Problems of the Philosophy of Marxism-Leninism'. It is a telling commentary on the long shadow cast by Stalinism that virtually every self-proclaimed Marxist-Leninist party in the world would likely have adopted the same resolution 60 years later. The few remaining Marxist-Leninist parties today would probably still endorse it:

> The Marxist-Leninist philosophy – dialectical materialism – is the only scientific theory which gives the proletariat a complete world view and weapon in the struggle for the proletarian dictatorship and the socialist reconstruction of society. It is the outcome of the whole accumulation of knowledge which mankind has achieved, and is confirmed by the everyday experience of the class struggle and every step forward of scientific research.[22]

Marxism-Leninism After Stalin

Stalin's death in 1953 opened up the possibility of major adjustments in Soviet policy and the Marxist-Leninist ideological assumptions he had bequeathed his successors. But from the outset, these possibilities were limited by the fact that Marxism-Leninism had anointed the CPSU's inviolate domination of Soviet society as the only possible form of the 'dictatorship of the proletariat' and proclaimed the system's centralized command economy the only possible model of socialism.

Still, there was a need for change. The limitations of the administrative-command system were beginning to appear in the economy and the suffocating intellectual climate in the country was exacting a toll in the subordination of science and art to the immediate conveniences of party power. The new leadership had also seen at first hand the negative political consequences – to say nothing of the personal perils – inherent in the investment of unchecked power in a single individual. Without in any degree weakening the hegemony of the party center, the new leaders wanted to reassert their collective authority over the system. Finally, Soviet leaders – keenly aware of their vulnerability to US nuclear power – were open to new approaches which might help defuse superpower tensions. The challenge to the party leadership, therefore, was how to distance itself from Stalin the individual while defending both the ideology and the 'socialist path' he had charted.

Probably going further than most party leaders felt comfortable with, Khrushchev denounced Stalin in his famous secret speech to the 20th Congress of the CPSU in 1956, but concluded that the panoply of terror, murder and 'departures from socialist norms' was due to 'the cult of personality' built around Stalin during those years and did not reflect any problems endemic to the system Stalin had built.

Twenty-five years later, the editors of *Kommunist*, the CPSU's theoretical journal, would continue to demonstrate their fealty to Stalinism as the only legitimate Marxism of the contemporary world:

> Stalin did not introduce anything into the Marxist-Leninist science
> that would essentially disagree with its fundamental conclusions ....
> That means that there can be no question whatsoever of any
> 'Stalinism' as an ideological current within the Marxist-Leninist
> science or transcending its limits .... In Stalin's day, the Soviet
> Communist Party confidently and unswervingly followed Lenin's
> course in the principal and essential areas of activity .... The
> personality cult did not change the general direction of Soviet
> society's stage-by-stage advance to the economic, socio-political and
> ideological maturity of socialism.[23]

In the final analysis, official Marxism-Leninism continued to exalt
Stalin's 'development' of Marxist-Leninist theory even while Stalin
himself was conveniently being whited-out of Soviet history:

> It would be wrong to think that the development of Marxism-
> Leninism came to a standstill after Lenin .... After Lenin's death, the
> CPSU contributed conspicuously to the development of scientific
> communism .... The Party formulated the fundamental principles of
> scientific communism concerning the building of socialism and world
> development .... The theory of the country's socialist industrialization
> and the collectivization of farming was elaborated in decisions of
> Party congresses. Heading the construction of the world's first
> socialist society, the CPSU enriched scientific communism with
> important propositions concerning key aspects of the socialist re-
> structuring of the economy, economic planning and management, and
> the development of social relations. Theoretical studies were carried
> further concerning the socialist state, the cultural revolution, the
> relations among nations in a multinational state, problems of ideol-
> ogy, and socialist culture.[24]

Except for the claim that the CPSU under Stalin 'unswervingly followed
Lenin's course', there is little reason to disagree with these appraisals.
For the fact is that Marxism-Leninism and Stalinism are inseparable.
Not only was Marxism-Leninism brought into being by Stalin, it took
shape as the ideological reflection of the society that was built on
Stalin's conception of socialism: the administrative-command economy,
the omnipotent and ubiquitous role of the state under socialism, the
infusion of the dictatorship of the proletariat with the absolute authority
of the party, and the omniscience of the party and its Marxist-Leninist
ideology on all questions.[25]

As Joe Slovo, then general secretary of the Communist Party of
South Africa, noted in reviewing the roots of Stalinism,

> A sizable portion of the diet of so-called Leninism on which we were
> all nourished is really re-packaged Stalinism. Much of it was Stalin-

ism in search of legitimation. The technique was to transform moments of specific revolutionary practice into universal and timeless maxims of Marxism which served to rationalize undemocratic practices.[26]

Marxist-Leninist Variants

Orthodoxy inevitably breeds schisms, and Marxism-Leninism was no exception. While numerous grouplets and sects have laid claim to the Marxist-Leninist mantle ever since the ideology was born in the Soviet political struggles of the mid-1920s, only two variants on the Stalinist orthodoxy merit our attention: Trotskyism and Maoism; Trotskyism because it has remained the main ideological umbrella for critiques of orthodox Marxism-Leninism from the left; and Maoism because, for a period, it was the dominant ideology of the world's largest Communist Party and a significant influence in several Third World revolutionary movements. (It also enjoyed a brief flurry as a non-Trotskyist alternative to Soviet orthodoxy in communist movements in the developed capitalist countries during the 1970s.)

In terms of political power, mass following, ideological concert or unified action, neither variant is comparable to the creed which originated with and was shaped by Stalin. And each, in turn, has given rise to additional variants likewise claiming to be the true faith.

Trotskyism

Leon Trotsky was, in many ways, the most mercurial figure among those who played a prominent role in the Russian Revolution. Lacking a clear-cut political base of his own – he studiously avoided commitment to any of the leading party organizations in the pre-1917 period – Trotsky's stature in the revolutionary movement rested not only on his impressive oratorical and theoretical talents but also on his visible public political activity. Returning to Russia from exile after the overthrow of the czar in the spring of 1917, Trotsky finally resolved his long-standing organizational ambivalence by throwing in his lot with Lenin and the Bolsheviks. He quickly became – next to Lenin – Bolshevism's most compelling public presence. After the Bolsheviks took power, Trotsky became the new state's first foreign minister and then, as the civil war raged, its minister of war. But it was only after Lenin's death in the struggle to determine Bolshevism's future course that one can speak of Trotskyism as a distinct current in revolutionary thought and politics.

Trotskyism's ideological core is the theory of 'permanent (or uninterrupted) revolution', which he himself summarized this way:

> It is, for us communists, that the revolution does not come to an end
> after this or that political conquest, after obtaining this or that social
> reform, but that it continues to develop further and its only boundary
> is the socialist society. Thus, once begun, the revolution (insofar as
> we participate in it and particularly when we lead it) is in no case
> interrupted by us at any formal stage whatever. On the contrary, we
> continually and constantly advance it in conformity, of course, with
> the situation, so long as the revolution has not exhausted all the
> possibilities and all the resources of the movement. This applies to
> the conquests of the revolution inside of a country as well as to its
> extension over the international arena. For Russia, this theory
> signified: what we need is not the bourgeois republic as a political
> crowning, nor even the democratic dictatorship of the proletariat and
> peasantry, but a workers' government supporting itself upon the
> peasantry and opening up the era of the international socialist
> revolution.[27]

Trotskyism has ever since been identified with the notion of continuous
communist-directed revolutionary activity aiming at the direct establishment in any particular country of the dictatorship of the proletariat and
a tendency to view compromises with that goal as 'betrayal'. As far back
as 1904 Trotsky had articulated a similar view of an exclusively
proletarian revolution, calling Lenin's concept of the democratic dictatorship of the proletariat and the peasantry an inherently contradictory
notion under which the working class would, in Deutscher's paraphrase,
'be obliged to forego posing the socialist task directly during the
impending revolution'.[28]

But Trotskyism's conception of 'uninterrupted revolution' was most
fully elaborated in its view of the struggle for socialism as a world-wide
process. Of course, such an outlook was hardly unique to Trotsky. Marx
and Engels had said as much as did all the major figures in early
twentieth-century revolutionary Marxism. And insofar as Russia was
concerned, hardly anyone imagined that socialism could succeed there in
isolation from revolutionary upheavals elsewhere. Virtually all held to the
idea that unless the revolution quickly spread to other countries, the
cause was doomed.

Trotsky, however, took this idea much further than anyone else,
arguing in 1906:

> Without the direct state support of the European proletariat, the
> working class of Russia cannot remain in power and convert its
> temporary domination into a lasting socialist dictatorship .... This will
> from the very outset impart an international character to the
> development of events and open the broadest perspectives: *the*

working class of Russia, by leading in the political emancipation, will rise to a height unknown in history, gather into its hands colossal forces and means and become the initiator of the liquidation of capitalism on a global scale ....

The Russian proletariat ... will meet with organized hostility on the part of world reaction and with readiness on the part of the world proletariat to lend the revolution organized assistance. Left to itself, the working class of Russia will inevitably be crushed by the counter-revolution at the moment when the peasantry turns its back upon the proletariat. Nothing will be left to the workers but to link the fate of their own political rule, and consequently the fate of the whole Russian Revolution, with that of the socialist revolution in Europe. The Russian proletariat will throw into the scales of the class struggle of the entire capitalist world that colossal state-political power which the temporary circumstances of the Russian bourgeois revolution will give it. With state power in its hands, with the counter-revolution behind its back, with the European reaction in front of it, it will address to its brothers all over the world the old appeal, which this time will be the call to the last onslaught: Proletarians of all lands, unite! [29]

In many ways, this promethean reverie captures all that is energizing – but also illusory – about Trotskyism. Pulsating with the spirit of the apocalypse, it advances its analysis with that hortatory disposition toward predictive certainty which *all* versions of Marxism-Leninism seem to share. Not only was Trotsky's vision of 'uninterrupted revolution' based on certainties which obviously were far from certain. Its logic is laced with fateful self-fulfilling prophecies.

Since the peasantry 'is certain to turn its back upon the proletariat', it is necessary to pursue policies – that is, rapid collectivization – virtually guaranteed to antagonize that class. Since the world proletariat is ready 'to lend the revolution organized assistance', there is no reason to make compromises with the international bourgeoisie, thereby assuring the latter's resolve to crush the new Soviet state. Since only massive external support can save the revolution, the Bolsheviks must use their fortuitous 'state-political power' to promote and support the revolution elsewhere – never mind that such a policy will undermine efforts to neutralize capitalist attempts to overthrow the workers' power.

Of course, Trotsky's speculative musings in 1906 had little practical significance. And since, at the time, the general political milieu in which he functioned shared the notion that the 'world revolution' was at hand, they were by no means considered extraordinary – although, as we have seen, Lenin sharply rejected Trotsky's analysis of the peasantry. But when Trotsky as a central figure in the highest reaches of Bolshevik power continued to insist on a political course based on this perspective in the radically changed circumstances prevailing after the revolution, the ensuing debate assumed enormous practical significance.

History has recorded this debate as a controversy between Stalin and Trotsky over the concept of 'socialism in one country'. But this is only partly true and, even then, only at a very high level of abstraction. In more practical terms, it was a debate over whether Soviet Russia would direct the main thrust of its policies toward consolidating the gains of the revolution within the USSR, or would, instead make the promotion of world revolution its principal task.

Both sides, of course, invoked Lenin as an authority to buttress their respective positions. But since Lenin had at different times advanced contradictory views, this exercise in quotation-citing was less than enlightening. Trotsky's supporters naturally turned their attention to comments made by Lenin in the period 1918–20, the years of civil war and 'war communism,' when the possibility of stabilizing the revolution in the face of capitalist hostility and peasant alienation seemed remote. They could thus cite the Lenin of 1919 who said: 'The work of construction depends entirely on the speed with which revolution achieves victory in the most important countries of Europe. Only after such victory shall we be able seriously to undertake the work of construction'.[30] Then there was Lenin a year and a half later: 'We have always stressed that we take an international view and that *a cause like the socialist revolution cannot be achieved in a single country*'.[31]

Stalin, on the other hand, pointed to Lenin's critique of the slogan calling for a 'United States of the World' because it 'may be wrongly interpreted to mean that the victory of socialism in a single country is impossible', when, in fact, 'the victory of socialism is possible first in several or even in one capitalist country alone'.[32] Lenin was to go even further in 1923, when he saw the development of a vast network of cooperatives in conjunction with the NEP as 'all that is necessary to build a complete socialist society', concluding:

> Our opponents told us repeatedly that we were rash in undertaking to implant socialism in an insufficiently cultured country. But they were misled by having started from the opposite end to that prescribed by theory (the theory of pedants of all kinds), because in our country the political and social revolution preceded the cultural revolution .... This cultural revolution would now suffice to make our country a completely socialist country.[33]

Although these remarks suggest that Stalin was on stronger ground than Trotsky in invoking Lenin's authority, neither claim was legitimate. For what both conveniently omitted from their polemics was Lenin's 1923 declaration that 'there has been a radical modification in our whole outlook on socialism'.[34]

Trotsky's critique of 'socialism in one country' assumed a concept of socialism – widely held by most Marxists prior to the Russian Revolution, including Lenin – that required a level of economic development commensurate with that of the most advanced capitalist countries. Likewise, Stalin's announced goal of building socialism in the Soviet Union was also based on the traditional view of socialism – as evidenced by the fact that this was precisely the kind of socialism he set out to build in 1929 with the 'Great Turn' and which, in 1936, he claimed had been completed. Neither view had anything to do with Lenin's radically new concept of socialism. (This issue is more fully considered in Chapter 4 on the transition.)

The oversimplified extremes of the debate – especially as continued by partisans of each side in the subsequent decades – has obscured the fact that there was considerable merit in both positions. Trotskyism's stress on 'world proletarian revolution' was a serious misreading of objective realities at the time and even more out of touch in subsequent years; but his charge that the attempt to construct the Stalinist model of socialism would inevitably lead to a system of suffocating bureaucratism has clearly been vindicated. Stalin, on the other hand, must be given credit for refusing to allow the fate of the Russian Revolution to be held hostage to the increasingly dim prospects of the world revolution; but his abandonment of Lenin's 'radical modification' – whatever else it may have accomplished – brought into being the very system which ultimately failed.

In the wake of these events, Trotskyism became an organized international trend in communism chiefly characterized by a 'world revolutionist' critique of all other forces on the left. Its most ambitious undertaking was the establishment of a Fourth International in 1938. But except in a few temporary and isolated cases, it never achieved a mass social base. As a result, it has been more significant as an intellectual rather than a political force. Its consequent political frustrations have inevitably provoked numerous splits, so that it is hardly possible today to regard Trotskyism as a single, coherent, unified ideology.

Maoism

Mao-Zhedong Thought marks a completely new stage in the development of Marxism-Leninism. It is Marxism-Leninism at the highest level in the present era. It is contemporary Marxism-Leninism for remolding the souls of the people. It is the most powerful ideological weapon of the proletariat.[35]

While Maoism ultimately became a theoretical prescription for what one western enthusiast would call 'the remaking of the human spirit,' its origins more properly rest in Mao's negative view of the policies of liberalization, social reform and rapprochement with the West introduced by Soviet leader Nikita Khrushchev in the mid-1950s.

In pursuit of this latter goal – clearly the precondition for a more normal peacetime economy and a measure of political democratization – the Soviets had taken a number of initiatives even prior to Khrushchev's assumption of power. They had helped bring the Korean War to what was a face-saving end for the US, while imposing significant concessions on the Vietnamese communists to facilitate a nominal settlement of France's doomed 'dirty war' in Indochina. In 1955, Khrushchev moved to heal the rift with Yugoslavia, conceding the possibility of 'a multiplicity of forms of socialist development'. Later that year, a Soviet policy shift led to an agreement ending the four-power occupation of Austria. Then came a four-power Geneva summit rapidly followed by a foreign ministers' conference in the same city, and soon the world was agog with 'the spirit of Geneva' and what was quickly seen as a 'thaw' in the Cold War. (Thirty years later, Gorbachev was to pursue a similar course.)

While this shift in the international climate was greeted with great satisfaction in Moscow, the view in Beijing was much more doubtful since the thaw did not seem to include China. A permanent American army of occupation was stationed in neighboring Korea, while US refusal to sign the Vietnam accords was seen in Beijing as part of a strategic design to encircle China. At the same time, war against the Chinese mainland was an open and frequent topic of discussion in Washington. Mao believed that US leaders would interpret Khrushchev's initiatives as evidence of weakness and that in the developing detente between the two superpowers – and with China heavily dependent on Soviet military and economic assistance – the Soviets were likely to begin negotiating away Beijing's own interests.

(This was not the first time that China's communists had chafed at Soviet policies. Mao rose to undisputed leadership of the Chinese Communist Party [CCP] in the 1930s only after a sharp struggle with a group of Moscow-trained '28 Bolsheviks' who had been sent back to China in hopes of reestablishing full Comintern control of the party. Mao also successfully resisted attempts by Stalin to force him into an anti-fascist coalition with Chiang Kai-shek during World War II, opting instead for a course which fought both the Japanese and Chiang.)

It would undoubtedly be simplistic to reduce the development of Maoism solely to these developments. There was fertile ground for its emergence, both in Chinese communism's own history and in the dynamics of the anti-colonial revolution where Maoist ideology has always had its most positive resonance. Still, ideological differences alone do not satisfactorily explain the Sino-Soviet conflict. Invariably, state-to-state conflicts reflect a clash of perceived interests – a clash which may then be expressed in ideological terms.

Clearly, significant political considerations were at work in Maoism's two defining features: an international line emphasizing the revolutionary struggle against imperialism rather than peaceful coexistence as the centerpiece of communist international strategy; and the belief – as exemplified by the Cultural Revolution – that a communist-governed country must introduce advanced forms of 'socialist' relations of production prior to building up its industrial base.

At the international level, Maoism focused on what it called Khrushchev's 'three peacefuls' – peaceful coexistence with the imperialist states, peaceful competition with them and peaceful transition to socialism. Dismissing the CPSU's view that nuclear weapons had changed the nature of war as 'nuclear fetishism' and 'the philosophy of out-and-out renegades', [37] the Chinese communists argued that imperialism was a 'paper tiger' and that the world balance of forces had already shifted decisively in favor of socialism ('The East wind prevails over the West wind.') They also argued that a third world war was increasingly likely, that it might very well be fought with conventional rather than nuclear arms, and that even a nuclear war would spell the absolute end for imperialism but not for socialism:

> If the imperialists should insist on launching a third world war, it is certain that several hundred million more will turn to socialism. Then there will not be much room left in the world for the imperialists, while it is quite likely that the whole structure of imperialism will utterly collapse.[38]

In the final analysis, Maoism rested on the view that national liberation movements in the Third World had become

> the storm centers of world revolution ... undermining the foundations of the rule of imperialism ... [so that] the whole cause of the international proletarian revolution hinges on the outcome of the revolutionary struggles of the people of these areas, who constitute the overwhelming majority of the world's population.[39]

Just as Trotsky was sure that 'socialism in one country' would inevitably lead to a 'betrayal' of the world revolution by the Soviet Union, so too Khrushchev's elevation of peaceful coexistence to the centerpiece of international policy was seen by the Maoists as inevitably leading to a Soviet 'betrayal' of the national liberation movements. (It is no small irony, of course, that it was Soviet *support* for these movements that constituted the principal stumbling block to detente with the US.) Aside from a deliriously optimistic appraisal of the world balance of forces and a cavalier dismissal of the consequences of nuclear war, the fundamental flaw in the Maoist analysis was that it attributed to the anti-colonial revolution a significance far beyond its capacity. Mao's thesis rested on the premise that China's experience had proven that successful revolution in a Third World country could lead directly to socialism, and that other countries – Korea, Vietnam, Cuba – were already demonstrating that this was a viable model of social transformation. But as subsequent events have shown, that premise can hardly be considered to have been verified. Indeed, the main development emerging out of the anti-colonial revolution has been the expansion and development of capitalism in the Third World, while those countries which set out on a socialist path (China most especially) are now trying to make up for lost time by increasingly turning to capitalist relations of production and distribution in their economies.

It is perhaps understandable that Khrushchev's shifts from fundamental Marxist-Leninist precepts combined with his unilateral moves toward a reconciliation with the US provoked considerable anxiety in Beijing. Could a Soviet Union reaping the presumed benefits of detente be counted on to defend Chinese interests when they clashed – as inevitably they would – with those of the US? Wouldn't a China dependent on Soviet economic support be hostage to the new Washington–Moscow relationship?

These questions led Mao to the conclusion that China could no longer rely on Moscow. Rather than tying its destiny to a Soviet-dominated 'socialist camp', China would have to become economically independent and, ultimately, self-sufficient. In this light, the timing of the Great Leap Forward (1958) can hardly be deemed accidental. This forerunner to the 'Great Proletarian Cultural Revolution' (1966) aimed to bring China quickly into the front rank of industrialized nations, Mao pledging to 'catch up with Britain in fifteen years'.[40] This ambitious program was founded on a view of social development which constitutes the philosophical core of Maoism.

'I stand for the theory of permanent revolution,' Mao had declared as he kicked off the 'Great Leap' in 1958. This startling pronouncement – which Mao warned his listeners not to 'mistake ... for Trotsky's theory of permanent revolution' [41] – is based on three fundamental principles that make up the ideological essence of Maoism.

First, that socialist relations of production are the precondition for a qualitative leap in the level of development of the productive forces: 'The revolution in production relations is brought on by a certain degree of development of the productive forces, but the major development of the productive forces always comes after changes in the production relations.' [42]

Second, there is an irreconcilable contradiction between the different forms of socialist ownership, and unless this contradiction is resolved quickly in favor of the 'higher' form, society will inevitably be back on the 'capitalist road'. Thus even collective farms must quickly give way to full state ownership:

The socialist state and socialist construction cannot be established for any great length of time on the basis of ownership by the whole people and ownership by the collective as two different bases of ownership. In the Soviet Union the period of coexistence between the two types of ownership has lasted too long .... We must resolve the contradiction between these two forms of ownership, transform ownership by the collectives into ownership by the whole people.[43]

And third, material incentives are a remnant of capitalism and undue reliance on them will subvert the efforts to build a socialist society. Moral incentives represent the new, advanced socialist consciousness: 'Individual material interest ... is in reality myopic individualism, an economistic tendency from the period of proletarian class struggle against capitalism manifesting itself in the period of socialist construction.' [44]

These principles comprise the theoretical foundation for Mao's Great Proletarian Cultural Revolution, namely that the heart of the socialist project is the ideological transformation of the masses. (The 'Revolution' is not so titled because the Chinese proletariat was leading it but because it was an effort to impose what Mao considered 'proletarian values' on the populace.) Everything else, including the development of a socialist economy, is dependent on this undertaking. All remnants of capitalism – not only private property, but economic and social activity based on 'individualism' and other bourgeois habits such as the distinctions between manual and intellectual labor – must be wiped out or socialism will be undermined. The Cultural Revolution thus became a political and ideological holy war designed to extirpate its heretics and, Genesis-like, create the 'new man' and his new culture out of the very dust of China:

> The proletariat ... must meet head-on every challenge of the bourgeoisie in the ideological field and use the new ideas, culture, customs and habits of the proletariat to change the mental outlook of the whole of society ... and to transform education, literature and art and all other parts of the superstructure not in correspondence with the socialist economic base.[45]

(Of course, this mass crusade also had a more immediate and practical purpose – to oust 'those Party persons in power taking the capitalist road,' many of whom 'are still nestling beside us'.) [46]

Just as Trotskyism shared a certain ultra-left terrain with Stalinism, so too did Maoism. Thus Mao cites Stalin's rapid collectivization of agriculture in the early 1930s as justification for his view that 'industrialization is not the precondition for collectivization' in agriculture [47] – a view which represents an almost total inversion of Marx, who argued:

> In acquiring new productive forces, men change their mode of production; and in changing their mode of production, in changing the way of earning their living, they change all their social relations.

> The hand mill gives you society with the feudal lord; the steam mill, society with the industrial capitalist.[48]

Maoism's most curious characteristic, in some ways, is its exaltation of Stalin. Politically and philosophically the two men seem light-years apart. Nor was their relationship particularly cordial. But, as we have noted with Mao's admiration of the Soviet experience in collectivizing agriculture, there was much in Stalin's history and methodology which had been incorporated into the basic assumptions of Chinese communism. And in light of Khrushchev's denunciation, Stalin became something of an ideological lightning rod for those who saw themselves defending the purity of Marxism-Leninism from Khrushchev's 'revisionism'. Mao may have been critical of Stalin's attempts to interfere in the affairs of Chinese communism, but he had no desire to diminish Stalin's version of proletarian dictatorship and the tight-knit monolithic party organization which were, after all, indistinguishable from his own.

China's defense of Stalin (70 percent good, 30 percent bad in the classical Maoist formula) is likewise connected to a certain understandable prickliness about the 'cult of personality' in light of the homage accorded Mao by the addition to Marxism-Leninism of that cumbersome dimension, 'Mao Zhedong Thought'.

Ultimately Maoism lost all semblance of any internal theoretical cohesion. Its earlier assertion that 'China must become the arsenal for the world revolution' [49] was unceremoniously buried in Mao's (really Deng Xiaoping's) 'Theory of the Differentiation of the Three Worlds' which called for a world 'united front' made up of China, the US and all the major capitalist powers as well as the Third World to oppose Soviet 'Social-Imperialism'. Likewise, its view that capitalism had been restored in the USSR and that reform-minded 'capitalist roaders' were pursuing a similar course in China became meaningless as Mao's successors scuttled the Cultural Revolution, rehabilitated its arch-enemies and set out on its own all-out path to an economy which now accords capitalist enterprise the dominant place.

Unlike Trotskyism which, never having been burdened with the pressures or constraints of power, can go on indefinitely as an unverifiable ideological resting place, Maoism had a meteoric rise and fall. In China itself, its utopian conception of social development burned out after wreaking untold disasters on the economy. It came into further disrepute after Pol Pot carried the suppositions of the Cultural Revolution to their logical conclusion in Kampuchea. Today it remains alive politically in the activities of groups like the Shining Path guerilla movement in Peru and a handful of tiny, super-revolutionary sects scattered throughout the capitalist world. But many of its utopian and voluntarist notions still have currency among certain influential Western left intellectuals who continue to believe that China's Cultural Revolution was a heroic attempt to establish a beachhead for 'real' socialism in the world.

2 Capitalism on the Rocks?

The reports of my death are greatly exaggerated.

Mark Twain.

Waiting for the Fall

Like Beckett's itinerants patiently awaiting Godot, Marxists have been anticipating capitalism's imminent demise for almost 150 years – and so far, at least, with the same results.

In 1848 Marx and Engels believed that capitalism had reached the point 'when the class struggle nears the decisive hour' [1] and that social-ist revolution in Europe was 'imminent'. They went so far as to predict that the coming 'bourgeois revolution in Germany will be but the prel-ude to an *immediately following* proletarian revolution' (emphasis added).[2] Seventy years later, implicitly acknowledging Marx's miscalcula-tion, Lenin concluded that sometime around the turn of the century capitalism had gone just about as far as it could go and was *now* rapidly approaching the end point of its development as a system. (Following the example of the British economist J.A. Hobson, he called the new system 'imperialism', thus signifying its qualitatively new global expanse.) 'The time when the new capitalism *definitely* superseded the old', he wrote, 'can be established with fair precision; it was the beginning of the twentieth century': [3]

> Imperialism is capitalism at that stage of development at which the dominance of monopolies and finance capital is established; in which the export of capital has acquired pronounced importance; in which the division of the world among the international trusts has begun; in which the division of all territories of the globe among the biggest capitalist powers has been completed.[4]

To Lenin, this new stage signified that capitalism had reached its outermost limits *as a system*. It might continue to grow quantitatively, but the system itself was now increasingly characterized by 'parasitism and decay'.[5] Imperialism was the final stage for the capitalist mode of production, he argued, because the growing domination of economic life by finance capital and increasing monopoly control of various industries by a handful of giant corporations would lead to economic suffocation, the stifling of competition, greater anarchy of production and the decimation of the small entrepreneur. As a result, capitalism's greatest strength – its constant drive to revolutionize the forces of production – would begin to decline. And with the overwhelming power of finance capital – especially as banking also became a monopoly-dominated branch of the economy – the owners of capital would be almost totally removed from the processes of industry and commerce. Therefore they would constantly be inclined more to speculation than to production and the system as a whole would be increasingly characterized by parasitism.

(Lenin qualified this appraisal by noting that the 'tendency to decay' does not 'preclude the rapid growth of capitalism .... In the epoch of imperialism, certain branches of industry, certain strata of the bourgeoisie and certain countries betray, to a greater or lesser degree, now one and now another of these tendencies'.[6] But it is clear from the overall thrust of his argument that Lenin regarded this phenomenon as principally *quantitative* growth which in no way negated the system's moribund character.)

At the same time, international monopolies (cartels) would be developing a similar stranglehold on the world economy. But with the individual nation-state remaining the dominant political form of capitalism, the intense struggle of distinct national capitals with each other would intensify. Therefore, since the world had already been carved up into colonies, dependencies and various spheres of influence by the rival imperialist powers, wars to redivide the world among the strongest national capitals were inevitable; likewise inevitable was the fact that such wars would pit coalitions of imperialist allies against each other, resulting in devastating world wars which would destroy the very economic wealth they were designed to ensure.

As Lenin saw it, both internal and external factors would inevitably bring socialism to the fore as an alternative. Monopoly's advanced forms of socialized production were proletarianizing entire populations; and the expansion of capitalism throughout the world would further swell proletarian ranks. Indeed, he argued, capitalist socialization of production had already brought into being – in the most developed capitalist countries, at least – the structural foundations for a socialist economy. Marx had earlier pointed to the fact that capitalism required and engendered ever-more socialized production on behalf of private appropriation as the system's inherent contradiction, the ultimate source of the revolution which would undo it. Now, Lenin argued, this contradiction had reached the point where continued private appropriation of the social product had become counter-productive to further economic development. By removing themselves from the processes of production, the owners of capital had become a parasitical class who could be dispensed with relatively easily once the proletariat took power. Or, to put it in the language of classic Marxist political economy, the forces and relations of production had become incompatible with each other.

As a result, capitalism's great revolutionary potential, saluted at length in *The Communist Manifesto*, had exhausted itself.

In addition, the wars being fought on behalf of imperialist interests by armies of proletarians engaged in killing each other were already setting the conditions for a mass revolutionary consciousness. Similarly, the rising tide of resistance to colonialism in the oppressed nations would be propelled toward revolutionary solutions and would link up with the proletarian mass in the 'mother' countries.

In sum, said Lenin, his analysis showed that:

> Imperialism is a specific historical stage of capitalism. Its specific character is threefold: imperialism is 1) monopoly capitalism; 2) parasitic, or decaying capitalism; 3) moribund capitalism. The supplanting of free competition by monopoly is the fundamental economic feature, the *quintessence* of imperialism .... Monopoly, which grows *out of* capitalism, is *already* dying capitalism, the beginning of its transition to socialism. The tremendous *socialization* of labor by imperialism produces the same result.[7]

Therefore, he concluded, 'Imperialism begins the era of social revolution'.[8]

(Rosa Luxemburg also believed that capitalism was in its last stage, but hers was a more mechanical analysis based on the idea that capitalism was incapable of carrying out expanded reproduction on its own foundation. As she saw it, capitalist expansion was dependent on its ability to continue integrating additional pre-capitalist structures. Therefore, once it had absorbed all such formations – feudal and semi-feudal agriculture, pre-capitalist societies in Asia and Africa, and so on – it would inevitably turn in on itself as each capitalist country sought to survive and expand at the expense of its rivals.)

At the time, the thesis that capitalism was in an advanced state of decline was not totally implausible. The First World War's unprecedented destruction of human and economic resources seemed to offer grim verification for the idea that out-of-control imperialist rivalry had reached a point of inexorable self-destruction. Then the Bolshevik victory in Russia seemed to establish that the alternative to this capitalist madness was at hand. The Treaty of Versailles confirmed Lenin's view that the driving force of the war had been the struggle over redivision of the world among the main capitalist powers, while revolutions in Germany and Hungary suggested that the overthrow of capitalism elsewhere in Europe was looming.

All these developments were summed up in Marxist-Leninist theory as signifying the onset of what would from then on be known as the 'general crisis of capitalism':

> a world historical process of the collapse of the capitalist mode of production and its revolutionary replacement by socialism. The first

and main feature of the general crisis of capitalism is that the world has split into two systems, the developing socialist system and the moribund capitalist one .... With the rise of the socialist economic system in Russia, the capitalist system ceased to be the sole one prevailing in the world.[9]

After Lenin's death Stalin expanded the thesis of 'moribund capitalism' to embrace the system as a whole, in the process introducing a concept of revolutionary immediacy which went beyond Lenin's most optimistic assessments:

Formerly it was the accepted thing to speak of the existence or absence of objective conditions for the proletarian revolution in individual countries, or to be more precise, in one or another developed country. Now this point of view is no longer adequate. Now we must speak of the existence of objective conditions for the revolution in the entire system of world imperialist economy as an integral whole; the existence within this system of some countries that are not sufficiently developed industrially cannot serve as an insuperable obstacle to the revolution, *if* the system as a whole or, more correctly, *because* the system as a whole is already ripe for revolution.[10]

But as the supposedly 'ripe' revolution failed to materialize, the issue of capitalism's viability again came under consideration. This time it was raised by Nikolai Bukharin, considered by many the foremost Soviet Marxist theoretician and, at the time, the head of the Comintern. Capitalism, he wrote in 1929, 'is again revealing the staggering wonder of technological progress, transforming scientific knowledge ... into a powerful lever of technological revolution'.[11]

Clearly attempting to take a more realistic view of capitalism's prospects, Bukharin's argument was advanced in the context of his bitter struggle with Stalin over the future direction of the Soviet economy. His thesis was that it was both unnecessary and a mistake to abandon the NEP and pursue the policy of forced collectivization of agriculture, because a lengthy period of capitalist stability would continue to give the Soviet Union breathing space to pursue a gradual and balanced process of industrialization. Stalin, meanwhile, argued that a new world war was brewing and that without rapid industrialization the new Soviet state would be one of its victims.

Over the long term, Bukharin's view that capitalism had not yet exhausted its possibilities turned out to be correct. But more immediate developments – the Great Depression of the 1930s, whose unprecedented scale crippled the world capitalist economy for a decade; the rise of fascism; World War II; – tended to reinforce the notion that the system was at the end of its rope. And, of course, the

Soviet Union was not only embroiled in the war; it became the conflict's principal battleground.

Contrary to many often-expressed expectations, however, World War II did not lead to the anticipated collapse of capitalism. In fact, the war itself provided the stimulus for advances in science and technology which were rapidly translated into yet another revolution in capitalism's productive forces and a vast expansion of its productive capacities. And while a 'socialist camp' expanded into Eastern Europe and East Asia in the wake of the war, the capitalist renaissance in Western Europe and Japan clearly turned out to be the more substantive and stable development.

But by this time Stalinism had thoroughly subverted theory to self-serving ideological predilections. Consequently, the thesis on capitalism's imminent collapse remained impervious to these new developments. Instead, communist theoreticians saw a further deepening of the capitalist crisis. The appearance of a socialist economic bloc, they argued, had ruptured the international hegemony of the world capitalist economy. In his last major pronouncement in 1952 Stalin declared:

> The disintegration of the single, all-embracing world market must be regarded as the *most important economic sequel* of the Second World War and of its economic consequences. It has had the effect of further deepening the general crisis of capitalism.[12]

The key factor in Stalin's analysis was that China and the countries of Eastern Europe

> broke away from the capitalist system and, together with the Soviet Union, formed a united and powerful socialist camp confronting the camp of capitalism. The economic consequence of the existence of two opposite camps was that the single all-embracing world market disintegrated, so that we now have two parallel world markets, also confronting one another .... It follows from this that the sphere of *exploitation of the world's resources by the major capitalist countries* (U.S., Britain, France) *will not expand,* but contract; that their *opportunities for sale in the world market will deteriorate,* and that their industries will be operating more and more below capacity. That, in fact, is what is meant by the deepening of the general crisis of the world capitalist system in connection with the disintegration of the world market.[13]

Not only was all this seen as a reaffirmation of the Marxist-Leninist thesis on the general crisis of capitalism, it also demonstrated that the decline was accelerating. Thus, in concluding this section of his work, Stalin posed two questions:

> Can it be affirmed that the thesis expounded by Stalin before the
> Second World War regarding the relative stability of markets in the
> period of the general crisis of capitalism is still valid? Can it be
> affirmed that the thesis expounded by Lenin in the spring of 1916 –
> namely, that in spite of the decay of capitalism, 'on the whole,
> capitalism is growing far more rapidly than before' – is still valid? I
> think that it cannot. In view of the new conditions to which the
> Second World War has given rise, both these theses must be
> regarded as having lost their validity.[14]

Stalin's crude stab at an image of modesty in these awkward third
person refinements of his and Lenin's earlier estimates was quickly
translated into a further theoretical elaboration. With Communist Parties
coming to power in Eastern Europe, China and North Korea, Soviet
theoreticians asserted, the general crisis of capitalism had arrived at a
new, second stage whose:

> principal feature was that socialism had exceeded the bounds of one
> country to become *a world system* ... The departure of new countries
> from the world capitalist system led to a further shrinkage of the
> sphere of capitalist exploitation and to the loss by world capitalism of
> vast markets, sources of raw materials, and fields of capital invest-
> ment.[15]

Undismayed by the fact that the West was enjoying a remarkable
postwar recovery, Soviet theoreticians went on to designate the disintegration of the colonial system as a 'third stage' in the general crisis of
capitalism. Thus, at the end of the 1960s the world's Communist Parties
would make yet another imaginative leap in the time-table of capitalism's
mortality, asserting that: 'Imperialism can neither regain its lost historical initiative nor reverse world development. The main direction of
mankind's development is determined by the world socialist system, the
international working class, all revolutionary forces.' [16]

World events in the 1970s lent a measure of credence to this
optimistic view. It was during this period that undisputed US military
hegemony came to an end as the Soviets managed to overcome
Washington's edge in strategic nuclear weaponry, thereby imposing a
situation of rough military parity between the leading powers of the
world's 'two camps'.

At the same time, world capitalism was severely jolted by a series of
international political/military reverses in the Third World. Chief among
these was the US defeat in Indochina, quickly followed by the victory of
Soviet-backed liberation forces in Angola and Mozambique. (The deployment of Cuban troops in Angola came as a particular shock to
Washington, since it suggested a new level of intervention by members
of the 'socialist camp' in Third World liberation struggles.) These

setbacks temporarily paralyzed American military power, which was unable to prevent the ouster of pro-US regimes in Ethiopia, Nicaragua, Iran, Afghanistan, Grenada and South Yemen. An anti-US government came to power in Libya. US clients in the Philippines, South Korea, Chile, Pakistan and South Africa were under siege and Latin America as a whole seemed poised for an anti-Yankee political explosion.

By the end of the decade, Marxist-Leninists continued to be confident that capitalism's slide into oblivion was accelerating and irreversible:

> It can be concluded from an analysis of the events of the 1970s that the system of state monopoly capitalism is increasingly displaying an incapacity to ensure continuous development of world capitalism, carry through the scientific and technological revolution, and stabilize capitalism's political position.[17]

But once again, Marxist-Leninist assessments outran reality. The capitalist countries proved more resilient than expected. A US global counter-offensive in the 1980s reversed many of the setbacks of the previous decade and helped bring the Soviet bloc's already developing internal crisis to a head.

Undismayed, Marxist-Leninist theoreticians continued to come up with new evidence showing that capitalism was in the grip of a deepening economic dilemma. Phenomena of radical change – if not always of crisis – were not hard to find. The deep recession of the early 1970s, the relatively weak recovery from it and yet another recession in 1980–81 certainly demonstrated that capitalism had not escaped the pattern of cyclical crisis which has been one of its permanent characteristics. The world capitalist economy also faced major dislocations during this period, flowing from the shifting relationships between its three main economic centers – Western Europe, Japan and the US. Similarly, the explosion in science and technology forced major alterations in the very structure of world capitalism.

Marxist-Leninists seized on these phenomena – invariably describing them in a one-sided fashion – to renew their claim that there was only darkness at the end of the capitalist tunnel; and that the end was getting closer all the time. Having been burned so many times before, there were the obligatory warnings not to underestimate 'the still available strength of monopoly capital and its economic and political possibilities'.[18] But these were usually slipped in at the end of lengthy analyses detailing the anticipated woes sure to flow from the ever-deepening crisis. Some Marxist-Leninist political figures did not even bother with the cautions, suggesting instead that capitalism's long-awaited terminal point was almost at hand.

As usual, Boris Ponomarev was the herald of revived revolutionary tidings. Declaring that 'imperialism's once dominant position in the world is undermined for good', Ponomarev saw an aroused working class rejecting capitalist attempts to pay for restructuring by cutting back on workers' earlier social and economic gains:

> Class battles are developing on a vast scale. As Communists predicted, the strike movement is acquiring more and more the character of a direct confrontation with the state-monopoly system and government policy. The country-wide upsurge of the working class movement in Britain, ... the unprecedented strikes in the Federal Republic of Germany, the large-scale class battles and the activization of the left forces in Italy, France, Japan and other countries, and the persistent struggle of the people in Latin America – all these are just a few of the recent events showing that the capitalists are being soundly rebuffed in their attempts to get out of the crisis at the expense of the working people.[19]

The near-celebratory mood prevalent in official Soviet theoretical literature of the time was captured in another text which saw the apocalypse close to hand:

> The growing economic instability of the capitalist system is without precedent in the postwar period. Capitalism is showing its inability to overcome the structural crises in its economy, to solve urgent global economic and ecological problems on its own basis .... The cyclic and structural economic crises are developing into a general instability of the economic system, into major upheavals in the world capitalist economy .... The class struggle in the capitalist countries has entered a new phase when ... socio-political crises are shaking the whole system to the very foundations, threatening the rule of monopoly capital.[20]

US Communist leader Gus Hall was so impressed with the notion of a 'triple-tiered crisis of capitalism' – especially its 'structural crisis' (which he incorrectly called 'a newcomer on the economic scene') – that he permitted himself one of Marxism-Leninism's less salubrious extended metaphors:

> What we are seeing now is a world capitalism entangled in layers of crisis. In this situation, what is new is that capitalism does not have the capacity to cleanse itself. In the past capitalism was able to cleanse the system through cyclical crises. But capitalism's kidneys are worn out, the dialysis machines are too expensive, and it just can't mend itself. [21]

Indeed, as late as 1985 – six years after Margaret Thatcher came to power in Britain, while Ronald Reagan was basking in his landslide reelection triumph and a sustained period of capitalist economic expansion was well underway – the Soviet Institute of Social Sciences would still assert that 'today socialist transformations in the developed capitalist countries are quite imminent.' [22]

But far from proving fatal, the structural crisis – as has generally been the case in the past – engendered major house-cleaning alterations in the capitalist economies. By and large, these changes were at the expense of the working class, especially those sectors in unionized heavy industry. Nowhere was this more the case than in the US. There, ruthlessly implementing the results of the scientific and technological revolution, capital drastically reduced the size of the industrial workforce, severely weakened the trade unions, and neutralized or eliminated many social benefits won in earlier periods. The net result was to make labor more vulnerable to the demands of capital as millions of workers had to choose between 'concessions' and unemployment. In the end, as one US Marxist economist noted, 'the crisis that restructuring posed for the working class was a boon for capital'.[23]

Errors in theory are inevitable, which is why trial-and-error is rightfully considered a linchpin of the scientific method. But the perpetuation of theoretical misconceptions long after they have been undermined by reality has nothing in common with science. In this sense, nothing has discredited Marxism-Leninism's claims to 'science' more than its adherents' stubborn insistence on retaining Lenin's thesis that by the beginning of the twentieth century capitalism had entered its final and moribund stage. Certainly with world capitalism's dramatic recovery and expansion in the post-World War II period, the theory was becoming less and less credible. But the refusal of the Marxist-Leninists to subject Lenin's paradigm to a sober reappraisal when it was already being refuted by history signified that ideological attrition which became a hallmark of that system's theoretical irresponsibility. Despite a growing body of evidence to the contrary, Marxist-Leninist theoreticians continued to base their analyses of capitalism and its prospects on 'principles' rather than concrete realities. As wishful thinking replaced hard-nosed assessments, every blip on the capitalist radar screen was viewed as a step closer to the apocalypse, while every sign of working-class militancy was hailed as the beginning of a new mass revolutionary upsurge.

Such in briefest form is the actual history of Marxism-Leninism's thesis of capitalism's impending last gasp. As even the most casual student of the subject knows, the comments cited above could be duplicated thousands of times over. No theme has been more pervasive or more insistently defended in communist theoretical literature. Refinements as to time, place and circumstance were added over the years. But the underlying presumption has remained a touchstone of Marxist-Leninist theory; indeed, one can hardly imagine Marxism-Leninism as a coherent theoretical system without it: the world – already split into two contending systems – is living through and in the process of liberating itself from capitalism's final and moribund stage; socialism, the next stage in human history, is already at hand and will shortly be extended through a process of proletarian revolution.

While somewhat understandable in light of prevailing conditions, Lenin's own miscalculations were also subjective, the result of trying to find a way out of the Bolshevik dilemma of being fated to bid for power in a revolution whose socialist prospects were remote. Since socialism in Russia was seen as dependent on the success of socialist revolutions elsewhere, the hope for those revolutions may well have influenced his conclusion that capitalism was now ripe for the taking.

But these errors – as with those of Marx and Engels – likewise reflect the limitations of all conjectural analysis. Lenin, after all, was extrapolating from the capitalism he knew, which up until then had shown few signs of the flexibility it was later to adopt in response to the Great Depression of the 1930s, the growing strength of the labor movement and the Bolshevik success itself.

What Lenin did not anticipate was the extent to which capitalism would continue to revolutionize the forces of production, including the development of entirely new technologies which in turn would stimulate a resurgence of entrepreneurial activity, open vast new markets and drastically alter the labor process. Similarly, it may have appeared that World War II confirmed his thesis on the inevitability of inter-imperialist war, but clearly Lenin did not foresee the relative political stability of world capitalism in the period since. (Inter-imperialist rivalry has hardly disappeared, of course. But it has not matured into a military confrontation between any of the leading capitalist rivals for almost half a century; nor does it show signs of doing so even though that rivalry is clearly a significant feature of the present-day world capitalist economy.)

Nor has the Marxist-Leninist analysis of the dire consequences to world capitalism of the passing of the colonial system held up. If anything, the end of colonialism has actually opened up a wider range of possibilities for capitalist expansion, by breaking the monopoly enjoyed by each imperial power in its own colonies. Certainly the Marxist-Leninist belief that a 'non-capitalist path' would be a viable option for newly liberated Third World nations was never realized. (This topic is more fully explored in Chapter 8.)

These phenomena were rarely discussed by Marxist-Leninists; when they were, it was usually to refute them by reference to and reaffirmation of 'principles'. To the extent that Soviet scholars and theoreticians had doubts or reservations about the sacred propositions, they could only express them – if at all – in the most guarded manner.

Finally, the unraveling of 'actually existing socialism' has plainly negated one of the fundamental assumptions underpinning Marxism-Leninism's theory of the general crisis of capitalism; that with the appearance of the new social order in 1917 and its subsequent growth and consolidation, the alternative to the old system had been constructed and was developing as a self-sufficient, independent new social order.

Taken as a whole, these phenomena demonstrate on a practical level that Lenin's thesis of capitalism's exhaustion has not been sustained by history. One might stop there and say no more on the ground that, by definition, any theory which is so at odds with the real world falls of its own weight. While this is virtually self-evident, such an approach avoids some critical theoretical issues which cry out for deeper consideration. Many socialists – and not just Marxist-Leninists – while acknowledging that the Leninist time-frame was off, remain locked into a theoretical construct which still holds that capitalism has exhausted its possibilities and is, therefore, now ripe for dismantling. In order to understand the contours of the present world, it is necessary to understand *why* capitalism has survived – and not only survived but dramatically developed and expanded – over the course of that century which, it was repeatedly and confidently predicted, would erect its tombstone.

By and large, Marxist-Leninists tended to view the very posing of this problematic as a heresy. As one Soviet scholar pointed out in retrospect:

Time was when subjectivist, rigid criteria were adopted – criteria of the 'correctness' of theory and practice proceeding, not from reality, but from ideological propositions taken for dogma. Those who did so constantly exaggerated the revolutionary potential of the oppressed and underestimated the ability of the capitalist regimes to resist them ... What is worthy of note today is the ability of capitalism to prolong its existence and the lack of any visible progress in the working class movement in developed West European countries and the United States.[24]

Lenin's Thesis Reexamined

A theoretical reexamination of Lenin's thesis requires us, first of all, to look at his formulation of the 'stage' question: that is, using Marxism-Leninism's own categories, is capitalism on the eve of the twenty-first century still at the same 'stage' of development that it was at the beginning of the twentieth century? Implicit in this question is the answer to another. Is the system analyzed by Lenin in 1916 capitalism's 'final' stage? I do not see how either of these questions can be answered affirmatively. This is not simply a matter of demonstrating capitalism's continued quantitative expansion. That much Lenin conceded was likely even after it had supposedly entered its 'moribund' period. Rather what must be examined is whether the defining structures and concepts of early twentieth century capitalism have been so altered that many critical categories and 'laws' of the earlier period no longer seem applicable or relevant.

Any serious investigation into this question cannot help but conclude that contemporary capitalism is as different from the system Lenin analyzed in *Imperialism* as that system was from the one analyzed by Marx in *Capital*.

Role of the State

Perhaps the main distinction between the two is the qualitatively enhanced role of the state in the economy.

To be sure, the state has always played a significant role in providing favorable conditions for capitalist expansion. Still, the capitalism examined by Marx was regulated principally by the market. The state, still a relatively minor customer in that market, had little economic power with which to influence the system. Nor did it have the political license to do so. Its main functions were to use its power to provide the system with an economic infrastructure, to limit restrictions on capital accumulation, to maintain law and order and to orchestrate international commercial activity to the benefit of domestic enterprise.

But beginning with the utilization of Keynsian economic theory in the 1930s, and accelerating even more sharply in the decades following World War II, state intervention in the capitalist economy has become an indispensable norm without which the system would have been torn apart.

From 1914 to roughly 1955 this system experienced a series of violent shocks: two world wars, the Russian Revolution, the rise of fascism, the Great Depression, the expansion of 'socialism' beyond the bounds of the Soviet Union and the anti-colonial upsurge. To Marxist-Leninists, these developments were clear heralds of capitalism's impending collapse. But the depiction of this panorama of catastrophe – endlessly repeated in the scientific analyses and somber resolutions of the international communist movement – was woefully one-sided. It either airily dismissed or simply ignored all evidence suggesting capitalism's recuperative powers. It likewise operated on the assumption that the conflicting interests of individual, corporate and national capital made it impossible for the system to develop a collective approach in trying to deal with its ripening contradictions. And finally, it rejected all intimations that the socialist economies were doing anything but inexorably closing the gap with their rivals.

Such a self-deceptive and self-serving methodology totally undermined Marxism-Leninism's capacity to make a materialist assessment of world events and the main trends in world development. It therefore overlooked the fact that far from undermining capitalism, the great traumas which shook capitalism in the two decades from 1930 to 1950 played the role of shock therapy for the bourgeoisie and its system.

In the US, the essential thrust of the New Deal ushered in by Franklin Roosevelt and the Democratic Party in 1933 was an unprecedented program of state intervention in the economy – especially the financial sector – on a scale never before imagined as being consistent with capitalism. Even the much-vaunted social programs – social security, unemployment insurance and so on – were the concrete expressions of the Keynesian emphasis on reviving and maintaining consumer purchasing power in order to stimulate business. Moreover, many of these programs enabled the state to refurbish and update the capitalist infrastructure. The New Deal also had the additional political virtue of ameliorating some of the hardships which capitalist crisis had imposed on the working class, thereby deflecting any possible 'revolutionary' alternatives which might prove attractive to the hardest-hit sectors of society. Then World War II further enhanced the state's supervisory/regulatory role in the capitalist economy.

But the state's new role did not stop with the end of the Depression and the war. The old capitalism dominated almost exclusively by the profit drives of monopoly trusts and corporations did not have the capacity to manage the system's pressing postwar agenda. Tasks such as organizing and financing the postwar recovery in Europe and Japan, regulating the modalities of a vastly enhanced level of international trade, supervising the production and use of nuclear power and conducting the Cold War required an expanded state apparatus with a significant measure of authority over privately owned resources and capital. But while this new role of the state may have appeared as a response to immediate, practical problems, it also reflected an inherent compulsion flowing out of the very size and complexity of a developed capitalist economy.

Just as monopoly capitalism could not return to its early days of 'free' competition, neither can today's capitalist economy return to the system that prevailed 60 years ago. This is not simply a theoretical assertion. Both Margaret Thatcher in England and Ronald Reagan in the US pledged themselves to return capitalism to a less regulated condition. All they accomplished, however, was to cut back on the social safety net of protections won by workers in previous decades – which was undoubtedly their real intention anyway. But the role of the state in British and US economic life can hardly be said to have diminished.

Today modern capitalism has incorporated and depends upon an unprecedented level of expenditures, regulation and coordination which goes far beyond the capacities of the market's 'invisible hand'. Not the least of these are military expenditures which, at least in the US, have poured hundreds of billions of dollars annually into the coffers of the country's largest monopoly enterprises and brought into being that vast 'military-industrial complex' which plays such a momentous role in the economy as a whole. In Germany, and even more so in Japan, the state has actively orchestrated an 'industrial policy' which effectively guides and channels investment decisions by the largest corporations, thereby influencing the direction of all domestic economic activity. Government bailouts for foundering banks and other enterprises have become commonplace, while state support for and direction of huge international economic institutions – the International Monetary Fund (IMF), the World Bank and the like – have brought into being a state-directed structure capable of influencing the world economy as a whole.

Ironically, Marxist-Leninist literature itself had already tacitly acknowledged the fact that contemporary capitalism represented a 'new stage' in the system's development. It did so by calling the present system 'state monopoly capitalism', thereby recognizing that the new role of the state was so significant as to need reflection in the very category used to describe it. Nevertheless, this development was viewed as a quantitative rather than qualitative change. Thus, a definitive 1963 Soviet text notes that 'the development of monopoly capitalism into state-monopoly capitalism ... represents merely the *completion of the material groundwork* for a new, socialist system of society'.[25]

Monopoly, Centralization and the 'Disappearing' Middle Classes

As Lenin noted, monopoly was an inevitable consequence of the earlier stage of 'free' capitalism because it grew directly out of the tendency toward concentration of production in large-scale enterprises. Such concentration heightened the process of centralized production as monopoly enterprises captured dominating portions of the national market in their respective spheres. These tendencies were also inevitable, Lenin said, since they reflected the technological advances of the industrial revolution of the late nineteenth century, which capitalist enterprises could ignore only at the peril of being bested by their competitors.

To Lenin, this development was another indication that imperialism – whose 'economic essence' was monopoly capitalism – was the system's final stage:

> Capitalism in its imperialist stage leads directly to the most comprehensive socialization of production; it, so to speak, drags the capitalists, against their will and consciousness, into some sort of a new social order, a transitional one from complete free competition to complete socialization. Production becomes social, but appropriation remains private.[26]

The market, of course, continued to play a defining role in early twentieth century capitalism. But the growth of monopoly and the more recent scientific and technical revolution of the post-World War II world have introduced a measure of planning and self-regulation which was not possible so long as the economy was dominated by small and medium-sized enterprises.

Lenin's overall thesis, maintained and fleshed out by Marxist-Leninist theory ever since, essentially argues three main points: (1) monopoly sharply reduces the economic function of the intermediate classes, thereby further dividing society into the two main antagonists – the handful of capitalists and the ever-growing working class; (2) as the owners of capital become ever more distant from production – hence 'parasitical' – they lose whatever functional utility they may once have had in the production process and their role is taken over by managers and technicians; and (3) socialized production and the growing trend toward centralization reflect the fact that capitalism itself is preparing the way for socialism.

To what extent has this thesis been verified? And has such verification had the consequences the theory predicted? The observations which follow are based principally on developments in the US, where if anything, monopoly is probably more dominant in the national economic life than it is in any other capitalist country.

Certainly all three tendencies described above have appeared in practice, although to different degrees. Clearly some sectors of petty capitalist enterprise have been undermined, and in some cases, even wiped out. This is especially true of the class of small, private farmers. Many small shopkeepers have encountered a similar fate, giving way to giant department stores, supermarkets and franchises. Nevertheless, the growth of monopoly has not eliminated non-monopoly enterprise as a significant economic force. Certain branches of agriculture in the US – wheat farming for instance – are still predominantly in the hands of 'family' farmers rather than monopoly agribusiness. (This phenomenon seems to be even more widespread in Western Europe and Japan.) Supermarkets, chain stores, shopping malls and fast food franchises have proliferated at the expense of small shops, but the competition between these new forms of property is hardly less intense. For the most part, these new types of enterprise cannot be categorized as *monopoly* capital. Small, family-operated shops have pretty much become anachronisms, but more often than not they have been replaced by larger, more efficient, better-stocked – though still hardly monopoly – ventures. In addition, there has been a proliferation of highly specialized retail establishments such as boutiques, repair services, and copying stores. And, finally, there has been a spectacular growth in service industries generally, from healthcare to rapid delivery enterprises.

Nor has monopoly completely taken over production. If anything, an interesting countervailing pattern has appeared as large enterprises have found total self-sufficiency uneconomical. Today there is a strong trend toward 'out-sourcing' many functions which giant companies used to maintain in-house, usually to smaller enterprises which are able to specialize in one or another operation. Until recently, small-scale production was generally considered a remnant of either pre-capitalist modes or of early capitalism. But with the explosion of new, more individualized products, the proliferation of bureaucracy and the accompanying high costs of overheads in large organizations, the growth of the service sector of the economy and the enhanced role of the 'human factor' in modern production, the once-hailed 'economics of scale' is increasingly giving way to decentralized small-scale enterprise.

The point here is that while the tendency toward monopoly has not slowed down, there is also a countervailing trend which has carved out a new role for small capital.

Dual tendencies can also be found in examining the separation between the owners of capital and production, although the trend identified by Marxist-Leninist theory of a growing disparity seems accurate. The explosion of merger mania, multibillion dollar buyouts, high-stakes wheeler-dealing in the financial markets and so on – little of which is related to advances in production or distribution of goods and services – are symptoms of the growing gulf between the holders of concentrated wealth and the economic foundation for that wealth in production. But that separation is far from absolute. Venture capital, for instance, plays a most important role in financing new technology and entire new branches of industry. (While such investors are themselves not usually involved in production, their economic activity bears a direct relationship to it.)

One must also take into account the fact that the disjuncture between ownership and production is not nearly as great in non-monopoly economic activity. Petty entrepreneurs and self-employed professionals obviously manage their own enterprises. But even the owners of relatively large-scale non-monopoly enterprises are more likely than not to be actively and directly involved in planning, administering and supervising production decisions. With the persisting (and growing) viability of this spectrum of economic activity, this sector of the bourgeoisie continues to have class interests which are, in many respects, objectively different from those of finance capital. This in turn gives rise to a political presence which often serves as a check on the interests of monopoly.

None of this is to deny the fact that 'parasitism' is becoming increasingly characteristic of capitalism as a whole. But there are also inherent reality checks – such as stock market crashes – which periodically serve as forceful reminders of the need to pay attention to the source of wealth in material production. Likewise, the modern bourgeois state can – and often does – assume responsibility for the continued viability of the system as a whole when parasitic depredations threaten to undermine it.

One difficulty in assessing Lenin's view that monopoly capitalism is preparing the way for socialism is that the characteristic features of socialism have not yet appeared in some historically verified form. (The systemic crisis engendered by 'actually existing socialism' and the radical turns toward a greater measure of capitalist enterprise in the surviving 'socialist' states mean that the only socialism the world has ever known cannot be used as a reference point.) Lenin, for instance, set great store by the fact that one consequence of monopoly was the greater centralization of production. But there has been a significant tendency away from centralization in recent years in both the private and public sectors of the capitalist economy; and the socialist experience itself has called into question the emphasis which Marxist-Leninist theory has placed on the centralization of planning, production, administration and authority as a defining feature of a socialist society. Indeed, we may now be witnessing the *limits* of centralized economic mechanisms in any developed industrial society, whether capitalist or socialist.

But even if we assume that capitalism is generating tendencies that will fully mature in a socialist system – an assumption I am quite willing to make – it does not follow that the appearance of such tendencies necessarily indicates any imminent transition to socialism. Socialized production, after all, is principally the consequence of new productive forces, which is why it is far more advanced in modern capitalist countries than it ever was under 'actually existing socialism'.

Imperialist War

Lenin's thesis on the *inevitability* of inter-imperialist war was a theoretical cornerstone of the theory that capitalism's proximate demise was at hand. Colonialism, he argued, had been a central feature in capitalism's earlier expansion. But by the beginning of the twentieth century, he noted, capitalism had completed:

> the final partitioning of the globe – final, not in the sense that *repartition* is impossible; on the contrary, repartitions are possible and inevitable – but in the sense that the colonial policy of the capitalist countries has *completed* the seizure of the unoccupied territories on our planet. For the first time, the world is completely divided up, so that in the future *only* redivision is possible, i.e., territories can only pass from one 'owner' to another, instead of passing as ownerless territory to an 'owner'.[27]

But given capitalism's uneven development and its inexorable search for markets, sources of raw material and cheap labor, the have-not capitalist countries were bound to try to bring about the redivision of the world, a process which – given the stakes – was bound to lead to war:

> What means other than war could there be under capitalism to overcome the disparity between the development of productive forces

and the accumulation of capital on the one side, and the division of colonies and spheres of influence for finance capital on the other? [28]

World War I seemingly provided the most vivid and convincing demonstration of his argument. Looking beyond the jingoist slogans, the national chauvinism and the demagogic pronouncements about 'making the world safe for democracy' and a 'war to end wars', Lenin argued that the conflict was nothing but the transfer of deep-seated capitalist rivalry onto the military battlefield. At the heart of the conflict was the attempt by German capital, by then the fastest-growing and most dynamic in Europe, to wrest its 'fair share' of the world's spoils from those older capitals – British and French in particular – who, between them, had incorporated most of Africa and Asia into their colonial empires.

It was a war without precedent. Where previously individual capitalist countries had engaged each other in combat, this war was fought on a world scale. The main military arena was Europe, but before it was done the conflict had encompassed millions on every continent. It was also a war of unprecedented scale and devastation. New implements of mass destruction made their debut against massed armies still being directed on the basis of outdated military doctrines, as a result of which battlefield casualties numbered 10 million killed and twice that many wounded. (More than 600,000 men were killed in one battle alone.) It was, in effect, the decimation of a generation of young men. The cost was $350 billion (in 1918 dollars) and left both victor and vanquished in dire postwar economic straits.

To Lenin, the war was living proof that capitalism in its imperialist stage had unleashed tendencies toward self-annihilation beyond its control. World War II which began as a conflict between two rival imperialist blocs – the German-Italian-Japanese Axis on the one hand and the Anglo-American-French alliance on the other – seemed to confirm Lenin's thesis further.

Lenin's framework continues to stand up as the most incisive explanation of the underlying sources of both world wars. But in light of the fact that the main capitalist powers have maintained peace between themselves ever since, his generalization that such wars are inevitable under capitalism – and that this itself is one of the most conclusive proofs that capitalism has reached the end of the line – has to be considered anew.

We might well start by recalling Kautsky's critique of Lenin's thesis precisely on this point:

The present imperialist policy [might] be supplanted by a new ultra-imperialist policy which will introduce the joint exploitation of the world by internationally united finance capital in place of the mutual rivalries of national finance capital. Such a new phase of capitalism is at any rate conceivable .... If it does lead to this, to an agreement between nations, disarmament and a lasting peace, then the worst of the causes that led to the growing moral decay of capitalism before the war may disappear. The new phase will, of course, bring the proletariat new misfortunes, perhaps even worse, but for some time ultra-imperialism could create an era of new hopes and expectations within the framework of capitalism.[30]

Kautsky's argument is clearly laced with questionable formulations and illusions. On the other hand, his projection of an 'ultra-imperialism' to supersede the system which had produced world war in 1914 – and was to give rise to it again in 1939 – certainly bears some resemblance to the actual state of affairs in the relations between the world's leading capitalist powers in the period since the end of World War II. The growth of transnational corporations (TNCs) has not eliminated contention between rival national capitals. But they do represent a countervailing and growing force within the world capitalist economy which tends to prevent presentday inter-imperialist rivalry from escalating into military conflict. Meanwhile, the realities of an increasingly integrated and interdependent world capitalist economy have given rise to international institutions – the World Bank, the IMF, the General Agreement on Tariffs and Trade (GATT), for example – designed to ameliorate the sharpest expressions of that rivalry.

Nor can we overlook the impact of nuclear weapons on Lenin's thesis. Traditionally, Marxist-Leninist theory has scorned such an approach, arguing that the compulsions of capitalist economic interest will, in the final analysis, tend to prevail over the 'rationality' of those who believe that a nuclear war would demolish victor and vanquished alike. Indeed, when Gorbachev asserted that the threat of human extinction as the result of a nuclear war was one of those common 'interests' of humanity which surpassed 'class interests', he was roundly pilloried by upholders of the faith for having abandoned Marxism.

In any event, there has not been a war between developed capitalist countries – singly or in coalitions – for almost 50 years. Nor does one seem likely in the foreseeable future. Wars there have been; and invasions too. But by and large, the major capitalist powers have not even threatened each other militarily. The possibility of such a war arising in the future cannot, of course, be ruled out. However, Lenin's thesis on the inevitability of such conflicts does not seem to have held up.

Retarding the Productive Forces

Central to Lenin's framework on the moribund character of modern capitalism was the view that monopoly capitalism inevitably 'retards' the further development of society's productive forces. What is often forgotten is that this was principally a *theoretical* assertion based on logical deduction rather than a body of evidence demonstrating this to be the case. Thus Lenin argued that with the decline of competition and the capacity of monopoly to fix prices, 'the motive cause of technical and, consequently, of all other progress disappears to a certain extent and, further, the economic possibility arises of deliberately retarding technical progress'.[31]

This view sounded very 'logical' at the time. But its underlying assumption – that the accelerating and inexorable trend toward monopoly would significantly retard technological development and thereby reduce capitalist competition as a factor of economic life – has not been borne out. For one thing, monopoly control is rarely (if ever) total. Rather, intense competition between a few giant corporations in the same industry has superseded the relatively wild competition between a few score (or even a few hundred) enterprises. There is also significant competition between monopoly industries within the same field: natural gas, nuclear power, oil and electricity, for instance, competing with each other as a source of energy for both consumer use and manufacturing. As a result, technological innovation and the search for more efficient utilization of resources do not appear to have waned. In addition, the continuing internationalization of the world capitalist economy – and particularly the emergence of powerful economic rivals to the US which was near-hegemonic in the immediate post-World War II period – has heightened competition and helped fuel the scientific and technological revolution of the past quarter of a century.

Once the ideological biases of the past are put aside, it seems clear, as Soviet scholar Victor Sheinis notes, that

> Neither the extensive involvement of the state in economic activity, nor the far-reaching monopolization have cut short the competition and the operation of uncontrollable market forces actively influencing price formation, structural shake-ups and cycles, and simulating or retarding technological progress.[32]

Certainly if we look at the system as a whole on a world scale, it hardly seems arguable today that capitalism has continued to revolutionize society's productive forces not once but many times over. It has engendered revolutions in energy (nuclear power), production (computerized automation), communications (television, satellite systems), information processing and retrieval (computers), and the physical sciences more broadly. It has brought into being whole new technologies, harnessing physics, chemistry and even biology to its economic development.

In light of these developments, Marx's theory on the inherent anarchy of capitalist production requires significant modification. Lenin had already noted the degree to which fairly sophisticated planning had become a part of the internal mechanisms of monopoly enterprises, seeing in this development the way in which capitalism was itself preparing the way for socialism:

> When a big enterprise assumes gigantic proportions, and, on the basis of an exact computation of mass data, organizes according to plan the supply of primary raw materials to the extent of two-thirds or three-fourths of all that is necessary for tens of millions of people; when the raw materials are transported in a systematic and organized manner to the most suitable places of production, sometimes situated hundreds or thousands of miles from each other; when a single center directs all the consecutive stages of processing the material right up to the manufacture of numerous varieties of finished articles; when these products are distributed according to a single plan among tens and hundreds of millions of consumers – then it becomes evident that we have socialization of production; ... that private economic and property relations constitute a shell which no longer fits its contents, a shell which must inevitably decay if its removal is artificially delayed. [33]

Since then, computerization has further maximized the efficient use of resources, further orchestrated the production process so as to limit unnecessary inventory growth and further enhanced the precision of market research. Today, 'market share' has become an accepted and operative concept in corporate planning; and while it has not eliminated competition to change the proportions of market share, it has somewhat reduced problems flowing from overproduction based on unduly optimistic expectations.

In the long run, Lenin's postulate that advancing socialization of production will outstrip the capacities of the private property social relation will probably prove to be true. But so far at least, capitalism has been able to incorporate the most advanced expressions of socialized production into its constant search for maximum profit. That there continues to be considerable waste in this system is undeniable. Still, that waste pales in comparison with the waste of raw materials, energy, agricultural products and finished goods characteristic of the administrative-command economies of the socialist countries. In any event, it would be ludicrous to try to maintain that capitalism in its monopoly stage *retarded* this process.

The ultimate irony, perhaps, is that the appropriate theoretical epitaph for Lenin's thesis on capitalism's looming encounter with extinction should turn out to be one of Marx's most fundamental observations about historical development: 'No social order ever perishes before all the productive forces for which there is room in it have developed'. [34]

Two World Systems

A central tenet of Marxism-Leninism, borrowed directly from the period immediately following the Bolshevik Revolution, is that with the appearance of the Soviet Union, the world was divided into two overtly antagonistic and mutually exclusive social systems – capitalism and socialism – and that ever since, world history has been shaped by their contention, which will inevitably culminate in the defeat of the former and the triumph of the latter.

The logic of Lenin's original conception, of course, is bound up with his view that only the rapid proliferation of socialist revolution to at least one and it was hoped several developed capitalist countries could enable Russia to become socialist. This thesis presupposed that victorious socialist revolutions elsewhere would enable proletarian Russia to compensate for the fact that on its own it had an insufficient material base for socialism. Almost by definition, therefore, the world would then be divided into two systems virtually at war with each other. Under such conditions, both would have to be self-sufficient.

In part, this view was fueled by the surge of revolutionary triumphalism which followed the Bolshevik ascendance to power as communists anticipated the early victory of socialism throughout the world. It was then reinforced by world capitalism's attempts at overt military intervention to throttle the new Soviet state at birth.

One can understand why the generation of communists caught up in the revolutionary fervor of 1917 and all that had preceded it would see themselves not only as the harbingers of world revolution but as its active catalysts as well. One can also understand why that generation and the next, facing the implacable animosity of the capitalist world, would likewise believe that their only hopes for survival rested on the construction of a totally self-sufficient economy and the expansion of their system to other countries.

Faced with hostility and a possible military assault by the capitalist countries – and itself openly declaring its intention to give active (and even military) support to anti-capitalist revolutions throughout the world – the Soviet Union adopted an autarchic approach to economic development, setting out to be self-sufficient in every area of economic life, from food to raw materials to all-sided production of both capital and consumer goods. In a hostile world environment, it could not afford to be vulnerable in any strategic area.

But while necessity may be the mother of invention, it does not follow that it can or should be the mother of generalization. And the theory of two world systems was precisely that – a generalization which attempted to make a socialist virtue (and principle) out of necessity. Yet that theoretical leap and the political strategy which flowed from it was, in the final analysis, self-defeating. Resting on unwarranted premises, it never provided the socialist project with the security it sought and was undoubtedly a major factor in its ultimate collapse.

Not only was the Soviet hope for supportive proletarian revolutions elsewhere misplaced. So were the assumptions on the possibility of building a viable, self-sufficient socialist system on Russia's limited material base. This was not readily apparent in the 1930s, when Stalin's crash program of industrialization enabled the Soviet Union to narrow the gap between itself and the most developed capitalist countries. Then significant progress could be measured in purely quantitative terms. But the autarchic system built during those years could not match the progress made by the most dynamic capitalist countries in the wake of the post-World War II scientific and technical revolution. For that sea-change likewise brought about a revolution in the capitalist mode of production, bringing into being a system which was beyond the capacity of an isolated state (or states) to sustain. Not even the US – with all its tremendous natural advantages – could have maintained its economic position in isolation from the world capitalist economy.

Perhaps the main consequence of the scientific and technical revolution and world capitalism's ability to harness its results to economic life has been the creation of a single world economy within which every country is obliged to function on pain of economic constriction and stagnation. The pronouncements by Stalin and subsequent Soviet leaders that the 'loss' of the countries of the 'socialist camp' would constrict capitalist expansion never really materialized; if anything, the capitalist countries were perfectly willing to restrict their business dealings with those countries in order to keep them isolated.

The futility of national autarchy in today's world was gradually becoming apparent even to the countries of 'actually existing socialism' in the 1970s. Deng Xiaoping's return to power in China in the mid-1970s was tacit acknowledgment that Mao's attempt to construct a communist autarchic system had failed and that China's way out of underdevelopment was inexorably tied to its participation in the world economy. In the Soviet Union, Gorbachev represented the same impulse – hence his willingness to cede victory in the Cold War to the United States and avail the USSR of the benefits of the larger world economy.

But beyond the particular circumstances demonstrating that the Marxist-Leninist concept of two world systems rested on false premises looms a larger question: Can it be presumed that the world transition from capitalism to socialism – assuming that it is on the horizon – will come about as a result of the overt contention between two contending world systems? All historical precedent suggests not. Such transitions from one mode of production to another on a world scale have always taken place over the course of many generations, during which time an uneasy coexistence between the two tended to prevail. And so long as uneven development remains a fact of life among the nations of the world, it would be far better to assume that the transition from capitalism to socialism will follow that pattern. Revolutions, after all, are fought to attain political power – and that can be won in a matter of a few years or even months. But economic changes cannot be made so precipitously. That being the case, it is much more likely that the transition to socialism will have characteristics of both modes of production in individual countries and in the world as a whole. Come to think of it, didn't Marx imply as much in his designation of socialism as itself the form through which the transition from capitalism to communism would be made?

In retrospect, we can hardly help but conclude that Marxism-Leninism's ritualistic sounding of capitalism's death knell for 75 years owed more to wishful thinking than fact. This is not to say that capitalism is trouble-free. The very scientific and technical revolution which generated a new array of productive forces and significantly aided another round of capitalist expansion has engendered major dislocations in the world capitalist economy. Even as centripetal economic tendencies pull competing capitalist centers toward each other, countervailing centrifugal tendencies pull them apart. The three main centers – Western Europe, Japan and the US – are each going through painful adjustment periods with all the potential that holds for engendering widespread social unrest. Meanwhile, proletarianization has impacted the consciousness of a growing mass of workers brought into capitalist production in the Third World.

Nevertheless, it would be quite foolhardy to conclude from these phenomena (and others, of course) that capitalism has exhausted its development potential or that it has lost the capacity to continue revolutionizing its productive forces. Buoyed by its proclivity for the historical sweep, the Marxist paradigm has tended to telescope social processes. Just as modern-day telescopes have made us aware of distant stars and galaxies, so Marx's social analysis has brought socialism into our field of vision. But the apparent proximity of a possible future socialist society may also have engendered a tendency to anticipate history, to forget that the decline of a social system – especially one as dynamic as capitalism has shown itself to be – is a lengthy process likely to unfold only over the course of many generations.

3 The Vanguard Party

The spontaneous struggle of the proletariat will not become its genuine 'class struggle' until the struggle is led by a strong organization of revolutionaries.

Lenin [1]

Invented by Lenin shortly after the turn of the century, the vanguard party is the most distinguishing characteristic of that line of socialism's development which runs from Marx through Lenin to Stalin and the International Communist Movement. The Leninist party is to its brand of socialism what the Catholic church has always been to its brand of Christianity. Both are the sole organizational manifestations of exclusivist doctrines with the inside track on truth – the former descending from Marx and Lenin, the latter from God. Both are the only authorized interpreters and developers of their doctrines. And both are managed by hierarchies with an overwhelming self-interest in upholding the sanctity of their respective belief systems and their own authority and privileges:

> The Party is the highest of all forms of organization of the working class and its mission is to guide all the other organizations of the working class. (It) consists of the finest members of the class, armed with an advanced theory, with knowledge of the laws of the class struggle and with the experience of the revolutionary movement.[2]

Today this entire structure is in disarray. The party which took power in Russia in 1917 and ruled the huge domain of the Soviet Union for more than 70 years is gone – finally driven from power when its resistance to change culminated in an aborted coup in 1991. The governing parties of the Eastern European socialist countries are likewise gone, their fate sealed when Soviet leaders refused to intervene and rescue them from mass uprisings against them. Communist Parties still hold power in China, Vietnam, Cuba and North Korea, but their prospects are not promising.

The non-governing Communist Parties are similarly in a state of advanced disorder. Virtually all have gone through splits. The few parties which once had a significant working-class base have declined sharply in numbers, strength and political clout, the only exceptions being one or two who changed their names as part of a process of forging new identities and distancing themselves from the Marxist-Leninist legacy.

Many small parties, having lost a major source of material support with the collapse of the CPSU, linger on only as pathetic testimony to the stubbornness of communist gerontocracies. (The major exception to this pattern is the Communist Party of South Africa which, thanks to its close and supportive ties to the African National Congress and its own history as an inter-racial organization in the anti-apartheid movement, has a substantial popular base.)

While this entire phenomenon is inexplicable outside the broader, all-pervasive crisis which has overtaken the ruling parties of the socialist world, the crisis of the communist movement pre-dates the collapse of 'actually existing socialism'.

In the years following the Bolshevik triumph, several newly formed Communist Parties achieved a significant measure of influence in the working-class movements of their respective countries. Communists also became prime contenders for the leadership of national liberation movements in a number of colonial and semi-colonial countries. These gains were due, in part, to the world capitalist crisis of the 1930s, the apparently remarkable achievements of the Soviet Union and the rise of fascism. But they also reflected the fact that the communist movement was better prepared for these developments organizationally than were their socialist rivals.

World War II and the immediate postwar period saw a further rise in the fortunes of Communist Parties. Their dramatic growth in France, Italy and the Balkans – achieved largely by their role in the anti-Nazi resistance and the prestige of the Soviet Union – was a direct spur to the Truman Doctrine and the beginnings of the Cold War. Communists in China, Yugoslavia, North Korea and Vietnam – unlike their counter-parts in most of Eastern Europe, who were escorted to state rule by the Red Army – won power principally through their own efforts.

By the end of the 1950s, however, this process had begun to ebb. As a result of capitalist economic recovery and Khrushchev's exposure of Stalin, the large Communist Parties of Europe arrived at what turned out to be the outer limits of their growth, while smaller parties steadily lost influence. Revolutionary parties did better in the Third World. But the Sino-Soviet split led to the appearance of contending communist formations, while the success of the Cuban Revolution similarly encour-aged those revolutionary-minded political forces in Latin America who were critical of what they considered the reformism of the traditional Communist Parties.

By the mid-1970s it was clear that the non-governing Communist Parties had reached an impasse. Their obligatory defense of the 1968 Soviet invasion of Czechoslovakia suggested a return to Stalinism and further exacerbated the process of defection in the ranks which had begun after Khrushchev's denunciation of Stalin. The New Left in Western Europe and North America proved much more appealing to radicalized youth than did the sterile orthodoxy which continued to characterize the Communist Parties. Likewise, new social movements – feminist, anti-racist, environmental, gay and lesbian – proved to be more receptive to a radical outlook and to have more political initiative than the traditional labor movement, which the communists continued to see as their main base. The rise of Eurocommunism in, not coincidentally, the only parties in the developed capitalist world which had a mass working-class following, was itself an attempt to reverse the communist decline by projecting a more realistic view of the world. Communist-led forces continued to score some gains in the Third World, but these were principally the result of effective positioning in the remaining anti-colonial struggles. On the socialist level, the intensification of the Sino-Soviet split and Maoism's dismal attempt to leap to communism via cultural revolution significantly weakened communist credibility. Meanwhile, Cuba's attempt to light a continental spark in Latin America had come to a sorry end in the mountains of Bolivia.

In short, by the time Gorbachev let the world in on the scale of the Soviet crisis in 1986, most of the world's non-governing Communist Parties had become thoroughly marginalized; and the ruling parties were on the verge of those events which would bury some – most significantly, the fount of world communism, the CPSU – and call into question the viability of the rest.

Parties bearing the name communist will undoubtedly continue to exist for some time, although they are clearly high on the endangered species list. Some may even continue trying to base themselves on the traditional Marxist-Leninist doctrine of the party, but it is hard to imagine a future for them other than as cults held together by nostalgia and a common subculture. Although new socialist organizations are bound to appear, it seems certain that the collapse of 'actually existing socialism' and its underlying ideology has brought the era of the Marxist-Leninist vanguard party to an end.

An examination of the theory of the Leninist party is more than an academic enterprise, however. If anything, the disarray of the communist movement has again brought the question of organization to the forefront of socialist thinking. In that light, a serious review of the vanguard party experience is mandatory. In undertaking such a review it is essential that we go beyond the formal enunciation of Lenin's theory of the vanguard party and focus on the *operative* theory too, the one which was actually forged in the real politics of the communist movement and which determined the practice and structure of all the Communist Parties.

It is also necessary to make a distinction between non-governing and governing parties, a distinction which Marxist-Leninist theory tended to obscure. At the broadest theoretical level, of course, there is a clear line of descent from the former to the latter. It is also fairly obvious that the Stalinist party, which was molded and took shape as an instrument of supreme state authority, profoundly influenced the organizational subculture of the non-governing parties. (The appetite for absolute authority, after all, tends to be irresistible for lesser satraps.) Nevertheless, the two are not the same. One speaks to the strategy for making revolution; the other to a particular conception of socialism.

In this section, therefore, we will examine the vanguard party as the force designated by Marxism-Leninism to lead the working class in the struggle for power. Later, in the section dealing with the dictatorship of the proletariat, we will look at the theory and practice of the vanguard party in the context of the socialist state.

A 'Party of a New Type'

Lenin's theory of the vanguard party was a striking innovation in the international socialist movement as it had developed up until that time. Although the first communists created political organizations in order to provide their theories with the necessary action component, the party question did not assume its subsequent overriding importance until the prospects of socialists winning at least a measure of political power began to emerge in the 1890s. Such possibilities began to appear as the development of capitalism brought into being a sizeable proletarian mass, thereby providing a political base for socialist parties to compete in the bourgeois electoral process – some of them winning significant representation in their countries' respective parliaments. These parties – whose structure was essentially the same as that of the other electoral parties – inevitably exercised the largest influence in the international socialist movement and its common organization, the Second International.

But in czarist Russia at the time, socialist politics was being shaped by strikingly different conditions. There, the political representatives of the rising bourgeois classes, chafing under the arbitrariness of czarist absolutism, were demanding democratic, Western-style political reforms. Many university students, swept up in the fervor of a period of crumbling ideological authority, began gravitating towards the relatively new (for Russia) ideas of Marxism. At the same time, industrial workers were demonstrating new-found strength in an unprecedented strike wave demanding amelioration of the oppressive conditions in Russia's young but growing mass enterprises.

These developments were also a stimulus to the Russian socialists. Operating outside the bounds of czarist legality, constantly harassed by the police, lacking any significant base in the working class, the socialists until then had been more of an intellectual than a political force. In the new climate of mass unrest, however, many socialists began establishing ties with the workers' movement. Buoyed by some initial successes in developing a mass social base, they founded the Russian Social Democratic Labor Party (RSDLP) in 1898. But the party did not, as yet, have a clear conception of itself, its political strategy or its organizational form. This was the political environment in which Lenin first began formulating the idea of a party of 'a new type' – a party based not just on politics but on an obligatory common ideology – whose members' lives would be completely organized around revolutionary activity.

No socialist party had ever posited such a tightly knit structure with so much authority invested in its leaders and with such all-sided demands on its members. In Marx's day, the various socialist parties were principally educational organizations with few, if any conceptions of fashioning the strategy – let alone tactics – of the workers' struggle. The parties of the Second International had a more overtly political action perspective, but this was mainly connected to work in the trade unions and the parliamentary process. Its emphasis was on immediate reform with socialism as, at most, a distant and ambiguous goal.

But czarist Russia – its burgeoning capitalism trying to burst the bonds of outmoded feudal structures and a political power fundamentally at odds with its economic system – was seething with revolutionary unrest on all sides. And while Lenin acknowledged that the focus of this tumult was hardly socialist, he believed that it was possible for the Russian working class, provided it was properly trained and led by a party of 'professional revolutionaries', to convert the coming bourgeois-democratic revolution into a process that would enable the communist-led proletariat to take power.

It was painfully obvious, however, that the RSDLP could never play the role Lenin – speaking in the name of history – had assigned it. Its social base was still quite small. It lacked both a common ideology and a political program. Its structure was loose and amorphous. The various local organizations which had combined to form it were not accountable to each other or to a single center. Such an organization could never agree on – let alone carry out – Lenin's ambitious agenda. Calling organization 'the most urgent problem of our movement' and 'its sore point', Lenin saw the unification and transformation of the RSDLP into a 'party of a new type' as the prime socialist task of the moment.[3]

The 'Advanced Detachment' of the Working Class

At the heart of Lenin's new vision was the view that while the proletariat represented the most revolutionary force in Russia, it would not arrive at revolutionary consciousness nor consistently take up revolutionary tasks on its own. Focused primarily on its own immediate economic struggle, the working class could only fulfill its mission under the leadership of a new kind of political party, a 'vanguard' which would undertake to raise the workers' political sights and guide them through all the complex twists of strategy and tactics sure to emerge in the course of the revolution.

Such a party, he argued, could only grow out of the socialist movement, for it alone understood – in a way that the workers themselves could not – the historical destiny and significance of the working-class movement. But the socialist movement was likewise doomed to futility until it was rooted in a critical mass of workers capable of turning socialism into a real political force:

At first socialism and the working class movement existed separately in all the European countries. The workers struggled against the capitalists, they organized strikes and unions, while the socialists stood aside from the working class movement, formulated doctrines criticizing the contemporary capitalist, bourgeois system of society and demanding its replacement by another system, the higher, socialist system. The separation of the working class movement and socialism gave rise to weakness and underdevelopment in each: the theories of the socialists, unfused with the workers' struggle, remained nothing more than utopias, good wishes that had no effect on real life; the working class movement remained petty, fragmented, and did not acquire political significance, was not enlightened by the advanced science of its time.[4]

Lenin saw the vanguard party as the key to fusing these two strains. Ideologically consolidated around Marxism, united behind both the goal of socialism and a more immediate political program, and organizationally capable of acting in unison, the party would be recognized by the working class as its vanguard on the strength of its broader vision and by winning the adherence of enough workers (especially among the industrial proletariat) so that it would function as a real political force in society. In the process of fusion, said Lenin, the party would draw ever-larger numbers of workers into its ranks, thereby transforming itself from an 'outside' force into an internal component ('the organized detachment') of the working-class movement.

The Monolithic Party

While setting out to unite Russia's socialist movement into a single party, Lenin made it clear that he was not interested in bringing all its tendencies intact into one organization. 'Before we can unite, and in order that we may unite,' he declared, 'we must first of all draw firm and definite lines of demarcation.'[5]

As Lenin saw it, only a party united from the outset in a common set of ideological assumptions concerning strategic goals, broad political assessments, philosophy, methods of organization and so on would be up to the revolutionary tasks history had placed before it. Only on such a foundation would it be possible to create an organization capable of functioning as the 'general staff' of a mass working-class revolutionary 'army'.

Lenin's persistent use of military imagery in his description of the vanguard party and its tasks did not mean that he was concerned exclusively with armed struggle as the path to power, although he did believe that at a certain point the military aspect of the conflict would come to the fore. Rather, it was meant to underscore the fact that the party was organized to give leadership to one side in the class war which was an inherent feature of capitalist society. To fulfill this role, he believed, the party would require the discipline and hierarchical structure characteristic of the military. Otherwise – especially in the conditions of Russia – the party would prove no match for its class opponents, nor for its task of winning the confidence and support of the workers. But Lenin also understood the limits of the military analogy. The party, after all, was a *voluntary* organization and – unlike the army – its members could leave at any time. Thus, if for no other reason, the total lack of democracy in a purely military organization would not work for a political party.

The discipline, the subordination of the individual to the collective, the inherently hierarchical structure, the willingness to sacrifice and the staying power of an army of professional revolutionaries, he argued, could only be achieved on the basis of a conscious sense of common, historically significant purpose. If this vision implied a fervor characteristic of religious zealots, it would be based not on ungrounded faith but on the most advanced science – the science of society as unfolded by Marx and Engels:

> The shouts will rise that we want to convert the socialist party into an order of 'true believers' that persecutes 'heretics' for deviations from 'dogma', for every independent opinion, and so forth. We know about all these fashionable and trenchant phrases. Only there is not a grain of truth or sense in them. There can be no strong socialist party without a revolutionary theory which unites all socialists, from which they draw all their convictions, and which they apply in their methods of struggle and means of action. To defend such a theory, which to the best of your knowledge you consider to be true, against unfounded attacks and attempts to corrupt it is not to imply that you are an enemy of *all* criticism. We do not regard Marx's theory as something completed and inviolable; on the contrary, we are convinced that it has only laid the foundation stone of the science which socialists *must* develop in all directions if they wish to keep pace with life.[6]

Fixated as he was on overcoming the prevailing lack of cohesion in socialist ranks – and determined that a clear break with Bernstein's 'revisionism' should be the ideological starting point for the party of a

new type – Lenin had little patience with those he regarded as
nay-sayers. This was perhaps understandable. But his commentary
makes for ironic reading today in light of the enforced dogmatism,
witch-hunting and stifling conformity which became characteristic features of the world communist movement.

Democratic Centralism

In his 1899 series of articles proposing a major turn in Russian socialist
politics, Lenin began wrestling with the problem of how to make a
revolutionary organization effective while maintaining its democratic
character. He was convinced that what the revolutionaries needed most
was a highly centralized party with enormous authority ceded to its
leadership, thereby enabling it to plan, direct and carry out a broad
range of political activity. In part, his emphasis on centralism stemmed
from what Lenin felt was the inherent weakness of the dispersed and
highly localized Russian socialist movement at the time (it lacked even a
single national newspaper). But his principal concern was with the
repressive political conditions under which Russian revolutionaries had
to function:

> Against us, against the tiny groups of socialists hidden in the
> expanses of the Russian underground, there stands the huge machine
> of a most powerful modern state that is exerting all its forces to
> crush socialism and democracy .... In order to conduct a systematic
> struggle against the government, we must raise revolutionary organi-
> zation, discipline and the technique of underground work to the
> highest degree of perfection.[7]

In this context, Lenin tended to see the question of inner-party
democracy as somewhat secondary. He believed, for instance, that the
party's democratic character would be assured – conditions permitting –
by vesting final authority in an elected national congress which would
determine its various leading bodies. It also seems clear in reading the
debates of the time that a certain level of open and free debate in party
ranks was simply taken for granted. But responding to those who
insisted that the 'broad democratic principle' be the party's main
organizational underpinning, Lenin declared:

> Broad democracy in Party organization amidst the gloom of the
> autocracy and the domination of gendarmerie is nothing more than *a
> useless and harmful toy*. It is a useless toy because, in point of fact,
> no revolutionary organization has ever practiced, or could practice,
> *broad* democracy, however much it may have desired to do so. It is a

harmful toy because any attempt to practice 'the broad democratic principle' will simply facilitate the work of the police in carrying out large-scale raids, will perpetuate the prevailing primitiveness, and will divert the thoughts of the practical workers from the serious and pressing task of training themselves to become professional revolutionaries to that of drawing up detailed 'paper' rules for election systems .... The only serious organizational principle for the active workers of our movement should be the strictest secrecy, the strictest selection of members, and the training of professional revolutionaries. [8]

At the RSDLP's Second Congress (1903), he again pointed out that the heated debate over party rules was inexorably conditioned by the fact that it took place 'at a time when political discontent is almost universal, when conditions require our work to be carried on in complete secrecy, and when most of our activities have to be confined to limited, secret circles and even to private meetings'. [9]

The system which eventually emerged from this lengthy discussion was based on six fundamental principles of organization:

1) Submission of the minority to the majority. 2) The congress, i.e., an assembly of elected delegates from all duly authorized organizations, must be the Party's supreme organ; moreover, any decision by these elected delegates must be final. 3) Elections to the Party's central body (or bodies) must be by direct vote and must be held at a congress. Elections outside a congress, two-stage elections, etc., are impermissible. 4) All Party publications, both local and central, must be completely subordinate to both the Party Congress and the relevant central or local organizations of the Party. Existence of Party publications organizationally unconnected with the Party is impermissible. 5) There must be an absolutely clear definition of what Party membership implies. 6) In like manner, the rights of any Party minority must also be clearly defined in the Party rules.[10]

In light of subsequent practice, this last point is especially noteworthy, since it assumes not only the existence of minorities, but that they would have 'rights'. Compare this with subsequent Marxist-Leninist theory which held that: 'The demand that a minority should be given some kind of special rights is incompatible with the requirements of Party discipline.' [11]

After the revolutionary upheavals in 1905 brought significant political concessions from the autocracy, a special Unity Congress of the RSDLP in 1906 adopted a host of new, more democratic procedures regarding internal party affairs. It was only then that the term 'democratic centralism' came into widespread use. Thus, immediately after the congress, Lenin noted:

> We were all agreed on the principle of democratic centralism, on
> guarantees for the rights of all minorities and for all loyal opposition,
> on the autonomy of every party organization, on recognizing that all
> party functionaries must be elected, accountable to the party and
> subject to recall. We see the observance in practice of these
> principles of organization, their sincere and constant application, as a
> guarantee against splits, a guarantee that the ideological struggle in
> the Party can and must prove fully consistent with strict organiza-
> tional unity.[12]

Lenin's commitment to democracy – whether in the party or in society
at large – was, of course, far from absolute. 'Democracy for whom?' he
asked time and again, indicating that suppression of the political rights
of those classes from whom the working class would take power was
essential to the revolution's security. Similarly, democracy in the party
would always be mediated by circumstance – although unlike his political
successors, Lenin seems to have been fairly scrupulous in asserting when
the party was facing a democracy-limiting situation.

A telling case in point is the ban on inner-party 'factions' which
became a cardinal principle of democratic centralism. The rule banning
factions was first adopted at the Tenth Congress of the RSDLP in 1921
as part of a broader resolution on 'party unity' which placed a number of
temporary restrictions on inner-party norms. These emergency measures
were adopted in the wake of spontaneous mass opposition among
peasants, workers and rank-and-file military units to the draconian
measures of war communism, thus provoking the revolution's worst
crisis since the Bolsheviks took power. In response, Lenin proposed his
New Economic Policy (NEP), a sweeping change in course which would,
essentially, restore capitalism in the Russian countryside and permit a
wide range of private enterprise in the new Soviet system. Complicating
the situation was the fact that a significant 'left opposition' to the NEP
had emerged within the party in organized form. It was under these
circumstances that the ban on factions was proposed, Lenin noting:

> The banning of opposition in the party results from the political logic
> of the *present* moment .... *Right now* we can do without an
> opposition, comrades, *it's not the time for it!*... This is demanded by
> the objective moment, it's no use complaining .... The *present*
> moment is one at which the non-party mass is subject to the kind of
> petty-bourgeois wavering which in the *present* economic position of
> Russia is inevitable ... and we must show unity not only of a nominal
> but of a deep, far-reaching kind.[13]

Lenin underscored the extraordinary and limited nature of this resolution
in other ways. For one thing, he rejected a proposal that the ban on
factions be applied to elections for the next party congress. He also

noted that one provision – empowering the Central Committee to remove its own members –

> has nothing whatsoever to do with democracy or centralism .... The Congress elects the Central Committee, and by this it expresses the highest trust, bestowing the leadership on it. But that the Central Committee could have such a right in relation to its members is something our party has never tolerated. It is an extreme measure, especially adopted in consciousness of the dangers of our situation.[14]

Lenin's intentions here are unmistakable. Nevertheless, subsequent Marxist-Leninist theory holds that 'The decisions of the Tenth Party Congress on Party unity, and on the impermissibility of factions, became the *unshakable principle* of Party life and Party building'.[15]

Ironically, while the addition of the adjective 'democratic' to Lenin's centralism was adopted by the Russian communists largely to protect inner-party democracy, the term itself is now generally taken to mean a highly centralized, authoritarian system of party organization. In part, of course, this stems from Lenin's view of centralism as the absolute and democracy as a variable in party organization. Even more so, however, it is the consequence of seven subsequent decades in which all the parties of the international communist movement – whether ruling parties or not – have been characterized by an enormous expansion of central authority, limitations on if not outright hostility to democracy and a growing insistence on uniformity of views. For the most part, this has taken place with a formal nod to the democratic procedures and guarantees embodied in the early Bolshevik views of democratic centralism. But those concepts and procedures have been so tampered with by ecclesiastical interpretation, historical misrepresentation and the aggrandizement of power by party leaders that the term is now rightly associated with the limitations on democracy and an almost unchecked authority in the hands of a vested leadership with virtual lifetime sinecures.

The Vanguard Party: A Critical Appraisal

Although Lenin's 'party of a new type' won out in the internecine battles of the Russian socialist movement, it remained unique to Russia until the Bolsheviks took power. Then Lenin took what would prove to be a fateful step. After hastily convening a meeting to form the new Third International, he universalized the Bolshevik conception of the vanguard party, insisting that parties wishing to join it would have to be organized along similar lines; indeed, that the Comintern itself would be organized as one huge vanguard party.

In doing so, he institutionalized a form which took shape not only under the conditions of czarist autocracy, but in a predominantly peasant country in which the working class was a small minority and the labor movement was relatively underdeveloped. This is most striking in the party-building literature of the Russian revolutionary movement, much of whose argumentation is based on such factors. A large part of the success of the Bolshevik organization rested on the fact that its structure was in full harmony with the principle – found so frequently in nature, society, engineering and art – that form follows function. Or, as Lenin himself put it, 'the character of any organization is naturally and inevitably determined by the content of its activity'.[16]

The inner logic of the Bolshevik organizational structure stemmed from the assumption that the party's principal task was the preparation for and organization of insurrection. Its strength derived from the fact that in czarist Russia such was indeed the case. The clandestine character of its inner workings was appropriate to the conditions of political repression that prevailed in Russia. Its centralism and discipline were likewise appropriate to a party actively preparing for armed struggle. And in a country with a small working class, much of it only recently off the land itself, there was something to be said for the notion of a vanguard whose mission would be to 'train' the proletariat in the art of politics.

But were these conditions the same in the developed capitalist countries? Acknowledging the dissimilarities, Lenin tended to dismiss them as largely illusory and ultimately irrelevant. Bourgeois democracy might prevail in most capitalist countries, but since it was at bottom a sham which could be abrogated in an instant, it would be a mistake for the communists to base their organizational structure on any illusions about it. Contending political parties – even including nominally socialist parties – might take power through peaceful elections, but did anyone doubt that the struggle for a real *class* transfer of power would bring out the full military force of the capitalist state? The working class might be much larger in the industrialized countries of the West and enjoy a long history of self-organization, but it remained deeply under the influence of 'opportunism' and would need to be retrained in a revolutionary fashion.

Ultimately, however, it all came back to the assumption that the epoch of proletarian revolution had dawned. Communist-led insurrections might be defeated (as they were in Germany and Hungary), the revolution itself might be delayed, some capitalist countries might even show signs of economic stability. But the 'final conflict' had already begun – not just in Russia but on a world scale – and the communists had to be organized accordingly:

The parties affiliated to the Communist International must be built up on the principle of democratic centralism. In the present epoch of acute civil war the Communist Party will be able to perform its duty only if it is organized in the most centralized manner, only if iron discipline bordering on military discipline prevails in it, and if its party center is a powerful organ of authority, enjoying wide powers and the general confidence of the members of the Party.[17]

After more than 75 years, however, this rationale for the pervasive centralism and iron discipline of the democratic centralist party is wearing thin. Nevertheless, fealty to the vanguard 'party of a new type' has remained a cardinal principle of Marxism-Leninism. True, highly centralized, tightly disciplined parties have proven their worth in struggles against colonialism and for national independence, although the communists in those countries have hardly been the only ones to adopt such organizational forms. But in the developed capitalist countries, the worth of the vanguard party has been more questionable.

In particular, it has been a powerful force for sectarianism in the working-class movement. From the very beginning, it reinforced the hostility (on both sides) between the communists and the old Social Democratic Parties of the Second International. Marx and Engels had said that 'The Communists do not form a separate party opposed to other working-class parties.' [18] But the new vanguard parties were not only separate from other working-class parties. They saw all other contenders for dominant influence among the workers as 'class enemies'.

Attempts to build a 'united front against fascism' in the 1930s and, subsequently the impressive role of many Communist Parties during World War II, took some of the edge off these divisions for a while. But so long as the communists saw themselves as *the* vanguard – and was there ever a Communist Party that didn't? – sectarianism toward other parties and political forces on the left was inevitable. As the General Secretary of the Argentine Communist Party would point out during the burst of Marxist-Leninist introspection in the late 1980s, 'Our attitude to the other leftwing forces was determined by the sectarian assumption that we were the sole revolutionary force.' [19]

Marx and Engels had also argued that the Communists 'do not set up any sectarian principles of their own by which to shape and mould the proletarian movement'. [20] Yet a prime purpose of the vanguard party was not only to 'shape and mold the proletarian movement' according to 'principles' which the communists had developed. Its function was also to guide and direct that movement in a disciplined and 'scientific' fashion. (It might be argued, of course, that Marx and Engels had warned specifically against sectarian principles, but there has never yet been a revolutionary party which viewed its own principles as 'sectarian'.)

In time, a process which had begun in a spirit – however misplaced – of revolutionary zeal became little more than a parody of Lenin's 'party of a new type'. Ironically, the smaller any given party was the more it seemed determined to act out that dogmatic posturing and out-of-control hubris which became the classic stereotype of anti-communism.

Nothing, however, has discredited and disarmed the vanguard party more than its unsavory legacy of throttling inner-party democracy. The discrepancy between a formal adherence to democratic regulations and the realities of inner-party life in the communist movement is no secret. The movement made little attempt to disguise the authoritarian, hierarchical nature of its system. How could it? Not only was it a norm of party life; it was a system, members were told over and over again, reflecting a 'proletarian' world outlook. For the working class had little patience with those – clearly 'petty bourgeois individualists' – who were more concerned with the right of an individual to disagree with the party line than with the party's ability to move as a monolithic force.

'Proletarian' mythology pervaded the communist movement and was invoked to justify the entire authoritarian structure and its practices. Democracy? The vanguard party was the highest form of democracy. It was democratic in a way that no bourgeois political party could imagine, let alone consider for itself. The party was inherently democratic because it represented and fought for the interests of the working class, itself constituting the overwhelming majority of the people. Further, it was democratic because it was thoroughly based on majority rule and would not tolerate attempts by a minority to interfere with decisions made by a democratically elected leadership. Dissent? Members were guaranteed the right to criticize leaders and policies. Leadership accountability? Leadership was elected by periodic national congresses or conventions, the delegates to which were chosen by democratic vote at delegated congresses held at lower levels.

Even if one were to take the typical party's rules at face value, the power of the hierarchy as the sole interpreter of the rules makes the entire process a sham. For instance, all Communist Parties enshrine their members' rights to criticize. But their elucidation of this principle is invariably more bound up with restricting that right than with guaranteeing it. Thus, as a basic Marxist-Leninist text explains:

> The Party always distinguishes criticism which strengthens it from that which weakens it, which turns into criticism for criticism's sake, into mere carping. While granting freedom of criticism and calling to account those who stifle it, the Party at the same time allows no one to use this freedom for the purpose of weakening its ranks ... While granting extensive rights to its members, the Party at the same time naturally demands loyalty to its program, aims and ideals. It does not tolerate advocacy of anti-Party views ... Party discipline does not expect anyone to relinquish his own convictions if they are not at variance with the principles of Marxism-Leninism ... Party discipline also requires that Communists should not discuss inner-party questions outside the Party.[21]

Notably missing from all this is who makes the distinction between 'anti-party views' and party-strengthening criticism. Who determines which convictions are consistent with or 'at variance with the principles of Marxism-Leninism'?

Party congresses and leadership elections are similarly under the tight control and supervision of the central party apparatus. Agendas, speaking privileges, access to the party press are all closely micro-managed from the center – as is the delegate-selection process. The ban on 'factions' – clearly not applicable to the leadership even though it functions as such during inner-party struggles – enables the leadership to disenfranchise opponents before they have an opportunity to organize. Party finances are a closely held secret, with control in that area delegated only to a faithful 'inner core' whose loyalty to the prevailing leadership is beyond question.

To vanguard parties, democracy is not a system guaranteeing members' rights and the organization's vitality, but a 'problem' to be managed to make sure that its exercise does not jeopardize the organization's stability and continuity. Even in the early days of Bolshevism, party functionaries often focused more on curtailing members' rights to criticize than on facilitating them. A 1906 Central Committee resolution establishing 'limits within which the decisions of Party congresses may be criticized' was roundly lambasted by Lenin, who called it:

> A totally wrong conception of the relationship between *freedom to criticize* within the Party and the Party's *unity of action*. Criticism within the limits of the *principles* of the Party Program must be quite free not only at Party meetings, but also at public meetings. Such criticism cannot be prohibited. The Party's political action must be united. No calls that violate the unity of definite actions can be tolerated either at public meetings, or at Party meetings, or in the Party press .... Obviously, the Central Committee has defined freedom to criticize inaccurately and too narrowly, and unity of action inaccurately and too broadly ... The principle of democratic centralism and autonomy for local Party organizations implies universal and full *freedom to criticize* so long as this does not disturb the unity *of a_definite action;* it rules out *all* criticism which disrupts or makes difficult the *unity* of an action decided on by the Party.[22]

Where democratic centralism has become, in the hands of Lenin's heirs, an instrument to shore up the powers of the party hierarchy and to curtail democracy, to Lenin it meant a qualitative expansion of democracy in the party. In this framework, 'universal and full freedom to criticize' has become a principle, with restrictions needed only to guarantee unity around a *'definite'* action. Thus, in the statement above, Lenin went to great pains to underscore the word *definite* so as not to provide a blank check for party leaders to abuse their authority by suppressing theoretical debate or categorizing particular views as departing from Marxism, weakening the party, or being frivolous. Nor does Lenin wall off public discussion of political questions that may be taken up inside the party.

But as the received wisdom – and the determination of heretical deviations from it – became the exclusive province of party leaders with enormous organizational authority, minimal talent and extremely limited accountability, the 'party of a new type' became the breeding ground for time-serving apparatchiks with a natural bent for intellectual suffocation, who persistently evoked the need to defend the 'purity' of their ideology to justify their authority.

Contrary to the simplistic explanations to be found in most Marxist-Leninist texts, democratic centralism has not been merely – or even principally – a system for ensuring unity in implementing 'definite' party decisions. (Most political organizations, after all, expect minorities to abide by majority decisions. And since non-governing parties are, at bottom, voluntary organizations, mature leaders will think twice before trying to force reluctant members to carry out decisions they oppose.) Rather, it has been the organizational device by which entrenched party leaders have walled themselves off from the rank and file of party members and from broader social realities which might suggest a lack of political perspicacity in the leadership. It effectively nullifies the right to criticize when those being criticized have the power to determine the permissible terrain and content of dissent. It is a system which breeds complacency in the top leadership, toadying in the middle levels of leadership and passivity in the membership.

Democratic centralism encourages dogmatism, stifles political and theoretical initiative, fosters a need-to-know climate which gives the highest party bodies a monopoly on information regarding party affairs, and opens the door to petty corruption. It has enabled party leaders to suppress inner-party debate, buttress bureaucracy, grant (and withhold) privileges, punish critics, launch and carry through ideological witch-hunts and in every way transform parties into virtual political fiefdoms. Justified as a means of keeping the party secure, it has facilitated the infiltration of government spies and agents. And far from maintaining the party's 'unity,' it has forced dissent underground, resulting periodically in ruinous splits. Worst of all, it has reinforced sectarianism, lent itself to voluntaristic enterprises, fostered a manipulative relationship to those whose cause the communists were nominally serving, throttled attempts at internal reform and perpetuated the leadership of political incompetents.

Its ultimate and perennial rationale is the sanctity of Marxism-Leninism. Thus a CPSU Central Committee member would declare in 1983:

The great theories of Marx, Engels and Lenin have entered the international communist movement as the sole scientific world view of the working class .... In matters concerning the scientific validity of Marxism there can be no compromises, no ideological-theoretical concessions. Departures from the theory of Marx and Lenin are no more than an ideological rupture with their cause, the cause of the socialist revolution and communism. Shoulder to shoulder with fraternal parties, the CPSU safeguards the purity of Marxist theory, repulsing every attempt to distort its class and scientific essence and sweeping away debris that is alien to its revolutionary-critical spirit.[23]

For more than 60 years, such statements have been the battle-cry for those who believe that there is only one truth and that the leading Marxist-Leninists (that is, party leaders) have privileged access to it. It takes no great leap of the imagination to figure out that 'repulsing' efforts to 'distort' the theory (read 'disagreeing with the party leadership') has time and again been readily convertible into a convenient pretext for suppressing political opposition. Appropriately enough, this paean to the spirit of Torquemada concludes with the prophetically ironic punctuation that Marxism-Leninism 'is the reason this (the international communist) movement is successfully fulfilling its function as the most influential political force of modern times.' [24]

Long before the political center of the international communist movement disintegrated, the revolutionary function of Lenin's 'party of a new type' – at least in so far as all the main capitalist countries were concerned – had receded into the realm of ideological fancy. Not only were prospects of proletarian revolution in those countries remote; the idea that Communist Parties would be the 'vanguard' of such revolutions was even more far-fetched. But the form remained, testament to the ideological hold of Marxist-Leninist mythology and the advantages to be gained from the Soviet Union's world position and largesse. It was this disjuncture which haunted and undermined those parties even before their world was irrevocably shattered in 1991.

Ideologically committed and organizationally structured to be the exclusive and ordained 'vanguard' of an increasingly distant workers' revolution, they were universally mistrusted by the rest of the socialist movement. Their unflagging support for the Soviet Union was a political millstone they could not afford to discard without cutting off a critical supply line and deeply splitting their own ranks. And Moscow, in turn, made it abundantly clear that any tampering with the Leninist party form would constitute the kind of break with Marxism-Leninism that was deemed intolerable. For it was precisely the democratic centralist structure which enabled the Soviet party to exercise control over the parties of the International Communist Movement through their close relationships with each party's leadership core.

Today the remnants of vanguard parties in all the developed capitalist countries are sad anachronisms. The Italian Communist Party – by far the largest of the non-governing parties and the one with the most substantial working-class base – has changed its name, shed the Leninist form and settled into being a new socialist-oriented Party of the Democratic Left. Others are more quietly abandoning the organizational strictures of yesteryear or preparing to do so. Most, however, have been reduced to brooding cults clinging to the fantasy that they are still the proletariat's vanguard and that a revived Soviet Communist Party will once again set things right.

Ironically, the long-range dire consequences of the 'party of a new type' had been anticipated by one of the leading revolutionary figures of Lenin's time. Long before the worst of her premonitions had been realized, Rosa Luxemburg warned the still fledgling communist movement:

> We can conceive of no greater danger to the Russian Party than Lenin's plan of organization. Nothing will more surely enslave a young labor movement to an intellectual elite hungry for power than this bureaucratic straitjacket which will immobilize the movement and turn it into an automaton manipulated by a Central Committee ... What is today only a phantom haunting Lenin's imagination may become reality tomorrow.[25]

Unfortunately, Luxemburg's phantom did materialize and exacted a heavier toll on both the party and socialism than even she had imagined. For what Luxemburg's prescient critique had uncovered was that buried deep in the concept and structure of the vanguard party were the seeds of a totalitarian culture which ultimately blossomed into the political norms of both 'actually existing socialism' and the International Communist Movement.

Now, in retrospect, it is hard to avoid the conclusion that in those countries with a distinct and honorable socialist tradition, where the leaders and activists of numerous mass democratic movements are every bit as 'conscious' – usually more so – than the vanguardists, where revolution is not on the agenda and where bourgeois-democratic norms prevail in the political system, the democratic centralist vanguard party has done socialism and those advocating it more harm than good.

4 The Transition: Stalin's Road to Socialism

Our ideas about Marxism and Leninism, about socialism in general, have come to us from Stalin.

Fyodor Burlatsky [1]

The touchstone of scientific socialism is the transition question. As materialists, Marx and Engels had little to say – except in the most general terms – on what a future communist society might look like. They scorned the utopian tradition of offering yet one more model of an ideally devised social system, arguing that socialism would be fashioned by future generations under circumstances which could not be determined in advance.

But they did devote considerable attention to the transition, exploring such matters as its material prerequisites, the role of classes and class struggle in bringing it about, and – in broad outline – some of the likely characteristics of the process. Marx also carefully noted that in all previous transitions from one social system to another, the new mode of production emerged alongside the property relations and within the framework of the old – a process which, historically, has taken place both before a political revolution and afterwards.

The Marxist-Leninist view of the transition, however, is based not so much on Marx (or Lenin) as it is on Stalin's 'revolution from above' – the crash program of 1929–36 which forcibly collectivized agriculture, totally nationalized industry and commerce, and brought into being the system of centralized planning and administration which characterized the Soviet Union for the next 60 years. Several generations of Marxist-Leninist theoreticians have obscured this discrepancy, chiefly by investing traditional Marxist concepts with a qualitatively different content and insisting that Stalin's all-sided, abrupt 'historical rupture' had settled the transition question once and for all.

During its initial period, when 'actually existing socialism' retained some significant measure of ideological authority, the Stalin version of the transition was considered such a fundamental principle of 'scientific socialism' that few Marxist-Leninists could imagine any other. It seemed only natural, then, that when after World War II the Soviet Union was orchestrating the spread of 'actually existing socialism' to Eastern Europe, it would do so on the basis of Stalin's transition framework.

Perhaps the most contentious problem Marx and Engels grappled with in contemplating the transition was the nature of the post-revolutionary society after the working class had taken power and while capitalist relations still dominated the economy. The first step in the revolution', they said in *The Communist Manifesto*, 'is to raise the proletariat to the position of ruling class, to win the battle for democracy'.[2] This would most likely be accomplished quickly, they believed, by extra-legal action; that is, a political revolution. But, materialists that they were, Marx and Engels also recognized that the subsequent economic transformation would unfold 'by degrees' through a complex and lengthy process.

The dilemma was this: if even a political changeover requires a measure of continuity from the old to the new, how much more so is this the case in transforming the economy? Even a short-term disruption in production and distribution could plunge it into chaos and undermine the revolution's political support. And this was so much more certain to be the case when the material base for the new social order was still primitive and backward.

Ultimately Marx and Engels came to the conclusion that a communist society could not immediately replace capitalism. Rather there would be, of necessity, a lengthy period of transition, one that would comprise an entire historical epoch. This transitional society they called socialism – or the 'lower stage' of communism.

Nominally accepting this theoretical framework, the CPSU – following Stalin's lead – completely trivialized and distorted it. Although the sharp historical rupture imposed on Soviet society by the 'revolution from above' seemed to work for a while – it certainly registered significant gains in industry – in the long run it turned out to be the main source of the calamity which ultimately overtook 'actually existing socialism'. Demonstrating this point requires a brief excursion into history.

The Russian Revolution

If Marx and Engels grappled with the transition as a theoretical question, Russia's revolutionaries confronted it as a practical one. There the fledgling communist movement, pledged to 'socialism', faced the dilemma of leading a proletarian revolution in a country which still awaited the completion of the transition from feudalism to capitalism.

Seeking to curb what he considered the unrealistic perspective of some members of the RSDLP who believed that the coming revolution would culminate in socialism, Lenin warned in 1905: 'We cannot get out of the bourgeois-democratic boundaries of the Russian revolution, but we can vastly extend these boundaries.' [3]

To Lenin, the limits imposed on the socialist mission stemmed from two related facts: Russia's relatively low level of capitalist economic development, and the overwhelming preponderance of the peasantry in the country's population. Therefore, he argued: 'The idea of seeking salvation for the working class in anything save the further development of capitalism is reactionary. In countries like Russia the working class suffers not so much from capitalism as from the insufficient development of capitalism.' [4]

But Lenin was also convinced that the Russian bourgeoisie would be unwilling or unable to make its own revolution a thoroughly democratic one – even in bourgeois terms – since the increasingly organized and militant working class would thereby gain enormous political initiative. Under such circumstances, he believed, a victorious bourgeoisie was likely to cut a deal with the autocracy which would be permitted to retain a measure of political power and privilege to be used against the workers.

Lenin's remarkable solution to this dilemma was a strategy aimed at bringing the bourgeois-democratic revolution under the leadership of an alliance between the working class and the peasantry. However, he cautioned, such an alliance could not be based on a socialist agenda:

> The peasantry is interested not so much in the absolute preservation of private property as in the confiscation of the landowners' land, one of the principal forms of private property. While this does not cause the peasantry to become socialist or cease to be petty bourgeois, it may cause them to be wholehearted and most radical adherents of the democratic revolution .... The peasantry will inevitably become a bulwark of the revolution and the republic, for only a completely victorious revolution can give the peasantry *everything* in the sphere of agrarian reforms that the peasants desire, of which they dream, and of which they truly stand in need (not for the abolition of capitalism) ... but in order to raise themselves out of the mire of semi-serfdom, out of the gloom of oppression and servitude, in order to improve their conditions of life as far as it is possible to improve them under commodity production.[5]

Although the 1905 revolution was defeated, revolt erupted again in February 1917. A major factor was Russia's sorry performance in World War I, then at its height with no end in sight. This time, undermined by the system's blatant military incompetence and resultant mass casualties in a largely peasant army, the czar was forced to give way. But the problems left behind proved too much for the provisional government which succeeded him. Locked into political positions dictated by bourgeois class interests, it could neither condone the spontaneous mass land seizures in the countryside nor move to extract Russia from the war. The conditions were thus set for Lenin and the Bolsheviks to win the effective leadership of the revolution, which, by October, they had accomplished. Their call for 'Peace, Bread and Land!' won the political support of large numbers of workers, peasants and soldiers; in October, when the opportunity presented itself, building on their years of disciplined preparation, they were able to move with dispatch and sureness of purpose and seize power.

The strength of the Bolsheviks rested not so much in their numbers or in the size of their conscious political constituency. True, they had grown spectacularly during 1917, from 24,000 in February to roughly 200,000 by October. But they were hardly the largest political bloc in the country. And in the elections for the Constituent Assembly held in November *after* they had taken power, they received only 25 percent of the vote. But they were the only organized force with a clear sense of the political possibilities of the moment and with the requisite boldness to exploit those possibilities to the hilt. Their triumph seemed to verify Lenin's strategic assessment that with capitalism in general rapidly approaching exhaustion, Russia's bourgeois-democratic revolution could be converted into a proletarian revolution.

War Communism

Despite Lenin's earlier warnings on the revolution's limits, the Bolsheviks pursued a much different course after taking power, instituting a draconian system of primitive socialist concepts they called 'war communism', subsequently described by one Soviet economist in this way:

> State enterprise lost its socio-economic independence and other forms of ownership were reduced to a minimum. Production was assessed by values produced, i.e. by volume, rather than the output of consumer values. Money was transformed into accounting units and thus lost its substance as the commodity of commodities, i.e. a universal equivalent. The market was completely excluded from the economy and regarded as the antithesis of socialism. All these measures were presented as the practical application of Marx's ideas.[6]

Marxist-Leninist mythology has tended to portray war communism simply as a series of temporary emergency measures forced on the Bolsheviks by the exigencies of foreign intervention and the civil war. But while wartime necessity undoubtedly was a practical impetus behind the policy, the Bolsheviks also saw it as a crucial step toward constructing a socialist economy. Thus early in 1919 the Russian Communist Party's Draft Program pledged to:

> Finish the expropriation of the bourgeoisie and the conversion of the means of production and distribution into the property of the Soviet Republic .... Continue steadily replacing trade by the planned, organized and nation-wide distribution of goods. The goal is the organization of the entire population in producers' and consumers' communes that can distribute all essential products most rapidly,

systematically, economically and with the least expenditure of labor by strictly centralizing the entire distribution machinery .... Strive as speedily as possible to introduce the most radical measures to pave the way for the abolition of money.[7]

Significantly, the Draft Program makes no mention of the worker-peasant alliance, citing instead 'the proletarian and semi-proletarian elements of the countryside' as the main forces on which the party will rely. The emphasis here is on new 'socialist' property relations rather than on production.[8]

Clearly such a perspective went far beyond a plan for dealing with the crisis of the moment. As Trotsky later pointed out:

War communism was, in essence, the systematic regimentation of consumption in a besieged fortress. It is necessary to acknowledge, however, that in its original conception it pursued broader aims. The Soviet government hoped and strove to develop these methods of regimentation directly into a system of planned economy in distribution as well as production. In other words, from 'war communism' it hoped gradually, but without destroying the system, to arrive at genuine communism.[9]

Acknowledging that the policy was an otherwise inexplicable 'theoretical mistake', Trotsky adds an enlightening note:

All calculations at the time were based on the hope of an early victory of the Revolution in the West. It was considered self-evident that the victorious German proletariat would supply Soviet Russia, on credit against future food and raw materials, not only with machines and articles of manufacture, but also with tens of thousands of highly skilled workers, engineers and organizers.[10]

The effect of war communism on the already staggering Russian economy was catastrophic in both industry and agriculture. The harsh measures brought about a calamitous fall-off in production and seriously undermined the Bolsheviks' political base. The early enthusiasm of the peasant masses for the revolution vanished as abrupt nationalization of land negated the earlier policy of land redistribution. Armed violence in the countryside and mutinous uprisings in the armed forces – such as the famous Kronstadt Rebellion which would shock some of the Bolsheviks into reassessing their course – were direct consequences of the harsh policy. Ultimately, Lenin would sum it up this way:

In attempting to go over straight to communism we, in the spring of 1921, sustained a more serious defeat on the economic front than

any defeat inflicted upon us by Kolchak, Denikin or Pilsudski.[11] ....
The surplus-food appropriation system in the rural districts... hindered the growth of the productive forces and proved to be the main cause of the profound economic and political crisis that we experienced in the spring of 1921.[12]

Nevertheless, subsequent Soviet accounts of the period had little to say about war communism except to argue that 'victory in the civil war would have been impossible without' it, [13] a view which then became the standard Marxist-Leninist summation of the period. This benign judgment – like so much else of Marxism-Leninism's historical accounting – bears a distinctly self-serving political imprint, since Stalin's 'Great Turn' in 1929 incorporated many of war communism's theoretical assumptions, was pursued with similar (albeit even more extensive) coercion and was likewise explained as imposed on the Bolsheviks by the threats of foreign intervention.

The New Economic Policy (NEP)

Faced with the crisis engendered by war communism, Lenin developed what turned out to be the most daring and significant innovation in socialist thought on the transition question since Marx's time: the New Economic Policy (NEP). Like so many important theoretical breakthroughs, the NEP was first conceived largely as a short-term practical response to the disastrous state of the Russian economy. It was, said Lenin, 'a strategical retreat [from] our previous economic policy ... [which] assumed that there would be a direct transition from the old Russian economy to state production and distribution on communist lines.' [14]

The central motor of the NEP was the 'tax in kind', a measure which replaced war communism's system of forced requisition of the peasants' surplus by a tax which could be paid in product. Such a step, Lenin acknowledged,

> means reverting to capitalism to a considerable extent .... For the abolition of the surplus-food appropriation system means allowing the peasants to trade freely in their surplus agricultural produce, in whatever is left over after the tax is collected – and the tax takes only a small share of that produce. The peasants constitute a huge section of our population and of our entire economy, and that is why capitalism must grow out of this soil of free trading.[15]

The purpose of this opening to capitalism, Lenin noted, was three-fold: 'a) to develop the productive forces of peasant farming; b) to develop small industry; c) to combat the evils of bureaucracy.' [16]

This concession to capitalism in the countryside implied and was accompanied by other significant compromises: private trade was legalized; many state-owned enterprises were leased to private capitalists; small businesses were allowed to reopen; state-owned enterprises were placed on a cost-accounting basis; foreign capital was encouraged to invest in Russia and permitted to repatriate profits. At the same time, large-scale industry, banking and foreign trade – the 'commanding heights of the economy' – remained in state hands. Finally, understanding that state-sponsored capitalism not only engendered but required a measure of capitalist ideology, Lenin said that 'Every important branch of the economy' – whether in the private or the state sector – 'must be built up on the principle of personal incentive'.[17]

The NEP was an almost immediate success. In just two years – from 1921 to 1923 – industrial production doubled. By 1926, the increase was five-fold and finally surpassed the prewar (1913) level. In the same five-year period, electricity production went from 520 million kilowatt hours to 3.5 billion – twice the prewar level. Steel manufacture rose from 183,000 tons to more than 3 million. Agriculture also got back on its feet, as the grain harvest of 1926 more than doubled the 1921 output. Exports, while still far below prewar totals, increased nine-fold.[18]

The NEP was not without its problems, of course. The revolution's initial measures – land reform and the liquidation of the bulk of the kulaks (the wealthiest peasants) – broke up the large estates which had produced much of the nation's food supply. Now with the dismantling of war communism's first attempts at forced collectivization, the NEP fostered two contradictory tendencies: increased production for the market by the remaining kulaks and middle peasants; and a strengthening of the 'natural' (subsistence) economy among the poor peasants.

At the same time, urban workers, negatively affected by the state's inability to maintain price controls and guarantee employment, increasingly resented the *nouveau riche* 'NEP-men' who took full advantage of the new openings for profit-based production and trade. Consequently, the Bolsheviks – most of whom were ideologically uncomfortable with the NEP to begin with – had mixed feelings about the sudden economic upsurge. They were relieved that production was at last on the upswing but fearful of the proliferation of capitalist enterprise and, with it, a resurgence of bourgeois ideology. Many wondered whether Lenin was selling out socialist 'principle' for economic expediency.

But Lenin stuck to his guns, arguing that there was no choice: Russia needed a massive dose of capitalism. The real issue was how to supervise it while finding the appropriate forms through which a socialist economy could begin to develop and compete with traditional private enterprise.

Two years after launching the NEP as 'a strategical retreat', Lenin believed that such a form had been found in producer cooperatives. Like the NEP itself, this notion also came as a shock to many Bolsheviks. Traditionally Marxism had derided cooperatives both for promoting fantasies about the path to socialism and as, at best, a modified (and somewhat disguised) form of capitalism. But now, said Lenin, 'Since political power is in the hands of the working class, since this political power owns all the means of production', cooperatives would prove to be the answer to the transition conundrum:[19]

> We have now found that degree of combination of private interest, of private commercial interest, with state supervision and control of this interest, that degree of its subordination to the common interests which was formerly the stumbling-block for very many socialists. Indeed, the power of the state over all large-scale means of production, political power in the hands of the proletariat, the alliance of this proletariat with the many millions of small and very small peasants, the assured proletarian leadership of the peasantry, etc. – is this not all that is necessary to build a complete socialist society out of cooperatives, out of cooperatives alone, which we formerly ridiculed as huckstering ... Our practical workers look down upon our cooperative societies, failing to appreciate their exceptional importance, first from the standpoint of principle (the means of production are owned by the state), and second, from the standpoint of transition to the new system by means that are the *simplest, easiest and most acceptable to the peasant!* [20]

While this represented a drastic change in both vision and policy – 'We have to admit that there has been a radical modification in our whole outlook on socialism', said Lenin [21] – it was, nevertheless, a logical extension of the worker–peasant alliance he had projected two decades earlier. But, he added, 'given social ownership of the means of production, given the class victory of the proletariat over the bourgeoisie, the system of civilized cooperators is the system of socialism.' [22]

Clearly Lenin saw his new outlook on socialism as singularly appropriate to Russia. But since his first words on the subject were also his last, we cannot say for sure to what extent he might ultimately have seen their relevance to the transition process in the more developed capitalist countries. Nevertheless, Lenin's corrective on the voluntarist transition attempted by war communism represented a major deepening of Marx's notion of socialism as the transition from capitalism to communism. Now, in advancing the notion that the 'system of civilized cooperators' was the 'system of socialism', he was projecting a vision of socialism as a mixed economy containing significant elements of both capitalist and socialist modes of production.

In this sense, Lenin's intellectual discovery has a significance that goes beyond the Soviet particularity. While the transition to socialism in the most developed countries clearly will not be based on 'peasant cooperatives', similar forms may well be appropriate in those sections of agriculture which still depend on extensive human labor, as in California's San Joaquin valley, for example. More broadly, however, capitalist relations and institutions – in particular, forms of private enterprise, the market, commodity production and so forth, as well as political processes and ideological traditions – are quite likely to continue to exist in the new society even as communist relations and institutions begin to develop. Nor can the former simply be eliminated by fiat or at will. They can only give way if and when the new forms prove superior not only in attempting to realize egalitarian ideals (which, after all, are dependent on a certain level of economic development), but in fashioning a more efficient, productive, environmentally sound, democratic and intellectually enlightened system.

'Revolution from Above'

The central tragedy of the Bolshevik Revolution was that Lenin's new understanding of socialism failed to survive his passing. Stalin's 1929–30 'revolution from above', which brought the NEP to an end by forcibly collectivizing agriculture and eliminating every vestige of capitalism in the economy, set the Soviet Union and the entire socialist project on a collision course with those historical limitations of which Lenin had become so keenly aware. In doing so, Stalin and his supporters posited a new kind of Marxism (now Marxism-Leninism) which would be permanently at the service of a utopian/voluntarist conception of socialism and which could only be held in place by ideological terror, political repression and intellectual suffocation.

Stalin's pretext for scuttling the NEP was a crisis in agriculture, specifically a sharp drop-off in the marketed portion of the harvest. (Grain production itself had actually increased dramatically after the policies of privatization and the 'tax in kind' were adopted.) The reasons for the grain shortage were well understood by economists at the time. Chief among these was that a severe shortage of consumer goods had left the market-oriented peasantry with little to buy after they sold their grain – even at free-market prices. In addition, arbitrarily low prices had been set for the grain the peasants were obliged to sell to the state. As a result, a growing number of peasants – especially the most productive – withheld their surplus grain, preferring to use it either to feed their livestock or to hoard it in hopes of driving prices up. Meanwhile, the Bolsheviks had become increasingly frustrated with the slow pace of development in heavy industry, which, despite its initial spectacular recovery under the NEP, began to come up against the limitations of an aging industrial plant and weak infrastructure.

Just as the civil war and foreign intervention of the 1918–20 period were taken by the Bolsheviks as the green light for war communism, so the economic difficulties of the mid-1920s were seized upon by Stalin as the reason for getting back on the 'true socialist path'. On the ideological side, Stalin's supporters were those who had never been comfortable with the NEP. As they saw it, the revolution could not afford to get mired in such a seemingly contradictory configuration in which both communist and capitalist forms existed side by side. To them it was only logical – indeed, a point of principle – that the Bolsheviks should utilize their political power to 'build socialism'. So far as they were concerned, Lenin's concessions to the peasantry may have been necessary to get the new Soviet state out of a power-threatening crisis. But after that, the worker–peasant alliance simply became an impediment to what they saw as their ordained socialist agenda. (Stalin was also helped, in no small measure, by the already numerous and career-oriented bureaucrats in both party and state whose aspirations for power could best be realized in a state-dominated economy.)

It was in this context that Stalin discovered the virtues of a thesis called 'The Fundamental Law of Socialist Accumulation', earlier advanced by one of Trotsky's supporters, a young economist named Evgenii Preobrazhensky.[23] (A member of the party Central Committee's secretariat in 1920, Preobrazhensky had been an enthusiastic supporter of war communism, seeing it as the harbinger of fully developed socialism. Ousted from his post when the NEP was adopted, he then became an early and outspoken opponent of the new policy, denouncing it as a departure from socialist principle. When it was first formulated in 1924, Preobrazhensky's 'Law of Socialist Accumulation' approach was rejected. In 1927, Preobrazhensky himself, along with other supporters of Trotsky, was expelled from the party and exiled to Siberia.) According to Preobrazhensky, there was only one way to obtain the resources necessary for massive socialist industrialization: by expropriating the surpluses produced by the peasantry. Here was an approach which seemed to provide answers to a host of problems: obtaining the peasants' hoarded grain; financing rapid industrialization; and, most of all, getting on with the true socialist mission.

Stalin, of course, never acknowledged his debt to Preobrazhensky, who, as Carr notes, was so 'impressed by the conversion of Stalin and the party majority to policies of industrialization more intensive than had ever been advocated by the opposition', that he broke with Trotsky and was readmitted to the party.[24]

What followed is well known. Stalin called on the party to adopt a new policy 'To extend and consolidate our Socialist key positions in all economic branches in town and country and to pursue a course of eliminating the capitalist elements from the national economy.' [25] In agriculture, this meant an end to all private holdings, including the cooperatives. Collectivization became the order of the day. Subsequent Soviet literature tried to justify collectivization; first, by asserting that it was, in essence, what Lenin meant in referring to cooperatives, and second, by denying that it was forced. But neither of these claims stand up to scrutiny. The poor peasants, Lenin believed, would be attracted to the cooperatives because (a) they would be voluntary and could be left at any time; (b) the peasants would retain rights to their land in the context of mutual assistance, cooperative farming and joint distribution; (c) the cooperatives would be autonomous, retaining control over production and distribution decisions; and (d) they would prove more efficient and financially rewarding to the peasants than the activity of those who chose to remain individual proprietors. Lenin expected that the cooperatives would be particularly attractive to the poor peasants who would then be able to enter the market alongside and in competition with those – mostly peasants with larger and more productive holdings – who chose to remain individual proprietors.

Subsequent Soviet assertions that collectivization was carried out on a 'voluntary' basis are even more spurious. Following Stalin's blunt call for an 'offensive' aimed at the 'elimination of the kulaks as a class', [26] collectivization was imposed on the Soviet countryside by physical and ideological coercion. The holdings of the wealthiest peasants were simply expropriated. Middle peasants, who produced a sufficient surplus to be prime suppliers of the market, were conveniently labeled 'kulaks' and also had their holdings expropriated. Indeed, any peasants who balked were similarly treated on the ground that their refusal to join the collective process showed that they harbored kulak aspirations.

Nor were the poor peasants so universally enthusiastic at the call to collectivize as official Soviet history would subsequently claim. Some, of course, were. They, after all, had the most to gain from the new arrangement. And, in time, most acceded to a combination of ideological pressure, threats (they could see what happened to those who resisted) and promises that the new collective farm system would give them 'ownership' of the lands, machinery and livestock of the expropriated wealthier peasants.

But the party was not prepared to let collectivization rest on the small holdings, less arable land and manual labor of the poorest peasants. It needed the more productive acreage, the livestock and implements of the wealthier peasants – in short, that section of the peasantry which had the least interest in collectivization and which was most likely to resist it.

As a result, despite Stalin's formal admonition to pursue collectivization 'gradually ... not by pressure, but by example and persuasion', [27] an all-out war was launched in the Russian countryside. Historian Roy Medvedev describes it thus:

Lenin's principle of voluntary collectivization was violated almost everywhere under pressure from Stalin and his closest aides. Organizational and explanatory work among the peasants was replaced by crude administrative fiat and force directed against the middle peasants and even some of the poor peasants. They were forced to join collective farms under threat of 'dekulakization'. In many areas the rule was quite simple: 'Whoever does not join collective farms is an enemy of the Soviet regime.' [28]

The human toll of collectivization was monumental. Millions of peasants were driven off the land and forcibly shipped to Siberia and elsewhere where conditions were harsh and prospects were poor. Many were killed. Countless others died of disease, exposure and malnutrition. One direct consequence of collectivization was a devastating famine in the Soviet countryside.

Roy Medvedev's somewhat cautious figures estimate a minimum of 10 million people uprooted from the land, somewhat less than half of whom died. He also believes that, in addition, the famine took 6 million lives.[29] 'The very fact of a massive famine was denied', says Medvedev. 'Any reference to it was prohibited in the Soviet press until 1956; in fact, during the thirties many people were arrested as "counterrevolutionary agitators" for uttering the words "famine in the south".' According to a Soviet demographic specialist, 'probably no less than three million children born in 1932–34 died of starvation.' [30]

The scale and speed of collectivization – from 3.6 percent of the cultivated land in 1929 to almost 100 percent by 1935 – and the zeal with which it was pursued, testify to the party's belief that the changeover in agriculture was the indispensable first step in the broader industrialization of the economy as a whole. The need for industrialization was not itself a disputed point. Without it, the new Soviet state would remain mired in economic backwardness and the working class – presumably the social foundation for socialism – would continue to be a small percentage of the population. The real questions had to do with where the resources for industrialization would come from and at what pace it would proceed.

Stalin's answer was the classic one of Russian history, pre-dating the revolution: it would come from the peasants. This was the real practical point of collectivization – to take over the lands, livestock, implements and harvests of the wealthier peasants to obtain the capital needed to industrialize. Thus, in the name of socialism, collectivization was designed – and turned out to be – a form of that 'primitive accumulation of capital' (to use Marx's phrase) which had played such an important role in jump-starting capitalism.

Finally, in launching his 'revolution from above', Stalin advanced what became the Marxist-Leninist theory of the intensification of the class struggle under socialism. Ideological authority for this thesis was found in Lenin's warning in the first days after the Bolshevik seizure of power that 'The abolition of classes requires a long, difficult and stubborn class struggle, which after the overthrow of the power of capital... does not disappear but merely changes its forms and in many respects becomes even fiercer.' [31]

To the above, Stalin added his shorthand summary: 'The abolition of classes *by means of the fierce class struggle of the proletariat* – such is Lenin's formula.'

Here is the archetype of Stalinist theoretical practice. First he cites the ultimate authority, Lenin. Then he condenses Lenin's comment to a 'formula', in the process eliminating the far from insignificant modifier 'in many respects.' Next he highlights the word 'fierce', dropping Lenin's 'long, difficult and stubborn'. Most important is the subtle shift from the passive voice 'becomes' (implying an objective process) to Stalin's 'by means of', in which Lenin's observation becomes the justification for a subjective undertaking.

Stalin's simplistic prescription for class war was, of course, a self-fulfilling prophecy. The forcible assault on the holdings and persons of that section of the peasantry which, only a few years earlier, had been encouraged to follow an entrepreneurial path in agriculture, naturally provoked a political response which, often enough, took a violent form. In addition, for the next half-century Stalin's dictum of the 'intensification of the class struggle under socialism' – whether domestically or in the international arena – provided the ultimate rationale for the tyranny, the mockery of law, the mass murder, the suppression of dissent and the ideological terror which followed.

Although Stalin clearly put his own unique stamp on the theory of the transition, he was hardly alone. The resuscitation of the ideas of war communism represented the natural ideological bent of most Bolsheviks at the time, who believed that free trade, commodity–money relations, individual forms of distribution and consumption and the rest were incompatible with socialism.

Not coincidentally, the Bolshevik shift was closely linked to a radical turn left in the international communist movement. For with it began the Comintern's notorious 'Third Period', probably unmatched for its record of sectarianism and revolutionary posturing. Stalin himself tied his struggle 'against the right deviation' in the CPSU to combating what he considered to be 'rightist' tendencies regarding international developments. In both cases, his particular target was Bukharin. In part, this can be attributed to Stalin's typical style of party politics, in which all of an opponent's views, policies and statements became fair game for the ideological sledgehammer. Yet it would be inaccurate to reduce the struggle simply to the tactics of power politics. The fact is that Stalin and Bukharin were on two different ideological and political trajectories, each – regardless of their individual histories – representing broader historical impulses not only in the CPSU but in international communism as well.

Thus Stalin criticized Bukharin's assessment that 'capitalism is reconstructing itself', arguing instead that 'in Europe the conditions are

maturing for a new revolutionary upsurge'. Facing 'a period of preparation of the working class for future class battles', he called on the
communists to step up the fight against social democracy:

> In Bukharin's theses it was stated that the fight against Social-
> Democracy is one of the fundamental tasks of the Sections of the
> Comintern. That, of course, is true. But it is not enough. In order
> that the fight against Social-Democracy may be waged successfully,
> stress must be laid on the fight against the so-called 'Left' wing of
> Social-Democracy, that 'Left' wing which, by playing with 'Left'
> phrases and thus adroitly deceiving the workers, is retarding their
> mass defection from Social-Democracy.[32]

Stalin won this battle too, of course. But it was a pyrrhic victory. As
with his 'triumph' in ending the NEP, the sharp turn left internationally
also had tragic consequences. For in a period when fascism was on the
rise in Europe and the times called for a broad united front of
democratic forces to head it off, the communists began playing at
revolution; and in keeping with Stalin's injunction they targeted their
most logical allies, the 'left' social democrats, as their principal enemy.
This sectarian turn was corrected five years later, but by that time Hitler
had come to power in Germany and valuable time had been lost.

Trotskyist and Maoist Conceptions of the Transition

The voluntarist/utopian spirit of Stalin's thesis of the transition is
likewise characteristic of the other principal strains of Marxism-Leninism: Trotskyism and Maoism. In this sense, all three share the same
ideological terrain.

Unlike Stalin, who does not seem to have had a strong ideological
center of his own, Trotsky's views were consistent. Back in 1906, in the
period when he was critical of Lenin's vision of a 'dictatorship of the
proletariat and peasantry', Trotsky had asserted:

> Coming into the government not as helpless hostages but as the
> leading force, the representatives of the proletariat will by virtue of
> that alone smash the demarcation between the minimal and maximal
> program, i.e., *place collectivism on the order of the day*. [33]

The telling phrase here is Trotsky's 'by virtue of that alone', clearly
signifying that it would be absolutely appropriate for 'the representatives
of the proletariat', (that is, the party) to impose its will on a vast
peasantry comprising 80 percent of the population. To Trotsky, therefore, 'revolution from above' was hardly an alien concept.

Formally a backer of the NEP after Lenin introduced it in 1921, Trotsky tended to emphasize the policy's temporary nature. One finds no echo of Lenin's 'radical modification in our whole outlook on socialism' in any of his writings. Instead, immediately after Lenin's death, Trotsky began pressing for a restriction of the NEP, calling for higher taxes on those peasants whose greater productivity had been most stimulated by the new policy, greater emphasis on collectivization and a program of more rapid and more extensive industrialization.

Still, the charge that Stalin ultimately adopted Trotsky's program is quite unfair – to Trotsky. For despite his advocacy of policies to curtail important elements of the NEP, Trotsky was appalled at the extent of Stalin's radical turn and the lack of preparation for it:

> The temporary 'extraordinary measures' for the collection of grain developed unexpectedly into a program of 'liquidation of the kulaks as a class'. From the shower of contradictory commands ... it became evident that on the peasant question the government not only had no Five Year Plan, but not even a five months' program.[34]

Although Trotsky was quite sympathetic to the impulse behind the Great Turn – asserting that it was forced by 'the necessity of finding some salvation from the consequences of the policy of 1923–28',[35] – he still argued that:

> The real possibilities of collectivization are determined, not by the depth of the impasse in the villages and not by the administrative energy of the government, but primarily by the existing productive resources .... These material conditions were lacking (and)... an exaggeratedly swift collectivization took the form of an economic adventure.[36]

In the final analysis, Trotsky's strategy for transition came back – as it always did – to the logic of world revolution he had first enunciated in 1905: 'The contradiction between a workers' government and an overwhelming majority of peasants in a backward country could be resolved only on an international scale, in the arena of a world proletarian revolution.' [37]

The Maoist view of the transition, on the other hand, is a direct ideological descendant of the 'great turn' and helps explain why communist China continued to include Stalin in the pantheon of 'great Marxists' after Khrushchev's denunciation of him. That conception was embodied in the 'Great Proletarian Cultural Revolution' – also orchestrated from above – which was designed to make an overnight leap into socialism despite the country's low level of economic development. And, as in Stalin's own great leap, this would be effected by the defeat of the capitalist-roaders (in the one case Bukharin, in the other Liu-Shao-chi),

intensification of the class struggle 'under socialism' and the utilization
of new 'socialist relations of production' to compensate for the backward
state of the productive forces.

Finally, the view that new socialist relations of production *precede* the
development of society's productive forces – perhaps the central point of
Mao's Cultural Revolution – assumes that the chief distinguishing
characteristic of an economic system, its new relations of production,
can become dominant principally as the result of ideological persuasion
even before the material basis for a socialist society exists. The first
terrifying refutation of that proposition occurred in the Soviet countryside, where Stalin's precipitous forced collectivization undermined Soviet
agriculture. In later years, it was the principal underlying cause of the
stagnation and ultimately overall failure of the Soviet economy as a
whole.

The Theory of the Transition as 'Historical Rupture'

That accelerated industrialization was an urgent need for the Soviet
Union at the time of Stalin's 'Great Turn' is unquestionable. And,
under the prevailing circumstances, there is even a certain logic in
seeing agriculture as a source for at least a portion of the capital that
undertaking would require. But Stalin had far more ambitious goals
for his 'revolution from above'. He was also going to 'build socialism'.

This notion of 'building' something called 'socialism' has become so
ingrained in communist intellectual discourse that it has taken on the
quality of an unimpeachable sacred mission, departure from which is an
obvious betrayal of socialist ideals. And yet, especially as undertaken in
the Soviet Union and subsequently raised to the level of universal 'law'
by Marxist-Leninist theory, the concept represents a flagrant breach of
historical materialism that reeks of voluntarism and utopianism.

As we have pointed out previously, Lenin's conception of a lengthy
transition in which 'state capitalism' could grow into socialism principally
by way of cooperatives was an attempt to come to grips with the
dilemma of communists holding power in a country where the material
conditions for socialism had not yet matured. But rather than confronting the implications of Russia's backward state for the socialist project,
Stalin fused two distinct goals – rapid industrialization and the immediate 'construction' of socialism.

Ever since, Marxism-Leninism has justified this 'Great Turn' as a
reflection of the 'laws' of the transition. Contradicting Marx – and,
ironically, anticipating Mao – Marxism-Leninism developed a new
theory, namely that 'the material prerequisites for socialism can be
created ... through restrictions placed on [capitalism] in economic, social
and political spheres by the revolutionary forces which consider socialism their ultimate goal.' [38] Of course, Stalin did far more than 'restrict'

capitalism. While Lenin had argued that Russia needed more capitalism in order to bring into being the conditions for socialism, Stalin undertook to wipe it out all at once by administrative injunction, military force and ideological compulsion. In its place he installed a command economy he called 'socialism'.

Over time, Stalin's transition – along with his conception of socialism – became two of the main building blocks of Marxist-Leninist theory. It was a strange hodge-podge which contradicted Marx, distorted Lenin, borrowed from (but hardly acknowledged) Trotsky, and effectively owed its parentage to Stalin.

Thus, in summing up his theory of the transition, Stalin offered his own variant of Trotsky's 'uninterrupted revolution': 'The transition from capitalism to socialism and the liberation of the working class from the yoke of capitalism cannot be effected by slow changes, by reforms, but only by a qualitative change of the capitalist system, by revolution.' [39]

Many socialists would endorse this statement, seeing it principally as an argument against reformism in the struggle to overturn capitalism. However, the 'revolution' to which Stalin is here referring is not the *political* revolution by which the working class takes power, but rather the subsequent social and economic transformation of society after the political revolution has triumphed. Thus the *History of the CPSU (Short Course)* – written directly by Stalin or under his close supervision – sees the 'Great Turn' as, in essence, the *socialist* side of the process, 'A profound revolution, a leap from an old qualitative state of society to a new qualitative state, equivalent in its consequences to the revolution of October, 1917.' [40]

Seeking Lenin's imprimatur to justify the 'Great Turn', Marxism-Leninism cited his assertion that 'all the objective conditions for the achievement of socialism had matured within the old society'. [41] In the mind-numbing climate of the communist movement in those years, this startling assertion went unchallenged. But the puzzled reader going back to Lenin would find that the Marxist-Leninist authors of this text had conveniently omitted the fact that Lenin here was speaking only of the most developed capitalist countries and not Russia, 'a peasant country, one of the most backward of European countries ... [in which] socialism cannot triumph *directly* and *immediately*'. [42] (As it turns out, of course, Lenin's assessment about the ripeness of objective conditions in even the most advanced capitalist countries was itself unduly optimistic.)

Generalizing the Soviet experience as a 'law' of historical development, Marxism-Leninism asserted:

As soon as the working class takes political power into its own hands, its primary task is to eradicate the production relations inherent in the bourgeois society. On this basis, the dictatorship of the proletariat executes its principal creative function – that of building socialism.[43]

Concentrated in this single paragraph is Marxism-Leninism's idealist essence. For the fact of the matter is that in the Soviet Union and in every other country which presumably 'built socialism' in the past 50 years, the 'primary task' of the revolution was not the eradication of bourgeois production relations but the qualitative development of the country's productive forces so as to meet its economic needs and lay the material foundations for a revolution in the relations of production.

But one searches in vain through this formula – to say nothing of the ideological thunderbolts Stalin hurled at those who opposed the voluntaristic proclamations of the 'revolution from above' – for any recognition that, in keeping with historical materialism, there might be objective, economic prerequisites for the new social system. This is not some textual oversight. The fact is that despite occasional obligatory references to them, Marxism-Leninism does not recognize such limitations.

Another new Marxist-Leninist proposition on the transition asserted: 'Socialist production relations do not take shape within the framework of capitalist society, and here lies the main specific feature of transition from capitalism to socialism as compared with the previous stages of social development.' [44]

This notion, which in effect, argues that 'socialist production relations' somehow spring full-blown from the minds of socialist Minervas, is yet another rupture with historical materialism. All history has shown that in the past the transition from one social system to another always took place as new modes of production grew up within the old. Thus capitalism appeared and took root in the midst of feudal property relations. The view that somehow socialism would develop otherwise was, bluntly stated, an *ex post facto* rationalization of Stalin's 'revolution from above', but had nothing to do with the actual processes in capitalism already under way.

Historical precedent aside, this Marxist-Leninist innovation flies in the face of numerous observations by Marx and others on how capitalism's own inexorable tendency toward the socialization of production is already bringing socialist forms into being. That socialization, Lenin noted, 'drags the capitalists, against their will and consciousness, into some sort of a new social order'.[45] In fact, he declared: 'Socialism is merely the next step forward from state-capitalist monopoly. Or, in other words, socialism is merely state-capitalist monopoly *which is made to serve the interests of the whole people.'* [46]

Elsewhere Lenin cites the state-run postal service as an example of the fact that 'the mechanism of social management is here already to hand'.[47] And these remarks were made long before the emergence of vast utility companies and state-run social services further demonstrated that socialist forms of organization – or, we might say, forms of organization which will undoubtedly be common to both capitalism and socialism – were already appearing in social and economic life.

In addition, as the Soviet experience with war communism showed, the turn to a new mode of production cannot be effected instantly or by the same methods used to secure the political revolution. This has also been the experience of every country which has tried to follow Stalin's prescription for a second 'revolution within the revolution'.

China and Vietnam, both presently scrambling to restore capitalism in many areas of the economy, are the most clear-cut examples. Cuba, which was cushioned from the harsher economic realities for more than two decades by massive Soviet assistance, is starting to take the first tentative steps in that direction – and would probably do more along those lines were it not for the overarching threat of US intervention. Other countries which set out on the 'socialist path' – such as Angola, Nicaragua, Mozambique and Ethiopia – have been forced to abandon it. What were often called attempts at 'capitalist restoration' in these societies have been, in effect, nothing but the impulse toward correcting the voluntarism of the Stalinist model by developing a mixed economy combining state-administered public ownership with private enterprise and a market system. (Even the seemingly headlong rush toward capitalism in the Soviet Union and Eastern Europe seems likely to wind up with significant features of public ownership still retained.)

Most important of all, perhaps, Stalin's vision of an abrupt historical rupture trivializes Marx's profound insight that the transition to socialism will take place 'by degrees', or that socialism, as itself the transitional society from capitalism to communism, will be 'in every respect, economically, morally and intellectually, still stamped with the birthmarks of the old society'.[48] In Stalin's framework and in subsequent Marxist-Leninist theory, these 'birthmarks' were seen mainly as holdovers of capitalist ideology – traces of individualism, superstition and the like – or such economic leftovers as the use of money, the limited applicability of 'the law of value' and what Marx called the 'bourgeois right' of paying workers on the basis of 'to each according to his labor'. There is no place in the Stalinist framework for the notion that these 'birthmarks' might include actual capitalist forms of entrepreneurship or that socialism might be based on a mix of capitalist and communist economic forms. In fact, Marxism-Leninism has obscured the very idea of socialism itself as a transitional society. Instead we have one of Stalin's typically stacked-deck juxtapositions:

> We cannot go on indefinitely basing the Soviet regime and socialist construction on two different foundations, the foundation of the most large-scale and united socialist industry and the foundation of the most scattered and backward small commodity economy of the peasants.[49]

Posed this way, the thesis sounds unimpeachable. But Soviet industry in 1929 had hardly arrived at this 'large-scale and united' stage, as a result of which there did not yet exist the technical (let alone ideological) foundation for large-scale agricultural cultivation. Stalin likewise posed his scheme of forced collectivization as the only alternative to 'the most scattered and backward small commodity economy of the peasants', completely dropping Lenin's conception of voluntary cooperatives which – taken in conjunction with private cultivation – would be conducive both to large-scale farming and the continuation of the worker-peasant alliance. And despite Stalin's use of the cautionary word 'indefinitely', it was quite obvious that he believed time had already run out. For, he argued, 'if we turn away from it [this task] and do not accomplish it ... a return to capitalism may become inevitable.' [50]

Marx and Engels had a different view:

Question: Will it be possible to abolish private property at one stroke?

Answer: No, such a thing would be just as impossible as at one stroke to increase the existing productive forces to the degree necessary for instituting community of property. Hence, the proletarian revolution, which in all probability is impending, will transform existing society only gradually, and be able to abolish private property only when the necessary quantity of the means of production has been created.[51]

In other words, Marx fully expected that socialism – precisely because it is itself the 'transition' – will be characterized by the coexistence of both capitalist and socialist economic forms and production relations. This is precisely the point Lenin came to, almost in passing, with the NEP. But the 'radical modification' of his outlook on what socialism might turn out to be was entombed with him. Instead, Soviet socialism and those following its prescriptions was shaped by Stalin and his ideological descendants, for whom, as one presentday Soviet critic put it:

Social reality is not an organic system of relations among people that develops according to its own laws, but a material, a clay, from which it is possible to shape anything one wants, given the requisite political will, strong organization and powerful instruments of coercion.[52]

Finally, what are we to make of the proposition that 'socialist production relations do not take shape within the framework of capitalist society' in the context of a single world economy? Unless one wants to postulate the unimaginable prospect of the transition from capitalism to socialism taking place on a world scale almost simultaneously, we can expect that both the old and the new relations of production will appear and operate for some considerable time within that single world economy. The countries of recently existing socialism tried to deny the reality of a single world economy, but their attempts to escape from it were self-defeating. Assuming that new (and improved) socialist countries will emerge in the future, and further assuming that the compulsions for all countries to function within the framework of a single world economy will be even greater then than they are now, does it not follow that socialist production relations will take shape within the framework of that economy which will be de facto a single world *mixed economy*?

In all these propositions we can see Marxism-Leninism's voluntarist and utopian tendencies at their most naked: voluntarist because the drastic alterations in property relations did not proceed from ready-to-hand economic necessities; utopian because they assume that the main features of an entirely new mode of production can be known with scientific certainty even before they have appeared in life.

Thus was 'actually existing socialism' born, from the beginning infected by the voluntarist viruses that would ultimately destroy it. For without a material foundation, the system required an extraordinary and *permanent* level of revolutionary enthusiasm and ideological commitment not only by the revolution's vanguard but by the great mass of the population. Popular enthusiasm is, of course, a critical factor at the revolutionary moment when power is taken; and is likewise a significant source of strength in consolidating the revolution's gains. But no system can survive – let alone develop – principally on such a basis. The inevitable result was a system which, unlike capitalism, could not reproduce itself or expand on the basis of its internal logic. Nor could it advance on the basis of a rapidly diminishing mass revolutionary enthusiasm which, over time, turned into mass alienation and demoralization.

October: Was It Really a 'Proletarian Revolution'?

In the Marxist-Leninist framework, the uprising in February 1917 which overthrew the czar was that long-anticipated historical turning point for Russia – the bourgeois-democratic revolution. (Lenin called it 'a revolution of the proletariat, the peasantry and the bourgeoisie in alliance with Anglo-French finance capital against Czarism'.) [53] In that same framework, Marxism-Leninism has designated the Bolshevik seizure of power later that year in October as a proletarian revolution – ergo, the only 'true' Russian Revolution.

(The first edition of the official *History of the CPSU [Short Course]* – the one personally supervised by Stalin – goes so far as to claim that 'the Bolshevik Party ... overthrew the Czar and set up Soviets of Workers' and Soldiers' Deputies.' [54] The subsequent 1960 edition, revised after Khrushchev came to power, is somewhat less self-serving. Acknowledging that the earlier revolution had brought about 'the overthrow of Czarism' and that 'the masses themselves created the

Soviets of Workers' and Soldiers' Deputies', it credits February 1917 with 'opening the way to the abolition of capitalism and the establishment of socialism'.) [55]

Now it is time to take another look at the sharp divide Marxist-Leninist theory has erected between these two events. Clearly the two revolutions had contradictory political goals. February was the bourgeois-democratic revolution the Bolsheviks had long anticipated. Its aim – to break the political power of the autocracy and remove the restrictions on capitalist development – was readily evident. In this sense, the revolution spoke to the outlook of one portion of its social base – the relatively new bourgeoisie. But that class had no intention of responding to the growing demands of the worker and peasant masses who wanted an end to the war, the breakup of the feudal estates and their distribution to the peasants in the countryside and relief for the workers in the cities.

It was under those circumstances – and because the workers and peasants comprised the overwhelming majority of the revolution's social base – that Lenin drew up his famous 'April Theses', calling on the Bolsheviks to lead the masses to the revolution's 'second stage which must place power in the hands of the proletariat and the poorest strata of the peasantry'. [56] That goal was the essential political program of the October Revolution which brought the communists to power.

But the mere act of taking power did not change the objective character of the Russian Revolution. The conditions which had first led Lenin to declare that 'We cannot get out of the bourgeois-democratic boundaries of the Russian revolution' had not substantially changed. Russia was still a predominantly peasant country and its capitalism was still relatively undeveloped. The Bolsheviks knew this. In fact, a number of Bolshevik leaders were hesitant about moving to seize power – some openly opposed Lenin's call to do so – on the grounds that Russia was still not ready for socialism.

However, there was one significant difference between 1905 and 1917: the disastrous consequences of the war, Lenin believed, had brought into being revolutionary conditions throughout the capitalist world. As a result, Bolshevik success in Russia might – Lenin was sure it would – trigger proletarian revolutions in the main capitalist countries of Europe. If only two or three of these succeeded, he believed, socialism would become a practical reality in Russia too.

Although hopes that October's socialist mission would be realized through the support of other revolutions never materialized, the mission now began to assume a practical form. The first attempt (war communism) almost brought Bolshevik rule to an end in 1921; the second – Stalin's 'revolution from above' and the administrative-command system which that revolution brought into being – set socialism on the course that ultimately did it in.

Therefore, without in the least diminishing the motives or second-guessing the tactics of the Bolsheviks in those electrifying days when it seemed that socialism might be converted from a dream into a reality, it seems to me that history has already rendered a judgment. Despite the intense efforts which spanned the next 70 years, the Bolsheviks were not able, as Lenin had said, to 'get out of the bourgeois-democratic boundaries of the Russian revolution'. February and October, it turns out, were different episodes in a single bourgeois-democratic revolution, the failed effort to go beyond those boundaries demonstrating that objective reality does not permit political actors, no matter how determined, to surpass historical possibilities.

Why has it been so difficult for ruling Communist Parties to recognize this historical imperative? The answer underscores the basic contradiction and historic tragedy of the Marxist-Leninist theory of the transition. Because the Stalinist model flew in the face of objective limitations, Stalin and his supporters posited a new kind of Marxism (now Marxism-Leninism) which would be permanently at the service of a utopian/voluntarist conception of socialism and which could only be held in place by ideological terror, political repression and intellectual suffocation. Its principal instrument was the all-powerful ruling Communist Party without accountability to the populace as a whole – or even to the working class whose mandate it claimed. And because, in this model, the party-state machine directs and operates the entire economy, it likewise generates an enormous bureaucratic apparatus whose resistance to change is rooted in its own vested personal interest in the prevailing social arrangement.

In this sense, the real test for the Bolsheviks was not whether to seek power but, having won it, what they would do with it. Stalin finally settled that question in 1929 with the 'revolution from above'. Yet the system fashioned by that rupture with history proved to be lacking in the flexibility and openness of thought that might have enabled it to adapt to social realities. Efforts to modify that system, to bring it more into line with historical possibility, were time and again frustrated by that powerful social force which had developed such a significant stake in perpetuating it.

As a result, as one Soviet reformer said in 1990:

A 70-year experiment is coming to an end, an experiment the essence of which was an attempt to establish a new system by arbitrary means, outpacing the development of productive forces, violating the basic ideas of Marxism, and disregarding the opinion of outstanding Marxists like Plekhanov. It was a purely utopian attempt. No one doubts the sincerity of the majority of revolutionaries of Lenin's time, no one doubts that early in this century there were already preconditions for movement toward socialism, but the actual experience of the first years of the revolution showed that these attempts were premature, and therefore the chosen path could only be a path of bloody violence perpetrated by a minority against the majority.[57]

Now all that remains is to change the tense of the opening sentence above to reflect the fact that this experiment has already come to an end.

5 Actually Existing Socialism: Utopian and Unscientific

Existing socialism is the most dynamic social system full of energy and capable of impressive historical accomplishments. [Its] advances ... are striking evidence of the new system's inexhaustible potentialities and its indisputable advantages over capitalism.

Peter Fedoseyev [1]

Adherents of ideologies claiming omniscience – whether by divine revelation or the laws of science – tend, almost inevitably it seems, to foster a culture of self-congratulation. Marxist-Leninists, in keeping with a history unrestrained by either materialism or modesty, justified such intemperance on the ground that 'actually existing socialism' demonstrated the viability of their theory.

Now with the collapse of the system Marxism-Leninism pointed to as 'verification', a postmortem on both 'actually existing socialism' and its ideological overhang requires a reexamination of the historical record and the system's main principles.

'Socialist Construction'

Stalin's 'Great Turn' had three objectives: rapid and massive industrialization made particularly urgent by the necessity to lay the economic and technological foundations for a military buildup in anticipation of war; the mechanization and collectivization of agriculture to generate an agricultural surplus that would provide the capital for a new industrialized infrastructure; and the construction, in relatively short order, of a 'socialist society'.

Although industrialization was the driving force behind this perspective, for the ideologically oriented communists, even this goal had to be filtered through the prism of that 'higher' objective of building socialism. As Stalin saw it, socialism – by which he meant a totally nationalized economy organized and directed by an all-powerful centralized state apparatus – would facilitate industrialization. (The socialist character of this system was assured, the Bolsheviks believed, by the fact that it would be under the direct and complete control of a Communist Party representing the real interests of the working class.)

Once this course was charted, Lenin's NEP was abruptly brought to an end. One of the first great reforms enacted immediately after the seizure of power in 1917, the Decree on Land, was declared 'a private-ownership vestige' and private property rights in all but a tiny fraction of agricultural land was abolished. Within a few years, the prevailing system was almost totally replaced by a vast network of collective farms.

In industry, all the numerous private companies and cooperatives which had sprung up under the NEP were transformed into 'public' property and placed under the direct control and supervision of the state. Numerous enterprises simply stopped functioning as the new central planning apparatus consolidated production and assigned resources based on the push for industrialization as well as extra-economic 'socialist' priorities. The framework within which the NEP had functioned – a mix of public, private and cooperative enterprises, commodity–money relations, a market economy, self-support and self-financing of enterprises and so forth – was scrapped.

The culmination of Stalin's socialist logic was the establishment of a vast new planning mechanism which brought virtually all economic activity under centralized state control, not only large-scale industry but light industry, agriculture, small business and distribution down to and including the retail level. In this system, an all-powerful administrative apparatus determined all investment, set priorities, assigned resources (including labor), managed all enterprise-to-enterprise relations, fixed prices, established wage levels and employment norms, assigned quotas for all enterprises, chose locations for entire industries, and altered the plan as it saw fit. Not least, the central authority had the power to appoint, promote, transfer and remove managers and directors at every level of the economic hierarchy.

The overhaul was so all-encompassing and proceeded so quickly that by 1936, seven years after launching his 'revolution from above', Stalin would proclaim that, 'Our Soviet society has already achieved socialism in its basic elements. We have created a socialist system, what Marxists call the first or lower level of communism.' [2] Three years later he declared that:

> By the end of the Second Five-Year Plan ... the socialist system of production began its unchallenged domination of the entire Soviet economy: it accounted for 99.8 percent of the gross output of industry, 98.6 percent of agricultural output ... and 100 percent of commodity circulation.[3]

With these pronouncements, Stalin and the CPSU completed their negation of Marx's view of socialism as itself the transition from capitalism to communism. In the Stalin construct – subsequently replicated by the other countries of the 'socialist camp' – socialism was now a fully developed, distinct mode of production in which an all-powerful proletarian state took over not only all private property but also the direction, planning, supervision and day-to-day management of virtually all economic activity.

(Formally speaking, state control was not absolute. Nominally, the collective farms were outside the 'publicly owned' sector and, after meeting obligations to the state under the plan, could dispose of their surplus on the 'collective-farm market'. Individual collective and state farm households could work small personal plots and were permitted to own a cow and some poultry. They, too, could dispose of their surplus as they saw fit. But the state owned the land and the means of production, determined collective farm quotas, owned and operated the transport system and storage facilities, dispensed tractors and other heavy machinery, exercised absolute control over commodity exchange, and had a thousand other economic and extra-economic means of influencing collective farm decisions. Similarly, individual farm households were circumscribed in their purchases of farm implements – especially those that might enable them to mechanize their production – and were not permitted to hire labor. Consequently, these 'exceptions' had little impact on the plan's authority over the economy.)

In time, Marxism-Leninism accorded this system the status of a universal model, the concrete expression of the 'objective laws' of socialism:

> There is only one *scientific model of socialism*, common to all countries. It is the logical conception of socialist society, shared by all Marxist-Leninists, produced on the basis of the knowledge of the objective laws to which the transformation of capitalism into socialism is subject, and containing the key characteristics of the new society showing its main features. The *general model of socialism* is a logical inference from the *general theory of socialism* .... All other models of socialism ... lie outside the domain of scientific communism.[4]

The main precept of this model is the near-omnipotent administrative-command mechanism. As one authoritative Soviet text put it 40 years after Stalin had declared socialism in the USSR:

> The universal laws of the transition from capitalism to communism find their practical expression in the *centralist* principle of organization of socialist society. Rational management from one center is the principal guarantee of popular control over the most essential social relations and of their further purposeful improvement.[5]

Ideological authority for these pronouncements was not hard to find. *The Communist Manifesto*, after all, had stated that, after taking power, the proletariat would 'centralize all instruments of production in the hands of the state, i.e., of the proletariat organized as the ruling class.' [6] And Engels, noted a Soviet text on *Scientific Communism*, had declared that:

> To begin with, management of industry and all branches of produc-
> tion will be ... run by the whole of society, according to a common
> plan .... Since industrial management by individuals presupposes
> private property ... private property will have to be abolished as well
> and replaced by the common use of all instruments of production
> and the distribution of all products according to common agreement
> .... Abolition of private property ... is therefore rightly advanced by
> the Communists as their principal demand.[7]

But, by taking these comments out of context, Marxism-Leninism
accorded them a completely unintended meaning. For instance, while
Marx and Engels undoubtedly assumed that, aside from personal possessions, private property simply would not exist in a communist society,
they did not imagine that such a fundamental social and economic
transformation could take place immediately or all at once. To begin
with, they assumed that socialism would first become a practical issue
'in the most advanced countries' where a relatively high level of
socialized production had already been reached. And even then, they
believed centralization would proceed 'by degrees'.[8]

Similarly, the citation from Engels on private property (taken from an
1847 piece on the *Principles of Communism*) describes what he considers
to be the main features of a fully developed *communist* society. Nevertheless, the Soviet text in which it appears – an anthology of passages from
longer works by Marx, Engels and Lenin – includes it under the heading of
'Socialist Transformations in the Period of Transition from Capitalism to
Socialism', thereby placing it in a context Engels clearly never intended. To
make matters worse, the phrase 'To begin with' – implying that Engels
believed in the immediate abolition of private property after a successful
proletarian revolution – does not appear in the original at all. Instead
Engels starts this passage with the words 'Above all', suggesting that the
abolition of private property is the 'highest principle' of communist society
rather than the first practical step in the transition. In fact, elsewhere in
the same article Engels makes a point of stressing that 'private property
will not be abolished at one stroke', that the revolution 'will transform
existing society only gradually', and that it would be impossible for the
revolution 'to take place in one country alone'.[9] None of these remarks,
needless to say, are to be found in the Soviet text.

Marxist-Leninist theorists also enlisted Lenin on behalf of their
universal laws. Thus a 1974 study approvingly quotes the revolution's
ultimate authority to the effect that:

> Communism requires and presupposes the greatest possible centrali-
> zation of large-scale production throughout the country .... To
> deprive the all-Russia center of the right to direct control over all the
> enterprises of the given industry throughout the country ... would be
> regional anarcho-syndicalism, and not communism.[10]

But this citation is equally dishonest. Missing from it is the information that Lenin's comment – made in 1918 – was an argument for war communism, a system he later declared responsible for the Bolsheviks' greatest setback in the immediate post-revolutionary period.[11] (See Chapter 4.)

Therefore, Marxist-Leninist declarations notwithstanding, Stalin's agenda for socialist construction and the 'laws of socialism' which followed in its wake represent a startling inversion of Marxist theory. For Marxism had long held that socialism, like any new mode of production, could only arise on the basis of a revolutionary advance in society's productive forces, which itself would undermine the foundations of the old system's class structure.

Stalin's path to socialism, by contrast, proceeded from the other end of the spectrum: new 'socialist' relations of production would bring about the revolution in the productive forces that socialism required as its material base. (This principle has resonated in Marxist-Leninist theory and communist practice ever since. It was the underlying tenet of Mao's Cultural Revolution in China and guided 'socialist construction' in Eastern Europe, Cuba, North Korea and other Third World countries where communist-led national liberation movements came to power.)

Therefore, in an attempt to make Stalin's essentially voluntarist conception of socialist construction compatible with historical materialism, Marxist-Leninist editors and theoreticians were forced to hone their skills at that dolorous art of quotation-juggling which, unfortunately, became a hallmark of their craft.

The significance of these and countless other tawdry exercises in historical manipulation goes far beyond the intellectual irresponsibility they reveal. They were among the prime devices employed to obscure the realities of the socialist system and to reinforce the authority of those who ruled over it. They were used to browbeat not only opponents, but other socialists who had the temerity to question the policies of Soviet leaders or the system's underlying premises. And they helped promote a culture of utopianism and arrogance in the world's Communist Parties.

But it wasn't all quotation-juggling and theoretical fraud. In the framework of Stalin's mechanical Marxism, it was enough to know that Marx had once declared that socialism's triumph over capitalism was, in terms of the Hegelian dialectic, a 'negation of the negation'. ('Capitalist private property is the first negation of individual private property .... But capitalist production begets, with the inexorability of a law of nature, its own negation. It is the negation of negation.') [12] For Stalin, the meaning and applicability of this statement was both clear and convenient. Socialism *demanded* the negation of every aspect of capitalism, from the market to even the most minute forms of private or individual enterprise. By the same token, 'bourgeois-democracy' would be negated by the dictatorship of the proletariat, bourgeois ideology by proletarian ideology, bourgeois art by socialist realism, and bourgeois man (sic) by the 'new Soviet socialist man.'

Nevertheless, lashed by Stalin's war against his 'right-opportunist' opponents and spurred by their own pretensions, the party overwhelmingly endorsed the precise theoretical and practical leap Marx, Engels and Lenin had all warned against, effecting a changeover from a system based principally on economics to one driven by administrative dictates.

The result was a system which, at first, registered impressive accomplishments. If nothing else, Stalin's breakneck program of 'socialist construction' transformed backward Russia into a relatively self-sufficient industrialized state. (Years later, cynical economists – socialist as well as capitalist – would call it 'the most impressive nineteenth-century industrial infrastructure in the world, seventy-five years too late'.) [13] At the same time, the new system brought Soviet citizens a higher and more egalitarian standard of living, along with guarantees of employment, free healthcare and public education without precedent elsewhere in the world. These gains were particularly noteworthy among the non-Russian nationalities, enabling the communists to forge what appeared to be a harmonious union between the scores of different peoples and nations of the old czarist empire.

Still, the much-vaunted Soviet economic and social accomplishments of the 1930s were far from the unmitigated triumph which official Marxist-Leninist history has celebrated. Many claims were exaggerated and some were simply untrue.

The Failure of Collectivization

The history of communism in Russia is, in one sense, a narrative of how the Bolsheviks wrestled with their most stubborn problem: how to build socialism in a predominantly peasant country. Clearly a socialist economy could not be based on small-scale, individual farming. But the main thing the revolution had promised the peasants was land. And it was on that basis that they supported the revolution.

Keenly aware of the need to socialize agriculture, Lenin was equally alert to the danger of alienating the peasant masses and turning them against Bolshevik power. Thus, as early as 1917, even before turning to the NEP, Lenin had warned the Bolsheviks – most of whom had little knowledge or experience of the realities of rural life – that:

> Joint cultivation of the land is a difficult business and it would be madness for anybody to imagine that it can be decreed from above and imposed on people, because the centuries-old habit of farming on one's own cannot suddenly disappear, and because money will be needed for it and adaptation to the new mode of life .... Changes in

the life of a people are not made on the advice of a party. Tens of millions of people do not make a revolution on the advice of a party, and such a change would be more of a revolution than the overthrow of the weak-minded Nicholas Romanov.[14]

But, along with the NEP, Lenin's warning was unceremoniously scuttled when Stalin collectivized Soviet agriculture.

In order to justify this dubious enterprise, Marxist-Leninist theory promulgated a linguistic charade which muddied the historical categories used to differentiate property forms in the countryside. Broadly speaking, Lenin had recognized three main categories aside from private ownership: cooperatives, collectives and state farms.

In cooperatives – predicated on a market economy – membership was voluntary. Peasants would maintain title to their holdings and would assist each other by pooling resources, organizing joint work brigades, making investments in new machinery and setting up common marketing mechanisms. They could even leave the association if they chose.

In the collective farms, the existing land titles would gradually lose significance as the land was transformed, over time, into collective property. Peasant income would depend on what was left after the collective sold its harvest, paid its bills and allotted funds for common social projects and the following year's purchases. Remuneration would be based on labor time, skill and so on. The enterprise would be self-managed by a directly elected leadership body subject to removal from below.

State farms, while envisioned as the ultimate, long-range goal of socialist agriculture, were accorded limited significance. They would mainly focus on highly mechanized, non-food industrial crops such as cotton. The land would no longer be the property of individuals or the collective, but of the state. The peasants would constitute an agricultural proletariat paid a set wage for their labor irrespective of the degree of success of their 'factories in the field'.

The cooperatives, Lenin believed, would be the dominant form in Soviet agriculture for a lengthy period. His hope was that cooperation would gradually convince the peasants through their own experience of the advantages of collectivization and that the changeover would take place voluntarily.

Stalin thoroughly obscured these distinctions and – in the course of a few years – transformed the Soviet countryside into a mammoth network of collective farms which bore little resemblance to Lenin's conception of how 'socialist agriculture' would develop. Totally bound to central planning with virtually no independent marketing rights, the collective farms were, for all practical purposes, seen as 'socialist forms' only one step away from state farms. The main distinction between the two forms was that peasants on state farms were agricultural laborers working for a wage whereas the income of peasants in collective farms was tied to output and the collective income. About the only concession to the spirit of the NEP was that peasant families were permitted to cultivate small private plots. These were relatively insignificant during the Stalin years, but over time – especially after 1956 – these private plots became the source of a major portion of the fresh vegetables and produce made available to urban consumers. Long operating in a grey area of the economy, this lingering form of private entrepreneurship – as was the case with the extensive black market that grew up in the Brezhnev years – was a de facto expression of the impulse toward a mixed economy which 'actually existing socialism' could never completely eliminate.

In the final analysis, collectivization not only eliminated the kulaks as a class. It destroyed Lenin's concept of the worker–peasant alliance and eliminated the *peasantry* as a class. Official ideology maintained the continued existence of a peasant class; but, given the actual relationship of the collective farms to the overall administrative-command system, the peasants became little more than an agricultural workforce, albeit with fewer social and economic guarantees than the industrial workers had.

As late as 1952 Stalin would assert that in agriculture, 'the state disposes only of the product of the state enterprises, while the product of the collective farms, being their property, is disposed of only by them.' [15] Twenty-five years later, when it finally became possible openly to cite the differences between official Marxism-Leninism and social reality, a senior research worker at the Institute of World Economy & International Relations of the USSR Academy of Sciences would comment:

> One reads this section [Stalin's statement] with special bitterness. How was it possible to imagine the collective farms as sort of 'Rochdale cooperatives' concerned only with the interests of their own members, who don't wish to get involved in the state plan and who dispose of their own produce in a mercantile manner? And to say this ... when the state had literally tied the collective farms hands and feet with the state system of obligatory purchases and payment in kind for work performed by the machine-tractor stations [and] when the greater part of the collective farm produce was 'paid for' at prices which didn't cover even delivery to the procurement centers.[16]

Nor did collectivization ever provide 'actually existing socialism' with a productive and reliable agricultural base. Although Marxism-Leninism has celebrated it as a shining example of socialist success, collectivization set back agricultural production and condemned the Soviet country-side to decades of stagnation. Looking back on the period, Gorbachev would conclude that:

Enormous damage was done to agriculture. The numbers of livestock and agricultural production dropped sharply, supply to cities grew worse, and consumption in the villages decreased .... The level of agricultural production reached before the beginning of collectivization was exceeded only twice in the prewar years – in 1937 and 1940.[17]

Nevertheless, state procurements of grain during those years actually increased, testimony to the fact that the famine in the countryside (with its estimated 5 million dead) and the general desperate plight of the peasantry were not due to unfavorable natural conditions but to the looting of the harvests by the state. Even Stalin acknowledged that collectivization's much-vaunted success was not so much in production gains, but 'primarily in the growth and consolidation of socialist agriculture on the one hand, and the downfall of individual peasant farming on the other'.[18]

But over and above the massive human tragedy from whose scars no society can be immune, the greatest damage of all *from a strictly economic point of view* was that millions of the Soviet Union's most experienced and most productive agricultural workers and entrepreneurs were lost – and never replaced. Even those 'kulaks' who cooperated with the new system were, as a rule, placed under constant supervision, barred from managerial positions and assigned the most menial jobs.

It was a tragedy from which Soviet agriculture never recovered. Half a century later, Gorbachev would somberly recount the true state of affairs in the countryside:

The reality is this: We do not produce enough agricultural output. The state is forced to make large purchases abroad of grain, meat, fruit, vegetables, sugar, vegetable oil and certain other products. We continue to trail behind developed countries – large and small – in labor productivity, in crop yields from fields, in livestock productivity and in the variety and quality of foodstuffs. The gap is not getting smaller, it is growing .... Mismanagement carries off up to 20% of everything produced in the countryside – and for some products the figure is as high as 30% to 40%.

The countryside is far behind the city in social and cultural development. The lack of good roads is a problem that affects all regions .... The extent to which the countryside is provided with up-to-date, well-appointed housing, municipal services, schools, and medical and cultural institutions is extremely poor. A person often has to travel dozens and sometimes hundreds of kilometers to obtain medical assistance, to obtain basic consumer services, to buy the simplest goods.[19]

Industrialization and the Mobilization Economy

Unlike agriculture, industry registered substantial gains after the 'Great Turn'. During the first Five-Year Plan alone, according to Medvedev,

> 1,500 big enterprises were built and the foundations were laid for branches of industry that had not existed in Czarist Russia: machine-tool production, auto and tractor manufacturing, chemical works, airplane factories, the production of powerful turbines and generators, of high-grade steel, of ferrous alloys, of synthetic rubber, artificial fibers, nitrogen, and so on. Construction was begun on thousands of kilometers of new railroads and canals .... A modern defense industry was established.[20]

Even so, the Marxist-Leninist penchant for analyzing economics through the prism of 'socialist realism' disguised the fact that Soviet industrialization was far from the unalloyed triumph usually celebrated.

For one thing, the disastrous results of collectivization effectively nullified the underlying premise that 'socialist accumulation' of the agricultural surplus would provide the capital for industrialization. At the beginning of the first Five-Year Plan, for instance, almost 50 percent of the agricultural surplus was used for industrialization. By 1932, this figure had dropped to 18.1 percent. And, as Medvedev, notes, 'At the end of the first five-year plan, the starving villages were hardly able to help industrialization.'[21]

For another, according to Medvedev, the glowing official figures on economic growth during the 1930s were riddled with exaggeration and dubious statistical methods. Contrary to claims of plan overfulfillment, most goals for various commodities were not met. Increases there were – in pig iron, steel, electricity, coal, building materials, tractors, mineral fertilizers, trucks and many others – but these were significantly less than called for in the plan. Production of consumer goods showed little growth, many items never surpassing pre-plan levels and some declining. Thus, says Medvedev:

> If fulfillment of the first five-year plan is analyzed not only on the basis of gross output but also on the basis of physical indices of goods produced, the results prove to be much more modest than the propaganda claimed. Toward the end of the plan almost none of the optimum goals as expressed in physical units, was reached. [23]

Latter-day Soviet economist Nikolai Shmelyov argues that, 'Using real as opposed to concocted figures, the annual industrial growth rate of the 1930s did not exceed 5–7 percent', compared to an average of '18 percent a year – the highest industrial growth rate in our entire history' in the NEP years 1921–28. [24]

Still, it cannot be denied that the first period of 'socialist construction' registered significant economic gains. But were these, as Stalin and subsequent Marxist-Leninist theory claims, due to socialism? Once ideologically imposed categories are dispensed with, all one can really say is that whatever success there was simply demonstrates the advantages of a mobilization economy for the realization of short-term goals. In more recent years it has not been at all uncommon for countries at lower levels of economic development to use state ownership and/or control over the means of production and state direction of the economy to accelerate economic growth.

The mobilization mode remained well suited to the exigencies of the war and postwar reconstruction, so little attention was paid to problems which had begun to appear in the economic mechanism. By the early 1950s, however, these problems had become significant and were mounting. Despite advances in mechanization, agriculture continued to be plagued by inadequate production. A severe labor shortage was attributed to wartime losses, but Soviet economists were beginning to realize that the problem was also due to the prevalence of labor-intensive production. In industry, rates of labor productivity remained low and gaps between the plan and end results were becoming commonplace. The main problem, however, was that the mobilization economy had spawned a huge government apparatus whose privileged position was directly tied to maintaining the system's norms.

Early Efforts at Reform

Stalin addressed some of these problems in his 1952 pamphlet, *Economic Problems of Socialism in the USSR*, especially criticizing 'voluntarist' tendencies in Soviet economic management. But he never considered the possibility that something might be wrong with the system itself. Typically, he placed the blame on subjective factors – executives and managers with an inadequate understanding of Marxian economics.

Post-Stalin Soviet leaders went further. Khrushchev encouraged Soviet economists to explore possible alterations in the economic mechanism and a measure of political liberalization. But a rather ambitious reform program which, in many ways, anticipated Gorbachev's perestroika 20 years later, was ultimately shot down by the resistant party-government administrative complex.

Still, the effort itself provided nourishment for a new crop of emerging Soviet economists aware of the scale of the country's economic problems and much more open to fundamental change. In an unprecedentedly blunt and confidential 1965 report on Soviet economic problems, Abel Aganbegyan, later to be Gorbachev's top economic adviser, told a group of Leningrad editors:

> In the last six years, the rate of growth of our economy declined by a factor of approximately three. In agriculture, there was approximately a tenfold decline .... Our industrial structure is the worst and most backward of all the industrially developed countries ... [Of] about two million machine tools ... only half are operational; the other half are either not in use or in repair .... Half the timber produced in the USSR is lost; from the remaining half, we produce three times less than the U.S., five times less than in West Germany, and eight times less than in Sweden .... We have a permanent disadvantage in trade with other countries. Essentially what we sell are raw materials because many countries (including socialist countries) are reluctant to buy finished products from us because their quality is not very high .... To smelt one ton of steel, we use three times as much coke as does the U.S. Natural gas is not delivered to metallurgical plants (there are no pipes, but the main problem is poor planning). Thus we keep expanding the coal industry and it devours enormous resources .... The regulating role of price and of value relations is virtually absent in our economy.[25]

Aganbegyan's report, however, never saw the light of day. Instead, the system disguised its predicament by such makeshift measures as an ever-greater use of labor-intensive production methods and by taking advantage of the high world price for its main natural resource, oil. Soviet consumers were told that their relatively low standard of living – as compared to the West – was due to the Cold War and the problems of capitalist encirclement. At the same time, economic statistics were rendered virtually meaningless by using quantitative rather than qualitative indices for production. Thus the glowing economic reports of the period focused on goods produced but ignored figures relating to matters such as distribution, sale, use-life and quality of finished products. In many cases, figures were simply falsified.

Meanwhile, the situation was growing worse. As the problems continued to mount – falling growth rates, low labor productivity, lags in technology, shortages in key products, (hidden) inflation and so forth – subsequent Soviet leaders tried to amend different aspects of the system. But largely due to the self-serving inertia of the bureaucracy, none of these efforts improved the situation.

At the same time, attempts to modify the system emerged in almost all the countries of Eastern Europe. Feeling that Khrushchev had given them a green light, Czechoslovakia and Poland experimented with reforms in the late 1950s. Other efforts were made in East Germany (1963), Bulgaria (1966), Romania (1967) and Hungary (1968). The most extensive and ambitious was the wave of reform encompassing not only the economy but also the political system in Czechoslovakia under the slogan of trying to construct 'socialism with a human face'. All of these efforts were aimed at modifying the rigid controls of central planning and introducing elements of private enterprise into the economy. None succeeded, most due to lack of serious implementation. The Czech experiment was finally crushed by Soviet troops in the summer of 1968.

During the 1970s, reformers working within the Soviet bureaucracy managed to get the ear of individual leaders and could even occasionally insert a call for reform into official speeches and publications. But they could not succeed in having this translated into practice. After a while, all they could do was wait for Brezhnev to die. When that finally occurred in 1982, the choice of the seemingly reform-minded Yuri Andropov as Brezhnev's successor encouraged many to try again.

A confidential study prepared for the new Kremlin leadership for the first time asserted that the administrative-command system could no longer ensure the 'full and effective use of the society's intellectual and labor resources'.[26] The reformers even went so far as to charge that needed changes were being stymied by what had become a ponderous bureaucratic apparatus employing ideological arguments to defend their own positions of power and privilege.

Impressed and influenced by the study, Andropov shortly thereafter sent out an even more urgent signal of distress:

> Why from vast capital investments do we now not get the return that we should? Why is production characterized by an unsatisfactory pace of scientific technological achievement?... At present, conditions are such that the economic law that Marx considered the first basic law of collective production, the law of economizing work time, does not operate among us in full force .... Even in industry non-mechanized hand labor reaches 40%. This is why the all-around acceleration of the tempo of scientific-technological progress and a more active utilization of its accomplishments are so relevant today.[27]

At the same time, in an effort to overcome these problems, a number of experiments in decentralization were begun. But Andropov's untimely death after just 15 months in office enabled the entrenched apparatus once again to reverse the reform process by installing the time-serving and ailing Konstantin Chernenko. A little more than a year later, Chernenko too was dead. But by then the country's economic difficulties were bordering on the intolerable. Even some of the political figures most closely associated with the Old Guard, such as Andrei Gromyko, could see the writing on the wall. As a result – and with Gromyko's backing – the CPSU Politburo finally bit the bullet and opted for reform by selecting its youngest and most reform-minded member, Mikhail Gorbachev, for its top leadership post.

But few people outside the inner circles of leadership were prepared for Gorbachev's open acknowledgment shortly after taking office in 1985 that the Soviet economy had been stagnating for almost two decades and was on the verge of calamity. The economic phenomena were grim: a sharply declining growth rate; falling labor productivity; an inordinate waste of resources; consistent shortfalls in plan fulfillment; the poor quality of finished goods and a totally inadequate service sector; seriously flawed distribution mechanisms; a wage-leveling process which was sapping individual incentive and promoting absenteeism and aliena- tion; the growing role of a 'shadow economy' capable of supplying at uncontrolled prices goods and services hard to obtain from the official economy; and widespread corruption and bureaucratic inertia.[28]

Adding insult to injury, 'Serious shortcomings ... were disguised with ostentatious activities and campaigns and celebrations of numerous jubilees in the center and the provinces. The world of day-to-day realities and that of make-believe well-being were increasingly parting ways.' [29]

The ultimate irony in these obscurantist exercises was that built into the advantages which enabled the administrative-command system to achieve its initial economic goals were the very problems that, in the final analysis, undermined it.

Centralized Planning

So long as Soviet economic goals were simple and could be calibrated quantitatively – tons of steel, kilowatts of electricity or numbers of tractors produced – centralized planning worked relatively well. Alec Nove, probably the most objective western analyst of the Soviet economy over the years, says:

> Planning worked in those sectors to which the state gave priority and whose needs could be easily quantified. This applied first and foremost to armaments, but also to electrical energy, where the product is homogeneous and thus readily 'plannable'. It also applied to production of oil and gas, and to the construction of a network of pipelines. In each of these fields the Soviet system scored impressive gains.[30]

However, as the Soviet economy became more complex, as the number and variety of products expanded, and as it became increasingly obliged to measure its performance against that of advanced capitalism, the system's inherent limitations and negative aspects were revealed.

The plan, it turned out, was really not a plan at all. Simply at the technical level, the central apparatus had no way to process – let alone absorb and evaluate – all the necessary information on resources, performance, transportation, warehousing, technology, consumer needs and so on that would have to go into developing a realistic plan. (Since computers might have made at least the gathering and processing of such information possible, the fact that Soviet planners never managed to ensure the full development and employment of a computer technology is itself highly suggestive of the plan's arbitrary character and the system's inherent inertia.)

Central planning did, of course, produce a vast quantity of goods. But its most successful product, by far, was the huge administrative apparatus which the ubiquitous nature of the plan – all production became subject to it – naturally generated. Originally it was thought that with the plan having the force of law, producers and managers would be forced to carry out social objectives irrespective of their personal interests. However the administrative-command structure generated a sociology of its own in which bureaucratic self-interest often proved a more powerful force than economic efficiency. As a result, the bureaucracy became supremely comfortable with this arrangement and could hardly imagine any other, the more so since its own well-being was bound up with it.

Over time the plan degenerated into a somewhat cynical negotiating process between producers and planners. The producers, who tried to keep goals deliberately low so as to maximize their chances of meeting them, simultaneously tended to overstate their requirements for resources for the same reason. The planners' bottom-line weapon then became the principle of 'planning from the attained level', that is, simply assigning a percentage increase in production from the previous year's output.

Soviet economist Gavriil Popov has described with painful accuracy the broader socio-political significance of the system's inexorable pull toward bureaucratism:

> Power became a special force standing above everything else. In this sense, there is no particular problem of bureaucratism, for the administrative system itself is bureaucratic, that is ... the apparatus not being controlled by anybody but the apparatus forces themselves .... In the administrative system all types of bureaucracy merge: the bureaucracy of the party apparatus, the bureaucracy of the state and the bureaucracy of the apparatus of the social organizations .... The strength of the bureaucracy lies not only in the giant machinery of reprisals but also (which is most important) in its right to dispose of huge material resources, to intervene in the distribution of material values.
>
> An exceptionally important feature of administrative bureaucracy is total ideologization, the stamping of everything with its ideas and the argument for the necessity of this system as serving these ideas and the proclamation of any resistance to the system an ideological-moral crime.[31]

With such an unchecked hold over society, the bureaucracy became quite adept at resisting reforms that would sap its authority. As a result of the bureaucratic inertia thus fostered – and in the absence of such objective checks as competition, a market in which consumers would have alternatives to offered products, enterprise accountability to cost-efficiency, and the possibility of political challenges – the system's flaws were reproduced at an ever-expanding rate.

Private Property, The Market and Monopoly

A fundamental premise of 'actually existing socialism' was that private property (other than one's personal possessions) was incompatible with a planned economy. In part, this was a profound ideological prejudice with roots in anarchism and utopian socialism whose proponents saw private property as something inherently evil. 'Property', said Proudhon, 'is theft.' And hadn't Marx and Engels themselves declared that 'The theory of the Communists may be summed up in the single sentence: Abolition of private property?' [32] Conveniently overlooked by Stalin and his followers was that Marx and Engels saw the abolition of private property occurring in stages. But full and immediate abolition was a requirement of the Stalinist model, for how could the state manage and control the country's human and material resources if significant economic decisions could be made independent of its authority?

Marxist-Leninist hostility to the market ran almost as deep as its antagonism to private property. For it was in the process of sale and exchange that one could see most graphically that most pernicious of all capitalist processes – profit-taking. Even more to the point, perhaps, a genuine market – in which consumer demand functions as a critical objective mechanism in the determination of production – would compromise the authority of the centralized administrative agency over the country's economic life.

At the producers' level there was not even the semblance of a market. Based on the plan, enterprises calculated their needs for raw materials, equipment, energy and labor power and then received authorization to place orders – usually with particular suppliers – and to hire workers. Finished products were disposed of in similar fashion. If factory managers were dissatisfied with the quality of materials delivered by a particular supplier, they had to make do or run the risk of failing to fulfill the plan.

Distribution at the retail level, on the other hand, gave the appearance of marketing because money actually changed hands when consumer goods were sold through huge state-owned department stores and shops. But the Soviet economy was not regulated to any significant degree by a market *relationship*. Their prices arbitrarily set by central planners and bearing little relation either to the cost of production or supply and demand, retail stores were merely distribution centers whose lack of concern, shoddy merchandise and perennial shortages became the system's most visible hallmarks. Without a market and competition, there was virtually no objective pressure on producers, distributors or managers to improve quality or take consumer concerns into account.

Consequently, managers of retail establishments could and did manage their enterprises like feudal fiefdoms, making the whole system fundamentally user-unfriendly. Long lines waiting to purchase scarce products transformed consumers into supplicants, afraid to complain of poor quality or service for fear of retaliation. Consumers unhappy with apparel or equipment being sold in one store could try another; but, in general, they would only find more of the same. There was also little incentive to improve customer services at the retail level, where archaic methods of purchase and payment prevailed. Three decades after supermarkets had become the distributive norm in developed capitalist countries, they remained exotic establishments of fantasy in the lands where 'socialism' had triumphed.

Individual travel was, more often than not, a nightmare that had to be experienced to be believed. In terms of passenger comfort, services and convenience, Soviet planes and trains operated far below the minimum norms deemed acceptable by travelers in the West – especially on domestic carriers. Seats were uncomfortable and cramped; bathroom facilities ranged from unclean to unsanitary; waiting rooms, check-in procedures and baggage handling were chaotic.

Another irony of the system's cumbersomeness was its promotion of and reliance on monopoly. Having learned from Marx the wastefulness of competition and from early industrial capitalism the advantages of economy of scale, Marxist-Leninists early on enshrined monopoly as the epitome of socialism.

But the Soviet system went even further than the capitalist countries in fostering monopoly. Somewhere between 30 and 40 percent of all Soviet commodities – including many of the country's basic industrial goods – were produced entirely or almost entirely at single sites.[33] Even where the same product was made at several locations, the central plan obliged customers to make their purchases from a particular plant or outlet. Shopping around – whether at the producer or consumer level – was virtually unheard of. And, of course, all industry was controlled from a single center in one or another ministry.

Certainly the abrupt abolition of private property, the elimination of the market and the prevalence of state monopoly made the work of the central ministries much easier. Since the state owned all land, resources and the means of production, it could simply issue directives to every economic sub-unit. Its absolute control over the dispensation of finances, raw materials, prices, commodities and labor ensured that its decisions became enforceable commands.

Contrary to the belief that this system would be more efficient, less costly and more productive, it bred waste, corruption and economic backwardness. The effective monopoly of the administrative-bureaucratic apparatus over the economy – and the vast network of privilege to which that arrangement gave rise – effectively destroyed the concept that 'state property' was the common property of all, replacing it with the attitude that public property belonged to no one. No less than capitalist private property, state property came to signify the alienation of labor. This alienation was expressed in extraordinarily high rates of absenteeism, rampant abuse and misuse of state property and a widespread public cynicism concerning the proclaimed ideals of socialism.

At the same time, the bureaucracy itself became adept at fashioning the system to its own convenience and advantage – more often than not at the expense of sensible economic practice. For those in the administrative apparatus, report-padding, bribe-taking, toadyism and disregard for laws became a social norm. Inevitably, such practices became commonplace in the broader culture.

Ironically, neither private property nor the market were ever fully abolished in the Soviet Union. For the most part, they were simply driven underground, rushing to fill the numerous economic vacuums left or, in many cases, created by the plan. As a result, a vast shadow economy – capable of supplying goods, services and food products in short supply or quality merchandise unavailable in state shops – came into being. Whether as purchaser, middleman or supplier, almost everyone was involved in it to one degree or another. Over time, this informal black market based on theft, smuggling, illicit private production, private use of state equipment and illegal currency exchange became indispensable to the functioning of the Soviet system. (According to some Soviet estimates, between the shadow economy and private peasant plots, roughly a quarter of the country's actual GNP was accounted for by private property forms.)

Given the poor quality of many big-ticket consumer items and the glaring inadequacy of state-owned repair services – to say nothing of the it's-not-our-responsibility attitude of manufacturers – private trade in services was especially widespread. Individuals who could repair automobiles, refrigerators, washing machines or television sets were in constant demand. But they would need spare parts and, in general, these could be obtained only by appropriating state property. Hence the extraordinarily high rate of thievery from factory warehouses.

During the 1970s and 1980s, pilferage of state property had become commonplace. One Soviet expert, confronted by speculation that the theft of concrete and other construction materials had been so great that nuclear reactors had been rendered structurally unsafe, laughingly dismissed the concern by noting: 'Under the Soviet system, 30 percent theft of building materials was assumed and taken into account before construction began.' [34]

This network of petty crime paled in comparison, however, to the entrepreneurial buccaneering of strategically situated administrators and directors who – working in conjunction with their party counterparts –

managed to appropriate state property and illegally produce goods for a market hungry for consumer-products. The most notorious example was the case of the Uzbekistan cotton scandal in the early 1980s in which a vast network of party and republic officials conspired to bilk the Soviet state of some four billion rubles.[35] Economic crime, of course, is hardly exclusive to the command economy. Honor of place in that regard certainly goes to capitalism whose scandals – one need only mention the Savings & Loans fiasco in the US in the late 1980s – readily dwarf even socialism's most notorious swindles.

The 'Law of Value'

With the entire system oriented to quantitative growth, cost-effectiveness became, at best, a secondary consideration. Consequently, little attention was paid throughout the 60 years of the administrative-command economy to Marx's postulate that the value of any commodity was determined by the amount of 'socially necessary labor time' required to make it; and that this value was demonstrated through the process of exchange.[36]

A prevailing Bolshevik prejudice in the early years after the revolution held that this thesis – the kernel of Marx's Law of Value – reflected the underlying dynamic of capitalist economics but had little relevance for socialism. Trying to make production conform to it, they argued, would negate socialism's ability to plan production in accord with social needs rather than profitability.

In practice, Soviet leaders tried to have it both ways, citing the Law of Value when trying to exercise some measure of control over production costs and overriding it when its application might interfere with highly prized goals. For Stalin, the Law of Value 'exercise[d] its influence' principally in the production of consumer goods, whereas in industries such as steel, machine-building and energy production, which were supposedly laying the foundation for socialism, its role was minimal. But in general, he declared, 'The Law of Value has no regulating function in our socialist production.' Were it otherwise, 'we should have to cease giving primacy to the production of means of production in favor of the production of articles of consumption.'[37]

In fact, the central planning mechanism never even made the consumer goods sector consistently accountable to the Law of Value. For one thing, heavy industry was such a dominating sector of the Soviet economy that its modus operandi inevitably spilled over into the rest. For another, the system had in its first years what seemed to be an inexhaustible supply of manual labor and raw materials so that little attention was paid to the inherent costs of these resources. Finally, and not least, the centralized apparatus had neither the inclination nor the knowledge to let such concepts as cost-accounting and profitability weaken its authority. After all, if enterprises were accountable to the Law of Value, they would be that much less accountable to the planners.

With plan fulfillment the overriding criterion for judging economic performance, administrators and enterprise heads learned how to protect themselves by hoarding labor power, raw materials and energy. Having little need to be concerned with costs, managers would maintain a larger workforce than necessary to make sure that absenteeism did not affect production figures. Similarly, enterprises would build up large reserves of raw materials and energy supplies as a hedge against poor quality and uncertain deliveries. The system likewise generated a tug-of-war between the central planning authorities and officials at the lower levels, in which the latter tried to keep their assigned production goals as low as possible.

After the initial period of rapid industrialization, the cost of operating this system was enormous. With state subsidies compensating for inefficiency at the enterprise level, managers had little incentive to improve economic performance. In fact, one of the great ironies of the system was that it actually encouraged waste.

The broader economic and social consequences of such waste were to be found in devastating comparisons between the productivity of the foremost capitalist and socialist countries. For instance, while the US economy significantly and consistently outproduced the Soviets in finished commodities, it did so with a much smaller industrial work force. Agriculture employed over 25 percent of the Soviet workforce, compared to 3 percent in the US. At the same time, the US was a net exporter of farm products, while the USSR long had to import grain to feed its population. Likewise, right up until its collapse the Soviet Union used more than twice the amount of metal and 23 percent more fuel than the US for each $1 billion of its Gross National Product (GNP). It also consumed 30 percent more raw materials to produce each ton of food.

Not only did the cost of subordinating quality to quantity take a devastating toll on the system's resources; what was worse, it obscured the fact that the Soviet economy had been normalized at a second-rate level. Pre-1985 official Soviet statistics, it will be recalled, regularly celebrated the accomplishments of socialism by citing spectacular increases in the GNP and by using figures showing the USSR was the world leader in the output of steel, pig iron, crude oil, gas, iron ore, mineral fertilizers, tractors, reinforced concrete structures, woolen cloth, shoes and so on. But after glasnost freed Soviet economists from the constraints of official hyperbole, a radically different picture emerged.

GNP growth was largely based on increasing quantitative inputs of capital and labor rather than increased labor productivity based on advances in technology.[38] Many of the impressive production figures were actually misleading because they reflected only industrial inputs and not finished products. These, Anders Aslund points out, were 'needed in such large quantities because of the excessive material intensity of the

Soviet production apparatus'. [39] As Aganbegyan notes, while the Soviet Union smelted 156 million tons of steel annually – more than doubling US output – the USSR wound up with a significantly smaller volume of steel-based end products.[40]

The wasteful use of the most readily accessible raw materials and fuels – such as oil, gas, coal, iron ore, timber – added yet another formidable expense to the Soviet economy. As a result of extremely high Soviet rates of extraction, Aganbegyan noted in 1986, 'good deposits and favorable fields are rapidly becoming exhausted, and ... it is necessary to transfer to new, more difficult deposits, deeper fields and worse conditions.' A massive shift in the extracting industries to the lands east of the Urals, particularly Siberia, began to take place at immense cost. Not only did new fields have to be opened up; a vast workforce had to be relocated and new cities, houses, railroads and highways – along with an accompanying social infrastructure – had to be built.

Over the years, Soviet manufacture became notorious for its poor quality and waste of resources. A 1987 quality control program – instituted to force improvements in finished products – rejected 6 billion rubles' worth of products.[41] According to Aganbegyan, due to structural defects, more than 2,000 television sets catch fire every year in Moscow alone.[42]

One devastating consequence of the poor quality of Soviet equipment is that at any given time much of it was under repair. In many cases, machinery had to be replaced long before earning back its capital investment costs. Similarly, many consumer products simply did not last as long as their Western counterparts. Of course, the need for early replacement is a goad to further production – the USSR, for instance, annually produced more than twice as much leather footwear as the US [43] – but this merely reflects socially unnecessary expenditures which aggravated an already deficit-plagued state budget.

Poor quality likewise reduced exports, thereby sharply curtailing the possibility for accumulating much-needed hard currency. Even the most optimistic Soviet estimate acknowledged in 1988 that only 14.2 percent of Soviet products conformed to world standards. More cautious estimates put the figure at between 7–8 percent.[44]

In economics, as in nature and art, form tends to follow function. And the administrative-command mechanism – brought into being precisely to facilitate extensive production – inevitably generated modes of planning, divisions of labor, work plans, production methods, technologies, relationships, habits and attitudes reflecting that fundamental orientation. But the command system's heavy-handed methods for realizing highly focused, short-term, quantitative goals could not efficiently manage a modern industrial society trying to satisfy the complex and increasingly sophisticated needs of a vast population.

Consequently, once the initial mobilizing phase of industrialization

was past, continued reliance on the old model often induced economically irrational decisions. Referring to an extensive literature produced by
both Soviet and Western economists, Nove points out how the plan, by
positing goals the only way it knew how – for instance, rubles of
turnover, tons produced or transported – actually encouraged the
unnecessary use of heavier and more expensive materials while discour-
aging economies in resources and energy.[45]

An even more voluntarist approach to socialist construction was
embodied in both the theory and practice of China's 'Great Proletarian
Cultural Revolution'. Many of the central theoretical precepts of that
catastrophic undertaking were first developed and put forward by Mao
during the Great Leap Forward of 1959–60. Using as his departure
point two Soviet works – *Political Economy* and Stalin's *Economic
Problems of Socialism in the USSR* – Mao critiqued a number of the
concepts we have discussed above and criticized the Soviets for not
going far enough down the voluntarist road.

Thus, in his *Critique of Soviet Economics*, Mao disputes a statement
in the *Political Economy* text that 'socialist industrialization is the
precondition for agricultural collectivization'. After all, he says, collectivization in the Soviet Union was 'basically realized between 1930 and
1932' prior to extensive mechanization in the countryside, neglecting to
mention the subsequent grave consequences for Soviet agriculture as a
result of collectivization.[46]

Elsewhere in this same work, Mao goes to great lengths to defend
the thesis that 'new production relations ... clear the way for the
development of new social productive forces'.[47] On this basis he
criticizes any intimation that 'material incentives' (a remnant of capitalism) might take priority over revolutionary motivation (a central element
of new 'socialist' production relations).

Finally, noting that this is the 'critical' question, the one which really
'joins the issues', Mao criticizes the Soviets for 'making too much of the
effects of the Law of Value'. In doing so he offers the following rather
remarkable statement:

> We did not carry through the Great Leap on the basis of the
> demands of the Law of Value but on the basis of the fundamental
> economic laws of socialism and the need to expand production. If
> things are narrowly regarded from the point of view of the Law of
> Value, the Great Leap would have to be judged not worth the losses
> and last year's all-out effort to produce steel and iron as wasted
> labor. The local steel produced was low in quantity and quality, and
> the state had to make good many losses. The economic results were
> not significant .... But there was great value to the campaign because
> it opened wide a whole economic construction phase.[48]

It turned out, of course, that both the embryonic revolution of the

'Great Leap' and the more elaborate Great Proletarian Cultural Revolution, far from opening a 'wide phase of economic construction', set China's economy back more than a decade. Eventually, as objective reality asserted its inescapable compulsions, the whole procession of great leaps and revolutionary surges which characterized Mao's version of 'permanent revolution' collapsed in a paroxysm of unrealizable fantasy.

'To Each According to Labor'

Contempt for Marx's Law of Value generated the most cavalier attitude toward another closely related Marxist precept – the law of distribution according to labor. Theoretically, the system upheld this concept, generally expressed as 'From each according to ability, to each according to work.' As a practical matter, it cultivated a culture of egalitarianism in which little differentiation was made between the skill levels or social value of labor performed – or even between socially necessary and unnecessary labor.

In part, this is a bias against intellectuals and toward the 'industrial proletariat'. Thus doctors and teachers were notoriously among the most underpaid of Soviet workers. (These professions were also heavily dominated by women – surely no coincidence.) Even within industry, this leveling tendency showed up in a narrowing gap between skilled and semi-skilled (or even unskilled) workers. And engineers often received lower wages than skilled industrial workers. After conducting a historical study of the subject, Soviet economist Vsevolod Kulikov reports:

> In Czarist Russia, the incomes of the engineers were about ten times more than the wages of the workers. After the Revolution, the ratio changed as follows: during NEP, it was approximately 4:1; on the eve of the Great Patriotic War, 2.15:1; and in 1960 – 1.5:1. By the mid-1980s, the average wages of workers and engineers were practically leveled out.[49]

But it is also part of that same primitive perception which heralded the administrative-command economy as the triumph of socialism. Marx had always predicated his conception of communism on the assumption that society would, by then, have arrived at a level of economic development capable of fully satisfying all human material needs. 'Only then', he said, would society be able to 'inscribe on its banners: From each according to ability, to each according to need.'[50] Concerning distribution under socialism until then, he said, 'the same principle prevails as that which regulates the exchange of commodities, as far as this is exchange of equal values.'

Leveling under 'actually existing socialism', of course, did not appear as literal equality of income. Various categories of work were assigned different wage scales. And within each category, there were wage differentials based on labor time and seniority. Rather, the principle of 'to each according to labor' was distorted in a less obvious but no less economically destructive a fashion. Thus Kulikov notes:

> The problem of unprofitable enterprises or those which bring but small profits has become one of the most acute for the socialist countries. In the Soviet economy, for example, their share by the mid-1980s has been 40 percent. It is obvious that no economy could function normally with such a brake on it. The question naturally arises: how could these enterprises have existed for whole decades? The answer is clear enough: the state took away the profit from the efficient work collectives and passed it to those at which the matters were bad. Under such conditions, it became senseless to work efficiently, while the losses did not create any panic: the state will come to the rescue. As a result, subsidies to unprofitable and not sufficiently profitable enterprises devoured a substantial part of the state budget revenues and were one of the reasons for its deficit character. Thus it has come about that the natural connection between labor (its results) and income was violated.[51]

A significant cause of the high rate of unprofitability in Soviet enterprises was the attempt to put into practice not only Marx's precept on remuneration according to labor but a socialist guarantee of full employment. However, this admirable objective – long pointed to by Marxism-Leninism as socialism's most compelling feature – is one of those 'rights' which, Marx warned, 'are in no way calculable by equity' [52] and which 'can never be higher than the economic structure of society and its cultural development conditioned thereby'.[53]

In trying to implement the guarantee of work to all by administrative edict, the communists condemned 'actually existing socialism' to economic inefficiency. The practice of feather-bedding (hiring more workers than needed) became one of Soviet industry's most characteristic features. Enterprise managers indulged in it in order to cover themselves in the drive for maximum output, secure in the knowledge that the state would pick up the tab at the end. Central planners went along with the practice for the same reason – and because of the party-exerted pressure to provide employment for all. Not the least of the ironies resulting from guaranteed employment is that it promoted frequent labor shortages, since the hoarding of labor by one enterprise was frequently matched by a lack of available workers at another.

The price exacted for these violations of basic economic logic was measured in the growth of parasitism, lack of concern for property and resources, loss of initiative, poor work habits and, of course, staggering budget deficits. It also fostered a culture of passivity which placed greater store on the redistribution of existing surpluses than on their increase. Leveling also led to a resurgence of private enterprise. For while 'socialism' provided insufficient rewards for initiative and productivity, the shadow economy did not.

For a long time, the financial consequences of ignoring considerations of real value were hidden by the simple expedient of printing money. The inflationary effect of this practice was likewise hidden by the system of controlled prices. But economics can be suppressed only so long. Resources for replacing and modernizing the aging infrastructure became less and less available. The shadow economy grew up in response to the artificial valuelessness of the 'socialist' exchange mechanism. Hard currency became increasingly difficult to obtain as – aside from oil and other raw materials – Soviet exports were largely ignored by countries outside the 'socialist camp'.

Social Consequences

Inevitably, the social impact of this waste was felt at home. For after years of subsidizing inefficient industries and socially unnecessary labor, the initial gains in improving the living standards of the Soviet citizenry leveled off and, in many crucial areas, began to deteriorate.

One of the most glaring declines has been in the availability and quality of healthcare. From 1950 to 1985, the proportion of national income allocated to health dropped from roughly 10 percent to 4 percent. In 1985, the Soviet Union ranked fiftieth in the world in infant mortality rates (26 deaths per 1,000 births), while life expectancy for Soviet men (63 years) and women (73 years) ranked well below the figures in every advanced capitalist country and many Third World countries.[54]

These dismal figures are directly tied to drastic inadequacies not only in the Soviet healthcare system but in the cavalier approach taken to problems of pollution, safety and a variety of environmental and occupational hazards. For instance, the Soviet Union had roughly 10,000–13,000 cases of typhoid fever annually (compared to 100–300 in the US), largely due to polluted drinking water. In 1989, the USSR had a total of 62 CAT scanners, compared to 4,000 in Japan and 4,800 in the US. A pronounced shortage of disposable needles and disposable syringes reduced the number of treatments offered and, in many cases, led desperate doctors to reuse equipment that should have been discarded. In the countryside, 69 percent of rural hospitals functioned without hot water and 27 percent had no sewage systems. [55]

A 1990 *Izvestia* investigation into monitoring of agricultural production and food-processing reported that:

the overwhelming majority of our public-health and chemical 'customs inspectors' are armed with equipment that should have gone to museums long ago. Using this equipment to monitor the quality of food products is as hopeless as trying to build a space station with a stone axe.[56]

The pressure of plan-fulfillment was a significant factor in poor monitoring and the reluctance of enterprises to scuttle below standard products. 'It takes four days to get back the results of a standard test', the *Izvestia* report noted. 'But when a test sounds the alarm because, for example, a batch of onions is almost bursting with pesticides, it turns out that those onions are already being sold at market stalls.'

A provincial official in Kazakhstan told the investigator:

People work with sick cattle for decades, risking their health, and they don't even receive a bonus for hazardous working conditions because there supposedly aren't any tubercular cattle on the livestock farms. According to the existing instructions, such cattle are to be slaughtered immediately. But tell me, how can this be done? How can they slaughter cattle and, at the same time, fulfill and even overfulfill the demanding plans and socialist commitments that come down from above? So it's turned out that, while hovering on the verge of disaster, they've sent triumphal reports to the higher-ups and received Orders and Hero of Labor stars.

Soviet labor-intensive coal fields had the worst of two worlds: high accident rates and low productivity. From 1979 to 1989, some 10,000 Soviet miners died on the job – roughly eight times the US figure; life expectancy for the Soviet miner was 49 years compared to 70 years for a US miner. At the same time, while 2.5 million Soviet miners were producing 800 million tons of coal a year, 140,000 US miners were producing 1 billion tons.[57]

Serious shortcomings also prevailed in education where funding fell from 10 to 7 percent of the national budget in the years from 1950 to 1985, and in housing, where the proportion of capital investment declined from 21 percent in 1960 to 14–15 percent in 1985.[58]

But nothing more graphically illustrates the system's failure in the realm of the people's social welfare than the environmental and ecological destruction it engendered. The 1990 *Izvestia* investigation, reporting that Novosibirsk Province in Siberia was awash with toxic waste, then asks: 'What about Moldavia, stuffed to the gills with herbicides? Or the Moscow area with its glut of heavy metals – mercury, cadmium, lead and arsenic? Or Central Asia, saturated through and through with nitrates and defoliants?' [59] Many of the worst problems were in the non-Russian republics, a provocation which loomed large in the nationalist upsurge which finally led to the breakup of the Soviet Union. 'From an ecological point of view', says

Malik Rozykulov, head of the English language department at Radio Tashkent,

> Uzbekistan is a disaster area. A long time ago there was a decision made in Moscow that Uzbekistan should become the Soviet Union's main producer of cotton. Everything was subordinated to this. Now we are living with a calamity which is, in many ways, as bad as Chernobyl![60]

Because Uzbekistan's vast new cotton domain required extensive irrigation, the two main rivers feeding the Aral Sea – once the world's fourth largest lake – were diverted to the cotton fields. The result? Over the past 20 years, the Aral lost more than half its water. As the fish disappeared, fishing villages were abandoned. Many of these can still be seen today, 40 miles from the receding shore line. At the same time, the cotton fields were inundated with chemicals. Ultimately the toxic materials filtered back into the region's rivers and ditches. This had a catastrophic impact on the area's water supply. In the Karakalpak Autonomous Republic, part of Uzbekistan, two-thirds of the population suffer from liver disorders, typhoid fever or cancer of the esophagus. Infant mortality rates are among the highest in the world.

In Estonia, arbitrary decision-making by the centralized administrative-command mechanism also had a devastating environmental impact. 'We have had much experience with such decisions', says Siim Kallas, a reform-oriented communist elected as a deputy to the Supreme Soviet in 1988. 'Almost all the pollution here in our lakes and rivers and also in the Baltic itself comes from enterprises – especially chemical plants – established and controlled by ministries in Moscow.' [61]

And, as the world knows by now, while communist leaders were proclaiming that the Soviet nuclear industry was 'ecologically the safest in the world',[62] it was actually more accident-prone and dangerous than its capitalist counterparts. (Of course, nuclear facilities in the US and other capitalist countries are hardly paragons of safety and sound environmental precaution. Ironically, however, while popular protest movements in the West forced the correction of some of the worst nuclear plant abuses, such movements were suppressed in the USSR.)

The 1986 catastrophe at Chernobyl in Ukraine is the most notorious example of the nuclear irresponsibility of the command system. But it is hardly the only one. Following an explosion at an atomic fuel plant in east Kazakhstan in 1990, an emergency investigating commission concluded that 'the accident was the logical outcome of years of accumulating violations and miscalculations, ranging from shop design to elementary disregard for safety regulations'. [63] Today, as the secrecy of the past has been penetrated, there is a growing body of evidence that news of numerous other 'accidents' was suppressed.

But this deplorable record cannot be ascribed simply to 'accidents' or careless individuals. Responsibility for it rests with the planning mechanism itself whose production norms had so thoroughly infused the Soviet Union's technocratic culture that the voices of warning and caution simply went unheard.

Science and Technology

Perhaps the most telling evidence of the command economy's failure, however, was its inability to absorb and apply the latest developments in science and technology to the Soviet economy. As Gorbachev noted:

> At a time when the Western countries started a large-scale restructuring of their economies with the emphasis on resource saving, the latest science and state-of-the-art technology, scientific-technical progress slowed down (in the Soviet Union) ... mostly because the economy was not responsive to innovation.[64]

This unexpected revelation seemingly confounded one of Marxism's prime axioms – that while capitalist relations of production had become 'fetters' on the further development of the productive forces, socialism would foster the process of revolutionizing them.[65] But far from being the 'dynamic system [whose] ... inexhaustible potentialities and indisputable advantages over capitalism' were being demonstrated daily, the Soviet system, Premier Nikolai Ryzhkov acknowledged, 'was held back by an insurmountable barrier of inertia in all economic systems and by a lack of receptivity to ... scientific and technical progress'.[66]

The problem was not new. Twenty years earlier, an article in the prestigious *Literary Gazette* had noted that:

> Only 30 percent of new inventions are taken up by industry. In view of the fact that 16,000 inventions are registered annually and each one used in a small enterprise would mean an average saving of 50,000 rubles (of course, the vast majority could be used in more than one place), it is quite easy to imagine the extent of the waste involved.[67]

Even the usually sanguine Brezhnev warned the CPSU's 25th Congress in 1976 that 'the application of scientific and technical achievements is still a bottleneck in many branches' and that 'a sharp reduction of the proportion of manual labor and comprehensive mechanization and automation of production' were 'indispensable' for further progress.[68] Five years later, at the party's 26th Congress in 1981, Brezhnev would claim that 'the scientific and technical revolution [STR] is developing in scope and depth', but would then go on to note 'intolerable delays in introducing promising innovations into production'.[69]

In 1982 Oleg Bogomolov, director of the Institute of Economics of the World Socialist System, reported that over the previous two decades the socialist countries had 'failed to take due account of the latest scientific and technological advances. This has had a [negative] effect on the quality and reliability, the energy and material-intensiveness of production, that is, on the key criteria of efficiency.' [70]

None of these comments, however, addressed the causes of the growing technological gap between the capitalist and socialist countries. Only dissidents like Roy Medvedev argued that 'very important aspects of economic life in socialist countries, far from facilitating technological progress, even work to inhibit it'. [71] But warnings that these problems signified a fundamental problem in the command economy's structure and orientation or in the objective sociology of the administrative apparatus did not fall into the category of permissible criticism.

In truth, as Soviet commentator Fyodor Burlatsky has pointed out, the rigidly hierarchical planning system feared the very reforms – 'transition to operational and financial autonomy in industry, transition to the team-contract and family-contract system in farming, and the development of cooperatives in the service sector' – which might have made the economy more receptive to the scientific and technical revolution. For the essence of these reforms was to break the vise-like grip of the centralized state–party mechanism over the economy – a change which inevitably would increase pressure on the political system for greater democratization.[72]

As a result, the system actually encouraged 'extensive' to the detriment of 'intensive' development. As Aganbegyan points out, the planning mechanism makes

> scientific and technological progress unprofitable and fail[s] to guarantee advantage to those who raise the quality of production. It encourages new construction but makes work on technical reconstruction unprofitable. The system hoards the depreciation funds, perpetuates the output of old products, and does not push enterprises to renew their funds and products.[73]

Citing studies made of the Soviet energy industries, Aganbegyan documents a variety of ways in which narrow departmentalization – useful for enhancing quantitative goals – resulted in missed opportunities for technological innovation. For instance, he reports, it took years before a new, more reliable and efficient vortical furnace, used in the production of thermal energy, was utilized. The new furnace needed a smaller boiler, required less housing, cut loading time in half, reduced fuel consumption and atmospheric pollution, and was easier to repair. The only 'flaw' was that the boiler used 25 percent less metal; since plan-fulfillment indicators for boiler construction factories were based on the amount of metal used, the factories went on producing the old models.[74]

In another instance, due to the rigidities and overspecialization of the planning mechanism, it took 15 years before a new high-technology cutter for the extraction of coal from thin beds could be put into production. 'The cost of this delay', Aganbegyan estimates, 'exceeds the total value of all the capital expended on coal machine-building in the Soviet Union and the total expenditures over many years on geological research'.[75]

These examples are only the tip of the iceberg. Although the Soviet Union pioneered humanity's venture into space – thereby demonstrating a scientific capacity that was the match of its capitalist rivals – it lagged far behind in the development (and, even more, the application) of computer technology, cybernetics, robotization, new energy sources, chemically-created construction materials, biotechnology and the like. Its principal success – achieving nuclear parity with the US during the early 1970s – actually underscored the system's contradictory pulls. As it had in the past, the administrative-command economy demonstrated its strengths when it came to research, development and production for military uses. In this area, the Soviet high military command itself instituted quality controls and effectively pressured the planning mechanism to prioritize its needs. (Of course, over time, the cost of the resources spent on the Soviet military buildup had a decidedly negative impact on the rest of the economy. In the long run, the fact that US military development was based on a more efficient and productive economy became a decisive factor in the final resolution of the Cold War.)

Research, development and especially production in the civilian economy were another story. Here, where the bureaucratic mechanism wielded unchecked power, stagnation and inertia prevailed. And nowhere was this lethargy more evident or more costly than in the system's failure to utilize adequately the scientific and technical revolution. For it was on this battleground perhaps more than any that 'actually existing socialism' lost the economic competition with capitalism.

The word one keeps coming back to in all this is waste: waste of energy and raw materials; waste of state funds on poorly produced equipment and goods; waste of financial and human resources on socially unnecessary labor; and waste of people's time – to say nothing of the abuses to their dignity.

The ultimate irony, however, is that the command economy was itself a principal cause of the very ailment it was supposed to overcome – the waste generated by capitalism's anarchy of production. For under conditions of state monopoly and without either a market or reliable political checks, 'actually existing socialism' functioned on the basis of subjective judgments and the self-interest of the bureaucratic apparatus. And as a result the Soviet system, notorious for its shortages, was also plagued by overproduction, dubious investment policies, environmental irresponsibility, shockingly low rates of labor productivity and huge budget deficits.

Those who tried to alert the Soviet public to the reality behind the officially orchestrated celebrations of socialist 'success' were castigated as petty-bourgeois malcontents or enemy agents. One can only wonder how history might have been different if Soviet citizens had been allowed to hear Roy Medvedev's suppressed 1971 warning:

> Between 1948 and 1964, the effectiveness of productive investments in all branches of industry except electro-energy and metalworking fell two to three times, which had never happened since the establishment of Soviet rule. Although at the end of the Seven-Year Plan the list of goods in short supply was very large and continuing to grow, factories flooded the market with huge quantities of unsalable goods. The retail network had in stock a year's supply of all types of unsold fabrics, knitwear, clothing, and sewing machines, and six months' worth of toys. Many enterprises had warehouses packed with items rejected by the retail system .... In 1964, the value of unsold consumer goods (excluding food) piled up in retail warehouses alone was approaching 20 billion rubles, more than in the U.S. during recession years.[76]

Instead, the inexorably ripening crisis was papered over with a new proclamation: Soviet society had advanced to a higher stage called 'developed socialism'!

Developed Socialism

Sometime in the early 1970s, Soviet theoreticians began using the phrase 'developed socialism' to characterize their system. Brezhnev's official declaration of the new juncture described it as

> a stage in the maturing of the new society ... reached when the repatterning of the totality of social relations on the collectivist principles intrinsically inherent in socialism is completed. Full scope for the functioning of the laws of socialism, for the manifestation of its advantages in all spheres of social life, the organic integrity and dynamism of the social system, its political stability and indestructible intrinsic unity – such are the major distinguishing features of the developed socialist society.[77]

The new stage did not, however, imply an alteration in the fundamental Stalinist model:

The economy of developed socialism shares the same principles as the economy built in the Soviet Union when the foundations of socialism were being laid. Both the economy of the 1930s–1950s and our current economy are based on the same form of public ownership, on the same economic laws, the laws of socialism, and on the use of the same, key principles of economic management.[78]

Predictably, the discovery of a new stage in the socialist project was hailed as 'a major achievement of Marxist-Leninist thought in our time' [79] and 'a new page in Marxism-Leninism'.[80] But in view of subsequent events, there is little point in dissecting the hyperbole used to justify it. Suffice it to say that, as in the past, the new theory's claims of verification based on presumed Soviet achievements in planned management, intensive-style production and the development and uses of science and technology bore little relation to reality. More to the point is to understand why Soviet leaders thought it necessary to promote this self-indulgence.

In one respect, the theory of developed socialism attempted to correct an even more improbable formulation bequeathed from the Khrushchev era: that 'The building of a communist society has become an immediate practical task for the Soviet people.' [81] This assessment was so much at variance with the readily perceived Soviet reality that its main effect was to reinforce a popular cynicism which was already a rising problem for party and state authority.

But the CPSU was not prepared to renounce Khrushchev's thoroughly idealistic thesis completely. It needed a theoretical construct that would reinforce the Soviet Union's special status as the 'leading force' and ultimate source of authority in the world communist pantheon. The concept of developed socialism fulfilled this function while enabling the Soviets to beat a graceful retreat from an untenable proposition.

This became particularly important after 1968, when reverberations from the invasion of Czechoslovakia were feeding into centrifugal tendencies both in the 'socialist camp' and in the broader international communist movement. The theory of developed socialism helped sanction Moscow's avowal of a right to intervene in the 'defense of socialism' as a whole by declaring that 'developed socialist society ... is the most complete, integrated and purest expression of the essence of socialism.' [82] Further, since 'existing socialism now has ... a theoretically substantiated and practically tested strategy for resolving its problems as it builds communism',[83] departures from that strategy represented a threat to the socialist project as a whole.

Still more pointedly, the theory held that a central feature of developed socialism was 'the growth of the leading role of the Marxist-Leninist party.' [84] Thus, any attempt to weaken the party or compromise its 'leading role' by legitimizing other political forces or suggesting alternatives to its absolute hegemony could be seen as a betrayal of socialism itself. (Even more than various experiments in economic reform, this was always a bottom-line test for determining whether any country was following the true 'socialist path'.)

Finally, the theory of developed socialism also fortified the CPSU in its struggle to isolate the virus of Eurocommunism which threatened Soviet hegemony over the non-governing Communist Parties.

To Karl Marx, ever the materialist, socialism's superiority over capitalism would not be demonstrated primarily by its promise of a more equitable distribution of the social surplus. For socialism would not succeed, he believed, if it merely redistributed the same amount of wealth that capitalism was capable of producing. To fulfill its promise, the new system would have to prove itself *economically* superior to capitalism. It had to be more efficient in its use of resources, more cost-effective in its production processes, more capable of revolutionizing society's productive forces. (Today, a Marxist would have to include in these criteria environmental and ecological considerations, a point not so readily apparent in the nineteenth century.) Socialism could and would do this, Marx believed, because it would replace capitalism's 'anarchy of production' with a system of planned production that would be inherently more rational.

Today it is apparent that 'actually existing socialism' never demonstrated – either in fact or potential – its economic superiority to capitalism. This reality was disguised for a long time because, *when compared to pre-revolutionary Russia,* the Soviet Union registered significant economic gains. But ultimately that comparison loses its significance.

For one thing, as the record of other developing capitalist countries at the time shows, a bourgeois-democratic revolution undoubtedly would have achieved many of the same economic results. More importantly, at some point the new system would confront capitalism in its most developed form – not simply in ideological terms but in a real life struggle. And the outcome of that struggle would inevitably be determined by which system was economically superior. This is the test that 'actually existing socialism' failed.

It failed because the administrative-command system gave rise to an economy which was less efficient, less flexible, more resistant to innovation, less self-reproducing and more unstable than capitalism. This system fostered its own socialist 'anarchy of production' which was, in many respects, even less rational than capitalism's. Because the system lacked objective checks on the subjective economic judgments of a vast bureaucratic apparatus – and because the power-wielders within that apparatus were themselves distant from the production process and not directly accountable to the consequences of their decisions – all the supposed advantages of centralized planning and administration turned into their opposite. Instead, it became a system of bureaucratic suffocation which proved unable – and unwilling – fully or consistently to bring considerations of quality, efficiency, value, productivity and the economic use of resources to the economic process.

The system's fundamental flaw, in Marxist terms, was that its relations of production – reflecting a voluntarist communist utopianism – were in contradiction with the level of development of its forces of production. Gorbachev's attempt to reorchestrate the Soviet concept of socialism came too late. The entrenched state-party administrative apparatus, stubbornly defending its authority and privilege, refused to permit a peaceful transition to new economic-political arrangements that would more accurately reflect real possibilities.

But the attempts to move in the direction of a mixed economy in other socialist countries make it clear that the impulse which gave birth to perestroika in the Soviet Union reflects a basic problem with the administrative-command model of socialism. The most obvious example is China, where the disastrous Great Proletarian Cultural Revolution made it easier to experiment with new forms of property and new relations of production.

The real tragedy, however, was political. And here the CPSU clearly bears the main responsibility. Not only did it generate and reify the administrative-command system; it failed to muster the political will for drastic reform even as it should have been painfully obvious to Soviet leaders that the system was failing. Instead, fueled by a hubris which reflected nothing so much as its own deep-seated political insecurity, the party constantly claimed that under its leadership the Soviet Union had achieved an ever-expanding, ever-improving crisis-free society in which the one challenge was to continue 'perfecting' an already eminently successful system. To maintain this extravagant fiction, the party imposed rigid ideological controls which obscured the more problematic aspects of 'actually existing socialism' and prevented its supporters from making realistic appraisals of its accomplishments, shortcomings and potential.

In essence, 'actually existing socialism' needed to be rescued from its own ideological dogmas. But the party, which owed its authority to that same dogma, was not up to the task. And since the party had also suppressed any possibility for alternative political forces to develop and mature, the center could not hold and there was nothing to take its place.

6 Dictatorship of the Proletariat

Only he is a Marxist who extends the recognition of the class struggle to the recognition of the dictatorship of the proletariat ... This is the touchstone on which the real understanding of Marxism should be tested.

Lenin [1]

In keeping with Lenin's injunction, the theory of the dictatorship of the proletariat has become the central tenet of Marxism-Leninism. But in its evolution from the writings of Marx to the political system which became the ruling mechanism of 'actually existing socialism', the theory underwent a major metamorphosis.

Marx and Lenin on the Dictatorship of the Proletariat

To Marx, who credited the Paris Commune of 1870–71 with originating the phrase, the dictatorship of the proletariat was fundamentally an objective phenomenon. Viewing the political essence of capitalism as the dictatorship of the bourgeoisie, he believed that the proletarian dictatorship was bound to be the 'corresponding period in the political sphere' to the transformation from a capitalist to a socialist economic system.[2]

This sweeping abstraction became much more concrete after the experience of the Commune. In the actions and institutions established by that short-lived working-class upheaval – including the elections and recall of all public officials, the executive power directly accountable to popularly elected representatives, government service paid for at no more than typical workers' wages – Marx detected 'the political form at last discovered under which to work out the economical emancipation of labor'.[3] He saw particular significance in the Commune's forcible replacement of the old state apparatus with its own authority, along with a host of democratic procedures assuring popular control over that authority. As Engels was to say 20 years later, 'Look at the Paris Commune. That was the Dictatorship of the Proletariat.' [4]

Unfortunately, Marxists all too often have taken Engels' comment as a statement of doctrine rather than the expression of enthusiasm it more properly would seem to be. For by reifying Marx's view of the Paris

Commune as a kind of roadmap for constructing the proletarian dictatorship, communism has tended to emphasize unduly the subjective side of the proposition. This approach has obscured Marx's main point – that the dictatorship of the proletariat is fundamentally an objective political expression of a socialist economy.

> The working class has ... no ready-made utopias .... They know that in order to work out their own emancipation, and along with it that higher form to which present society is irresistibly tending by its own economical agencies, they will have to pass through long struggles, through a series of historic processes, transforming circumstances and men. They have no ideals to realize, but to set free the elements of the new society with which old collapsing bourgeois society itself is pregnant.[5]

With the collapse of the Paris Commune, the concept of proletarian dictatorship became little more than a doctrinal footnote in the socialist movement. It was Lenin who, for better and/or worse, brought Marx's theoretical discovery back to life. (References to the 'dictatorship of the proletariat' in the subject index to Lenin's *Collected Works* take up four-and-a-half pages consisting of more than 1,000 entries, many of which are several pages in length. The fullest statements are in *State and Revolution* and *Proletarian Revolution and the Renegade Kautsky*.) For nestled in the innermost recesses of Marx's pungent phrase Lenin found what he believed to be the central theoretical principle of the revolution: the necessity for exercising power unrestrained by law *after* the revolutionary victory.

To Lenin, the revolution's need for dictatorial power was self-evident:

> It would be extremely stupid and absurdly utopian to assume that the transition from capitalism to socialism is possible without coercion and dictatorship .... Firstly, capitalism cannot be defeated and eradicated without the ruthless suppression of the resistance of the exploiters, who cannot at once be deprived of their wealth, of their advantages of organization and knowledge, and consequently for a fairly long period will inevitably try to overthrow the hated rule of the poor .... Secondly, every great revolution, and a socialist revolution in particular ... is inconceivable without civil war which ... implies a state of extreme indefiniteness, lack of equilibrium and chaos ... The misfortune of previous revolutions was that the revolutionary enthusiasm of the people ... did not last long .... It was this historical experience of all revolutions, this world-historic – economic and political – lesson that Marx summed up when he gave his short, sharp, concise and expressive formula: dictatorship of the proletariat.[6]

In Lenin's framework, both sides of the formula were crucial – dictatorship as well as proletariat. The latter gave the concept its social base and democratic underpinning. But given what he considered tendencies toward an ill-advised concern for formal democracy in the socialist movement, he particularly stressed the former:

> The scientific concept of dictatorship denotes nothing less than power which is unlimited, unconstrained by laws or by any *kinds of rules* and directly dependent on violence. That is what 'dictatorship' entails, no more and no less – and don't you forget it! [7]

Responding to the criticisms of the German socialist Karl Kautsky a decade later, when the question of power emerged as an urgent practical question, Lenin reiterated the thought: 'The revolutionary dictatorship of the proletariat is rule won and maintained by the use of violence by the proletariat against the bourgeoisie, rule that is unrestricted by any laws.' [8]

In *State and Revolution*, Lenin made a great point of citing Marx's references to the dictatorship of the proletariat and his tribute to the Paris Commune for offering the first practical example of it. But he was not about to wait for revolutionary Russia spontaneously to produce the next example. Sooner or later, in every revolution, the key strategic question becomes the identity of that political force which functions as the practical realization of power. And it was on this point that Lenin broke fateful new ground, asserting that the 'dictatorship of the proletariat is possible only through the Communist Party'.[9]

Marx and Engels, of course, never even contemplated such a role for the communists, particularly since those who called themselves such had not yet established themselves as a significant political force and were still at a most primitive level of organization. What they would have advocated in Lenin's place we will never know, although one should not assume that they would necessarily have rejected Lenin's approach.

To Lenin, however, the necessity for the party to be the exclusive instrument of the dictatorship of the proletariat was obvious. Certainly it was an eminently practical and sensible response to the intense struggle which broke out immediately after the Bolshevik seizure of power. No revolution – least of all one as sweeping and ambitious in vision as the Bolshevik-led uprising – can avoid or eschew the use of force or the exercise of arbitrary power.

But in the Marxist paradigm, the dictatorship of the proletariat is not simply a system of rule for the relatively brief period during which a revolutionary seizure of power is consolidated. It is the form of political *power throughout the entire historical epoch of the transition from capitalism to communism!* [10]

However understandable Lenin's emphasis on the exigencies of power in the immediate post-revolutionary period may have been, his failure to situate 'rule unrestricted by law' and dictatorial authority vested in a singularly centralized party precisely in and exclusive to that period was a costly one. His 'oversight' – if we can call it that – did not go unnoticed at the time. Thus, while defending the Bolsheviks for their employment of terror in the immediate post-revolutionary period, Rosa Luxemburg declared with what now seems like uncanny prescience:

> It would be demanding something superhuman from Lenin and his comrades if we should expect of them that under such circumstances they would conjure forth the finest democracy, the most exemplary dictatorship of the proletariat and a flourishing socialist economy ... The danger begins only when they make a virtue of necessity and want to freeze into a complete theoretical system all the tactics forced on them by these fatal circumstances, and want to recommend them to the international proletariat as a model of socialist tactics.[11]

Fixated on ensuring the party's ability to suppress the forces of counter-revolution, however, Lenin adopted an uncharacteristically idealist view of how the masses would exercise ultimate political control over the system:

> The escape from popular accounting and control will inevitably become so incredibly difficult, such a rare exception, and will probably be accompanied by such swift and severe punishment (for the armed workers are practical men and not sentimental intellectuals, and they will scarcely allow anyone to trifle with them), that the *necessity* of observing the simple, fundamental rules of the community will very soon become a *habit.*[12]

Needless to say, this utopian vision was never realized. On the contrary: Lenin's failure to set limits to the arbitrary rule of the immediate post-revolutionary period bequeathed his successors a blank check to construct a system in which power was not subject to popular control. The consequences of that fatal error are well-known. Unlike capitalism which has devised a measure of separation of powers in order to regulate the struggles internal to the ruling class, a handful of men in the Communist Party hierarchy – and for almost three decades, one individual – exercised virtually absolute authority over every aspect of society in the name of the dictatorship of the proletariat.

The Marxist-Leninist Conception of the Dictatorship of the Proletariat

Lenin's emphasis on the subjective character of proletarian dictatorship, its extra-legal nature and the exclusive role of the Communist

Party in implementing it provided Stalin with the theoretical rationalization for the political system which managed 'actually existing socialism' throughout its life. Of course, that system was not principally the product of theory; nor did it simply reflect Stalin's insatiable appetite for power – although both played an important role in forging it. The crucial factor was that this political system was the natural and inexorable accompaniment to the administrative-command economy whose inner logic mandated an absolute and centralized concentration of power.

That system was not possible during the period of the NEP. For as long as substantial sectors of the Soviet economy functioned with some significant measure of independence from government control, the authority of the party-state apparatus was inherently less than absolute.

All that changed drastically after Stalin's 'revolution from above' which vastly expanded the realm of activity explicitly subject to dictatorial directive. Central planning eliminated all non-state enterprise in manufacture, trade and finance; and collectivization eliminated virtually all forms of private and cooperative enterprise in the countryside. As a result, all economic activity was brought under state supervision. To the party leadership, these measures also had the not inconsequential virtue of liquidating all other potential power bases that might develop in opposition to Bolshevik rule.

Consequently, it is not possible to evaluate the theory of proletarian dictatorship simply by going back to Marx or Lenin's writings. These are all relevant, but the most definitive text is the actual practice of proletarian dictatorship, first and principally in the Soviet Union, as well as by the other Marxist-Leninist parties who governed under its umbrella. Not all of them had a Stalin at the helm. But they all functioned under the same economic arrangements and subscribed to the same ideological framework.

For a considerable period, the practical advantages promised by this system were fairly obvious. Freed from the trappings of cumbersome parliamentarism and narrow-interest politics, decision-making can be expedited and quickly translated into practice. Special constituencies which thrive on legislative maneuver and the separation of powers characteristic of bourgeois rule can no longer hold the government hostage to their demands. Support for adopted policies – or, at least, lack of open opposition to them – is assured.

However, neither the theoretical assumptions nor presumed practical advantages of this system stand up to closer scrutiny. In particular, let us examine three key assumptions at the heart of the Marxist-Leninist theory of the dictatorship of the proletariat: the new and enhanced role of the subjective factor in the construction and functioning of socialism; the leading role of the party; and the distinction drawn between bourgeois and proletarian democracy.

The Subjective Factor

For all his proclamations that, having taken power, the Bolsheviks were going to 'build socialism', Lenin never lost sight of the fact that economic processes operate out of a social logic which cannot be altered on command. (He acknowledged that the Bolsheviks' departure from that fundamental Marxist thesis during the brief period of war communism was a costly error.)

The seizure of political power, he understood, was a relatively simple matter compared to the task of bringing into being a new mode of production. The former is the act of a particular historical moment and can be accomplished subjectively by a conjuncture of fortuitous circumstance with a concentration of forces and organization. But, as Marx stressed in laying claim to a science of society, substantive alterations in society's economic arrangements cannot be brought into being simply by subjective processes:

> In the social production of their life, men enter into definite relations that are *indispensable and independent of their will*, relations of production which correspond to a definite stage of development of their material productive forces. The sum total of these relations of production constitutes the economic structure of society, the real foundation on which rises a legal and political superstructure and to which correspond definite forms of social consciousness .... It is not the consciousness of men that determines their being, but, on the contrary, their social being that determines their consciousness. [Emphasis added.] [13]

Marxism-Leninism and the Soviet model of socialism on which it is based consigned this fundamental theorem of historical materialism to the 'pre-socialist' era. For according to a Marxist-Leninist theoretical text of the Brezhnev period:

> The laws of socialism do not operate automatically. The road to the triumph of communism can only be cleared by immense organizational work .... Under socialism, a key subjective factor of society's revolutionary reconstruction is the work of the governing Marxist party, which has all the conditions to enable it to play an active role and lead society along the road to communism in accordance with Marxism-Leninism's scientific postulates and conclusions on the laws governing the development of socialist society. The Communist Party's role grows in parallel with the advance toward communism.[14]

There thus appeared for the first time in history a mode of production dependent on human consciousness and 'immense organizational work' in order to function. Ergo, socialism, according to Marxism-Leninism, was a system in which its ruling authorities enjoyed an omniscience heretofore denied all previous historical actors: they had overcome, *at the societal level*, the perennial discrepancy between the intentions and results of human activity. Needless to say, of course, they hadn't. But the usefulness of such a doctrine to a vanguard 'conscious element' claiming permanent authority over all social activity seems too obvious to labor. For if 'the laws of socialism do not operate automatically', then an active agent of history – the Marxist-Leninist party – is *permanently* required to insure that they operate at all.

The notion that the 'laws of socialism' do not act automatically is an implicit acknowledgment that the administrative-command system of socialism was not objectively based. Accordingly, one of the chief functions of the dictatorship of the proletariat is to make sure that these 'laws of socialism' – so proclaimed by party congresses and dutifully echoed in Marxist-Leninist theoretical texts – remain operable even when they come up against contrary objective economic processes which, as Marx noted, operate independent of human will. This function – for example, subsidizing inefficient and uneconomic enterprises which otherwise would be unworkable – cannot be carried out for long without the arbitrary authority which only a dictatorship can provide.

Role of the Party

The concrete functional expression of the enhanced role of the subjective factor under the dictatorship of the proletariat can be summed up by transforming the old Bolshevik slogan 'All power to the soviets!' into a new axiom – 'All power to the party!' While usually dismissed as a canard by Marxist-Leninists, both Lenin and Stalin were quite straightforward on the subject. 'By the dictatorship of the proletariat we mean, in essence', declared Lenin, 'the dictatorship of its organized and conscious minority' – an unmistakable reference to the Communist Party.[15] Stalin spelt it out even more concretely in the Soviet context:

In the land of the dictatorship of the proletariat ... not a single important political or organizational question is decided by our Soviet and other mass organizations without guiding directions from the Party. In this sense it could be said that the dictatorship of the proletariat is in essence the 'dictatorship' of its vanguard, the 'dictatorship' of its Party.[16]

Since then, several generations of communists have said as much, continuing to assert that, 'The guiding and directing force of the dictatorship of the proletariat is the revolutionary party.' [17]

The marriage of Marxism-Leninism's concepts of the permanent 'leading role of the party' and its version of the 'dictatorship of the proletariat' assumes that certain individuals – when joined with others and subsumed into a vanguard party – are uniquely gifted by virtue of their grasp of Marxism-Leninism to chart society's course; indeed, that they are privy to the only scientific course of social development. Their social position thus permanently established by their consciousness – and armed with the equivalent of papal infallibility on virtually all matters – they have not only the right but the obligation to enforce that agenda by all the means at their disposal.

The effrontery of this utopian attempt at social engineering extended far beyond changes in the relations of production. Where Marx saw the mode of production as the foundation for changes in ideology, ethics and human behavior, Marxist-Leninists believed that they already knew what 'socialist' values, morality and aesthetics were. They then completed their break with historical materialism by consciously setting out to construct both the 'new socialist man' (sic) and his culture.

Such presumptuousness would have been ridiculous – but not so tragic – had the communists not abandoned, along with other forms of 'bourgeois democracy', the concept of separation of church and state. (Here I use 'church' not simply in a narrow, overtly religious sense, but as any reified ideology-based institution.) But when the dictatorship of the proletariat accorded Marxism-Leninism's assumed omniscience unrestricted state power, it shut off all the other processes – both spontaneous and those representing different outlooks – by which ideology and culture are shaped. Inevitably, this unnatural impediment to social development resulted in a system bereft of any 'natural' checks on its rulers' policies and actions.

According to Marxism-Leninism, this concentration of power is one of the greatest virtues of socialism:

> Massive and comprehensive control has become an inalienable component part of Soviet political democracy .... Permeating every sphere of inner-party life, the party's governing and guiding role extends to every aspect of state, economic and social activity ... [where] it promotes the normal functioning of the state and economic mechanism, injecting into economic and socio-political activity the necessary impulses of purposefulness, consistency and workmanship.[18]

The point of this system of sustained and total control over every aspect of society – control unrestricted by and unaccountable to law, other centers of power or institutionalized democratic processes – was that socialism needed (putting it in its most favorable light) a benevolent dictatorship as the only guarantee for its defense and progressive development.

And perhaps it did in the first years of the revolution. But it hardly requires a sophisticated sense of dialectics to recognize that the very mechanisms used to secure and defend power in one set of circumstances can turn into destructive fetters on social development in another. Even so, the party's power in the decade immediately following the revolution was far from absolute. The very existence of forms of property and economic activity not subject to dictatorial mandate during the period of the NEP was an objective limitation on the party's jurisdiction. Nor was the party then the monolithic institution it subsequently became. Lenin was its undisputed leading figure, but challenges to his authority and his opinions were commonplace. Even after Lenin's death, the very nature of the internal power struggle made it impossible to shut down political debate.

But with the advent of the period of 'socialist construction', the party's power became all-encompassing. For now it was the party apparat – operating through the economic planning mechanism and other state bodies – which made all the critical decisions relating to investment, expenditure and the disbursement of the social surplus at the national, republic, regional and local levels. The party thus became the locus of all political activity. Whether motivated by proletarian principle or personal ambition – and who is to say where one ends and the other begins? – all political actors could aspire to their goals only through its mechanisms.

The underlying assumption of this entire edifice is that the party is and always will be the sole repository and guardian of the true interests of the working class and therefore of society as a whole; and, in the unlikely event it goes astray, a self-correcting institution. As a trio of Soviet scholars would put it years later:

The party apparat's conviction that it is universally competent had ideological roots. It substantiates its special position and rights by appeals to the communist idea and the Marxist-Leninist doctrine. With this aim in view, the doctrine as such has been raised to the degree of state ideology, having been primarily subjected to at least two barbaric operations. First, Marxism-Leninism was seen as the final dogma. It was believed that Marxism alone was quite enough to resolve successfully all fundamental issues – whether in machine building, agrobiology, linguistics or any other sphere. Second, it was not enough simply to split the living doctrine into a number of dead formulae. There was also a need to stand guard over their purity and implant them in the mentality of citizens. It is the Party apparat that assumes the role of interpreter and guardian of the doctrine. It complements its function as supreme ruler with that of peculiar supreme priest. The Party apparat has produced a spiritual situation where its right to be society's leading force and its very existence have been elevated to the level of an historical mission.[19]

The consequences of making the party the sole and ultimate dispenser of power – presumably the great strength of its democratic centralist organization – were actually disastrous. For in the absence of any institutionalized checks on its authority, such a concentration of power inevitably leads to a system in which the party becomes a force separate from and standing above society.

One result of this accretion of power was that the character of the party changed. Not only did it increasingly attract the self-seeking, it generated an inexorable tendency toward self-serving activity even among those whose initial allegiances and motivations may have been principally ideological.

Ironically, these tendencies toward personal careerism seem to have been held somewhat in check during the Stalin years. For one thing, there were few material privileges to hand out during the industrializing stampede of the 1930s or the spartan years of war and postwar reconstruction. For another, overly conspicuous signs of privilege would have undermined the regime's ideological legitimacy at a time when the populist premises of the revolution were still a living force in the popular mind. And Stalin himself – better to be understood, it seems to me, as an ideological zealot than a pursuer of private gain – relied more on terror than the dispensation of privilege to retain the loyalties of the party hierarchy. (Even into the Gorbachev era there were many in the Soviet Union who thought of Stalin more as a harsh taskmaster intolerant of corruption than as a suborner of the revolution's ideals.)

But, over time, the unconditional power of the party bred a sociology of its own. As Stalin's successors tried to put the legacy of terror behind them, they increasingly turned to the indulgences of privilege, promotion and material benefits to hold the allegiance of the growing stratum of party and government bureaucrats who constituted the regime's actual social base.

The ritualization of this system took place through a mechanism called the 'nomenklatura', defined in the official manual on party development as 'a roster of the most important posts whose candidates shall be discussed, recommended and approved in advance by the Party committee in question (of the district, city, region, etc.)'.[20] The jobs filled in this manner were the real seats of power in the system. Those who filled them had decision-making authority and, in effect, constituted the party's inner core. Not least among the functions of this socialist elite was its self-perpetuation, along with an irresistible tendency constantly to expand its domain.

But while this system was explained and defended as a means of ensuring the selection of the most qualified individuals to positions of leadership, it actually functioned – especially during the Brezhnev years – as a widespread network of privilege and self-aggrandizement. Inevitably, this constantly expanding pattern of corruption generated a climate of cynicism in both the nomenklatura itself and society at large. Many instances of the degenerated moral climate became notorious.

One 1969 case, reported in a glasnost-era *Izvestia* article, tells of the wedding banquet given for her son by Uzbekistan leader Yadgar Sadykovna Nasriddinova at her own luxurious dacha outside Tashkent. According to the account:

> The nearly 800 guests included [Sharaf] Rashidov, the Republic party leader, the members of the Bureau of the Republic Party Central Committee, high-ranking party and state officials, and Ministers and economic executives. The wedding was catered by a staff of 150, while 200 chauffeurs shuttled guests between the dacha and their hotels. Entertainment was provided by the Republic's most famous singers, dancers and musicians. Characteristically, Nasriddinova, who was also a member of the CPSU Central Committee and a Vice-Chairman of the Presidium of the USSR Supreme Soviet, contrived to pay for the wedding with state funds .... When news of the extravaganza reached Brezhnev, his response was simply, 'You were stupid to hold a wedding like that.' [21]

Years later, after Nasriddinova had become chair of the USSR's Council of Nationalities, a long-stalled trial resulted in the conviction of 315 people closely associated with her on charges of bribe-taking and embezzling socialist property valued at more than 10 million rubles. Thirty-one of these were high-ranking government and judicial officials. Nevertheless, when the Party Control Commission recommended expelling Nasriddinova in 1976, pressure to rescind the resolution was exerted by both Brezhnev and Nikolai Podgorny, then chairman of the Presidium of the USSR Supreme Soviet. The recommendation was dropped and an official reprimand closed out the case. Twelve years later, *Izvestia* noted: 'Nasriddinova lives comfortably in a spacious Moscow apartment, has a state-owned dacha and automobile at her disposal and draws a large all-Union personal pension. Her Party reprimand was long ago expunged from her record.' [22]

An exception? In 1987, Gorbachev's bill of particulars demonstrating the need for a massive overhaul of the Soviet system, called attention to:

> Senior officials, vested with trust and authority and called upon to stand guard over the interests of the state and citizens, who abused their authority, suppressed criticism, sought gain, and some of whom even became accomplices in, if not organizers of, criminal activities.[23]

Since the appointed and elected officials who make up this entire nomenklatura network owe their positions – and the privileges that go with them – to the party, they inevitably become a loyal retinue of the system's ultimate wielders of power. Nor are there alternative routes to either privilege or influence. The dissatisfied cannot go public with contrary views or with criticism of their superiors, while attempting to form contending political organizations outside this framework is clearly an exercise in futility. Persisting in such behavior is a virtual guarantee of becoming unemployable except at the most menial level and at one time was readily seen as prima facie evidence of psychological disturbance.

As a result, anything remotely resembling serious political debate or efforts at significant reform can take place only within the confines of the party. But the possibilities for free and open discussion within the party – let alone the exercise of any degree of democratic control over its leadership – are not much better.

For one thing, as the system's only sanctioned political institution, the party's 'right' to select its own members becomes a means of excluding all others from public political activity. (Non-party people who manage to participate in such activity can do so only with the acquiescence of the party.) And it hardly takes a leap of the imagination to recognize that vocal disagreement with the party's line or criticism of party leaders are not recommended activities for those seeking invitations to join.

For another, democratic checks within the party are as elusive as they are in the broader society. Democratic centralism accorded power in descending order to higher party bodies who had the sole authority to appoint, promote, reward, discipline and expel. It also left control of inner-party discussions very much in the hands of its leadership, who established parameters beyond which one could venture only at great risk. As a result, it is the party hierarchy – overlapping and enmeshed with the state structure – which actually rules. In this structure, final authority is vested in the party Political Bureau (Politburo), where all policy is either formulated or is subject to its approval.

(Former Soviet Minister of Justice V.F. Yakovlev recalls that, 'All draft laws used to pass through the CPSU Central Committee's apparatus and be confirmed by the Politburo. After that confirmation, no one could change so much as a line in the draft law, which to all intents and purposes was already a law, which was then simply made official by the Supreme Soviet.') [24]

The 'democratic' side of democratic centralism – procedures for elections of leadership and free discussion and debate within the party – was a meaningless formality. Nominally, the highest authority was the Party Congress which elected its Central Committee and adopted the party's program. Composed of delegates elected through a series of intermediate bodies – local, district, regional and republic congresses – it really functioned as a rubber stamp for the Politburo which exercised tight control over the delegate-selection process. In addition to providing a detailed account of how this system worked,

Medvedev cites a samizdat article from the early 1970s which, he says 'accurately' describes the dynamics of party life at the primary level:

> Ordinary party members are in practice excluded from the process of making political decisions. Almost no information is available to primary organizations about the working of party bodies above them, right up to the Central Committee. Political questions are rarely raised at party meetings, and if they are, then only after the issue in question has already been settled by a higher authority. But as we know, it is a basic principle of democratic centralism that once decided, a question can no longer be discussed – only implemented. It is hardly surprising, therefore, that all discussion at party meetings on questions already decided is an empty formality which generally takes place in an atmosphere of total apathy.[25]

Further up in the party structure, particularly among the nomen-klatura, debate could occasionally be more free-wheeling – but virtually never in public view. Even then, only the foolhardy or the naive – and few of the latter could make their way into that privileged echelon – would openly advance unduly controversial views unless they had the backing of a powerfully positioned personage, preferably at the Polit-buro level. After all, good standing in the party, to say nothing of party membership, was not something to be jeopardized lightly when losing such status could well mean political and professional oblivion.

Appropriately, Brezhnev must be given credit for juridically enshrin-ing the party's absolute authority over society. This occurred in 1977 with the adoption of a new Soviet constitution which declared that 'The Soviet state is organized and functions on the principle of democratic centralism.' Now the same principles which enabled the party leadership to exercise unchallenged control over the country's only political institu-tion were made legally applicable to society in general.

Bourgeois versus Proletarian Democracy

The Marxist-Leninist theory of the dictatorship of the proletariat rests, in great measure, on the distinction it draws between bourgeois and proletarian democracy. Both are seen as class dictatorships. But the former is deemed fundamentally undemocratic because it is the dictatorship of the few over the many, while the latter is just the opposite.

As Lenin put it, 'Bourgeois-democracy, although a great historical advance in comparison with medievalism, always remains and, under capitalism, is bound to remain restricted, truncated, false and hypocriti-cal, a paradise for the rich and a snare and deception for the exploited, the poor.' [26] By contrast, its proletarian counterpart is truly democratic because it 'strikes at the exploiting minority in the interests of the exploited majority'. [27]

Arguing that formal elections and nominal individual liberties actually strengthened the bourgeoisie's dictatorship by promoting the illusion of majority rule, Lenin saw 'a democratic republic [as] the best political shell for capitalism'. [28] On the other hand, no matter how much it uses force to suppress its opponents, proletarian dictatorship is democratic because it uses such methods in the interests of the majority.

To be sure, many of Lenin's reductionist pronouncements (on one occasion he declared that 'Only supporters of capitalist slavery can favor bourgeois-democracy') [29] are polemics directed against those – personified by Kautsky – who faulted the Bolsheviks for overriding parliamentary norms in the struggle to consolidate power. But these hortatory declarations had a broader purpose as well. Believing that virtually the entire capitalist world was rapidly approaching a revolutionary crisis, Lenin saw a more general significance in the Bolshevik experience. In particular, he felt that a decisive ideological break with bourgeois democracy and an understanding of the necessity of proletarian dictatorship were immediately relevant to the class struggle wherever revolution was a ripening question.

Those expectations were dashed. But Lenin's caustic view of bourgeois-democracy and his panegyrics to 'coercion and dictatorship' [30] had a profound and ultimately deleterious impact on Marxist-Leninist theory, the political system which emerged in the Soviet Union and world communism in general.

Contempt for bourgeois democracy was particularly awkward for communists striving to build a working-class political base in the capitalist countries. Not only did it help keep alive the illusion of imminent revolution, thereby fostering sectarian and ultra-left tendencies in the communist movement; it also enabled their rivals in the working class movement to charge – with considerable justification, – that communist support for democratic rights was at best strictly tactical, and at worst hypocritical.

However, by far the greater damage was in the socialist countries themselves. There Lenin's scathing dismissal of bourgeois-democratic norms along with the simplistic definition of proletarian democracy as rule in the interests of (but not necessarily by) the majority was used to justify the elimination of all popular checks on the party's dictatorship.

This is a far cry from Marx, who envisioned the dictatorship of the proletariat as 'a government of the people by the people.' [31] By contrast, Marxism-Leninism holds that 'Proletarian dictatorship is always that of the majority ... even when the majority of the population mistakenly identifies bourgeois interests as its own or, conversely, believes proletarian power to run counter to its own interests.' [32] With this outlook and under circumstances in which the party was deemed the permanent, unchallengeable and only expression of working class interest, professions of democracy – while enshrined in law – became even more of a charade than their bourgeois-democratic counterparts.

The one-party system with its typically single-candidate elections makes voting, at best, a ratifying event. Nor does the party take any chances on the outcome of these elections. All candidates are either chosen by the party (the usual case) or subject to its approval. For, as one Soviet Marxist-Leninist puts it: 'Study by the party of the working and political qualities of candidates is a specific guarantee against any kind of accidents which might take place were the candidates to be nominated spontaneously.' [33]

(In some Eastern European countries, other parties representing the peasants or some other social stratum were permitted. Their acknowledged function was to win support for the Communist Party's policies among their constituencies by serving as a kind of lobbying group for them. One or two leaders might, under certain circumstances, be given a government post. But none ever exercised real power – nor could they aspire to do so.)

Consequently, the few opponents of official nominees have virtually no access to the media and, with all printing establishments under state control, almost no legal possibility of publicizing their views. Nor can they organize themselves as a concerted force with an alternative slate of candidates or political program. Meanwhile, party officials closely supervise the balloting and have little difficulty ascertaining the source of opposition votes.

Even then, only a small percentage of officials are subject to direct public election, usually representatives to local councils (soviets). These councils, in turn, select local government executives and elect delegates to higher legislative bodies. But most government officials and virtually all directors and managers of economic enterprises are appointed. And, needless to say, the most powerful officials of all – those who run the party – are not subject to public election or even ratification by publicly elected legislatures.

It almost goes without saying that the nominal authority vested in all elective bodies – whether in the government, trade unions or mass organizations – is entirely specious. Except occasionally at the most basic, local level, all elective posts are controlled by the nomenklatura, which micro-manages the whole process with the greatest care:

It is a secret to no one that our Communist Party really accomplishes political leadership of campaigns for elections to the soviets, defines their tasks, takes trouble over the election to the organs of popular power of worthy representatives of the working class, the peasantry and the intelligentsia. [The party] sees this as its obligation, and the concrete expression and manifestation of its leading and directing role in the system of socialist democracy.[34]

If the Marxist-Leninist conception of 'proletarian democracy' is not distinguished by an open electoral process which might enable the working class and other social sectors to exercise a check on party authority, neither does it have much use for such elementary concepts of democracy as free expression, public access to uncensored information or individual liberties. To be sure, all of these democratic rights were enumerated in the 1977 Soviet constitution. (Most of them are even to be found in Stalin's 1936 constitution as well.) But in both formal clauses and in actual social practice they were surrounded with qualifications which effectively undermined them.

For instance, freedom of speech, press and assembly were a guaranteed right – but only so long as their exercise contributed to the development and strengthening of the Soviet system. Likewise assured was 'freedom of scientific, technical and artistic creation' so long as such activity was 'in accordance with the goals of communist construction'.[25]

Of course, the ubiquitous restrictions on speech, press, the arts and other forms of expression under the dictatorship of the proletariat are hardly a matter of dispute. Those curbs have been proclaimed, defended, even celebrated over and over again by Marxist-Leninist theory, ruling Communist Parties and most of the international communist movement. Their purpose, according to Soviet regulations on the press, is to prevent

the use of the press for purposes of undermining or eliminating the established socialist system in the USSR, to propagandize war, to preach racial or national exclusivity or hatred and violence on a national, religious or other basis, to damage the country's security interests or defense capability or public order, or to publish materials incompatible with the requirements of public morality and protecting the population's health.[36]

In order to put these constraints in the best light, Marxist-Leninists traditionally have underscored the bans on pro-war and racist propaganda. But such a generous reading obscures the fact that their main point was to throttle real or potential political opposition, a term which, ever since Stalin's day, has been interchangeable with counter-revolution. One Soviet journal was quite explicit on this point:

Freedom for 'opposition' is a very different matter. The question is: Should the revolution grant freedom for counter-revolutionaries?... Demagogic clamor about denial of 'freedom of expression' must not be allowed to confuse the main issue – to whom is it being denied and for saying what? It is a particular feature of socialist democracy and communist humanism that their adherents are able to say loudly and clearly, without hypocrisy or pharisaism, without taking refuge in rhetoric about 'universal democracy', that in the name of happiness for millions, the dictatorship of the proletariat has the right, conferred on it by world history, to abolish freedom for counterrevolution.[37]

High-sounding pronouncements aside, however, in the Soviet Union against whom was the dictatorship applied and what did it suppress? The answer is painfully obvious. From Stalin, who executed a majority of the elected CPSU Central Committee, to Brezhnev, who slammed the door on the first attempts to introduce a climate of openness in Soviet society, the proletarian dictatorship was used primarily against other communists and supporters of socialism. What it suppressed were proposals for reforms which did not have the prior approval of the party leadership, criticism of party or state officials, opposition to government policies (for instance, the war in Afghanistan or the invasion of Czechoslovakia), expressions of nationalism (particularly among non-Russians), information contradicting official government claims and so on. Of course, a certain amount of debate, criticism and controversy could be found in the public media. But these appeared strictly at the sufferance of the authorities. For the plain fact is that so long as the party controls all means of public communication and is also prosecutor, judge and jury of its own critics, all 'rights' disappear.

The ultimate rationale for claiming that this arrangement is democratic is the principle of 'majority rule'. As long-time Soviet political commentator and analyst Fyodor Burlatsky puts it in retrospect:

We understood democracy as decision-making based on the expressed rights of the majority. But we did not see it as the inviolable rights of the individual, rights upon which no one can infringe, not even the state. In our pursuit of the phantom of universal equality, we sacrificed freedom. The will of the majority suppressed the rights of the minority; the state suppressed the individual.[38]

Leaving aside for the moment the not unimportant question of whether the Soviet system was really based on the principle of majority rule, such a concept of democracy is totally unsatisfactory. For in the absence of alternative sources of information, competing political opinions and criticism not subject to the suppression of the authorities – and with the holders of dissenting views subject to economic penalties as well as legally enforced suppression – majority support for official policy is neither surprising nor sufficient as an indicator of democracy.

In his famous polemic, Lenin chastised Kautsky for taking a non-class approach to democracy: 'He has forgotten to put the question: democracy *for which class?*' [39] Unfortunately, Lenin too 'forgot' that the

temptation to view any political opposition or criticism as the willful –
or even unknowing – expression of anti-working-class sentiments will
usually prove irresistible to the wielders of power. In 'actually existing
socialism's' version of the dictatorship of the proletariat it was always
the ruling Communist Party – whose self-interest in the matter was
painfully evident – that determined the boundaries beyond which dissent
became impermissible expressions of the 'class enemy'. Needless to say,
those boundaries did not venture far beyond official policy and ideology.

The fact is it has always been a relatively simple matter for
communist authorities to manipulate the legal system for their own
political and even personal purposes. Even Stalin sought a legal fig-leaf
for the terror of the 1930s. His successors brought the bloodbath to an
end, but the ready availability of mechanisms of unchecked social
control which the dictatorship of the proletariat provided was an
overwhelming lure. Soviet leaders were hardly the first or only governing
authority to seek ways to silence critics, curb political opponents, banish
dissidents and – particularly important in assuring the privileges of the
nomenklatura – protect their own. But with no political force representing individual rights or civil society, it was a relatively simple matter to
enact laws and structure the legal system to facilitate these ends.
Consequently, apologists for this system could claim that their suppression of political opponents was nothing more than enforcing the law and
fighting crime. As one of them has said:

> We do have in the Soviet Union individual persons who express
> views that contradict communist ideology; we also have some frank
> anti-Sovieteers, opponents of socialism. Some of them do find
> themselves in court: not for their views, however, but for actions that
> are counter to the law .... Subject to legal penalties are actions aimed
> at undermining or weakening the socio-political system of our
> country or attempts to spread deliberate falsehoods that discredit the
> Soviet state and social system .... The Soviet state has had to
> elaborate a number of protective measures to defend itself against
> constant massive acts of ideological subversion .... Our law states
> that slander against society as a whole – social defamation – is as
> punishable as slander which defames an individual. [40]

Among the 'crimes' for which Soviet citizens were prosecuted under those
regulations were reading and owning books or periodicals considered to be
'anti-Soviet', staging unauthorized showings of paintings by Soviet artists,
or charging that political critics were being confined to psychiatric hospitals. After 1985 the Soviet press was awash with such accounts, most of
which were documented by records of actual court proceedings. In one
such account we find that in 1982 a certain A.P. Churganov was sentenced
to a six-year jail term for having read books by Soviet historian Roy
Medvedev.[41] In another, S.B. Khmelevsky of Kiev was hounded by the

KGB and finally sentenced to three years in prison for writing and submitting critical reviews of officially praised plays and novels. After defending his ideas to a group of police investigators, Khmelevsky was sent to a psychiatric clinic for examination on the grounds that 'he is defensive during questioning. He claims he compiled these documents for the purpose of modernizing Soviet society'. [42]

As with political and civil liberties, there is an unbridgeable canyon between formal professions of legal protections for the individual and the actual practice of the criminal justice system under the dictatorship of the proletariat. The starting point for such protections must be an independent judiciary, a notion which – because it has the potential to thwart party policies or state decisions – is an intolerable affront to the unbounded authority accorded the party-state apparatus. 'The general principle for everyone – police, prosecutor, judge', notes a former judge who served for seven years under this system, 'was that we were all colleagues in law enforcement'. [43]

Individual judicial inclinations aside, the Soviet court system was designed to facilitate that principle. It was only after Gorbachev started to democratize the legal system that such concepts as 'presumption of innocence' or the inadmissibility of illegally obtained evidence and unsupported (and renounced) confessions were incorporated into the legal structure. Prior to that time, the prevailing view was that articulated by Andrei Vishinsky, the steely prosecutor who conducted most of the notorious show trials of the late 1930s. To Vishinsky, the idea of 'presumption of innocence' was 'bourgeois', while confessions by the accused 'inevitably assume the nature and significance of basic evidence'.[44]

Thirty years after the show trials and 15 years after Stalin's death, 'presumption of innocence' was still a suspect term in Soviet law. Legal scholar William E. Butler cites the case of Soviet criminal procedure expert M.S. Strogovich, who included the following in a 1968 book: 'We suggest that there are sufficient grounds to incorporate the formula of presumption of innocence in prevailing criminal procedure legislation as a separate legal norm.' That sentence went undiscovered until after the book was published. Then, at the insistence of a CPSU Central Committee member, the book was recalled and the passage removed (an entirely new signature was inserted) before the work was made available once again.[45]

None of this is to suggest that the Soviet system of criminal justice – especially in the post-Stalin era – was simply a sham. The vast majority of criminal proceedings undoubtedly were based on actual crimes and probably resulted in appropriate verdicts. But alongside and meshed with this system was the other ever-present reality which irretrievably compromised the legal system's integrity: the widely documented practice of 'telephone justice' in which party functionaries informed judges of the verdicts that were required in particular cases; the vulnerability of judges who could be removed from their posts by party decision; the lack of legal protections for those accused; the assumptions of guilt; the restraints on (and shortage of) defense attorneys; and the absence of a monitoring press.

Not surprisingly, acquittals were rare in the Soviet court system. Of course, that could be attributed to the conscientiousness of the police and prosecutors who might only have gone to court with airtight cases. An *Izvestia* investigative reporter took a somewhat more jaded view: 'Acquittal? That is, public and open admission that a person had been wrongfully accused? It was considered a political mistake – an extraordinary incident, an undesirable sensation that undermined the authority of the "organs".' [46]

Critique of the Dictatorship of the Proletariat

One cannot separate Lenin's view of the dictatorship of the proletariat from his assumption that the transition to socialism will take place by extra-legal methods. Under such circumstances, the revolutionaries will have little choice but to use all the resources at their command to suppress the inevitable attempts by the political representatives of the overthrown class to undermine the new regime. Likewise, the new regime must be prepared to exercise firm control over its political rivals whose maneuvering in the unsettled conditions that prevail in an immediate post-revolutionary period can easily facilitate a return to power by those who have been ousted.

It also seems obvious that any such revolution which undertakes to dismantle the existing institutions of authority and replace them with new working-class forms cannot do so using the old mechanisms of power. These new structures are, virtually by definition, forms of the dictatorship of the proletariat.

In the context of not only pre-revolutionary Russia but the pre-World War I capitalist world in general, Lenin's insistence that the dictatorship of the proletariat is the 'touchstone' of Marxism was eminently sensible. Whether the experiences of the rest of the twentieth century confirm such absolutism is another matter.

Increasingly, the old notion of the transition from capitalism to socialism taking place via an abrupt shift from one mode of production to another seems less and less likely. One can imagine, therefore, forms of transition in which the modalities of political and economic power are negotiated. (Such a process is actually underway today in South Africa.) In contemplating this possibility, there is no need to promote the illusion that such a transition will unfold free of tension or without extra-legal forms of struggle. But the resolution of those tensions in a mix of property forms, for instance, would clearly indicate forms of power and power-sharing which could hardly be termed proletarian dictatorship.

In Lenin's time, such a prospect seemed most unlikely. (Marx had considered the possibility of a peaceful transition in England and the US. But, as Lenin pointed out, 'In those days monopoly capitalism did not exist [and] in England and America there was no militarist clique then – *as there is now* – serving as the chief apparatus of the bourgeois state machine.')[47] Today, however, there is no reason for socialists to rule out a process of change in which dictatorship of the kind described by Lenin would be inappropriate.

However, the need for dictatorial rule in an immediate post-revolutionary period is not really the essence of the Marxist-Leninist theory of proletarian dictatorship. As we have seen, much more pertinent to that doctrine is the nature of power in the period of 'socialist construction' and throughout the entire epoch of socialism. It was under those circumstances that the main features of the Marxist-Leninist concept of the dictatorship of the proletariat came into being.

Ironically, as the collapse of those systems of rule in the Soviet Union and Eastern Europe demonstrates, the success of ruling Communist Parties in securing absolute power for themselves and stifling all expressions of political opposition turned out to be a pyrrhic victory. The exercise of dictatorial authority may have been a helpful component of the industrializing fury of the 1930s – and was certainly a boon to the constant reproduction of party domination – but in the long run it helped destroy the socialist project. Why is this so?

Disenfranchising the Working Class

To begin with, the Marxist-Leninist conception of the dictatorship of the proletariat objectifies and disenfranchises that force – the working class – which in class terms should be the foundation of socialist society. The justification for the dictatorship of the proletariat is that it is rule in the interests of the working class. But the critical question is: who decides what those interests are at any given moment?

In the Marxist-Leninist framework, there can be only one answer – the party. Yet, despite its own claims, the party is not omniscient; more to the point, the very nature of its dictatorship sets in motion compulsions which insistently compromise its dedication to those in whose name it rules. For it cannot escape the fact – especially in a society which is relatively backward economically – that power's access to privilege creates a tension which ideology alone cannot repel. As a result, the party's monopoly on power – and the enormous scale of authority it wields in a system in which all economic as well as social and cultural activity is organized and financed by the state – inevitably gives rise to a fairly large social stratum which stands above society and is not subject to its controls.

As a result of this privileged position, the party hierarchy invariably develops 'interests' which are quite likely to diverge from those of the working class. And here we must go beyond the petty and even large-scale corruption which unfailingly accompanies such a vast concentration of power. The more fundamental divergence rests on the fact that the party leadership increasingly cultivates and rewards loyalty to itself, rather than creativity, competence and criticism which might in any way weaken its own authority.

This development, in turn, breeds an ideology in which the party becomes the only conceivable mechanism for guiding socialist society, thereby equating continued unrestricted communist rule with socialism. But leaving aside for the moment the blatantly self-serving character of this argument, it simply does not follow that dissent, disagreement and opposition to party policy – or even party rule – necessarily reflects antagonism to socialism or working-class interests. On the contrary: in a state which has generated an all-powerful ruling stratum standing over society and not accountable to it, the real interests of the working class are more likely to find expression in an oppositional rather than an official institution.

Further, Marxism-Leninism holds that the party's rule cannot be weakened in any way – even if a popular majority or a majority of the working class should wish to alter its policies, replace the party's leaders or entrust power to some other social force. At bottom, this is the reason for the elaborate electoral charade played out in every country under the dictatorship of the proletariat. It is likewise the ideological justification by which the communists of the Soviet Union arrogated to themselves the right to determine the affairs of other countries where communist rule seemed to be threatened. As a result, it becomes impossible – short of violent revolution – for the masses to exercise control over the party. But without a legally structured system for bringing new political forces to power by democratic, peaceful and socially recognized means, all policy differences become potential social explosions, thereby further justifying totalitarian forms and a 'party-knows-best' intellectual climate.

In addition, the party itself does not operate along democratic lines. The party leadership bears the same relationship to its members that the party does to the public. Especially for a democratic centralist party exercising a monopoly on state authority, the realities of power politics are such that the party leadership has little difficulty in controling every aspect of party life and ensuring that the only changes that will take place are those which it sanctions. As a result, the dictatorship of the proletariat which was first modulated into the dictatorship of the party becomes, in effect, the dictatorship of the Politburo, in which every debate over policy sooner or later turns into a power struggle generally settled behind closed doors. Consequently, the public is kept ignorant of the real political struggles in the country and becomes further disenfranchised.

Finally, Marxism-Leninism's view of proletarian democracy is based on a limited conception of human rights. Thus, while the defenders of 'actually existing socialism' always pointed to its assurances of employment and low-cost (or free) housing, healthcare and education, guarantees of individual political rights and liberties were always conspicuous by their absence. As a result, the system's natural proclivity toward toadyism – only to be expected when there is a monopoly on power in a rigidly hierarchical social arrangement – went unchecked by open debate, public criticism, investigative journalism and organized protest.

A Closed Society

Most socialists believe that socialist society should and would be more open and democratic than any capitalist society ever could be. For despite the nominal freedoms assured by bourgeois society, it is the power of wealth – operating both through the marketplace and through its influence over politicians and opinion-makers – which determines who can realize those rights. Therefore, by curbing and ultimately eliminating that power, socialism would seem to provide the great mass of people with a terrain uniquely favorable to democratic control and political liberty.

One of the most desultory and ultimately self-destructive features of the dictatorship of the proletariat, however, was that it never realized that possibility. Instead it engendered a closed society which suffocated views and criticism the party considered threatening to its position in society, punished opponents of party rule and policy, rigorously controlled the flow and content of information, subjected science and art to rigidly ideological predispositions, and discouraged intellectual initiative and the give-and-take of constructive discourse.

There is probably no ruling group anywhere in the world that does not strive to set society's political agenda and orchestrate its public dialogue by controlling the information on which such colloquy depends. But where bourgeois society does this through the power of wealth – thereby allowing for a significant degree of contention within the ruling class and a limited space for free expression outside those ranks – the proletarian dictatorship exercises this control by administrative means and leaves no room whatsoever for anything but official information or a dialogue confined to approved subject matter and opinions.

In a telling passage from his Report to the 26th CPSU Congress in 1981, Brezhnev made clear the party's view of the function of mass media while tacitly acknowledging its less than satisfactory results. With Soviet newspapers and journals enjoying a circulation of 380 million copies and with 75 million television sets operational, he declared, 'This means that tens of millions of families can get the necessary explanations of the Party's policy and new information.' [48]

Nevertheless, he admitted, the party's ideological work needed a major overhaul:

> Propaganda should not shun sensitive issues and should not be afraid to deal with what are termed difficult questions .... Ideological education must be conducted in a vivid and interesting manner, without stereotype phrases and a standard set of ready-made formulas. When the Soviet citizen is spoken to in a thoughtless, bureaucratic language, when general verbiage is invoked instead of concrete living reality and actual facts, he simply turns off his TV or radio, or sets aside his newspaper.[49]

The 26th Congress was not unusual in this respect. Calls to improve the effectiveness of the party's propaganda were obligatory at such gatherings, though little changed. (Brezhnev really was looking for better techniques – the socialist equivalent of those feel-good Coca-Cola commercials US television advertising has honed into such a fine art.) But the party's ideological hegemony – to say nothing of the bureaucratic elite's inbred talent for self-preservation – requires both a monopoly on information and a careful orchestration of its dissemination.

The irony is readily apparent. By promulgating only official views and making the party the sole repository of the answers to every question, the dictatorship of the proletariat inevitably cultivates a climate of proletarian passivity.

At the same time, the task of assuring society's ideological purity engenders a further expansion of the purely bureaucratic side of the state. For officially managed censorship and information control require a force of ideological watch-dogs whose function is not only to forbid the unacceptable but to monitor, censor and edit all public expression. Naturally, the bureaucracy's finely tuned instinct for self-preservation serves as the unfailing guide for this office, which almost inevitably adopts the credo of all such missions: better safe than sorry.

Even if one were to acknowledge the need for a measure of official supervision, Medvedev – speaking from a vast storehouse of unwelcome experience – points out how this system actually works:

> There is nothing that cannot be misrepresented and banned by the censors. Any reasonable criticism of obsolete dogma can be viewed as 'revisionism' or even 'ideological sabotage'; honest historical research scrupulously based on facts may be denounced as 'slanderous'; an outstanding original novel or story can be rejected as 'anti-Soviet' or 'ideologically harmful' and classical works of art described as 'pornography'; a strictly scientific work on physics, chemistry, biology or astronomy stands every chance of being labeled 'pseudo-science' or 'idealism'; fair criticism of a government institution or individual leader may be viewed as defamatory, and the most

sincere appeal for the reform and improvement of socialist society seen as a 'disguised' call for its destruction.[50]

What makes this entire arrangement so suffocating and, in the long run, self-defeating is that it effectively abolishes all independent public activity. Virtually nothing can (legally) take place in such a society without the permission and supervision of the party–state apparatus. Of course, all kinds of organizations exist: scientific and professional associations, trade unions, social clubs, sports leagues, societies of hobbyists, amateur art organizations, self-help and discussion groups, parent–teacher associations, fan clubs, civic beautification and improvement bodies, non-official schools, and a great range of common interest groups based on social categories (seniors, veterans, women, youth, homosexuals) and a variety of ideological and political views. But none are exempt from or function independently of party and/or government supervision and control. Consequently, society has no legal or semi-formal space in which independent interests can be cultivated or defended and unsupervised ideas can find a hospitable environment.

Impact on Science and Art

Under 'actually existing socialism', the consequences of such ideological supervision and information control were devastating for science, the arts and scholarship in general. Much of the Soviet Union's lag in the development and application of the scientific and technical revolution can be attributed to this. History demonstrates a fateful connection between periods in which the forces of production develop rapidly and a concomitant development in the means of receiving, digesting and distributing information. For science – perhaps more than any other field of endeavor – demands the free exchange of knowledge, speculation and opinions.

But censorship of ideas, research and test results by ideological criteria makes it all too easy for well-situated heads of scientific institutes to stifle innovation, creativity and criticism. After all, some Soviet scientists must have been aware of the inherent structural weaknesses in the nuclear reactors at Chernobyl, or many of the environmentally destructive schemes hatched in the central planning ministries.

Likewise one must ask to what extent Soviet fears of unsupervised exchanges of information and ideas between ordinary citizens held back the development of computer technology and a computer culture. The proliferation of personal computers in the US certainly has produced much that is frivolous. But it has raised a new generation able to function in the information age and was a central factor in the widening gap between rates of labor productivity in the US and the Soviet Union during the 1970s and 1980s.

Clearly a system of firm ideological control must also embrace the arts; the dictatorship of the proletariat was no exception. During the 1920s, the party's role was largely limited to suppressing art that was explicitly anti-Soviet and counter-revolutionary. A 1925 Central Committee resolution on literature called for 'the greatest tact, caution and tolerance' and the need 'to banish the tone of literary command and every kind of pretentious, semi-literate complacent communist arrogance ... [and] amateurish and incompetent administrative interference in literary matters'.[51]

This resolution was a direct response to the Proletkult (Proletarian Cultural and Educational Organizations) and other super-Bolshevik zealots who were intolerant of the post-revolutionary cultural explosion in Russia. That explosion was fueled in great measure by a large number of artists and intellectuals who – while influenced by the wave of 'modernism' in Europe – were among the revolution's most ardent supporters. Proletkult followers, who considered much of this work 'the most harmful poison for the working people',[52] believed that the revolution should permit only art created by and for the proletariat.

The scope of what the party considered permissible in those days was underscored by Anatoly Lunacharsky, commissioner of Enlightenment (which included education and the arts) from 1917 to 1929:

> We need a flourishing, diversified literature. Obviously the censor should not allow clearly counter-revolutionary stuff to pass. But apart from that, everything that shows talent should have free access to the book market. Only when we have such a broad literature will we have a genuine loudspeaker into which all strata and groups of our enormous country will speak; only then will we have sufficient material, both in the subjective statements of these writers as representatives of these groups and in objective observations of our reality seen from various points of view.[53]

This climate of relative openness in the arts was abruptly brought to an end following Stalin's 'Great Turn' at the beginning of the 1930s. Just as Stalin's conception of 'socialist construction' borrowed much from war communism, so the party's new approach to the arts borrowed much from the crudely utilitarian pleadings of the Proletkult. Combining its fears of unrestricted expression with the communist penchant for social engineering, the party advanced and made mandatory a new Marxist-Leninist principle to guide artistic production: socialist realism.

According to Marxist-Leninist theory, 'scientific socialism demanded from art a strictly realistic approach to life.' But traditional realism was not adequate to this task, 'being restricted to a truthful recreation of the situation as it is'.[54] Marxism-Leninism required something more: 'Reality in its revolutionary development'.[55] To achieve such a goal, the socialist artist needed to know the course of history – not only what exists, but what is coming into being and what will be. Socialist realism, therefore, required of both art and the artist 'the Marxist-Leninist outlook which is the philosophical basis of its creative method'.[56]

The adoption of socialist realism as the only true and permissible proletarian art form was a major step in consolidating the party's power. With it, Soviet art became completely subordinate to the party's diktat. No one personified the new spirit of zealotry and the witch-hunting which followed better than Andrei Zhdanov, Stalin's main ideological alter ego and presumed political heir who is reputed to be the originator of the term socialist realism itself. Launching a post-World War II ideological offensive that went further than ever before in setting parameters for Soviet art, Zhdanov declared:

> We demand that our comrades, both as leaders in literary affairs and as writers, be guided by the vital force of the Soviet order – its politics. Only thus can our youth be reared, not in a devil-may-care attitude and a spirit of ideological indifference, but in a strong and vigorous revolutionary spirit.[57]

Zhdanov's crusading crackdown presaged a grim decade for Soviet artists who never knew when some zealous censor or high-ranking official might find an 'ideological deviation' in a novel, a play, a painting or even a symphony. Thousands were driven into exile or sent to labor camps. Jewish artists in particular were the victims of persecution and a number of them were secretly executed. Countless others were prevented from working at their professions. Art was made subject not only to the mindset of the party officialdom, but also to the political and artistic judgments of the censorial temperament – a temperament shaped by its willing obeisance to party instructions and a powerful compulsion to play it safe.

One of the hallmarks of the Khrushchev era was a significant relaxation of controls over science, the arts and scholarship. Ilya Ehrenburg's 1954 novel, *The Thaw*, became the harbinger of what would follow the famous secret speech of 1956, while works like Vladimir Dudintsev's *Not by Bread Alone* breached the hitherto forbidding strictures of socialist realism. As formerly banned writers were 'rehabilitated' (although not always published), a new generation of Soviet artists began challenging the old taboos with work on such previously forbidden subjects as anti-semitism, pre- and extramarital sex, labor camps, the existence of poverty and official corruption. Works which only a few years earlier would have earned both author and publisher the severest punishment – such as Alexander Solzhenitsyn's *One Day in the Life of Ivan Denisovich* – finally saw the light of day.

Such openness, however, owed at least as much to Khrushchev's concern with extirpating the grip of Stalin's heirs by demonizing Stalin than to any real commitment to the full democratization of Soviet society. A few, like the poet Alexander Tvardovsky who transformed the journal *Novy Mir* into the liveliest and most free-wheeling journal of the Khrushchev period, tried to go beyond those parameters. At a special Writers' Congress convened in 1959, Tvardovsky provided an insight into the norms of socialist realism in practice as he addressed questions which challenged some of the party's most important ideological assumptions:

> We cannot go on living in the old way is what we must say to our literary past and even to our today .... When it comes to literature, the first and most important thing is quality – hardly a new idea, but what can you do if it is not yet fully clear to all of us .... How many times have we heard the expression 'more and better' at this Congress, with 'more' receiving greater emphasis, since it is something much easier to achieve than 'better?'... The highest form of collective responsibility in our work is a real awareness of one's responsibility for oneself, not for 'literature as a whole' .... We haven't really very many writers who cope with this sort of responsibility.... We have more who eagerly take upon themselves responsibility for 'literature as a whole' – for supervising it, instructing it and directing it.[58]

But the Party was not about to surrender its crucial ideological outposts. Despite several sensational publishing events during this period, a countervailing 'go slow' tendency was sparked by certain top party leaders. Vasily Grossman's novel, *Life and Fate,* an account of life in the Stalin era written right after the 20th Congress, was stopped in its tracks even as two magazines were considering it for publication. According to Medvedev, the Politburo's chief ideologist, Mikhail Suslov, 'told Grossman that the novel could not be printed for another two or three hundred years'.[59] Also suppressed during this time was *Journey Into the Whirlwind,* Eugenia Ginzburg's memoirs of her 17 years in prison camps, the censor noting:

> Despite the urgency of the topic and the literary merits of this work, it should not be published in its present form, because it would have a harmful influence on young people, promoting pessimism and demoralization among them, and because the press in the imperialist countries would add this to their arsenal and use it against us.[60]

At the time and until the late 1980s when glasnost threw open the flood gates, socialist realism remained the official theory of art and the state still decided what could and could not appear in Soviet media. Khrushchev may have concluded that the system would be better served by a degree of openness in the country's intellectual life, but it was a decision which sent paroxysms of distress through much of the party's top leadership.

As a result, the thaw was short-lived. After Khrushchev's ouster in a

1964 Politburo coup, Brezhnev moved quickly to turn back the clock on the party's brief and relatively modest flirtation with broad-mindedness. The exposés of Stalin-era crimes came to a precipitous halt even as a number of party leaders called for Stalin's 'political rehabilitation' – an enterprise which was dropped as wiser political heads prevailed. Instead, the new period came to be known as 'Stalinism without Stalin'. A renewed ideological offensive against bourgeois trends in art was launched, most anti-Stalinists were removed from their publishing jobs, the trek of dissidents to jail and/or exile was resumed, and the more overtly propagandistic version of socialist realism was revived.

The 1966 trial of Jewish writers Andrei Sinyavsky and Yuli Daniel was a turning point. The anti-semitic and Russian chauvinist overtones of the vitriolic campaign against them were unmistakable. Charged with the crime of arranging for the publication of their work abroad, the two writers were sentenced to seven and five years respectively in corrective-labor camps. Over the next few years, scores of others suffered a similar fate. Solzhenitsyn was expelled from the Writers' Union. Underground circulation of *Let History Judge* led to Roy Medvedev's expulsion from the Communist Party. His brother Zhores, whose *Rise and Fall of T.D. Lysenko* was a landmark exposé of Stalinism's impact on Soviet science, was dismissed from his research job, arrested and sent to a mental hospital. Tvardovsky was removed as editor of *Novy Mir* and that journal was once again submerged in the mediocrity of the managed press.

The recidivist party leadership's hard-line cynicism toward the arts was on full display at the CPSU's 23rd Congress in 1966, where one top official declared:

> In our country every person who considers himself an artist has the right to work freely, to write as he sees fit, without the slightest limitation. But by the same token, our party and state institutions also enjoy full freedom in their choice of what to print.[61]

It was a fitting overture to the intellectual, scientific and artistic stagnation of the Brezhnev era.

Historical Failure of the Dictatorship of the Proletariat

The lessons of this historical experience seem painfully obvious. The dictatorship of the proletariat failed even by its own criteria. In the name of proletarian power, it disenfranchised the working class. Its transformation of proletarian dictatorship into party dictatorship fostered a concentration of power which alienated the communists from society and alienated society from the communists. While the communists claimed that their system of 'proletarian democracy' offered greater freedom and was more efficient than the bourgeois democracy of capitalism, the opposite proved to be the case.

The relative openness of the latter – and the absence of a government monopoly on information and communication – facilitates political debate and economic competition within the ruling class, thereby enabling the system to self-correct and/or improve. While such a public dialogue opens space for the working class and social forces outside the Establishment – and even for those opposed to capitalism itself – this, too, is turned to good advantage, for it forces the bourgeoisie to make timely concessions and incorporate useful reforms which it might otherwise reject. (Social security, unemployment insurance, minimum-wage laws, and the like, not only forestall more radical politics; as Keynes understood, they help the capitalist system overcome what Marx saw as one of its most fundamental contradictions: the immiseration of the working class and the consequent shrinking of consumer purchasing power.) Bourgeois democracy also enables the system to recruit the most promising and talented from the ranks of other classes to help manage its economy, its politics, its ideological institutions and civil society in general.

The dictatorship of the proletariat, however, walls off those in power from any meaningful political and social checks. It thereby rewards the time-servers and the incompetent, recruits on the basis of loyalty rather than ability, penalizes the innovative and suppresses reform-promoting dialogue and criticism. (While similar tendencies exist under capitalism, economic competition and bourgeois politics often work to circumscribe and impede them.)

Further, by imposing preordained ideological values on society – and using that ideology to rationalize their unbounded power – the Communists encouraged dogmatism and toadyism, thereby stifling unauthorized impulses toward innovation, reform, criticism and democratization.

Most damaging of all, the dictatorship of the proletariat with all its much-vaunted principles – the one-party state, the suppression of political liberties, the arbitrary establishment of a single ideology for society, the ubiquitous control of all social activity, the elimination of the institutions of 'natural' or civil society, and the refusal to countenance political change within the framework of socialism – surrendered the capacity to adjust and change course other than by the conscious self-correcting activity of those in power.

The most important lesson of all, perhaps, is this: far from being outmoded appurtenances of bourgeois democracy, elementary civil liberties – freedom of speech, press, assembly and thought, open and competitive elections based on unhindered rights of political association, constitutional checks on authority, and the rights of both individuals and political minorities – are not merely desirable, they are indispensable in a socialist society.

7 World Revolution

Part I 'Workers of the World, Unite!'

The communist revolution will be no merely national one .... It is a worldwide revolution and will therefore be worldwide in scope. Engels [1]

The idea that socialism will replace capitalism by way of a world revolution is a central assumption of the Marxist paradigm. Now, with the collapse of the most ambitious attempt ever to bring about a world socialist transformation, it is clearly time to reexamine the idea that this will be brought about by an overt, centrally directed world revolution. Not only has this vision – whether as an event occurring in a relatively limited time-frame, a rapidly spreading contagion, a consciously directed assault on the bastions of capital or a more long-term 'world revolutionary process' anchored and guided by the 'socialist camp' – failed to materialize; in my view, the proposition itself has been fatally flawed from the outset.

The Marxist Legacy of World Revolution

Probably more than with any other facet of their doctrine, Marx and Engels' vision of a pending working-class revolution that would overthrow the capitalist order bequeathed their ideological heirs that sense of being central to history which would sustain them in those times when their goal seemed most distant. Every advance of the workers' cause was seen as another building block in the edifice of revolution. Every sacrifice was the price one paid for being allowed to be part of the greatest historical project ever undertaken. By the same token, every setback was not only temporary but a learning experience, a loss that could be turned to profitable uses in the revolutionary cause.

No revolution has ever succeeded without such a devoted core committed to imparting that same vision to millions of others who alone could translate it into reality. But that same spirit would also contribute to the zealotry and sense of historical impatience which, time and again, has propelled the socialist movement down politically dubious and inherently sectarian paths.

It was, perhaps, inevitable that Marx and Engels, having uncovered the working class as socialism's agency for revolution, should conclude that it was already being called on by objective processes to take the historical stage. As early as 1848 they argued that capitalism was rapidly approaching – if it had not already arrived at – the end of its developmental possibilities. Indeed, much of their theoretical work is imbued with this sense of impending apocalypse. Thus, they asserted, just as feudalism was 'burst asunder!' when its 'relations of property became no longer compatible with the already developed productive forces', so too 'a similar movement is going on before our own eyes.' [2]

Germany in particular, they believed, was 'on the eve of a bourgeois revolution that ... will be but the prelude to an *immediately following* proletarian revolution'. (Emphasis added.) [3] Ten years later, Marx was still arguing that 'on the Continent, the revolution is imminent and will immediately assume a socialist character'. [4]

But the coming socialist revolution, they asserted, would be no mere national revolution. For capitalism itself had made the proletariat an international class whose mission was to liberate all of humanity and bring into being what a later American IWW song would call a 'commonwealth of toil'.

The concept of world revolution is so deeply embedded in socialist culture, it is hard to imagine what that ideology would be like without it. From *The Communist Manifesto*'s heady call on 'Working men of all countries to unite' to the stirring strains of 'The Internationale' urging the wretched of the earth to bring a better world to birth, an international frame of reference has been central to the Marxist legacy.

To Marx and Engels, the international character of the struggle for socialism was rooted in the very nature of capitalism:

> Large-scale industry, already by creating the world market, has so linked up all the peoples of the earth, and especially the civilized peoples, that each people is dependent on what happens to another .... The proletarians in all countries have one and the same interest, one and the same enemy, and one and the same struggle. The great mass of proletarians are, by their very nature, free from national prejudices and their whole disposition and movement is essentially humanitarian, anti-nationalist[5]

Accordingly, it was not only appropriate but necessary for the communists themselves to be organized as an international force. In 1864, Marx established The International Working Men's Association (the First International) which lasted until 1876. The Second International, founded in 1889, was based mainly in the Western European labor movement and still survives today as a loose association of world socialist parties. But unlike their successors, these Internationals did not see themselves as the engineers of world revolution. As Marx put it: 'The international activity of the working classes does not in any way depend on the existence of the International Working Men's Association.' 6

The idea of an international association of parties acting in unison to bring about the world revolution, guiding it and ultimately taking power in the name of the world proletariat actually began with Lenin, who launched the Third International in 1920 largely as a split from the Second. It was dissolved in 1943 as a gesture of unity in World War II. Trotskyists set up a Fourth International in 1938, and there are a number of rival claimants to that mantle today. Stalin created the Cominform (Communist Information Bureau) after World War II as a coordinating body for the countries of the new 'socialist camp' plus the major mass Communist Parties of Western Europe.

Subsequently Communist Parties constituted themselves as the International Communist Movement, a body which from the outset foundered on the contradictions resulting from the coming to power of Communist Parties in separate states through separate revolutions – in particular, contradictions between the Communist Parties of the Soviet Union and China. In time it became a gathering of parties dependent – to one degree or another – on the CPSU.

The most significant thing about all these efforts to internationalize the socialist revolution was that none of them even came close to succeeding. The revolution's time-frame has been adjusted. Elaborate explanations for the unexpected delay in its appearance have been offered. And, especially after Stalin's consolidation of power in the Soviet Union, it was projected in a framework that departed substantially from the idea of world revolution first raised by Marx and Engels and further developed by Lenin. But it has never been abandoned.

After the collapse of the Paris Commune of 1871, Marx's 'simultaneous' world revolution gave way to the idea of the revolution beginning in one country and subsequently spreading beyond its borders. Poland, Italy, Hungary, Spain and ultimately Russia were identified as countries where the 'final conflict' might begin. And while Marx and Engels never relinquished the notion of world revolution, their later writings clearly are not imbued with the same sense of immediacy that is to be found in the pages of the *Manifesto*.

Despite their own paeans to capitalism's enormous capacities, Marx and Engels clearly underestimated its staying power and resiliency. Perhaps the very grandeur of Marx's sweeping historical vision led him to sound a premature death knell for the system he both admired and detested. Doubtlessly the contrast between the wonders of capitalism's shattering revolutions in material production and the social misery engendered by them must have influenced Marx to believe that the existing socio-economic structure could not last long.

If so, he would hardly have been the first to become impatient with the relatively plodding pace of historical change. The gap between logical reasoning and the concrete unfolding of social processes has ever been larger than the philosophers can imagine. And even Marx, for all his attempts to base his forecasts on 'science', could not avoid the virtually irresistible tendency to telescope historical development in keeping with his own deductions. But history builds on itself and a constantly changing reality whose consequences cannot be known in advance. As a result, those who venture into a predictive mode, even the practitioners of 'scientific socialism', can, in this connection, be regarded only as speculators rather than prophets – a point which the reification of Marx's work into 'Marxism' (and, even more so, 'Marxism-Leninism') has tended to obscure.

In any event, Marx and Engels failed to see the extent to which capitalism would continue revolutionizing the productive forces, thereby escaping from its own crises and, in the process, enhancing its own economic efficiency. Likewise, they misjudged capitalism's capacity to adapt itself politically and make timely concessions to the demands of a rapidly growing working class.

Although it was becoming obvious that the proletarian revolution would be longer in arriving than they had first imagined, Marx and Engels – as with Lenin's generation of revolutionaries half a century later – never reconsidered their vision of a rapidly maturing world revolution which would usher in the dawn of the communist epoch. As a result, the concept of a unified worldwide revolutionary movement objectively based in capitalism's decline and the proliferation of the proletariat remained a central feature of the Marxist legacy.

Lenin: New Dimensions to the World Revolution

In the three decades following Marx's death in 1883, the socialist movement's earlier dream of a world proletarian revolution gave way to the far more parochial concerns of a growing European labor movement. In the most industrially developed countries of Europe – Germany, Britain, France, Belgium, for example – Social Democratic parties built mass followings in the trade unions, gained parliamentary representation and maintained a semblance of internationalism through congresses and conferences of the Second International. Few took seriously the notion of a concerted worldwide assault on the bastions of capital.

But there were dissenting voices in the Second International, chief among them Lenin who challenged the dominant opinions in the mass European Social Democratic Parties, arguing that world revolution was an even more timely and practical question than it had been in Marx's time. Lenin's critique of the Second International was, of course, powerfully influenced by conditions in Russia, where it had been clear since the turn of the century that a revolution was brewing. Appraising the lineup of class and political forces there, Lenin glimpsed the possibility that, led by the

Bolsheviks, the Russian working class – in alliance with the mass of Russian peasants – might be tempered into a force that could actually take power in the coming Russian Revolution. But could this alliance hold power? And could it begin the process of building socialism on a terrain rendered inhospitable by Russia's economic backwardness?

Lenin revolutionized Marxist theory by concluding that these questions could be answered in the affirmative *provided* the Russian Revolution would trigger a chain reaction in which the working class elsewhere – at least in Germany and one or two other developed capitalist countries in Europe – would also rise up against their respective bourgeoisies. 'We will make the Russian political revolution', he wrote in 1905, 'the prelude to the socialist revolution in Europe'.[7]

But Lenin also had to explain why the revolution had not yet appeared in the developed capitalist countries and why there were so few indications of revolutionary consciousness in the working classes of those countries. One reason, he said, was 'the domination of bourgeois ideology ... [because it] is far older in origin than socialist ideology, it is more fully developed, and it has at its disposal *immeasurably* more means of dissemination'.[8]

Such an explanation is, of course, quite obvious. But it has become over the years a somewhat complacent rationale which tends to obscure more fundamental wellsprings for the workers' low level of revolutionary consciousness. For isn't the grip of bourgeois ideology on society as a whole itself a reflection of the relative stability of bourgeois rule and capitalist property relations?

Lenin himself was never fully satisfied with this explanation. As he began to deal more extensively with the problems of the socialist movement, he sought other reasons for working-class passivity. At another point he attributed backward ideas in working class ranks to the influence of non-proletarian class forces:

> In every capitalist country, side by side with the proletariat, there are always broad strata of the petty bourgeoisie, small proprietors. Capitalism arose and is constantly arising out of small production. A number of new 'middle strata' are inevitably brought into existence again and again by capitalism. These new small producers are just as inevitably being cast again into the ranks of the proletariat. It is quite natural (therefore), that the petty-bourgeois world outlook should again and again crop up in the ranks of the broad workers' parties.[9]

Theory of Opportunism

However, the problem continued to weigh on Lenin's mind, especially as he contemplated the fact that revolutionary consciousness was rising in Russia, a predominantly peasant country, while it was stagnant and worse in those countries where the industrial proletariat was larger and had the longest history. Ultimately he arrived at an explanation which would become a central theme of his outlook: the Theory of Opportunism.

According to this theory, the chief obstacle to the proletariat's political maturation was the fact that the working class was not the homogeneous entity originally envisioned by Marx. Rather, it was split between its more privileged and better-organized sections and its then largely unorganized proletarian mass whose conditions of life and labor were sharply distinct from each other. Through leaders reflecting their outlook, the former – in effect, a 'labor aristocracy' – actively collaborated with the ruling capitalist class in its broad political and economic objectives in exchange for benefits and privileges not available to the mass of proletarians. This 'insignificant minority' of the working class was nevertheless enormously influential because it dominated the ranks of labor's only viable organizational form, the trade union movement.

Lenin's analysis built on earlier explanations of the failure of the world's workers to unite in concerted opposition to the rule of capital. Foreshadowing the apocalyptic rhetoric which would characterize subsequent Marxist-Leninist theory, those explanations also viewed the unexpected delay in proletarian insurrection as a temporary phenomenon constantly on the verge of coming to an end. Thus Engels, in 1892, held that when England finally lost its dominance of world industry – a process he believed was already well underway – 'either the country must go to pieces or capitalist production must'. [10] One consequence of the coming crisis, he believed, would be the renewed radicalization of the English proletariat:

> During the period of England's industrial monopoly, the English working class have, to a certain extent, shared in the benefits of the monopoly. These benefits were very unequally parcelled out amongst them; the privileged minority pocketed most, but even the great mass had, at least, a temporary share now and then. And that is the reason why, since the dying out of Owenism, there has been no socialism in England. With the breakdown of that monopoly, the English working class will lose that privileged position; it will find itself generally – the privileged and leading minority not excepted – on a level with its fellow-workers abroad. And that is the reason why there will be socialism again in England. [11]

In the unfolding struggle in the Second International, Lenin wholeheartedly adopted Engels' analysis, finding evidence of the approaching revolution on every hand. In 1908 he saw 'social revolution approaching in Britain'.[12] In 1911 he saw the German workers 'becoming welded ever more strongly into an *army of revolution*, and this army will deploy its forces in the not so far distant future'.[13] In 1912, he cited the report that the US socialist weekly, *Appeal to Reason*, was nearing a circulation of one million as evidence showing 'the kind of revolution that is approaching in America'.[14]

While Lenin's proclamations on the imminence of revolution in this period were laced with 'revolutionary optimism', World War I placed the issue in an entirely new context. Tens of millions of proletarians fighting and dying for their respective bourgeois governments suggested that the workers' ideological allegiance to the system ran far deeper than any had suspected. But the war also indicated, Lenin said, that capitalism had reached a point 'in which bourgeois states, with their national boundaries, have outlived themselves'.[15] Further, he believed that the war had brought about 'a revolutionary situation ... in most of the advanced countries and Great Powers of Europe'.[16] Yet while Lenin, Luxemburg and other 'left' socialists militantly opposed the war and saw in it new revolutionary possibilities, most leaders of those Social Democratic Parties which had developed a mass base in the trade unions and a parliamentary voice supported their governments' policies.

As a result, the festering ideological division within the Second International erupted in a bitter internecine battle which effectively split the world socialist movement. The war, said Lenin, had brought into being the very conditions which the socialists had for so long anticipated – a breakdown of the relatively stable capitalist world order and the foundations for mass proletarian upheaval. Therefore, he said, those working-class leaders who actively supported any capitalist government in this war – most particularly their own – 'have patently betrayed socialism', thereby demonstrating 'the monstrous and disgusting victory opportunism (in the form of social-chauvinism) has gained over the labor movement in Europe'.[17]

Earlier, commenting on the collapse of the Second International, Lenin had explained that:

Opportunism means sacrificing the fundamental interests of the masses to the temporary interests of an insignificant minority of the workers or, in other words, an alliance between a section of the workers and the bourgeoisie, directed against the mass of the proletariat .... By social-chauvinism we mean acceptance of the idea of the defense of the fatherland in the present imperialist war, justification of an alliance between socialists and the bourgeoisie and the governments of their 'own' countries in this war, a refusal to propagate and support proletarian-revolutionary action against one's 'own' bourgeoisie, etc. It is perfectly obvious that social-chauvinism's basic ideological and political content fully coincides with the foundations of opportunism. It is one and the same tendency.[18]

Now Lenin went beyond Engels' observations on the British working class and posited opportunism as an international phenomenon with a material basis:

The receipt of high monopoly profits by the capitalists in one of the numerous branches of industry, in one of the numerous countries, etc., makes it economically possible for them to bribe certain sections of the workers, and for a time a considerable minority of them, and win them to the side of the bourgeoisie of a given industry or given nation against all the others. The intensification of antagonisms between imperialist nations for the division of the world increases this urge. And so there is created that bond between imperialism and opportunism which revealed itself first and most clearly in Great Britain, owing to the fact that certain features of imperialist development were observable there much earlier than in other countries.[19]

Moreover, the influence of opportunism was not a recent phenomenon:

Opportunism was engendered in the course of decades by the special features in the period of the development of capitalism, when the comparatively peaceful and cultured life of a stratum of privileged workingmen 'bourgeoisified' them, gave them crumbs from the table of their national capitalists, and isolated them from the suffering, misery and revolutionary temper of the impoverished and ruined masses.[20]

But where Engels had principally cited England's 'industrial monopoly' as the source of the bribery, Lenin took account of colonialism as an additional and possibly now the main source of 'super-profits' which provided the means for buying off the labor aristocracy:

In the epoch of imperialism, owing to objective causes, the proletariat has been split into two international camps, one of which has been corrupted by the crumbs that fall from the table of the dominant-nation bourgeoisie – obtained, among other things, from the double or triple exploitation of small nations – while the other cannot liberate itself without liberating the small nations, without educating the masses in anti-chauvinist, i.e., anti-annexationist, i.e., 'self-determinationist' spirit.[21]

It was this objective split in the working class, Lenin argued, which had produced the split in the socialist movement. The struggle against opportunism, therefore, had become 'the fundamental question of modern socialism'.[22]

Many trenchant insights are embodied in Lenin's theory of opportunism. Clearly it is based on a far more realistic view of working-class dynamics than are those largely sentimental paeans to class unity which, both in Lenin's time and since, have tended to obscure the profound divisions in the working class. It is to Lenin's credit that he did not

flinch in the face of these realities, and indeed sought to find a
materialist explanation for them.

Nevertheless, there are a number of problematic concepts in the
theory which limit its usefulness. For example, central to Lenin's
argument was his view that the privileged workers were 'an insignificant
minority' and that capitalism would be unable to extend the privileges
granted the labor aristocracy to ever-larger sections of the class. Perhaps
that was true in Lenin's time, although I doubt that 'insignificant'
captures the scope of the phenomenon even then.

But whatever the size of that minority, it can hardly be denied that it
has since been enlarged considerably – especially in the decades after
World War II. It also seems rather obvious that in an international
context, the vast *majority* of the working class in the most developed
capitalist countries enjoys a privileged position relative to their Third
World counterparts. As a result, the anomaly first noticed in the last
years of the nineteenth century – that working-class revolutionary
consciousness is least developed in the very countries which are,
supposedly, the most ready for socialism – has become a more
prominent feature of the world political landscape since.

Likewise questionable is Lenin's mechanical emphasis on 'super-
profits' derived from colonial exploitation as the main source of the
means capitalism has used to 'bribe' the privileged sectors of the
working class in its home territory. Colonial investments certainly
yielded high returns – thanks largely to the aggrandizement of natural
resources and industrial crops – but they still comprised a relatively
small percentage of each country's total capital investment. Nor does
Lenin's thesis explain why Germany, with extremely limited colonial
holdings, also enjoyed the advantages of a privileged sector of the
working class comparable to those in France and Britain, the two
colonial giants. Today, under the conditions of a thoroughly internation-
alized capitalist economy, any significant distinction between profits –
both relative and absolute – derived from Third World investments and
investments at home or in the other developed capitalist countries seems
difficult to sustain.

Further, Lenin's belief that the success of the anti-colonial movement
would cut off the material foundations for those privileges which bred
opportunism has not been borne out. Quite the contrary. Just as the
elimination of slavery cleared the way for a phenomenal expansion of
capitalism in the US, so did the end of colonialism make possible a
further expansion of capitalism throughout the world.

In the final analysis, the fundamental flaw in Lenin's theory of
opportunism is that it is based on the assumption that capitalism had
reached the end of the line. This is why he underestimated the size of
the privileged sector of the working class and overestimated the
revolutionary readiness of the proletarian mass. It is also why he was
unable to recognize that capitalist accumulation was expanding in an

all-sided way and not principally from the 'super-profits' derived from colonialism.

But if this was indeed the case – that is, if capitalism was *not* in its 'moribund' stage and proletarian revolution was *not* really on the agenda of the developed capitalist countries – of what significance is the term 'opportunism' in the Leninist sense of the word? A socialist might wish that trade union leaders would hold to a revolutionary perspective; but those who pursue a policy of reform within the system can hardly be regarded as allies of the 'class enemy' at a time when socialism has not yet emerged as a practical question.

Lenin's view was that reformism – which he equated with opportunism – was the inevitable outlook of the labor aristocracy, whereas the proletarian mass, by contrast, was ready for a revolutionary ideology. In fact, as subsequent developments have clearly demonstrated, the proletarian mass in all the major capitalist countries has also directed – and continues to direct – its politics principally toward winning social and economic reforms and concessions within the framework of the prevailing capitalist property relations. Indeed, it is hardly coincidental that it is the mass-based Communist Parties (in Italy, France, Spain and Japan) which have become the most 'reformist'.

Significance of the Anti-colonial Movement for the World Socialist Revolution

Perhaps Lenin's most innovative contribution to the theory of world revolution was his extension of it to include the colonial and semi-colonial world. Needless to say, he was not the first to do so, as witness the writings of individuals such as Jose Marti and W.E.B. DuBois, among others. But he was the first of the European Marxists to break out of the old ideological mindset which, while sympathetic to the plight of colonized peoples, did not attribute any particular *socialist* relevance to the still embryonic movements for national independence in the colonies. Some even saw colonialism as a necessary evil which was, at least, bringing 'backward peoples' into capitalism, thereby hastening the day when genuine liberation would be on their historical agendas.

Even when the socialist movement upheld the right of nations to self-determination, its focus was primarily on the subject nations of Europe rather than the colonies. Thus a resolution adopted by the Second International at its 1896 Congress in London calling for 'the full right of all nations to self-determination' notes the 'yoke of military, national or other absolutism' but never mentions colonialism at all.[23] Some went so far as to argue that socialists should 'not reject all colonial policies in all circumstances, such as those which, under a socialist regime, could serve a civilizing purpose'.[24]

To a certain extent socialists tended to underestimate the significance of the anti-colonial movement because, in general, it was led by nascent bourgeois and petty bourgeois class forces. Rosa Luxemburg, for instance, ridiculed the principle of self-determination as 'a mere platitude', seeing in it a diversion from the class struggle and, in fact, a bourgeois attempt to divide the workers along national lines in order to prevent them from uniting along class lines. Although her concern, typically, was with movements striving for national separation in Europe, she failed to make a distinction between those and movements in the colonies and, indeed, totally ignored the latter. [25]

Lenin's scathing rejoinder to Luxemburg laid out the theoretical foundations for what would ultimately become the Comintern's statement of principles concerning the national and colonial questions:

> Rosa Luxemburg has lost sight of the most important thing – the difference between countries where bourgeois-democratic reforms have long been completed, and those where they have not .... In Eastern Europe and Asia the period of bourgeois-democratic revolutions did not begin until 1905 .... By supporting the right to secession, we are told, you are supporting the bourgeois nationalism of the oppressed nations .... Insofar as the bourgeoisie of the oppressed nation fights the oppressor, we are always, in every case and more strongly than anyone else, in favor .... But insofar as the bourgeoisie of the oppressed nation stands for its own bourgeois nationalism, we stand against.[26]

In an immediate sense, Lenin's polemic with Luxemburg stemmed from the situation in Russia at a time when every possibility seemed to exist to draw the subject peoples of the czar's vast empire into the developing revolution. But this could not be done, he believed, unless the revolution pledged itself to the right of self-determination for the peoples of that 'prison-house of nations'. Still, Lenin emphasized, he was not proposing secession for these nations – only the *right* to secession. The real point of self-determination, he argued, was 'to facilitate and accelerate the *democratic* association and merging of nations'.[27] In other words, the union of peoples and nations was desirable, but it had to be voluntary and on the basis of equality.

However, Lenin's thinking was not confined to the Russian circumstance. While upholding the right of self-determination as a general proposition regarding all oppressed nations – whether colonies, semicolonies or nations forcibly amalgamated into larger states (Poland, Serbia, Finland, and so on) – he underscored the particular significance of the liberation movements in the colonies as a critical component of a broader world revolutionary process which would link the oppressed people of the colonies with the revolutionary proletariat in the most powerful capitalist countries. This was not simply a theoretical analysis. In 1916 he would declare:

Socialists must not only demand the unconditional and immediate liberation of the colonies without compensation; they must also render determined support to the more revolutionary elements in the bourgeois-democratic movements for national liberation in these countries and assist their uprising – or revolutionary war, in the event of one – against the imperialist powers that oppress them.[28]

Still, Lenin did not advocate independence of nations per se. 'We have always advised and shall continue to advise all the oppressed classes in all the oppressed countries, the colonies included, *not* to separate from us, but to form the closest possible ties and merge with us.' [29]

Later, after the Bolsheviks had come to power, Lenin would make another remarkable theoretical leap:

The socialist revolution which is impending for the whole world ... will not be solely, or chiefly, a struggle of the revolutionary proletarians in each country against their bourgeoisie. No, it will be a struggle of all the imperialist-oppressed colonies and countries, of all dependent countries, against international imperialism.[30]

Here was a declaration which went far beyond previous general statements of support for the anti-colonial movement. It heralded the appearance of a new kind of socialism, one which situated the struggle against colonialism directly at the center of the struggle against capitalism. And however extravagant in terms of assessing the possibilities of a unified, coordinated and mutually supported world revolution against the main capitalist states – who were, naturally, the main colonial states as well – it nevertheless became a battle-cry which enabled the communists to play a significant and, in some cases, decisive role in the anti-colonial movement. Further, in a world where imperial armies were constantly engaged in war against 'rebellious natives', the communists were making a profound and probably costly political commitment to work for the military defeat of their own governments in its colonial wars.

(The strains on these parties over the ensuing decades were readily apparent. On numerous occasions, communist movements in the colonies registered complaints about the inactivity and complacency of their counterparts in the colonizer nations. Ho Chi Minh directly castigated the Communist Parties of Britain, France, Belgium and Holland at the Fifth Comintern Congress in 1924, declaring, 'What our Parties have done in this domain [the anti-colonial struggle] amounts to almost nothing.' [31] The spirit of proletarian Internationalism might flourish at international communist congresses, but the West European workers the Communist Parties needed as a political base were not nearly as enlightened as communist rhetoric of the day suggested.)

By itself, however, Lenin's extension of the world revolution to the peoples subjugated by imperialism did not resolve the much more complex question of what the real content of 'emancipation' would mean. Neither the 'bourgeois' anti-colonial movements nor the anti-Leninist socialists posed the question of emancipation for the colonies in socialist terms. The former, by virtue of their own class outlook, sought an indigenous capitalism free of foreign domination, while the latter remained committed to the traditional view that the material conditions for socialism did not exist in the colonies.

Here Lenin made another break with Marxist orthodoxy:

> Are we to consider as correct the assertion that the capitalist stage of economic development is inevitable for backward nations now on the road to emancipation? ... With the aid of the proletariat of the advanced countries, backward countries can go over to the Soviet system and, through certain stages of development, to communism, without having to pass through the capitalist stage.[32]

Although Lenin was careful to tie this new proposition to the anticipated success of the socialist revolution in the capitalist heartlands (his phrase, 'with the aid of the proletariat of the advanced countries', implies the working class holding power), this idea of a non-capitalist path to socialism became incarnated in subsequent Marxist-Leninist doctrine and continued to be propagated long after the immediate post-revolutionary enthusiasm of the international communist movement had given way to harsher realities. We will return to this question in the next chapter where we examine 1960s and 1970s Marxist-Leninist doctrine on the world revolutionary process and the path of 'socialist orientation' for developing Third World countries.

Lenin's revolutionary new view of the struggle against colonialism represented a remarkable ideological shift for the socialist movement. Certainly it was decisive in enabling new indigenous Communist Parties affiliated with the Third International to win leadership of their countries' liberation struggles – as in China and Vietnam. Ho Chi Minh became a communist, he recalled, after reading the Comintern's *Theses on the National and Colonial Question* and becoming convinced that only the communists were fully committed to the anti-colonial struggle.[33]

Still, a distinction must be made between those insights which uncover new political realities and the broad conclusions which are drawn from them. Lenin's appreciation of the historic importance of the anti-colonial movement was a major theoretical breakthrough in the attempt to develop Marxism further under the conditions of twentieth century capitalism. The same cannot be said, however, about the strategic conclusions he drew from this analysis. In retrospect, one can see that the success of the national liberation movements consisted principally in bringing the colonial system to an end, certainly no small accomplishment. But Lenin's vision of an organic link between these movements and what he believed would be their revolutionary counterparts in the imperialist countries failed to materialize. Following Marxist-Leninist precepts, some liberation movements tried to set their countries on a 'socialist path'. But virtually all such efforts have come to grief and, in a number of cases, those revolutionaries who tried to pursue such a course have been forced out of power. Almost without exception, the liberated countries now find themselves obliged to seek entry into the world capitalist economy.

The Comintern: An International of a 'New Type'

Although Lenin had made constant reference to the developing revolution in the West, the Bolsheviks felt they had to do more than count on the revolution spreading spontaneously. Within months of taking power, they openly announced their intentions of using 'every means at [our] disposal' to push the revolution forward elsewhere:

> Confident that the working-class revolution is maturing persistently in all belligerent countries and is preparing the full and inevitable defeat of imperialism, the Congress declares that the socialist proletariat of Russia will support the fraternal revolutionary movement of the proletariat of all countries with all its strength and with every means at its disposal.[34]

Ultimately, all talk of a consciously directed world revolutionary process comes down to questions of practical politics and organization. Many of the Second International's pronouncements pledged the world socialist movement to high-sounding internationalist and revolutionary principles. But as a loose federation of totally autonomous parties, it lacked the capacity for concerted action. Still, this was not primarily an organizational flaw. Rather, there was no basis in ideology, politics or power relations for the large, mass-based socialist parties to subordinate themselves to an international body which, in their view, needed them more than they needed it. The trade unions which comprised their main social base had little interest in revolution, nor did there exist objective conditions external to their association which might propel them toward a common strategy or coordinated activity.

The Second International was unable to survive the outbreak of war in 1914 when the bulk of its constituent parties lined up in support of their respective warring governments. While some (derisively called 'centrists' by Lenin) tried to keep the door open to a possible postwar reconciliation of the socialist movement, Lenin immediately began calling for the establishment of a new Third International. 'Two world outlooks, two appraisals of the war and the tasks of the International, two tactics of the proletarian parties', he argued, demonstrated that hopes for regrouping the forces who made up the old movement were futile and, ultimately, counter-productive.[35]

Yes, he acknowledged, the Second International had done 'useful preparatory work' in the previous 'peaceful period' when capitalism had enjoyed rapid progress and was generally quite stable. But the war, he said, had brought that period to an end. The hour of the world revolution had arrived. Barely two months after the war began, Lenin was calling for a new organization:

> To the Third International falls the task of organizing the proletarian forces for a revolutionary onslaught against the capitalist govern-ments, for civil war against the bourgeoisie of all countries for the capture of political power, for the triumph of socialism! [36]

At this point, three years before the Bolsheviks would take power, Lenin's perspective was based strictly on the paradigm first charted by Marx and Engels: the revolution would be sparked and led by the proletariat in the most developed capitalist countries. Only then would it be possible for the Russian working class to use Russia's coming bourgeois-democratic revolution as the springboard to power. However, the inability of those who first overthrew the czar to resolve the dilemmas of Russia's continuing role in the war and the frustrated demands of the land-hungry peasants rendered this latter qualification inoperable. And so, contrary to Lenin's expectations, the Russian working class could and did take power. (It has been argued, of course, that it was the Bolsheviks, not the workers, who seized state power. But there seems little doubt that by then the Bolsheviks had achieved political hegemony among the proletarians.) Despite this alteration in his broader scenario, Lenin still held that the ability of the Bolsheviks to hold and consolidate power remained dependent on proletarian revolu-tion in the West.

But he also concluded that while conditions might be ripe for revolution in the main capitalist countries, one essential condition was missing: 'Europe's greatest misfortune and danger is that it has no revolutionary party.' [37] Six months later, at Lenin's behest, the Bolshe-viks convened a gathering of like-minded parties and split-offs from the Second International to bring a new international into being.

The hasty establishment of the Comintern had a dual purpose. In an immediate sense, it was an act generated by the Bolshevik view that their own struggle remained dependent on – indeed, was doomed without – the speedy spread of the revolution to at least one and, it was hoped, several European countries. Yet the Comintern's founding cannot be reduced solely to the compulsions of revolutionary Russia. Granted that Lenin and the Bolsheviks could not help but be influenced by the concrete circumstances of their own revolution, there is no reason to doubt the internationalist standpoint which clearly was at the core of their outlook. The Bolsheviks' need for the revolutionary 'contagion' to spread was self-evident. But Lenin and virtually all the Bolshevik leaders had long been committed – by intellect, ideology and logic – to the cause of world revolution.

And so in March of 1919, what Lenin would call the 'world party of revolution' came into being. However, it was not a very representative grouping that came together in Moscow to found the new Communist International. The German Spartacists, for instance, after the Bolsheviks the largest and most influential of the revolutionary contingents, were not at all convinced that the timing was right. Their reservations were based on two significant considerations which would loom large in the ensuing years. First, they argued, the new 'Communist International should be definitively established only when, in the course of the revolutionary mass movement now gripping nearly all the countries of Europe, Communist parties have sprung up.' [38] Second was the concern, voiced on a number of occasions by the Spartacist leader Rosa Luxemburg, that if the new Communist Parties owed their standing principally to the Comintern rather than to their respective political constituencies, they would inevitably be molded too rigidly into the Bolshevik model.

In addition, some who welcomed the new International and subscribed to its principles also wanted to keep the door open to others – especially prominent socialist leaders of trade unions and other popular organizations as well as other 'honest', hardworking socialists not yet completely won over to Bolshevism.

Lenin, however, was adamant on establishing the Comintern at once. Soviet power was under siege, not only from invading bourgeois armies but also from the still-influential leaders of the old Second International who maintained a constant ideological barrage against the Bolsheviks. And, he believed, the revolutionary moment was at hand, waiting only the development of new political forces capable of organizing and leading it. For these reasons, Lenin had little patience with those who would conciliate the upholders of the discredited policies of the old Second International. If the Comintern were to become the headquarters for world revolution, he stressed, it could not tolerate the presence of reformists and vacillators. For 'as long as the reformists remained what they were they could not but sabotage the revolution .... Victory in the proletarian revolution cannot be achieved, and that revolution cannot be safeguarded, while there are reformists and Mensheviks in the ranks.' [39]

To no one's surprise, the newly established Comintern quickly embraced the entire pantheon of what was already being called Leninism – Lenin's theses on imperialism, the prospects for world proletarian revolution, the vanguard party of a new type, the dictatorship of the proletariat, the nature of and struggle against opportunism – in short, all the key propositions that had shaped Bolshevism ideologically.

To ensure that it would become the 'ideological and political headquarters of the revolutionary movement',[40] the Comintern adopted Lenin's vanguard party principles not only for its constituent organizations but for the International itself. Thus, where the Second International was a loose federation with minimal ideological coherence and no mechanism for common action, the Comintern's rules declared: 'The Communist International should represent a universal Communist Party, of which the parties in every country form individual sections.' [41]

Accordingly, democratic centralism became obligatory not only for each affiliate party but for the Comintern itself. This meant that all constituent parties were obliged to carry out all Comintern decisions and to refrain from publicly airing disagreements with adopted policies. Members of each party were similarly obligated. Needless to say, the Comintern's democratic centralism guaranteed Soviet hegemony within the International.

The differences between the two Internationals were striking. Where the Second International's strength had rested in the mass, union-based, parliamentary Social Democratic Parties of Germany and Western Europe, the Comintern's power base was Soviet Russia. For the first time world socialism embraced an apparently successful revolution and included a country where a working-class party actually held power. Immediately the new Soviet power became – in terms of resources and prestige – an ideological and organizational magnet for a wide array of political forces: some of Lenin's old allies in the Second International; many of the now rootless socialists; new revolutionary-minded workers and intellectuals appalled at the destructive magnitude of the war and attracted by the ideas and energy of the Russian Revolution; and radical-minded forces in the anti-colonial movement.

(Shortly thereafter, and undoubtedly in response to the Comintern's founding, a number of prominent figures of the Second International – with the tacit encouragement of the most powerful capitalist governments – scrambled to resurrect their organization. Ramsay MacDonald of the British Labour Party played a particularly important role in this effort, which led to a conference in Berne in 1919 that reconstituted a now miniaturized Second International. Another more left-leaning assemblage gathered in Vienna in 1921 and created what briefly came to be known as the Second-and-a-Half International. Despite some ideological differences, both saw their power base in the relatively better-off unionized sectors of the working class, while sharing a common hostility to the Bolshevik Revolution. In 1923 these two groupings merged.)

Perhaps a split in the international socialist movement was inevitable. The shameless support for the war that the leaders of mass socialist parties demonstrated, to which one must add their naked hostility to the Bolshevik seizure of power in Russia, indicated antagonisms in the world movement so fundamental that any attempt to reconcile them would probably have failed.

The split was, in a sense, an application of the principle of the dictatorship of the proletariat to the politics of the socialist movement. Just as proletarian dictatorship was based on the notion that the working class could not simply take over the already existing state apparatus but rather had to create a new state of its own, this too was the case with international socialism. The new revolutionary forces, Lenin believed, needed an organization of their own creation, shaped by its own purposes, based on its own forces. Did Lenin recognize that the new organization – in its program, structure and personnel – would inevitably reflect the power shift of international socialism from the mass parties of prewar western Europe to the Communist Party of the Soviet Union? It is hard to imagine otherwise.

All protestations to the contrary, the split and the principles on which it was based inexorably set the communist movement and its new International on a sectarian and ultra-left course. Not only were the assumptions about the timeliness of proletarian revolution misguided; ultimately, that same assumption influenced and distorted every political and ideological question which came before it. From the outset, therefore, the Comintern adopted a mode which almost routinely denounced all contrary views as a 'counter-revolutionary' surrender to the bourgeoisie. In addition, the very nature of the split and the conditions under which the Comintern came into being established the pattern of Soviet domination which Luxemburg had cautioned against. Given the enormous gap in real power between the CPSU and the other parties of the new International, the conception of the Comintern as a single international communist party organized on the basis of democratic centralism inevitably assured ubiquitous Soviet control.

Socialism in One Country: The World Revolution on Hold

In 1921, three years after declaring that 'victory on a *world scale* is very near and easy',[42] Lenin had to face up to some hard facts: the hoped-for European revolution was not an immediate prospect; and Russia itself could not proceed directly to building a socialist economic system.

As a result, he said, it was time for a 'retreat'. Domestically, Lenin's NEP launched a system of communist-supervised 'state capitalism' in which the base of power would be not only the Russian working class but the peasantry as well. The prerequisite for making the peasantry a reliable base for the revolution was the maintenance and defense of private property in the countryside and the enhancement of (capitalist) light industry. Internationally, world revolution was put on hold, a shift concentrated in a single word in a Comintern resolution: 'The 4th World Congress reminds the proletarians of all countries that the proletarian revolution can never triumph *completely* within a single country; rather, it must triumph internationally, as world revolution.' [43]

The introduction of the word *'completely'* into this traditional formulation bespoke a revolution in Marxist theory, paving the way for the communist movement to shift its emphasis from world revolution as an immediate and practical goal to support for the NEP and defense of the Soviet Union as the main strategic tasks of the period. Formally, the Comintern remained committed to world revolution. But now it became a historical question rather than a practical one – destined to happen sooner or later but not likely in the near future. The Comintern would concentrate on helping Communist Parties sink roots in the working class in their respective countries; and it would continue to advance a revolutionary ideology. But no longer would it be prepared, as it had pledged in 1918, to support the world revolution 'with every means at its disposal'.

Lenin died in 1924 still believing that the world revolution was 'proceeding', but acknowledging 'not along as straight a line as we had expected'.[44] Within months, Stalin, then having succeeded to the leadership of the CPSU, took this assessment one step further and announced a radical departure from earlier Bolshevik precepts:

> Formerly, the victory of the revolution in one country was considered impossible, on the assumption that it would require the combined actions of the proletarians of all or at least a majority of the advanced countries to achieve victory over the bourgeoisie. Now this point of view no longer fits in with the facts. Now we must proceed from the possibility of such a victory, for the uneven and spasmodic character of the development of the various capitalist countries under the conditions of imperialism, the development, within imperialism, of catastrophic conditions leading to inevitable wars, the growth of the revolutionary movement in all countries of the world – all this leads not only to the possibility, but also to the necessity of the victory of the proletariat in individual countries.[45]

A year later, a resolution at the 14th CPSU Conference, spelled this position out further:

> Leninism teaches that the *final* victory of socialism, *in the sense of full guarantee against the restoration* of bourgeois relationships, is only possible on an international scale .... But it *does not follow* from this that it is impossible to build a *complete socialist society* in a backward country like Russia without the 'state aid' of countries more developed technically and economically.[46]

(The italics in this text are not in the original resolution but were added some time later by Stalin in an effort to prove that the 'Great Turn' had been theoretically sanctioned by Lenin. Thus the distinction between the 'final victory' of socialism and the building of a 'complete' socialist society in Russia is not to be found in Lenin's works. Stalin similarly doctored other statements by Lenin in order to justify his course. For example, Roy Medvedev points out that according to the official Soviet edition of Lenin's *Collected Works* [Vol. 27, p. 95], he reportedly declared at the Seventh Congress of the Russian Communist Party in 1918, 'There would doubtlessly be no hope of the ultimate victory of our revolution if it were to remain alone.' However, notes Medvedev, the word 'ultimate' does not appear in that sentence in the stenographic record of the Congress but was added later. Where it came from and when is not hard to figure out. The phrase 'ultimate victory' was accorded great significance by Stalin in his debate with Trotsky on the possibility of building socialism in one country, Stalin arguing that his theory was consistent with the views on world revolution previously articulated by Lenin.)

The Stalin-Trotsky Debate

Although the great debate over 'socialism in one country' was framed, to a large extent, as a struggle to carry out the true Leninist legacy, the fact is that both Stalin and Trotsky departed from Lenin in significant ways. Having recognized early on that the Soviets probably would have to go it alone for some considerable period, Lenin searched for and came up with what he believed was a strategy for defending proletarian power in Russia while building the material foundation for a future socialist society. Trotsky, on the other hand, argued:

> The specific alignment of forces in the national and international field can enable the proletariat to seize power first in a backward country such as Russia. But the same alignment of forces proves beforehand that *without a more or less rapid victory of the proletariat in the advanced countries* the workers' government in Russia will not survive. Left to itself, the Soviet regime must either fall or degenerate .... All the statements on this question made by the Bolshevik leaders from 1917 until 1923 ... lead to one conclusion: without a revolution in the West, Bolshevism will be liquidated either by internal counter-revolution or by external intervention, or by a combination of both.[47]

Trotsky's thesis was that while the Bolsheviks might be able to hold on to state power in the absence of new socialist revolutions in the West, they could not build socialism under those circumstances. At best, they would rule over a 'deformed workers' state'. Settling for such a paltry prize, he believed, would be a 'betrayal' of both the Russian Revolution and the world revolution, which were, in any event, inseparable. The principal task of the Russian communists, as he saw it, was therefore to utilize Soviet power to foster the ripening revolutions in the West.

Trotsky, of course, could point to numerous statements by Lenin and the Bolsheviks to support his views. Even so, Lenin never elevated his opinions to a categorical absolute. Thus Stalin cited other statements by Lenin which seemingly reflected a contrary position:

> The victory of socialism is possible first in several or even in one separate capitalist country. The victorious proletariat of that country, having expropriated the capitalists and *organized socialist* production, would stand up against the rest of the world, the capitalist world, attracting to its cause the oppressed classes of other countries, raising revolts in those countries against the capitalists, and in the event of necessity coming out even with armed force against the exploiting classes and their states.[48]

Stalin made a great point of this passage in his argument with Trotsky. Quoting it in *Problems of Leninism* he italicized the phrase 'organized socialist production', arguing that in using it Lenin clearly meant that it was possible for a single country 'to complete the building of a socialist society.' But the obvious inference from the context in which the article was written indicates that in holding out the possibility of a socialist victory in one country, Lenin was thinking principally of one of the developed capitalist countries, with Germany, France or Britain the most likely.

In addition, while Stalin quite properly was concerned with achieving a break-through on the economic front, he thoroughly muddied the theoretical waters by calling his crash-program of rapid industrialization and forced collectivization of agriculture the 'construction of socialism'. In doing so, he returned to the primitive conceptions of war communism and set about establishing absolute and direct state control over every aspect of Soviet economic life. Granted that a massive effort to accelerate industrialization was needed, the attempt to build an all-sided socialist society in the course of half a dozen years was poorly conceived from the point of view of theory and actually wasted enormous natural and human resources, permanently weakened Soviet agriculture, brought about a horrific loss of life, and established a model of 'socialism' which ultimately was consumed by its own internal contradictions.

Thus the decision to build socialism in the Soviet Union represented a momentous ideological shift – not only in the communist view of world revolution, but in its conception of socialism. Now defense of the Soviet Union – rather than the promotion of proletarian revolution elsewhere – became the central task of the world communist movement. Trotsky's charge that the new policy inevitably meant a subordination of the world revolution to the diplomatic needs of Soviet foreign policy was, of course, quite accurate. (Whether or not this was a 'betrayal', as Trotsky charged, or an eminently sensible policy judgment is, of course, a separate question.)

But Lenin himself had already taken a significant step in that direction. Responding to the economic crisis devastating Russia in 1921, he acknowledged that war communism had been a tragic error and launched his New Economic Policy. It was, he conceded, a 'retreat' to 'state capitalism' whose virtue rested in the fact that 'we gain time, and gaining time means gaining everything, particularly in the period of equilibrium when our foreign comrades are preparing thoroughly for their revolution'. [49]

As the new policy took hold, however, and the Russian economy began to revive, Lenin increasingly began to view the NEP as a long-term policy for a period of incubation during which socialist forms would be tested in competition with capitalist forms. In 1923, acknowledging that 'there has been a radical modification in our whole outlook on socialism',[50] Lenin would speak of the transition to socialism in Russia comprising 'a whole historical epoch'.

Thus, where once the fate of Bolshevik power had been linked to the progress of the revolution in the West, now Lenin adopted a whole new perspective. Not only could the Bolsheviks hold on to power without outside support from other revolutions, they could even begin an advance *toward* socialism in Russia itself. Nowhere does he give the slightest intimation of Trotsky's prediction that without revolutions in the West, Russia would inevitably become a 'deformed workers' state'.

On the basis of these comments, Stalin could legitimately argue that the *conception* of building socialism in the Soviet Union even before proletarian revolution had broken out and won elsewhere had some measure of theoretical justification in Lenin. But his abrupt turn toward quickly constructing what he conceived to be an all-sided socialist economy had little in common with Lenin's revised views on the nature of the transition and the character of socialist construction.

At the same time, party leaders continued to assert that they remained committed to world revolution. Thus Bukharin, then still Stalin's ally and the party's principal theoretical defender of 'socialism in one country', declared in 1925:

Despite the fact that our technology and economy are lagging far behind, nevertheless we can, step by step, construct socialism and we shall finish the construction of it unless armed interference from the capitalist power prevents us from doing so .... Can we be defeated by armed strength? We say: yes, we can. Can we therefore in all reality turn away from the course of international revolution? No, we cannot. International revolution is the sole guarantee against our being strangled by the capitalist powers. [51]

A year later Stalin would go even further in proclaiming fealty to the world revolution: 'What else is our country, "the country that is

building socialism", if not the base of the world revolution? But can it
be a real base of the world revolution if it is incapable of completing
the building of a socialist society?' [52]

To the extent that Trotsky's critique of the theory of socialism in
one country is based on an objective appraisal of the possibilities
confronting the USSR at the time, it has considerable merit, especially
his prescient prediction that the effort would inevitably lead to a gross
bureaucratic distortion of the socialist ideal. The same cannot be said,
however, of Trotsky's political conclusion – that the only principled
and practical course open to the new Soviet state was to spearhead a
world revolutionary assault on capitalism. His profound misreading of
the Western proletariat's readiness for revolution was patently out of
touch with reality and would undoubtedly have drawn the new Soviet
state into a confrontation with the West which it would have had
little chance of winning.

Still, Trotsky's prediction that the policy of building 'socialism in
one country' would inevitably abandon the world revolution – at least
in the sense that phrase had generally been understood by Marxists –
clearly was accurate. Soviet policy under Stalin and since – 'socialism
in one country', the United Front against Fascism of the 1930s, and
the postwar pursuit of 'peaceful coexistence' – all demonstrated that
the Soviets had significantly reduced their expectations of revolutions
in the West. Official Marxist-Leninist literature routinely promoted the
notion that prospects for revolution were constantly 'ripening' in the
developed capitalist countries, but Soviet foreign policy was clearly
based on more realistic assessments. Thus, while Mikhail Suslov, the
CPSU's foremost ideologist, would argue in 1971 that 'proletarian
revolutions [were] becoming the order of the day' in the major
capitalist countries,[53] negotiations were already underway that would
culminate in a Moscow summit meeting a year later at which
Brezhnev and Nixon would sign the protocols of 'detente'.

But in the 1920s the rhetoric of world revolution in the more
traditional sense still resounded in the Soviet Union and the Third
International, whose revolutionary pronouncements became even more
denunciatory of the capitalist states. (The Soviet Foreign Ministry
complained more than once that the International was negating its
diplomatic efforts at developing coexistence.) Likewise, the Comintern
became even more vituperative in its denunciations of Social Democratic Parties for pursuing reform rather than revolution. Even while
calling for unity of action against fascism, the communists emphasized
a 'united front from below' which was principally aimed at splitting
the social democratic rank and file from its leadership. Needless to
say, such ultra-left tactics made a mockery of the Comintern's calls
for unity.

The United Front against Fascism

Hitler's rise to power and, even more, his rapid and thorough consolidation of Nazi rule, forced many leading figures in both the social democratic Second International and communist Third International seriously to consider a change in course. While official Marxist-Leninist history attributes the change exclusively to the initiative of the communists,54 some of the first public calls for cooperation came from socialist leaders.

One of the first was a statement by the leaders of the Labor and Socialist International (LSI) in February 1933, declaring its readiness 'to negotiate with the Communist International with a view to common action [against fascism] as soon as this body is also ready'. The only condition posed by the LSI was the ending of mutual attacks. Later that year the French Socialist Party similarly declared its readiness for concerted action with the communists provided the latter put an end to 'insulting polemics between the two parties'.55

The first signal from the communist side came in May 1934, with the publication in *Pravda* of an article endorsing the political propriety of seeking united action with socialist leaders. With Stalin's imprimatur thus made public, the international communist movement began the process of a major shift in its line, culminating in 1935 with the Comintern's adoption at its seventh World Congress of the policy of building a United Front against Fascism.

In making this turn, the Comintern emphasized the 'changed circumstances' in Europe, especially fascism's rise to power in Germany. For Hitler's program was based on the view – so attractive to German monopoly capital – that the key to German resuscitation was expansion; and the most likely direction for expansion was the East: to the countries of Central Europe and ultimately the grandest prize of all, the USSR. (Hitler's virulent anti-communism was, in this sense, part of the ideological preparation for war against the Soviet Union.) In addition, the governments of both France and Britain made no secret of the fact that they would look tolerantly – if not benevolently – on a German move to the East which would serve the dual purpose of bringing down the Soviets and averting the threat of a German attack on them.

Still, a more critical appraisal of the ultra-leftism characteristic of the years leading up to the Seventh World Congress would have been both appropriate and helpful. Not only would it have made the task of reconciliation with social democracy easier, it might have altered the ideological climate within both the Comintern and the individual Communist Parties. But since such an admission would clearly have called into question the sectarian policies of the earlier period, and therefore Stalin's infallibility, the signal from the Kremlin was to eliminate any suggestion of self-criticism.

So, just as the economic crisis engendered by war communism led

Lenin to the NEP, Hitler's success shocked the leaders of the international communist movement into the realization that the 'united front from below', denunciations of social democracy as 'social fascism' and other ultra-left tactics of the Comintern's 'Third Period' ran counter to their own self-interest in light of the new political realities in Europe.

By contrast, the United Front against Fascism posited unity between the communists and social democrats from 'above', that is open and explicit cooperation between the two tendencies at the leadership level with the implicit understanding that sectarian attacks against each other would cease. Although many social democrats were understandably wary of the turn and many in the communist movement had a hard time trying to adjust to a spirit of cooperation with their old foes, the new policy helped change the political climate in Europe and North America. Inevitably, the communists found themselves cooperating not just with social democracy (in view of past antagonisms, that cooperation was, in many respects, quite shaky), but with bourgeois political figures who were themselves alarmed at the dangers posed by a revived, militarized and expansionist Germany.

The United Front against Fascism was probably the international communist movement's most signal political and theoretical accomplishment during the Stalin years. Closing down the illusion that the Comintern could or was going to orchestrate a world socialist revolution, it brought the communists into the mainstream of West European political life. In the US, the abandonment of earlier dual unionism and the revolutionary posturing of the 'united front from below' enabled the communists to win more influence in the labor movement – most particularly in the new Congress of Industrial Organizations (CIO) – and to develop a significant working-class base. More broadly, the communists became identified as the torch-bearers of anti-fascism. While the United Front against Fascism proved unable to prevent World War II, it laid the foundation for the Grand Alliance between the Soviet Union, Britain and the US which ultimately brought about Hitler's defeat.

One victim of the success of the new policy was the Comintern itself, which was dissolved in 1943. Although this event was, to a great extent, viewed pragmatically as a measure designed to reassure the US and Britain of Soviet allegiance to the wartime alliance, it had a deeper historical significance. In effect, the end of the Comintern signaled the surrender of the view that the Soviet Union would count on and, therefore, support proletarian revolutions in the most developed capitalist countries both for its own defense and as the course of the world transition from capitalism to socialism.

The question left unanswered by all this – as well as subsequent events – is why didn't the expected revolutions in the developed capitalist countries occur?

Trotskyists still attribute the revolution's postponement to Stalin's 'betrayal' of the true socialist cause. Maoists and diehard Stalinists blame Khrushchev and his 'modern revisionism' for subordinating both proletarian revolution and national liberation to peaceful coexistence. And those Marxist-Leninists whose outlook remains principally shaped by Stalin's theoretical constructs hold that both socialism and the world revolutionary process were actually proceeding apace until Gorbachev sold the whole cause down the river.

But in the final analysis, it all comes back to the misassessment of capitalism's staying power. Beginning with Marx and Engels, the inveterate error has been a grave misreading of capitalism's lifeline. Marx, it seems to me, was quite correct in declaring: 'No social order ever perishes before all the productive forces for which there is room in it have developed; and new, higher relations of production never appear before the material conditions of their existence have matured in the womb of the old society itself.' [56]

Nevertheless, sometime around the middle of the nineteenth century both Marx and Engels quite incorrectly concluded that capitalism had arrived at – or was rapidly approaching – the end of its developmental potential; and that the material conditions necessary to bring into being a working class-led cooperative social order had already matured in the capitalist womb. Considering that this conclusion was arrived at when the industrial revolution was still in its infancy – capitalism had not yet even harnessed electricity to either industry or its products, nor had such productive forces as the internal combustion engine and the wireless telegraph yet been developed – the magnitude of this error is hard to overstate. Further, while Britain's industrial revolution had begun in the middle of the eighteenth century, that in France, Germany and the US was still in the early stages. Nor had even bourgeois revolutions yet taken place in Germany, Eastern Europe and Russia, where feudal political relations were still holding back full capitalist development. As for the presumed 'engine of revolution' – the proletariat – it had only recently begun to organize itself into trade unions.

Succeeding generations of Marxists have tended to glide lightly over Marx's profound misreading of nineteenth century class dynamics, generally viewing the error as a slight miscalculation in timing. But almost 150 years later, when socialism's short-term prospects in any of the countries where the material conditions are presumably ripest remain dubious at best, the political and theoretical consequences of Marx's failed prediction clearly make it more than a simple mistake.

Lenin, who had earlier seen the Russian Revolution as catalyst for the world proletarian revolution, remained convinced throughout his life that capitalism was in its final, 'moribund' stage and that, objectively, the working class in the main capitalist countries was ready for revolution. He too concluded that the delay in capitalism's demise was due more to subjective than objective factors, the missing element being the proletariat's *international* revolutionary vanguard party whose principal task was to break the hold of 'bourgeois labor leaders' over the masses of workers. It was to this end that the Comintern was founded.

But this, too, was a profound misreading of capitalism's remaining potential and an unwarranted generalization of the Bolshevik experience. Lenin believed that capitalism could no longer expand because the main imperialist countries had already divided the entire world between them; as a result, they would be driven to war in various attempts to redivide the world. This analysis, however, was actually quite mechanical. For capitalist expansion did not consist solely – or even primarily – in extending its domain. The *linear spread* of capitalism throughout the world actually represents an early stage of expansion. The more significant and lasting expansion went beyond the colonialist aggrandizement of land, natural resources and agriculture. Even in Lenin's time, international capital had begun to draw new hundreds of millions into the world capitalist economy both as a new industrial laborforce and a growing world consumer market – a process which has accelerated rapidly since the 1960s.

Were Marxist expectations of revolution totally off base? It can hardly be denied, after all, that revolution has been a striking and persistent feature of the twentieth century. But this was also true of the nineteenth century, when bourgeois-democratic revolutions swept much of Europe and erupted, in one form or another, elsewhere as well.

Today, with the benefit of historical hindsight, we can see that what changed in the twentieth century was not so much the class content of revolution as the locale. Without exception, the revolutions of the past 90 years – including the Bolshevik uprising of 1917 and the various upheavals and wars of national liberation (among them the Chinese, Vietnamese and Cuban revolutions) against colonialism – were likewise bourgeois-democratic revolutions, even if some of them proclaimed socialist principles and aspirations.

World Revolution: the Trotskyist and Maoist Alternatives

If fidelity to Lenin's known views on world revolution were the principal criterion, Trotsky's claim to the Leninist legacy would have considerable merit, although it must be said on Lenin's behalf that all of his principles were laced with a tactical flexibility that Trotsky sorely lacked. But consistency is, at best, a dubious standard in the ever-changing world of politics. Thus Trotskyist insistence on the timeliness of world revolution may have the merits of consistency, but it still miscarries since, when all is said and done, it is based on the same original assumption that capitalism, having reached the point of no return, is ripe for the taking; and that the workers in the developed capitalist countries are only awaiting the leadership of a genuinely revolutionary party.

Certainly one would expect that if Trotsky's assessment of working-class readiness for revolution were accurate, some political evidence to buttress that thesis would be at hand. After all, revolutions can be 'betrayed', but historical processes cannot. If they are materially rooted, they will appear again and again. Lenin's misassessments in this regard are more understandable in light of the conditions prevailing – especially in Europe – during the first two decades of the twentieth century. But the stubborn insistence of Trotsky and his followers on the ready-to-hand possibilities for world revolution long after it had become quite apparent that whatever revolutionary moment might have existed imme-diately after 1917 had passed, bespeak a dogmatism which has kept Trotskyism out of the mainstream of class-based politics.

Mao also had a theory of world revolution. Unlike Trotsky, however, Mao shared Stalin's view of building socialism in one country. But in light of two decades of US military threats against communist China (the US fought the two major wars of the post-World War II era in Korea and Vietnam on China's borders) and Khrushchev's stress on peaceful coexistence, Mao saw revolutionary upheavals elsewhere as crucial to China's security. He entertained no illusions about the possibilities for revolution in the developed capitalist countries. Nor did he view the Soviet-dominated 'socialist camp' as a reliable 'anchor' for a world revolutionary process.

For Mao, the dream of world revolution – and, with it, the enhancement of China's security – rested on the potential represented by Third World national liberation struggles. His strategy, therefore, was to 'surround the cities' (the world's industrialized countries) 'by the coun-tryside' (the still largely agricultural Third World). Lending this thesis a measure of credibility was the fact that it was formulated at a time when the anti-colonial movement was at its height. Buttressed by the conse-quent flush of revolutionary enthusiasm among socialists and in the Third World generally, Mao asserted that the national liberation move-ments had picked up the vanguard mantle which had turned out to be beyond the capacities of the proletarians in the capitalist countries. (China's 'Great Proletarian Cultural Revolution' was supposed to demon-strate that a newly liberated, predominantly peasant Third World country could take charge of its own destiny and establish a truly egalitarian modern society.)

But Mao had assigned impossible tasks to the poor peasants of the Third World. Although sometimes embossed with socialist rhetoric, the anti-colonial movement was first and foremost energized by the struggle for national independence. (Even the communist Ho Chi Minh had declared that 'Nothing is more precious than independence.') Such a goal was within its reach. But despite some extravagant fantasies – advanced mainly by its supporters in capitalist countries – the movement did not aspire to, nor could it bring about the overthrow of international capital. At the same time, the disastrous consequences of Mao's Cultural

Revolution simply underscored the fact that attempts at some kind of socialist transformation in the newly independent Third World countries faced highly dubious prospects at best.

Although the Leninist prophecy has remained elusive, belief in the timeliness of proletarian revolution – either in one or more of the developed capitalist countries or on a world scale – has remained central to Marxist-Leninist theory over the decades. Even as late as 1985, official Marxist-Leninist doctrine was still proclaiming this 'the epoch of imperialism and proletarian revolutions'.[57] Still, if one goes beyond the official rhetoric and examines the actual policies followed by the Communist Parties, it is quite clear that as 'an immediate, practical question', proletarian revolution has not been on the communist agenda for some time.

Arguably, this has been the case ever since the mid-1920s when it became apparent that the Bolshevik Revolution was *not* going to trigger a broader uprising against world capitalism. By the 1950s, when neither the Great Depression nor World War II had played the role of revolutionary catalyst, the theory was fundamentally inoperable. Nevertheless, Marxist-Leninists over the decades have comforted themselves with what would become a perennial self-deluding strain – that the proletariat was on the verge of a breakthrough towards that revolutionary consciousness which would be ready for and eagerly seek the communists' vanguard leadership.

But even before the collapse of 'actually existing socialism' interrupted the general Marxist-Leninist reverie, adherence to this cornerstone of the Marxist-Leninist canon had produced a form of ideological schizophrenia in the world communist movement. On the one hand, it has simply become untenable to continue asserting that proletarian revolution is today – or has been for many decades – an 'immediate and practical question'. Socialism – which in the absence of a verified, viable model can only be postulated as the next stage of human development after capitalism – is undoubtedly beginning to make its presence felt in various forms and relationships that have emerged within the framework of capitalism. But the Marxist-Leninist notion of a rapidly maturing proletarian assault on world capitalism – even on capitalism in any of its major centers – would appear to be fairly worthless as the theoretical basis for a viable socialist politics and a sure-fire formula for political isolation and irrelevance.

On the other hand, since belief in the imminence of socialist revolution was the principal raison d'être for the existence of the Communist Parties and the justification for their organizational rigors, it could only be tampered with – let alone dropped – at the risk of undermining the institutions built up on the strength of those beliefs. The established church has long understood the importance of dogma in perpetuating its authority and, with it, the tenure of its hierarchy – and the communist movement has certainly been subject to the same dynamic.

In the Soviet Union, the defense of Marxism-Leninism was *ipso facto* a defense of the prevailing system and the perquisites that went with it. In the non-governing parties, lifetime investments in careers, organizational structures, and access to the authority and largesse of Soviet power likewise provided compelling reasons – over and beyond ideological conviction – for keeping the Marxist-Leninist faith.

8 World Revolution

Part II Building the World Socialist System

Although imperialism is desperately trying to restore the bourgeois order, it is powerless to regain its lost historical initiative and reverse the development of the modern world. The main course of human development is determined by the world socialist system, the international working class and the national liberation movement.

Soviet Text (1983)[1]

While the theme of world revolution has been a constant in the Marxist framework, the theory itself has undergone significant change.

For Marx and Engels, world revolution had a specific meaning: 'It will be a revolution taking place simultaneously in all civilized countries, that is, at least in England, America, France and Germany.' [2] Two main considerations went into this conclusion. First, the 'civilized' countries – by which they meant the most developed capitalist countries – were the only ones in the world where the material conditions for socialism had matured; this was reflected not only in the level of development of the productive forces, but in the growth of the working class to the point where it had become capable of leading a struggle for power. Second, given the international character of the bourgeoisie, they were sure that other capitalist governments would unite to suppress the revolution if it took power only in one country.

As we know, however, history did not fulfill Marx and Engels' expectations.

In light of the Russian experience and what he considered the influence of 'opportunism' among the workers in the most developed capitalist countries, Lenin advanced a new theory of the proletarian revolution based on the 'weak link'. According to this thesis, the revolution was most likely to begin in a major country but one whose capitalism was much weaker than the others and hence more unstable – that is, Russia. But such a revolution, lacking the material conditions for socialism, could only succeed if it were converted into a 'world working-class revolution.'

Still, despite what seemed to be extremely favorable conditions in a Europe devastated by World War I and the Bolshevik triumph in Russia, revolution did not break out in the capitalist heartland.

After Lenin's death, the Bolsheviks confronted a dilemma. Should they stick to their old analysis and use their new power base in Russia mainly to promote the revolution elsewhere in Europe – Trotsky's position? Or should they concentrate instead on trying to build socialism in the USSR – Stalin's position? We know who won that battle.

The World Revolution Redefined

Contrary to Trotsky's charge, Stalin did not abandon the concept of world proletarian revolution. Rejecting the traditional thesis of a direct and concerted assault on the bastions of international capital by the world proletariat, Stalin instead evolved a strategy for the steady expansion of the 'world socialist system' through the incorporation of more and more peoples and countries into it. Nominally, this expansion would occur as proletarian forces came to power in various countries and voluntarily joined the new system. In fact, to the extent that the 'Socialist Camp' did indeed expand in subsequent years, this mostly was the result of Soviet military successes in World War II and communist-led wars of national liberation in the Third World.

In effect, Stalin and his successors did not so much abandon world revolution as redefine it. Where Lenin had once assumed that revolutions in the West would supersede the Russian Revolution, Marxist-Leninist theory now adopted a new view: the Soviet Union had become the mainstay and ultimate arbiter of strategy for the World Revolution.

Stalin had actually inclined toward such a perspective as early as 1921 when he asserted that with the Bolshevik seizure of power, 'The Russian proletariat, which until now had been just one of the units of the international proletariat, henceforward became the vanguard of the world proletariat.' [3] (Needless to say, the Russian proletariat could play this role only under the leadership of its own vanguard, the CPSU.) Whether or not stated as forthrightly, it was a view many Bolsheviks held and was patently evident in the structure and political dynamics of the Comintern. Even earlier, in 1919, Lenin had envisioned 'the complete amalgamation of the workers and peasants of all nations in a single world Soviet republic'.[4]

But no prominent communist leader had gone as far as Stalin did. Even Lenin's comment was undoubtedly intended simply to convey the idea of an eventual single nation-state which would draw from the experience of the Bolshevik Revolution, not an expanding 'socialist camp' headed and dominated by the Soviet Union.

Stalin's new paradigm of world revolution in effect permanently established Moscow as the center of the developing alternative world system and provided the international communist movement with an old ideological raison d'être in new form. The goal was still world socialism, but theory was now in line with the real power relations of the International Communist Movement where strategy and politics were determined by the CPSU.

The full implications of this sea-change were not seen until after World War II when Soviet military might helped establish communist states in Eastern Europe. Backed by the Red Army which had liberated their countries from German fascism, Communist Parties came to power in East Germany, Poland, Bulgaria, Romania, Hungary and Czechoslovakia. Estonia, Latvia and Lithuania – detached from the old czarist Empire after World War I and 'ceded' to Moscow in a secret protocol to the 1939 Nazi-Soviet non-aggression treaty – were reincorporated back into the Soviet Union. (In Yugoslavia and Albania, Communist Parties came to power largely on the strength of their own roles in the anti-Nazi resistance, although political and economic backing from Moscow helped bolster them. Not coincidentally, these countries were the most independent of the Soviet Union.)

At the same time, Communist Parties were coming to power in Asia. The major development, of course, was the communist victory in China in 1949. In addition, Soviet entry into the war against Japan in the closing days of World War II helped communists take power in the northern portion of Korea, while communists moved to the van of the anti-colonial struggle in Vietnam when the French sought to regain their foothold in Indochina after the Japanese were ousted.

Marxist-Leninist theory saw all these developments as 'the most important historical event since the October Socialist Revolution in Russia', because 'socialism [has now] emerged beyond one country to become a world system.' [5] For the first time, Stalin's new theory of world revolution took on a practical aspect. While the western proletariat remained relatively dormant – at least in so far as the struggle for socialism was concerned – the transition from capitalism to socialism on a world scale was already taking place as Eastern Europe and parts of Western Asia became directly linked to the new world socialist system. Once again defying the traditional Marxist prescription for socialism to triumph where capitalism was most advanced, socialism's future now seemed to lie with countries contiguous to the Soviet Union and to those Third World countries where communist-led national liberation movements, having come to power, would establish close economic, political and military ties with the 'socialist camp.' Ironically, it was a thesis which held, in effect, that socialism would next come to those countries and peoples who, in classical materialist terms, were least ready for it.

The essential logic of Stalin's schema was that new socialist countries would have to put themselves under Moscow's protective wing or else face the certainty of being undone by world imperialism. They would also have to adopt the Soviet model of socialism for how else could a world 'system' ensure socialist economic integration. Refusal to join, or stay in or subordinate an individual country to the 'socialist camp' clearly would be an expression of opportunism and ultimately betrayal, since it would subordinate the cause of the whole movement to narrow national considerations. Countries choosing to be 'independent' would have little choice but to reach an accommodation with the other world system.

The same principle would apply to countries breaking out of colonial or semi-colonial domination. They could only be truly independent of imperialism by developing close political, economic and military ties with the Soviet Union and the whole 'socialist camp'. In a world composed of two contending systems, there could be no 'middle way'. Similarly, failure to make this link, while promoting illusions about 'independence', was an expression of 'petty-bourgeois nationalism' and yet another form of opportunism.

Consequently, Soviet policy remained cool – if not outright hostile – to the political leaders of newly emergent states who tried to steer a neutral course between the US and the USSR. In part because Tito played a central role in it, Stalin denounced the first efforts to form the Non-Aligned Movement. But others, such as Nehru and Nasser, were also attacked. A prominent Soviet historian notes, for instance, that Nehru 'was regarded as a henchman of British imperialism and not as the leader of the liberation movement in India'.[6] (Ironically, the main architect of US foreign policy during this period, Secretary of State John Foster Dulles, was equally distrustful of the Non-Aligned Movement. Like Stalin, Dulles had a you're-either-with-us-or-against-us view of the world.)

Meanwhile, Western condemnation of the incorporation of much of Eastern Europe into the new 'socialist camp' – 'From Stettin in the Baltic to Trieste in the Adriatic, an Iron Curtain has descended across the Continent', declared Churchill with Truman's obvious approval in 1946 – effectively buried any lingering hopes the Soviets might have had about extending the wartime alliance with the US and Britain into the postwar era. To Stalin, who believed that the Yalta summit had acknowledged Eastern Europe as a postwar Soviet sphere of influence, this breach of a wartime understanding meant only one thing: emboldened by the American nuclear monopoly, the West was returning to its long-standing aim of undermining socialism.

With the Cold War apparently confirming their thesis of two world camps and two world systems, the Soviets retreated to the more familiar ideological territory of world revolution. 'In the final analysis', noted a subsequent Marxist-Leninist text, 'the bourgeoisie and proletariat become international classes, and antagonism between them acquires an international character.'[7]

Khrushchev and Peaceful Coexistence

The most pressing question confronting Stalin's successors was how to avert the seemingly inexorable military confrontation with the US for which the Soviets – facing a foe whose nuclear capacity far outstripped its own – were ill-prepared. With the arms race aggravating strains on the Soviet civilian economy and a war-weary population frustrated by prospects of continued housing shortages and a scarcity of consumer goods, the need for a policy change was becoming increasingly apparent.

A brief internal power struggle in the post-Stalin Soviet leadership was played out in the shadow of these tensions. In the end, Nikita Khrushchev emerged as the incarnation of a previously suppressed impulse toward reform. A down-to-earth, shoot-from-the-hip communist of working-class background, Khrushchev sent shock waves through Eastern Europe and the parties of the International Communist Movement with his 1956 secret speech denouncing Stalin. This damning exposé of the man who had been hailed as the 'greatest Marxist of his time' when he had gone to join Lenin in permanent entombment in Red Square helped foster a climate more conducive to political liberalization, economic reform and an overhaul of long-standing Marxist-Leninist precepts.

Khrushchev's attempted reforms of the administrative-command economy are discussed in Chapter 5 above, which deals with 'actually existing socialism'. Here we will focus on Khrushchev's 'new thinking' in the international realm where the urgent practical problem facing postwar Soviet foreign policy was how to avert a war with the West while protecting the postwar changes which had brought the 'socialist camp' into being.

Stalin's answer to this challenge had been to argue that war between the US and its main capitalist allies was more likely than war between the US and the Soviet Union. Basing himself on Lenin's thesis that wars between rival capitalist countries were inevitable, he predicted that sooner or later Britain, France, (West) Germany and Japan would try to 'tear loose from American bondage and take the path of independent development', an eventuality bound to lead to another world war. In practice, he asserted, 'the struggle of the capitalist countries for markets and their desire to crush their competitors [will] prove to be stronger than the contradictions between the capitalist camp and the socialist camp.' [8]

Not everyone in the CPSU leadership was satisfied with this somewhat sanguine view of the nuclear threat facing them. Stalin acknowledged as much when he noted that his reassertion of the classic Leninist thesis on the inevitability of war was a response to certain unnamed 'comrades' (Khrushchev was probably one) who 'hold that, owing to the development of new international conditions since the Second World War, wars between capitalist countries have ceased to be inevitable'. [9]

The first tentative steps toward what would become a major change in both policy and theory was the 'thaw' of 1954–55. Consciously taking a less provocative stance toward the West, Moscow played a crucial role at the 1954 Geneva Conference which brought about peaceful settlements in both Korea and Indochina. (Vietnamese communists later noted that they were under intense pressure from the Soviets to make concessions in order to assure a settlement with the US.)

At home, the thaw began to dispel the climate of intellectual numbness which had prevailed in the Soviet Union and Eastern Europe during the years of Stalin's rule. The most significant and dramatic step, however, was Khrushchev's secret 1956 speech exposing Stalin, delivered at the CPSU's 20th Congress. The 'secret', of course, did not last long; and there can be little doubt that Khrushchev made sure that it was leaked, since it clearly was intended as a signal both to Soviet citizens and the international community – particularly the West – that the Stalin era was over. Demystifying the figure who, more than any other, was the human metaphor for 'actually existing socialism' was the essential precondition for a change in course. (The leak probably was also an end run around those in the Politburo who had grudgingly gone along with the exposé on condition that it be kept secret.)

In particular, the new Soviet leaders – Khrushchev more so than any – felt the need to ditch Stalin's policies via-à-vis the West and take a new look at all previously existing military and political theory. Stalin's anticipation of a new world war between the imperialist powers was being confounded by the unprecedented hegemony enjoyed by the US within the world capitalist system and by American success in welding the main capitalist countries into a tight alliance. Most sobering of all, however, was the danger of nuclear war. Soviet leaders knew that the US had seriously considered using nuclear weapons in Korea and had offered the French a nuclear bomb for use in Vietnam – an eventuality that could have drawn Moscow into a disastrous nuclear showdown with Washington.

Thus, contrary to Stalin's assertion that a third world war would result in the end of capitalism and the dawn of socialism on a world scale, Khrushchev warned that the awesome destructive power of nuclear weapons had not only made it impossible for any group of imperialist powers to achieve the goals for which wars previously had been fought, but that such a war would negatively affect socialism's prospects as well:

> There can be no doubt that a world nuclear war ... would inevitably result in the downfall of the capitalist system, a system breeding wars. But would the socialist countries and the cause of socialism all over the world benefit from a world nuclear disaster?... Marxist-Leninists cannot propose to establish a Communist civilization on the ruins of centers of world culture, on land laid waste and contaminated by nuclear fall-out.[10]

This somewhat belated understanding of the impact of nuclear weapons on traditional military doctrine – along with Soviet successes in space and in rebuffing Western attempts to roll back the postwar expansion of the 'socialist camp' – emboldened Khrushchev to propose a significant shift in Soviet foreign policy and a momentous alteration in Marxist-Leninist theory. Clearly concerned that the escalating Cold War could lead to a direct military confrontation with the US, Soviet leaders announced that henceforth peaceful coexistence had become not simply a goal of communist policy but the main aspect of the foreign policy of the socialist countries. To underscore the significance of this alteration, they likewise declared obsolete Lenin's thesis on the inevitability of armed struggle in the transition from capitalism to socialism, asserting instead that peaceful transition had become a definite possibility, especially in the system's most developed citadels in Western Europe, North America and Japan. In effect, this was an olive branch held out to the US and its allies that Communist Parties in the most developed capitalist countries would forswear any strategy based on an armed seizure of power. It was also a formal notice that under no circumstances would the Soviet Union come to the support of any effort to change the status quo in those countries by force. In addition, Lenin's thesis on the inevitability of war under imperialism was significantly altered to hold out the possibility that war between imperialist rivals as well as between the two social systems could be averted. Taken as a whole, these propositions reflected the beginnings of a theoretical adjustment to the implications of the nuclear age.

The new outlook represented the most sweeping initiative ever undertaken by a Soviet leader to develop a long-term non-antagonistic relationship with the world capitalist system. Previously, under both Lenin and Stalin, peaceful coexistence had been conceived in relatively narrow terms pretty much as an armed truce between the Soviet Union and the capitalist West. (Even the Grand Alliance of World War II was viewed as a temporary conjuncture of interests.) Inherent in the old view was the notion that peaceful coexistence would have to be imposed on the capitalist states by the growing strength of the 'socialist camp'.

But to Khrushchev, peaceful coexistence was more than a non-aggression pact with the West. It should include, he believed, coordinated policies for curbing the testing, deployment and use of nuclear weapons and armaments in general; cooperation in trying to defuse regional and international tensions; and normalizing trade and other economic relations. Previously peaceful coexistence had been seen as an adjunct to Moscow's world historic task of promoting and extending socialism. Now, he proclaimed, it would become 'the general line of the foreign policy of the USSR',[11] with support for socialist and national liberation movements the adjunct.

(A particular aspect of peaceful coexistence would be 'peaceful competition'; in effect, a pledge by both camps to pursue their distinct world agendas solely through economic and ideological means.)

Perhaps the most startling change, however, was Khrushchev's declaration that the communists now recognized the definite possibility of a peaceful transition from capitalism to socialism in the most developed capitalist countries. This was the precise heresy against which successive generations of communists had waged bitter ideological struggles ever since the days of Eduard Bernstein and the turn-of-the-century Second International and, more recently, Browderism – the apostasy associated with Earl Browder, head of the US Communist Party since the early 1930s. (During the Second World War Browder had dissolved the American Communist Party in favor of a Communist Political Association shorn of both its revolutionary rhetoric and mission. Advocating a peaceful transition to socialism in the framework of a new era of US–Soviet cooperation in the postwar world, Browder came to grief as Stalin switched back to a 'class struggle' line as the war came to an end in 1945. Condemned as a 'revisionist', he was expelled from the Communist Party in 1946.)

But with Khrushchev advancing similar propositions in Marxism-Leninism's own headquarters, the international communist movement was thrown into turmoil. A more provocative ideological alteration is hard to imagine – a fact which is itself a measure of the upgraded importance the Soviet leadership attached to it. For the new thesis, as with the broader conception of peaceful coexistence, was clearly intended as an unambiguous signal to the West that the CPSU would not support or countenance a strategy of armed struggle by Communist Parties in the capitalist heartland. Soviet leaders went so far as to assert that the USSR could actually become a *communist* society even while capitalism dominated the world economy – yet another message designed to reassure the West of Moscow's peaceful intentions. Likewise, Khrushchev's pronouncement that war was no longer inevitable under capitalism was yet another signal that Moscow was no longer speculating on a third world war as a potential catalyst for the world revolution.

No one was more unhappy with Khrushchev's 'new thinking' than Mao Zhedong and the leadership of the Chinese Communist Party (CCP). Charging Khrushchev with 'systematized revisionism', 'nuclear fetishism', and, ultimately, the 'restoration of capitalism in the USSR', the CCP mounted the most significant challenge to Soviet leadership in the history of the International Communist Movement.

(Underlying this 'ideological dispute', were compelling political considerations. In particular, Moscow's new enchantment with 'peaceful coexistence' did not seem to include any 'thaw' in the US attitude toward China. Washington clearly intended to go on supporting the Taiwan-based forces of Chiang Kai-shek who daily proclaimed their intention to overthrow the communist regime on the mainland. And with US troops stationed on China's borders in South Korea and Vietnam, and with US bases in Japan and the Philippines only a short distance away, Beijing had good reason to doubt that peaceful coexistence between the US and USSR would extend to US–Chinese relations. If anything, the new Soviet emphasis on peaceful coexistence intimated that Moscow might now be ready to cut deals with Washington that would not take into account Chinese interests and concerns. That Mao's concerns were more with immediate political considerations than with broader questions of Marxist principle became apparent a decade later, when he would eagerly embrace a new relationship with the US which went far beyond Khrushchev's 'peaceful coexistence' – a relationship which attempted to link China with the US in a crusade against 'Soviet social-imperialism', considered far more dangerous to the world than traditional US imperialism.)

Nevertheless, Khrushchev's ideological shift was significant in its own right. It clearly undermined the classic Marxist paradigm on world revolution and the transition to socialism. While the new line commanded majorities in most of the world's Communist Parties, almost all suffered splits – those departing for more revolutionary pastures accusing Khrushchev of everything from treason and revisionism to cowardice and simple-mindedness.

But the leftist charge that a naive (or treacherous) Khrushchev had jumped into bed with the capitalists and abandoned socialism simply refused to face the fact that in any confrontation with the US, the Soviet Union was still dealing from a position of relative weakness. Not only was there a significant gap in nuclear weapons capacity; economically, the USSR was barely at the pre-World War II industrial level of the capitalist countries and was already showing signs of that technological lag which would become such a prominent feature of the Soviet economy in the 1970s and 1980s. (While the Soviets were gradually catching up with the West in introducing new military technology, they were far less successful in harnessing the new industrial-scientific developments of the 1940s and 1950s to civilian production.)

Still, Soviet leaders were hardly chastened hat-in-hand supplicants to the West. Moscow had developed its own nuclear capacities years before expected and despite Washington's threats to start 'rolling back' communism, the 'socialist camp' had emerged intact following a decade of Cold War. Communist forces had fought the US to a stalemate in Korea and a communist-led national liberation movement had soundly defeated France in Indochina. Left-leaning nationalists were well positioned to come to power in a number of other Third World countries.

Within the 'socialist camp', the Soviet Union had been able to suppress breakaway tendencies in East Germany, Poland and especially Hungary without a US military response. Topping all this off, the Soviet Union had become the first to breach the frontiers of space, thereby demonstrating a scientific and industrial capacity which provoked consternation in the capitalist world. Consequently, Soviet leaders felt that the US and its allies also had some compelling reasons to explore a new relationship based on peaceful coexistence.

Although the push for peaceful coexistence was the most visible aspect of Soviet foreign policy during this period, the new Soviet leadership had not abandoned Stalin's perspective on world socialism arising as a result of the continuous expansion of the 'socialist camp' and the world socialist system. For them, peaceful coexistence was the primary task *of the moment*, a strategy for easing tensions with the US that would enable the countries of 'actually existing socialism' to consolidate their system and move it ahead economically while capitalism's own inner contradictions would continue to deepen.

In effect, this was a more sophisticated version of Stalin's strategy in which peaceful coexistence would shape Soviet policy in areas of its strategic weakness, while its 'revolutionary commitment' could be invoked when favorable opportunities for socialist expansion presented themselves.

Marxism-Leninism and The World Revolutionary Process

By the end of the 1950s Marxist-Leninist theory had developed a new scenario for world revolution: a 'world revolutionary process' composed of three elements – the 'socialist camp', the working-class movement in the capitalist countries, and the national liberation movements of the Third World. In this construct, the 'leading role' was assigned to 'the international working class and its highest achievement, the community of the socialist countries',[12] clearly a euphemism for asserting the dominant position of the Soviet Union in the revolutionary constellation. Implicit in this framework – and quite explicit in the actual political dynamic unfolded alongside the theory – was Stalin's new paradigm of world revolution, namely that socialism would gradually sweep the world as a result of the continued expansion of the existing world socialist system.

Underpinning the new theory was an assessment that as a result of changes in the world balance of forces an objective process of world revolutionary change had come into being:

> Our time, whose main content is the transition from capitalism to socialism initiated by the Great October Socialist Revolution, is a time of struggle between the two opposing social systems, a time of socialist revolutions and national liberation revolutions, a time of the breakdown of imperialism, of the abolition of the colonial system, a time of transition of more peoples to the socialist path, of the triumph of socialism and communism on a world scale.[13]

Setting the obligatory affirmations of revolutionary confidence aside for the moment, the practical political goals of the new theory were: (a) to develop a relationship of peaceful coexistence with the West at the state-to-state level in order to secure breathing room for the Soviet Union and to consolidate the gains made in expanding the 'socialist camp'; and (b) to bring the countries coming out of colonialism into the Soviet orbit while avoiding direct confrontation with the US in the Third World by down-playing the communist leadership of national liberation struggles and projecting a peaceful non-capitalist path toward socialism there.

In terms of practical politics, Khrushchev saw this new mix of peaceful coexistence and the world revolutionary process as laying the groundwork for a trade-off in which the West would acquiesce in the 'triumph of socialism' where it had already come to power, while the 'socialist camp' and the International Communist Movement would forswear the use of force in trying to bring down capitalism where there was little likelihood of undermining it anyway.

The Third World, however, was a gray area. Khrushchev emphasized that peaceful coexistence with the West did not preclude support for the anti-colonial struggle, albeit with the implicit proviso that Moscow would not deploy its own military forces in such conflicts. And it was also prepared – as it did in the case of Indochina – to help negotiate peaceful settlements in such wars and other regional conflicts.

Now let us more closely examine the three main actors in the scenario envisioned by the world revolutionary process.

The Socialist 'Anchor'

The basis for socialism to 'anchor' this revolutionary pantheon was the all-sided political, economic, military and ideological strength and con-solidation of the 'socialist camp'. And if we ignore, for the moment, the more long-term political and economic structural defects in the system, it is undoubtedly true that world socialism was stronger and more consolidated in 1960 than it had been a decade earlier.

The Warsaw Treaty Organization – the Soviet Union's response to NATO – was the largest and strongest military force in Europe. No one doubted its capacity to emerge victorious from any conventional war in Europe. Even on the nuclear front, it was rapidly closing the gap with the West. And the alliance which brought the military forces of Poland, East Germany, Czechoslovakia, Hungary, Bulgaria and Romania under direct Soviet command seemed to be more cohesive than the sometimes shaky unity characteristic of the NATO countries.

Economically, the 1950s had been a time of spectacular growth rates for the Soviet Union and the 'socialist camp' generally. Rapid postwar reconstruction of the economy was precisely the kind of undertaking for which the administrative-command system was well suited. And with the establishment of the Council for Mutual Economic Assistance (CMEA or Comecon), the bloc began to coordinate and integrate planning, produc-tion and trade through a 'socialist division of labor'. (The incorporation of Cuba and Vietnam into Comecon in the early 1980s indicated the way in which the world socialist system would continue to expand in the future.)

Politically, the restlessness in Eastern Europe which had produced protests and uprisings in East Germany, Poland and Hungary during the 1950s seemed to be giving way to a period of relative calm and a new, more collegial climate. The restoration of good relations with Yugoslavia helped ease tensions throughout Eastern Europe. And in the wake of the dissolution of the Comintern and the quiet passing of the Cominform, a new, somewhat informal association of the world's Communist Parties was taking shape, its ideological foundations cemented by the theoretical journal, *World Marxist Review*.

On the strength of these developments, Marxist-Leninists held that 'the fraternal socialist countries have created an effective alternative to the international capitalist division of labor.' [14] They alone could extend the necessary aid to national liberation movements and to new countries taking the 'socialist path'. Likewise, only the Soviet nuclear umbrella – especially after the USSR had achieved a rough nuclear parity with the US in the early 1970s – could protect the socialist countries and designated national liberation struggles from all-out attack by the US.

Later in the 1960s, the idea of consolidation went beyond devising a system to make the 'socialist camp' impervious to outside subversion and assault. It also came to mean preventing attempts to alter each country's institutions without Moscow's consent or any other actions seen as weakening the relationship between each of the socialist countries and the Soviet Union.

Moscow had always used both threats of military intervention and actual intervention to suppress movements threatening communist rule in Eastern Europe. But the invasion of Czechoslovakia by Warsaw Treaty troops in 1968 introduced a major innovation in both the theory and practice of 'socialist consolidation' – the 'Brezhnev Doctrine'. Naturally, the countries of the 'socialist camp' never used that pejorative phrase. They preferred the term 'socialist internationalism', by which they meant, as one Soviet historian puts it, 'the Party and state leadership of each socialist country is responsible not only to its party and the people but also to the entire world system of socialism.' [15] But the operative term, acknowledged as such by Brezhnev, was that the countries of the 'socialist camp' – with the exception of the Soviet Union, of course – enjoyed only 'limited sovereignty'.

For as the Czech invasion demonstrated, the Brezhnev Doctrine accorded the Soviet Union the right to intervene in the internal processes of each socialist country even when these had been initiated and were being guided by the Communist Party of that country itself. It likewise unmistakably demonstrated that Marxism-Leninism recognized only a 'single model' of socialism based on and conforming to the Soviet system. By definition, therefore, attempts to modify that system in a manner not acceptable to Moscow were proof of an intent to depart from 'the socialist path' and 'restore capitalism'. (Invariably, programs of substantive reform –

such as Czechoslovakia's attempt to devise 'socialism with a human face' –
were attributed to CIA-sponsored subversion.) Finally, the doctrine reinforced the Soviet Communist Party not only as ultimate arbiter of what
constitutes socialism, but as enforcer of the measures to 'protect' it.

As illustration, in his posthumously published autobiography, the
ousted Czechoslovak president, Alexander Dubcek, reports a conversation
in the Kremlin in which he tried to defend his country's reforms to
Brezhnev. The Soviet leader's response, Dubcek notes, was that Czechoslovakia

> was part of the Soviet security zone and that the Soviet Union had
> no intention of giving it up. What had worried the Soviet Politburo
> most about Prague Spring had been our tendency toward independ-
> ence: that I did not send him my speeches in advance for review,
> that I did not ask his permission for personnel changes. They could
> not tolerate this.[16]

The broader implications of the new doctrine were underscored in 1979
in Afghanistan when, for the first time since the end of World War II,
Soviet troops were sent to fight outside the confines of the Warsaw
Treaty Organization countries. Attempting to shore up a tottering pro-
Soviet regime, Moscow's unprecedented move signalled a new willingness to expand the world socialist system through military force. This
extension of the Brezhnev Doctrine to include newly established communist regimes in the 'irreversible' category was therefore taken by the
West as the return to a more aggressive policy of socialist expansion.

Soviet boldness thus exhibited in Afghanistan was based on Marxism-Leninism's perennially optimistic estimate of yet another 'shift in the
world balance of forces' – this one stemming, at least in part, from
Moscow's sense of its own growing military strength and what it
perceived to be, in the wake of the US defeat in Vietnam, an
unaccustomed lassitude on the part of the West. Thus a 1974 retrospect
on US–Soviet relations concludes:

> While, in the 1950s, imperialism had the power to export counter-
> revolution and thereby to reduce or even nullify the chances of
> victorious revolutions in small states, this power is now largely
> paralyzed – as events showed in Hungary and Egypt in 1956, and in
> Cuba and Czechoslovakia during the 1960s. This applies both to
> attempts at military intervention and to economic sanctions and
> blockades, and to attempts at eroding the socialist awareness of
> nations.[17]

Although claims that counter-revolution had been 'paralyzed' were clearly
overstated, there was enough of a factual basis in the Soviet estimate to
permit ideological predilection to influence Moscow's policy decisions –

especially after the Soviet Union reached what amounted to a nuclear standoff with the US. At the very least, Moscow's military capacities seem to have discouraged any overt attempt to 'roll back' communism in Eastern Europe even when relatively favorable opportunities to do so existed. (There was even, during this time, considerable speculation by top-ranking Soviet military figures that Moscow might actually be able to prevail in a nuclear showdown with the US.)

Likewise, in Vietnam Soviet strength was clearly a factor in Lyndon Johnson's decision to pursue a 'limited war' which did not envision either an invasion of North Vietnam or the use of nuclear weapons. But US defeat in Indochina suggested that, short of using nuclear weapons, Washington could no longer blithely assume that it could succeed where its colonialist predecessors had failed; and the aptly named thesis of 'mutually assured destruction' (MAD) underscored how parity with the Soviets had made nuclear arms a dubious option.

Subsequently, the fall of the shah of Iran, along with the successes of Soviet-backed, left-led liberation struggles and coups in a number of Third World countries – Angola, Mozambique, Guinea-Bissau, Ethiopia, Nicaragua, Grenada, Afghanistan and Zimbabwe – suggested that the Soviet Union might indeed be capable of anchoring a world revolutionary process. (Moscow actually backed a losing faction in Zimbabwe, but quickly switched its support to the ultimate victors.) As a result of this 'revolutionary wave', the Soviet conception of peaceful coexistence increasingly reverted to its Stalinist meaning in which socialist expansion, directed by Moscow, became a more active ingredient in the formulation of Soviet strategy.

The Third World and the Path of 'Non-capitalist Development'

In its original formulation in 1960, the International Communist Movement had listed the three main components of the world revolutionary process in the following sequence: 'The peoples who are building socialism and communism, the revolutionary movement of the working class in the capitalist countries (and) the national liberation struggle of the oppressed peoples.' [18]   (It also was seen as attracting 'the peasantry, the working intelligentsia, urban petty bourgeois strata, students, democratic elements of the armed forces and, in some countries, segments of exploitative classes – anti-imperialist elements of the national bourgeoisie'.)[19]

Brezhnev's 1976 report to the CPSU's 25th Congress introduced a subtle but highly significant shift in this progression. 'Actually existing socialism' was still first in the hierarchy of forces. But now 'the victories of the national liberation movement [which were] opening up new horizons for countries that have won independence' was cited as the second component. In third place was 'the class struggle of the working people' which, while 'gaining in intensity', was no longer referred to as a 'revolutionary movement'.

This elevation of the national liberation movements and down grading of the workers' struggle in the advanced capitalist countries was a major theoretical and political shift for the Soviets. In part, it was a reflection of the real political dynamic in the world indicating where the only successful challenges to imperialist hegemony were taking place. But the shift was also the culmination of almost two decades during which Moscow had – with some significant success – sought to expand its influence in the Third World.

As the colonial system began to collapse in the 1950s, an urgent political question presented itself to Soviet leaders. In a world characterized by the 'struggle between the two opposing social systems', which way would the newly independent countries go? From a classic Marxist point of view, it would seem almost inevitable that such countries, without the material prerequisites for socialism, would have to develop their economies along capitalist lines. But if this were the case, such countries clearly would be drawn into – or, more precisely, remain in (albeit under somewhat altered terms) – the world capitalist economy.

The theoretical answer to this dilemma was the thesis of the 'non-capitalist path' of development, subsequently called the 'path of socialist orientation'. According to this thesis, economically underdeveloped countries can by-pass capitalism – or significantly shorten the period in which capitalist production relations are extant – 'by a strict and consistent reliance on a union with states in the world socialist community'.[20] A subsequent Marxist-Leninist text called the thesis of 'non-capitalist development': 'a concept of the transformation of economically backward countries into socialism, bypassing or terminating the capitalist stage at an early phase .... The concept is an integral part of Marxism-Leninism.'[21]

According to this theory, a country taking the path of 'non-capitalist development' would not attempt an immediate socialist transformation. Its aim, rather, would be to develop and give priority to non-capitalist economic forms while curtailing and strictly limiting the sphere of activity of the remaining capitalist institutions – especially those controlled and dominated by the most powerful capitalist banks and institutions. Large industry would be gradually nationalized while middle and small capital would be regulated and increasingly restricted. Agriculture would be collectivized very slowly, beginning with a system of voluntary cooperatives. A socialist system would be built incrementally, principally by prioritizing and expanding the state sector. Replacing the role previously played by large-scale foreign capital would be a policy of 'broad cooperation with the socialist states'.[22] Ultimately the country would be drawn into and integrated with the world socialist system.

Similarly, the political system of such a state would be closely modeled after the Soviet form of the dictatorship of the proletariat. Such states, according to the most definitive Soviet text on the subject, 'reject bour-geois-democracy' and, along with it, insistence on such forms as 'bourgeois parliamentarism, pluralism of political parties, and individualistic concepts of the rights and liberties of citizens'.[23] To implement this program, a 'vanguard revolutionary party' would be indispensable, its role being to direct the country's course 'in accordance with the basic principles of scientific socialism'.[24] The party-state relationship which operates in all the countries of 'actually existing socialism' – where the ultimate authority in all matters rests with the party rather than the state – is likewise seen as the form of rule in 'socialist oriented states'. Accordingly:

> The party must actually determine the political course, guide and constantly control the functioning of state bodies and public organi-zations ... [and] strive to turn state power into a chief instrument for building a new society and the party into society's guiding force .... The party guides the establishment of a new system of state power, the power of the working people, and the work of all state bodies. The party guides the working people's revolutionary activity ... by reinforcing state bodies with politically conscious and competent party workers. [25]

Finally, and never to be forgotten, is that 'the objective prerequisite' for the 'non-capitalist' path 'is the existence of the world system of socialism, which determines the main direction and the basic tendency of historical progress'.[26]

This scenario proved attractive to a number of newly independent Third World governments for several reasons: it promised an infusion of Soviet aid – military as well as economic – to governments with few resources; it provided developing countries with a bargaining lever to be used with capitalist investors; and it provided 'socialist' legitimacy for nationalist-oriented one-party military regimes, many of whom had come to power by way of coups. (Later, the phrase 'non-capitalist develop-ment' would be gradually replaced by 'the socialist oriented state'.)

The virtue of this approach for Moscow was that it corrected the self-defeating, sectarian policy which, in emphasizing the unreliability of the 'national bourgeoisie', had kept the Soviet Union isolated from the main political currents in the Third World. Now it could seek warm relations with countries such as Egypt, India, Indonesia, Algeria and Guinea headed by those (like Nehru and Nasser) who had become newly designated 'national democrats'. Further, the realignment of the Third World (or a major portion of it) with the world socialist system would undermine the foundations of imperialism economically and thereby provide the impetus for the radicalization of the workers in the developed capitalist countries.

The catch in this theoretical construct, however, was that there was virtually no basis in the actual conditions prevailing in any of the dominated countries for socialist consciousness or socialist relations of production to take hold. These countries were still far removed from even the level of industrialization in Russia of 1917. Of course, the theory had carefully noted that 'socialist orientation' was not the same as socialism. But in practice, its actual scenario of curtailing capitalist development amounted to the same thing, since it was a program for interfering with the very economic processes these countries needed in order to overcome underdevelopment.

This theoretical shift heralded the beginning of a massive Soviet economic and political offensive. Extensive aid – generally provided at much lower interest rates than the West was offering – focused on helping the recipients build up the state sector of their economies. Among the major beneficiaries were India's state steel industry and the Algerian oil industry. The new direction was warmly welcomed by many Third World leaders who saw in it a means for both industrializing on the cheap and completing the break with their former masters. In a number of cases, local Communist Parties became supporters of regimes which previously they had been trying to overthrow.

In the short run, this turn in Soviet policy was aimed at weakening the West's hegemonic presence in the Third World. But it was also part of that long-range strategy which continued to see expansion of the Soviet-dominated 'socialist camp' as the course of the world transition to socialism. As a Soviet political analyst in the glasnost era 30 years later put it:

> As to the policy in the Third World, it was believed that peaceful coexistence could not apply to this part of the globe. It was there that the antagonistic contest between the two systems was being decided ... that the center of the military rivalry with the US was located. The focal point of policy in the Third World was the desire to put as many countries as possible under our control and do as much damage as possible to the other side's interests. This was veiled by the philosophy of solidarity with progressive regimes and support for social transformations, although in reality the ideological motives and, all the more so, a real assessment of the nature of the regime and its policy vis-a-vis its people did not have substantial meaning .... We promoted the creation of regimes in different parts of the world that tried, under the banner of anti-imperialism, to implement in their own conditions the administer-by-command model and therefore counted on us in everything.[27]

Class Struggle in the Capitalist Countries

No Marxist-Leninist theory of world revolution could completely omit the newly downgraded third pillar of the world revolutionary triad – the working-class movement in the most advanced capitalist countries. All other considerations aside, the Communist Parties in those countries would have balked at any formulation that did not refer to the forces they supposedly led as playing one of the main roles in it. But, as a practical matter, the inner circle of those who constituted the leadership of world communism had long since given up the notion that the working class in the capitalist heartland was imbued with a revolutionary outlook, let alone preparing for revolution.

This did not prevent Marxist-Leninist propaganda from hailing the growing 'revolutionary consciousness' supposedly sweeping proletarian ranks everywhere in the capitalist world. Thus, even as anti-working-class offensives in Britain, Germany and the US were scoring major successes, a 1981 Soviet text announced that 'The class struggle in the capitalist countries has entered a new phase when ... socio-political crises are shaking the whole system to the very foundations, threatening the rule of monopoly capital.' [28]

Undismayed by the inroads of Reaganism and Thatcherism – and their equivalents elsewhere – a 1983 Soviet assessment held that 'The formation of the essential subjective conditions for the transition from capitalism to socialism' in the imperialist countries 'can be seen from the growth of the consciousness and organization of the working class, from its readiness for mass revolutionary action'.[29] Two years later, a definitive Marxist-Leninist study cited 'Documents of the fraternal communist parties' to show that 'today socialist transformations in the developed capitalist countries are quite imminent'.[30]

All this was hard to take seriously even at the time. In fact, further description of the actual class struggles of the period focused much more on such phenomena as strikes and parliamentary gains by communist and socialist parties. Even these were exaggerated, however, as strikes were transformed into 'unprecedented strike waves' and elusive 'leftward shifts' in the trade unions and other sectors of the population were constantly being discovered.[31]

It is tempting to attribute such perennial optimism to ideological blinkers; and, perhaps, in middle and lower levels of leadership in the communist movement, this was the case. But in the higher echelons of the movement, among those who were responsible for formulating policy, these extravagances were not simply the fruits of dogmatism. Reminiscent of capitalism's perennial claim in the midst of economic difficulties that 'prosperity is just around the corner', party leaders felt the need constantly to renew the ideological underpinnings of the party faithful in order to keep the light of revolutionary commitment blazing in otherwise depressing circumstances. Such reassurances were needed not only for communists toiling in the capitalist vineyards but also for the peoples of the socialist countries since the spread of socialism to the developed capitalist countries, was expected to bring the scarcities and other hardships of life under 'actually existing socialism' to an end.

Likewise, leaders of national parties in the capitalist world needed a record of accomplishments in order to retain their posts and accompanying privileges – such as control over Soviet-supplied funds and access to Soviet leaders. Reliable Soviet Marxist-Leninists were happy to help out these loyal deputies by quoting their own self-estimates and lending them the ultimate theoretical authority only publication in a Soviet theoretical text – or an invitation to speak at a Soviet-sponsored congress – could provide. Nay-sayers could then be dismissed as lacking confidence in the working class, clearly the first step down the path of revisionist perdition.

In truth, Soviet strategists had long since written off the prospects for revolution – let alone communist-led revolution – in the capitalist core. At best, the communists might be able to help create a favorable ideological climate for peaceful coexistence and to assist the trade unions in maintaining pressure on the capitalist economy. These may be useful – indeed admirable – goals. But they have one shortcoming. Their pursuit hardly requires an ideologically tempered, disciplined pro-Soviet vanguard party. And without that broader vision of being part of the process of bringing about world socialism, there would be little basis for the level of commitment required to maintain the sacrifice and discipline of those who saw themselves as a revolutionary vanguard.

The International Communist Movement

While the theory of the world revolutionary process emphasized three component parts, a fourth *operational* component was, in the final analysis, the crucial one:

> The unity of revolutionary forces is achieved through purpose-oriented, conscious activities of the most active political force of today, i.e. of the International Communist Movement. The communist parties which are the most trained and conscious detachment of revolutionary forces, equipped with the truly scientific theory of social development, cement the entire revolutionary process. They are the core of the fraternal union of the socialist countries and various detachments of the international working class and national liberation movements, promoting cooperation with revolutionary democratic parties and all the democratic and progressive forces in the world.[32]

Identifying the omniscient force which is to direct the world revolutionary process as the International Communist Movement is, of course, a common euphemism in the Marxist-Leninist vocabulary. Much more precise is Boris Ponomarev: 'The Communist and Workers' Parties of the socialist countries form the advance detachment of the International Communist Movement. Under their leadership the prototype of a new society for all mankind is being created.' [33]

In the framework of the operative power relationships between Communist Parties, the hierarchical categories delineated for leadership of the world revolutionary process – the International Communist Movement as guiding force; the governing parties as the 'advance detachment'; the Soviet Union, as ever, 'heading' the 'socialist camp' – it is readily apparent that the theory was rooted in the paradigm of a world transition to socialism through the continuous expansion of a Soviet-dominated 'socialist camp' directing a world socialist system modeled after and integrated into the Soviet Union's administrative-command economy.

Critique of the World Revolutionary Process

When first advanced, the world revolutionary process appeared to be a more sensible strategy for serving the cause of socialism than previous theories of world revolution. The theory put to rest the fantasy of a direct, coordinated assault on the heart of world capitalism, a venture which inevitably would have led to a nuclear showdown between the US and the Soviet Union. Nor does it assume, despite the obligatory rhetoric to the contrary, that the workers in the capitalist countries are ready for revolution or that the newly independent countries of the Third World could quickly build socialism. And its positing of the 'socialist camp' as the anchor for the international class struggle certainly seemed more realistic than reliance on these other class and political actors.

For a while, the new policies enjoyed some success. Significant Soviet economic assistance combined with aggressive political support for the Third World at the United Nations and in international relations generally facilitated a greater Soviet presence in the Middle East than ever before. One result was the undermining of the Central Treaty Organization – a US attempt to forge a NATO-like Middle East military alliance stretching from Turkey to Pakistan. Supporting Vietnam, aiding and (in effect) protecting Cuba, supplying needed resources, capital and expertise to countries such as India, Egypt and Algeria, the Soviet Union increasingly was seen as the Third World's champion against the other superpower.

But the theory of the world revolutionary process was rooted in quicksand. Long before the Soviet collapse made the entire issue moot, the thesis had foundered in the canyon between the optimistic assessments on which it was based and world realities. By far the most damaging were the false assumptions about the capacity, strength and viability of 'actually existing socialism' and the systems and institutions it spawned.

How Strong the 'Socialist Anchor'?

A resolution adopted at the 1960 meeting of the Communist and Workers Parties concluded that as a result of the expansion of socialism and the gains of the anti-colonial movement, there had been a

> shift in the balance of forces in the international arena in favor of socialism encompassing the sphere of the economy in which existing socialism steadily gains momentum in its development; ... it extends to the military-strategic area in which a strategic-military parity has been achieved ...; it also covers the moral and political sphere in which the authority of the world revolutionary forces and international communist movement has immeasurably grown.[34]

Shortly thereafter, the 1961 program of the CPSU predicted that by the beginning of the 1970s the Soviet Union would surpass the US in production and would become, sometime in the 1980s, a fully communist society. By then, the program stated, economic scarcity would be completely eliminated so that money would no longer be needed. All active citizens would work eight hours a day for the benefit of society and obtain whatever they needed or wanted from state-run warehouse stores. The social surplus would be so large that non-active members of society – the young, the infirm and the aged – would likewise have all their needs met.

These appraisals notwithstanding, however, the combined economic-military strength of the US and its allies was far superior to that enjoyed by the Moscow-led bloc. By the beginning of the 1980s, the NATO countries' sum of economic indices was more than 2.5 times higher than the USSR's. Nevertheless, the USSR – with a much smaller economic base – was spending twice the percentage of its national income on military purposes than the US was. And unlike the US, the Soviet Union could not count on any tangible assistance from its allies.

Consequently, while Marxism-Leninism could continue to trumpet capitalism's crises and socialism's strengths, the real strengths and weaknesses of the various forces represented by the two systems, the two blocs and the two superpowers, and the actual relationship between them, began to assert themselves.

Soviet leaders may have derived satisfaction from being accorded the 'leading role' in the world revolutionary process. But, as always, there was a quid pro quo. However great the honor, being the 'anchor' (and banker) of a process embracing national liberation movements in underdeveloped countries, desperately poor and densely populated Third World countries, relatively backward socialist countries and resource-scarce Communist Parties (to say nothing of the arms race) came with a price tag.

National liberation movements – particularly those facing US-backed counter-insurgencies – needed supplies, resources and relatively sophisticated arms with which to conduct their struggles against oppressive regimes and to manage liberated areas. In some cases they might need troops – and whether these came from other socialist countries such as Cuba or from the Soviet Union itself (as in Afghanistan), the bill would ultimately wind up in Moscow. In the case of Vietnam, which faced sophisticated American weaponry and 500,000 US troops, the material aid supplied by the Soviet Union was enormous.

Likewise, by trying to draw various Third World countries into close relations, the Soviet Union found itself making costly unfavorable trade deals, loans with little likelihood of repayment and massive arms 'sales' with limited prospects for collecting on their invoices.

At the same time, most of the countries of the 'socialist camp' – themselves locked into the economically inefficient Soviet model of socialism – had to be subsidized. Add to all this a period of stagnation during which the Soviet economy barely grew, together with Moscow's own growing burden of expenditures in order to achieve and then maintain military/nuclear parity with the US, and the costs became astronomical. In short, the assistance rendered a variety of peoples, governments and movements may have been admirable, but it was far beyond the Soviet system's actual capacities.

As a result, when the US, under the Reagan administration, launched its 'Empire-Strikes-Back' counter-offensive of the 1980s, the already existing strains in the Soviet economy began to approach breaking point. Something had to give. Moscow could not maintain its support for national liberation movements, Third World allies and the other countries of the 'socialist camp', and, at the same time, keep up with the US in the arms race and continue to subsidize inefficient factories and farms at home.

The signs of trouble were everywhere. The 'revolutionary wave' of the 1960s and 1970s was rapidly receding. Costly civil wars in Afghanistan, Angola, Ethiopia and Kampuchea were draining Soviet resources. Already huge economic subsidies to Cuba and Vietnam were growing. A popularly based opposition movement in Poland was barely under control. Some Third World allies began switching their allegiances, turning to the US for help. The promise that Nicaragua and El Salvador would expand the socialist beachhead in Central America was fading rapidly. Adding to Soviet economic woes, world oil prices had been dropping drastically since the mid-1970s, thereby reducing Moscow's main source of hard currency. And looming over this impending debacle was the omen of a newly intensified arms race with a US government seemingly determined to undo the losses of the previous two decades.

The CPSU's turn to Mikhail Gorbachev in order to defuse the

crisis of Soviet foreign policy and bring the country out of economic stagnation was itself the most telling reflection of the fact that the role of 'anchor' for the world revolutionary process was becoming an intolerable burden for the Soviet system. Central to Gorbachev's hotly debated 'new thinking' in the realm of international affairs was the effort to ease and, where possible, rid the Soviet Union of that burden.

How Deep the Crisis of Capitalism?

Locked into Lenin's thesis on the 'moribund' nature of world capitalism, Marxism-Leninism either obscured or derided all phenomena suggesting the contrary. Downturns were exaggerated while upswings were pooh-poohed. Structural adjustments to the growing internationalization of the world capitalist economy were characterized as an ominous 'structural crisis' further deepening the 'general crisis of capitalism'. And Soviet theoreticians saw the scientific and technical revolution more as the harbinger of yet another 'crisis' for capitalism rather than a source of renewal. Only socialism, they declared in the face of a growing body of evidence to the contrary, could truly and fully utilize this development.

Marxism-Leninism also thoroughly misread the impact that the end of colonialism would have on world capitalism. Asserting that the demise of the colonial system represented a 'new [third] stage in the general crisis of capitalism', Marxism-Leninism saw postcolonial capitalism as simply trying to replicate the old relationships between colony and mother country:

> The imperialist monopolies are doing everything they can to prevent the industrialization of the developing countries which they are trying to retain as hewers of wood and drawers of water for the industrially developed capitalist world. [35]

Based on old formulas, this analysis failed to grasp the actual historical processes at work in both the developed capitalist countries and the Third World. Although virtually all the imperial powers strongly resisted their colonies' demands for independence– France fought two bitter and costly wars in a vain effort to retain Vietnam and Algeria – the end of colonialism was, in many ways, a boon for world capitalism as a whole.

For as mechanization drove growing numbers of peasants off the land in the former colonies, world capital found in the newly independent states a vast new potential from a new cheap laborforce which could now be harnessed to industry. Aided immeasurably by the revolution in science and technology, giant corporations were now able to fine-tune their division of labor on a world scale, assigning different processes and functions to their plants in different countries. New financial instruments of expansion – transnational banks and corporations – facilitated investments in and trade with the new states. Third World countries such as South Korea, Thailand, Brazil, Egypt, Singapore and Taiwan went through a period of rapid industrialization and have already taken a share of the world market in certain industrial products away from the more developed capitalist countries.

In addition, because along with political independence came the end of the economic monopoly each colonial country enjoyed in its own possessions, the former colonies could now attract investment and trade from a large number of sources. None of this is to suggest that the fuller expansion of capitalism into the Third World has been an unalloyed blessing for these countries who now enjoy – even more than before – all the benefits of capitalist exploitation. But contrary to Marxist-Leninist predictions, world capitalism does not seem to have suffered at all from the fall of colonialism; nor is it scheming to prevent industrialization in the Third World.

How Viable the Path of 'Non-capitalist Development'?

Following formal adoption of the thesis at a meeting of the International Communist Movement in 1960, Marxist-Leninist theoreticians set out to demonstrate that the idea of 'non-capitalist development' had its origins in the writings of Marx, Engels and Lenin. This unfortunate habit of seeking ideological authority from the ikons of 'scientific socialism' has led Marxism-Leninism down many an ingenious path, but few more makeshift – and costly – than this one.

As a result of this legitimating effort, Soviet theoretical texts on 'non-capitalist development' or 'socialist orientation' are replete with general assertions and judiciously edited quotations from the founding fathers suggesting that such a path was not only possible for economically 'backward' countries, but absolutely certain. One went so far as to assert that Engels believed that 'the colonial countries...were sure to bypass capitalism'. [36]

It is worth reviewing this attempt to find ideological authority for the concept of 'non-capitalist development', not simply to demonstrate Marxism-Leninism's theoretical irresponsibility. More to the point, the comments by Marx, Engels and Lenin help to demonstrate the ways in which the Soviet version of this concept was riddled with non-materialist assumptions.

An examination of their writings on the subject – and they are few and far between – shows that Marx and Engels, to the extent they considered 'non-capitalist development' a possibility, always tied it to two absolutely essential conditions. First, they believed it applied only to peoples living in predominantly pre-capitalist societies, – that is, countries at a fairly low level of economic development in which capitalist relations of commerce and production had barely appeared; and second, that the main bastions of world capitalism would already have tumbled and that socialism would have been established there. Thus Engels writes:

> It is not only possible but inescapable that once the proletariat wins out and the means of production pass into common ownership among the West European nations, the countries which have just managed to make a start with capitalist production and where tribal institutions or relics of them are still intact will be able to use these relics of communal ownership and the corresponding popular customs as a powerful means of considerably shortening their advance to socialist society and largely sparing themselves the sufferings and the struggles through which we in Western Europe have to make our way. But an inevitable condition of this is the example and active support of the hitherto capitalist West. Only when the capitalist economy has been overcome at home and in the countries of its prime, only when the retarded countries have seen from their example 'how it's done', how the productive forces of modern industry are made to work as social property for society as a whole – only then will the retarded countries be able to start on this abbreviated process of development. But then their success will be assured.[37]

Lenin fared no better at the hands of the quotation-mongers, whose most frequent citation was the following:

> Are we to consider as correct the assertion that the capitalist stage of economic development is inevitable for backward nations?... We replied in the negative. If the victorious proletariat conducts systematic propaganda among them, and the Soviet governments come to their aid with all the means at their disposal – in that event it will be mistaken to assume that the backward peoples must inevitably go through the capitalist stage of development.... With the aid of the proletariat of the advanced countries, backward countries can go over to the Soviet system and, through certain stages of development, to communism, without having to pass through the capitalist stage.[38]

Like Marx and Engels, Lenin also emphasized that the absolute precondition for countries bypassing capitalism was the triumph of socialism in those countries where capitalism had reached its productive and technological pinnacle. But the Marxist-Leninist version of 'non-capitalist development' drastically altered these propositions even while citing their authors as legitimating authority for its own theory.

The most significant change, of course, was substituting the 'world socialist system' for the 'hitherto capitalist West' as the source of the economic support and ideological example that would make a non-capitalist path possible. This theoretical sleight-of-hand overlooked the crucial considerations which had led Marx, Engels and Lenin to their conclusions.

For one thing, the overthrow of imperialist regimes in West Europe and North America would remove the one force most likely to fight, militarily and economically, to prevent Third World countries from taking the non-capitalist path. If the West became socialist, the very strength of the old capitalist system could be turned against it as new economically advanced socialist countries would be able to assist the most underdeveloped countries. But the actual 'world socialist system' was far from being the economic equal of world capitalism. It was, in fact, a secondary world system which, instead of representing a new, advanced mode of production based on breakthroughs in the productive forces, was based on and locked into the already outmoded productive forces. In short, the world socialist system simply did not have the wherewithal or the potential to play the role assigned it by the theory of the world revolutionary process.

For another, the theory of 'non-capitalist development' also ignored Marx and Engels' qualification that such a path might be possible *only* in those countries where capitalism had not yet – or just barely – appeared. Instead, Marxism-Leninism looked primarily to those Third World countries where communist-led national liberation movements were the leading political force or to those where bourgeois-nationalist regimes (Egypt, Syria, Algeria, for instance) held sway.

The fact is that the theory of 'non-capitalist development' owes much more to Stalin than to Marx, Engels or Lenin. Just as Stalin's 1929 'Great Turn' was designed to use 'socialism' to create the material conditions for a socialist society in the USSR, so 'non-capitalist development' would play the same function in Third World countries. The theory thus reflects Stalin's voluntarist notions of the primacy of politics over economics and of the superstructure over the base, both of which may be applicable during the period immediately preceding and immediately following the revolutionary seizure of power, but never as a permanent condition of social development.

Suffice it to say, therefore, that the Marxist credentials of the CPSU's actual theory of 'non-capitalist development' are dubious. Even more to the point, however, the theory was hopelessly flawed by its own assumptions and perspectives. In practice, all the carefully constructed qualifications regarding the 'gradual' and 'voluntary' nature of the process went quickly by the board under the pressure of unchecked power politics. In the end, the main result of 'non-capitalist development' was to curtail the general economic development of those countries which had embarked on that path.

For virtually every Third World country has discovered that it needs investments of foreign capital in order to develop its industry and economic infrastructure. In no country of 'socialist orientation' was the Soviet Union able adequately to fill the vacuum left by the total expulsion of foreign capital. Today, all the countries which once trod the non-capitalist path are urgently seeking investment from international capital. (A more realistic policy would have been to try to negotiate better terms in that relationship.)

The bottom line in all this, however, is that the theory of 'non-capitalist development' stems from and is another form of Stalin's concept of the world's transition to socialism by way of continuous expansion of the 'socialist camp' under the leadership of the Soviet Union. Thus, Marxist-Leninist theoreticians insisted that the success of 'socialist orientation' was totally dependent on ever closer ties to the Soviet Union, to the point of 'a union with states in the world socialist community'.[39] (Indeed, the main precedent usually cited for the thesis was the 'socialist transformation' of the Soviet Union's Central Asian republics in the 1920s, a process which obviously presupposed their political incorporation into the USSR.)

Another text goes even further. Asserting that 'cooperation with the world socialist system is vital to the progress of developing countries', it declares that 'this cooperation is comprehensive; it comprises practically every domain of international relations: political, economic, cultural and military.' [40]

Still, 'socialist orientation' did enable the Soviet Union to break out of the earlier sectarianism which had kept it isolated from many of the most important forces in the anti-colonial movement. Enticed by offers of aid and trade on significantly more favorable terms than those proffered by the US, a number of newly independent Third World countries whose governments would earlier have been denounced as 'neocolonial puppets' developed close ties with Moscow. New and unprecedented economic links gave the Soviets a foothold in Africa and Asia where contacts hitherto had been limited to political relations with communist governments and communist-led national liberation movements. The new relationship was reflected at the United Nations, where the West openly fretted over the growing clout of what looked like a Third World–socialist voting bloc.

As the anti-colonial movement continued to register successes and a number of newly independent Third World countries declared themselves 'socialist'; as the US was stymied in Vietnam and successfully defied by Cuba; and as the elements of a political bloc between the Third World and the 'socialist camp' began to emerge, Marxism-Leninism hailed these events as proof of a new 'revolutionary tide' demonstrating that 'The historical tendency towards non-capitalist development in Asia and Africa is becoming irreversible.' [41]

These phenomena, however, were much more the hallmarks of the final stages of the anti-colonial movement than the beginning of a new

socialist surge. The downfall of colonialism was, of course, no small matter. But 'socialist orientation' was hardly the success Marxism-Leninism
claimed it to be. Soviet aid and investments – particularly given Moscow's emphasis on building up the state sector of the economy – proved
no match for the resources, skills and flexibility of capitalism. As a result, industrialization in countries pursuing 'non-capitalist development'
lagged considerably behind those where Western capital chose to invest.
In the end, just as the East European socialist states regarded their
West European counterparts with a degree of longing and envy, so too
most 'socialist-oriented states' could not help but notice the economic
advances of their more capitalist-oriented counterparts.

Examining 'socialist orientation' with the benefit of historical hindsight, it is clear that the theory was rife with contradictions, misassessments, dogmatic attempts to impose Marxist-Leninist formulas, wishful
thinking and no small degree of shortsighted political and ideological
pragmatism.

From the point of theory, perhaps its most fundamental error was
that it obscured the crucial distinction between bourgeois-democratic
revolutions and socialist revolutions. The anti-colonial revolution was
fundamentally a bourgeois-democratic impulse reflecting two facts: that
the colonial system had become a political and economic anachronism
which was holding back the full development of capitalism in the
colonized countries; and, to borrow Lenin's apt formulation for one of
the essential conditions for revolution, that the rising bourgeois classes
of the colonies could no longer 'live in the old way'.

But, as Marx was fond of pointing out, ruling classes rarely recognize
– let alone submit to – the fact that the existing order has become a
fetter on development. As a result, the Third World was vibrant with the
spirit of revolution, a reality which, in a number of cases, enabled
communists and other radicals to win leadership of national liberation
struggles. Coinciding with the Soviet Union's interest in weakening its
international adversaries and a radicalism-provoking alienation among the
young in the West, this tended to invest the anti-colonial struggle with a
significance which went far beyond its actual capacity.

The theory of 'socialist orientation' reinforced that tendency. Convinced, as ever, that world capitalism was in its death throes, Marxist-
Leninists saw the anti-colonial revolution as a new stage in the general
crisis of capitalism. The end of colonialism, they argued, would further
aggravate the deteriorating economic condition of the capitalist countries
while more and more countries would adopt the path of 'socialist
orientation'.

Unfortunately, this unwarranted and self-serving assessment obscured
the real gains of the anti-colonial movement. For by imposing an
ill-conceived and unwarranted 'socialist orientation' on the movement,
Marxism-Leninism raised expectations that inevitably were frustrated.
Ridding themselves of the yoke of open, fascist-like domination which is

the political hallmark of colonialism, the peoples of the newly independent countries opened up vast new possibilities for gaining a measure of
control over their individual and collective lives. In doing so they
brought into being more favorable conditions for the untrammeled
development in their countries not of socialism but of capitalism.

In addition, the theory was corrupted from the outset by Moscow's
aptitude for attaching the 'socialist' label to Third World countries
willing to cooperate with it. A few national liberation movements laid
claim to orthodox Marxist-Leninist principles, the most popular of
which was the concept of a one-party system headed by a (not
necessarily communist) vanguard. But attempts to implement the
economic prescriptions of the 'non-capitalist path' invariably foundered
– some rather quickly, others after the Soviet Union itself collapsed.

Much more common were states supposedly taking the non-capitalist
path by proclaiming a variety of 'African' and 'Arab' socialisms. The
fallacy in uncritically placing all of these under the 'socialist orientation'
umbrella was pointed out as early as 1977 by a leading Soviet scholar
on the Third World, who noted:

> Though there is a wide range of nuances, we are in effect dealing in
> all cases with an idealization of the historical past of the people in
> question, an idealization of patriarchal relations and patriarchal or
> even religious ideology, an ideology that is not only petty bourgeois
> but also at times nationalistic.[42]

A telling example of what such 'unique socialisms' mean was expressed
by Julius Nyerere, head of state of Tanzania, a country whose 'socialist
orientation' was perennially celebrated by Marxist-Leninist theoreticians.
To Nyerere, pre-colonial Africa had been 'socialist' until capitalism
corrupted it by introducing notions of personal enrichment:

> In traditional African life the people were equal, they cooperated
> together, and they participated in all the decisions which affected
> their lives .... Our task, therefore, is to modernize the traditional
> structure so as to make it meet our new aspirations for a higher
> standard of living. This can be done provided we hold fast to the
> basic principles of traditional living, while we adapt its techniques to
> those of the twentieth century.[43]

Whatever one may think of Nyerere's vision or of other forms of
African and Arab socialism, it is clear that they have little in common
with the Marxist-Leninist concept of 'socialist orientation'. The socialisms thus proclaimed may indeed have been 'petty bourgeois and
nationalistic' in outlook. But this was the natural tendency in states
where a majority of the population were small landholders and an
embryonic national bourgeoisie was seeking to undermine the power

of foreign capital and to remove all the old impediments to capitalist development.

The theory of 'socialist orientation' also glossed over many of the objective difficulties facing countries attempting to take that path. For one thing, their economies remained indelibly tied to and dominated by their former colonial 'mother' countries. Calls to end the ties with foreign capital may have a pleasing ideological ring but, in the absence of a viable alternative, are more than likely to go unheeded by business people, enterprise managers, technologists, government officials and the mass of the population seeking consumer products.

The theory also disregarded the question of what class base 'socialist orientation' would rely on. In a number of countries, the working class was miniscule; in others it was weak and/or poorly organized. In many cases the workers were still ideologically in thrall to outmoded ideas and fettered by traditional social ties. Even where wage-labor made up a large percentage of the population (30–50 percent), the overwhelming majority of such workers were employed as farmhands and day laborers.[44]

The peasants who often provided the mass base for national liberation struggles tended to be politically passive after independence was achieved; and, given the low level of mechanization in agriculture, were not particularly enthused by schemes that would subordinate their individual holdings to cooperatives, let alone state-supervised collectives.

Not surprisingly, Third World 'revolutionary' governments – many of whom came to power by way of military coups by young nationalistic officers – relied mainly on the armed forces, the urban petty and middle bourgeoisie, professionals, intellectuals and students. All of these were attracted to the notion of 'socialist orientation' principally by the promises of substantial aid from the 'socialist camp' as a means of overcoming their countries' economic backwardness.

Aleksei Kiva, one-time head of the Sector of the Working Class and Communist Movement at the USSR Academy of Sciences Institute of Oriental Studies, offers a behind-the-scenes insight into the way in which pragmatic political considerations distorted theoretical work:

> Shortly after Anwar Sadat's accession to power in Egypt, I wrote an article about new social and economic developments in that country. A scientific journal refused to publish the article for fear of offending Sadat even though the article did not attack either him or his regime but spoke merely of a reorientation of the country's development toward capitalism .... In editing an article on socialist-oriented countries written by the director of an academic institute, I crossed Egypt out of the list of those countries on my own initiative. But I was asked to put it back on the plea that otherwise the Egyptians would be offended. I had to comply. It was logic turned upside down.[45]

As Kiva points out:

The enthusiasm of non-proletarian supporters of socialism dwindled as our country entered the period of stagnation and we began to experience difficulties in rendering new states highly effective assistance, while the public sector, which we advertised for a long time as a sure means of achieving rapid economic progress, failed to meet expectations and cooperation in production miscarried almost everywhere.[46]

In terms of maintaining a 'socialist orientation', therefore, it was really the Soviet Union and the 'world socialist system' – a force external to the developing country – which were seen as guaranteeing the socialist path. In other words, designating a country as one of 'socialist orientation' was a means of seeking ideological legitimacy for the Soviet attempt to expand its influence in the Third World. This point was unmistakably driven home when, after the collapse of the Soviet Union and the 'socialist camp', most of the 'socialist-oriented states' found themselves unable to sustain the path of 'non-capitalist development' on the basis of their own resources.

But while the Soviet collapse clearly hastened the process, there was already abundant evidence indicating that Marxist-Leninist predictions of the viability of a 'non-capitalist path' for newly liberated Third World nations were foundering.

Efforts to follow a path of 'non-capitalist development' in countries as diverse as Mozambique, Nicaragua, Afghanistan, Burma, Laos, Ethiopia, Angola and South Yemen all turned out to be unworkable. In other cases, revolutionary movements – as in South Africa and El Salvador – made major adjustments in their programs which, in effect, recognized that attempts to curtail capitalist growth would be counterproductive. Vietnam has introduced significant elements of capitalism back into its economy, while China has embarked on an ambitious program of economic liberalization and rampant private enterprise which has resulted in an extraordinary rate of economic growth. (Held in place by a still powerful and authoritarian Communist Party, the system has been called – with no small measure of pointed irony – 'market-Leninism'.) [47]

Summing up the experience of the Sandinistas in Nicaragua, Victor Tirado, a central figure in that revolution, declared after the 1990 Sandinista electoral defeat:

The cycle of anti-imperialist revolutions conceived of in the 1950s is finished .... Today the best we can aspire to is coexistence with imperialism, even though it hurts to say so. To have good relations with them and that they let us develop. We cannot jump stages .... It is a lesson we must learn.[48]

Clearly it is a lesson that has been learned by virtually every country which attempted to implement the concept of 'socialist orientation'.

It continues to be argued by many defenders of the old dogma that these losses and 'retreats' are principally due to American-sponsored subversion – as though superior US military and economic strength is not itself an objective reflection of capitalism's capacities. But such arguments merely obscure the fact that neither 'socialist orientation' nor socialism had any real internal foundation in the Third World and instead were based on glaring misassessments of the supposed strength and 'maturity' of world socialism and the supposed debilitating condition of world capitalism. (Even in the case of Afghanistan, where Soviet military strength was far greater than the anti-government forces supplied with outside aid, the cause of a 'socialist-oriented' government still proved unavailing.)

Clearly it is time to recognize that earlier hopes that the Third World would turn into a bastion of anti-capitalism had little basis other than the wishful thinking of romantic revolutionaries and ultra-left socialists. Now it is necessary to face up to the fact that the appearance and growth of capitalism in new states emerging from colonial and imperialist domination is a historically progressive development. 'The bourgeoisie', Marx and Engels noted, 'has created more massive and more colossal productive forces than have all preceding generations together'.[49] And it is certainly not open to question that the unleashing of already known productive forces is the number one economic priority for developing countries. Indeed, it is this precise quality of capitalism that is crucial to setting the conditions that make socialism possible. Therefore, as Kiva points out, 'To oppose capitalist development when capitalism is on the rise and there is no real alternative to it nor a revolutionary situation would mean adopting a reactionary position.'[50]

Despite the consequent misery for millions, the expansion of nineteenth century capitalism could not be stopped. This is also the case with capitalist expansion into the Third World in this century and its further extension in the postcolonial period. No matter what the alignment of political forces, a return to pre-capitalist social formations is impossible. Nor will it be possible for these developing countries to establish socialist societies until and unless they achieve a level of economic development commensurate with that of the most developed capitalist countries. (Lenin's opinion that this process may be significantly shortened if and when socialism wins out in the capitalist heartland may still be valid, but that is not the situation at present, nor was it even when there was a Soviet Union and a 'socialist camp'.) Therefore, the likelihood of any imminent development in these countries of economies based on anything other than capitalist relations of production seems quite remote.

To be sure, the further penetration of imperial capital in the Third

World has produced dislocations and new forms of exploitation which, for tens of millions, has simply replaced old forms of alienation, misery and squalor with new ones. But it is far from inevitable that European, Japanese or North American capital will indefinitely dominate these countries. Indeed, there are already signs that certain of the newly industrialized countries may, sometime in the future, become serious rivals to those who presently dominate the world economy.

We can also expect that Third World capitalism will probably not simply replicate nineteenth century capitalism as it appeared in Western Europe and North America. In the past, socialists tended to view the anti-imperialist struggle in the Third World as an objectively anti-capitalist struggle, when in fact it was, in essence, a national revolutionary struggle principally aimed at ending foreign political and economic domination. That struggle continues in the Third World today. One of its main forms is the struggle for more equitable relations of investment and trade with the major capitalist powers and their international institutions.

Similarly, we can expect that with the rapid growth of an industrial proletariat in the developing countries there will be a corresponding rise in trade unionism and broader working-class consciousness that will be expressed in an intensifying struggle over the conditions of labor. In addition, crucial environmental questions – barely thought about when capitalism was flowering in nineteenth century Europe – have today become burning issues in the Third World. Thus, the uniqueness and strength of the conflicts already sharply emerging rest in the inter-relationship of both the national democratic and the class struggles in the Third World.

Export of Revolution

In the final analysis, the theory of the world revolutionary process was based on a concept which Marxism-Leninism formally eschewed but, which in fact, was central to its framework: the export of revolution.

Heatedly denying such a charge, Soviet communists pointed out that (1) they had never fostered or supported revolutionary activities in the developed capitalist countries; (2) revolutions in the Third World had emerged spontaneously out of the conditions of colonialism and foreign domination and not as the result of Soviet intervention; and (3) to the extent that the military forces of socialist countries had been used to support national liberation struggles, this had always been in response to US attempts to export counter-revolution.

In fact, under Stalin as well as his successors, not only did the Soviet Union use military power to export its revolution, such efforts were militantly defended by most of the international communist movement.

The various revolutions in Eastern Europe which established the 'socialist camp' were certainly a Soviet 'export'. Possibly two or three of the East European countries would have taken a socialist path on their own. But it is hardly deniable that the 'socialism' ultimately imposed on those countries was not the result of popular support but of Soviet military might. Nor can it be denied that it was Soviet arms which, contrary to popular will, kept communist regimes in power there for more than 40 years.

A legitimate case can be made, of course, that after the experience of the Nazi invasion (and a long history of invasions from the West), Moscow had good reasons for insisting on a European security zone along its western frontiers. But it does not follow that this gave the Soviet Union the right to install communist governments in the countries on its border or to impose a particular economic and political system on them.

'Rights' aside, however – no country, after all, bases its international policies on respect for other countries' 'rights' – it is now fairly obvious that the attempt forcibly to impose 'socialism' in Eastern Europe weakened rather than strengthened Soviet security.

One only has to look at the example of Finland, which had been a Nazi ally during the war, to see that there were more satisfactory alternatives. Although postwar Finland never had a communist government, was never a 'People's Democracy', had a thoroughly capitalist system and never was a member of the Warsaw Treaty Organization, it filled the role of 'buffer' for the USSR more effectively than any of the East European communist governments ever did.

In the countries of the 'socialist camp', Soviet domination and totalitarian rule fostered ideological alienation and forms of political resistance highly susceptible to collusion with the US. As a result, Moscow felt obliged to maintain occupation forces in most countries of the bloc and to intervene militarily when mass opposition threatened continued communist rule – all of which proved quite costly in both political and financial terms. But Finland presented no such problems to the USSR. Successive Finnish governments may have chafed somewhat at the objective limits on their foreign policy, but the country was politically stable, relatively well-off and not a drain on Soviet resources. (Why was Finland 'permitted' to go its own way instead of being incorporated into the Soviet bloc? Because it had not been occupied by Soviet troops. A somewhat similar situation prevailed in Austria, where US, British and Soviet troops shared in the country's liberation.)

Soviet security concerns aside, however, the arbitrary imposition of socialism in Eastern Europe demonstrated again the futility of trying to export revolution. Although there was a measure of improvement in the lives of most workers, socialism never won genuine mass support in those countries – particularly since the socialism they received came with all the unattractive features of the Soviet administrative-command system and without the virtue of having its own national character. Recognizing the futility of standing up to Soviet military strength, the peoples of Eastern Europe accorded the system no more than a grudging acquiescence – and even this was frequently breached. Consequently, 'nationalist deviations' in Eastern Europe became Moscow's recurring nightmare until Soviet leaders no longer had the will or the capacity to resist them.

To be sure, Moscow made no effort to export revolution to the main capitalist countries. But clearly this owed more to the readily apparent unprofitability of such enterprises than to any ideological forbearance. (Likewise, the 'Moscow gold' sent to a number of western Communist Parties – those of France, Italy and the US in particular – had more to do with maintaining influence over those organizations than with any serious expectation that the parties might be able to take power.)

But the same can hardly be said of Soviet policy in the Third World. Moscow's strategy of trying to direct the anti-colonial revolution on to the 'non-capitalist path' was, in essence, an effort to intervene in the internal processes of a country's development in order to draw it into the world socialist system. Soviet economic aid to 'socialist-oriented states' was orchestrated so as to encourage growth of the administrative-command system. This strategy was as much a failure as was Moscow's Eastern Europe policy. Certainly it did nothing to build socialism in these countries. If anything, it distorted their natural path of economic development and left these countries poorly prepared to deal with world capitalism when ultimately they had to. Nor did the 'socialist camp' have the massive resources that would have been needed in order to establish a material base for socialism in these countries. As it was, Soviet expenditures on assistance to Third World countries and national liberation movements were a significant factor in the limitations imposed on domestic social spending and the system's mounting budget deficits.

In the end, the world revolutionary process turned out to be every bit as voluntarist as the other schemes for world revolution which had preceded it. What Soviet historian Elgiz Pozdnyakov has called 'state Messianism' [51] stems from the notion that the 'socialist camp' – both to protect itself and as a matter of 'internationalist' principles – was obliged to follow an expansionist strategy.

More to the point, perhaps, it was a policy which in the long run failed. It left the Soviet Union trapped in an arms race for which the US and its allies were far better equipped. And to the extent that Soviet influence did expand in the world, it left Moscow with huge financial obligations which took an enormous toll on its economic capacities.

One consequence of trying to impose 'socialism' on countries not ready for it – and insisting that the process is 'irreversible' – is that it inevitably leads to a system of political repression and all-round centrally administered social control. For when the low level of industrial development hampers the socialization of labor; when the backward state of agriculture is not conducive to collectivization; when the absence of large-scale production turns central planning under state ownership into a fetter on production; and when the population is not ideologically prepared for the new social and production relations of socialism – then governmental authority becomes inherently unstable and no one can be trusted.

All this makes the attempt to export revolution dubious enough. But when, in essence, it is really an attempt to export a social system which is unsound even in a supposedly more favorable habitat, then the process becomes even more problematic. And, in the final analysis, the model of socialism the Soviets were trying to export was itself not workable.

It could be argued, of course, that the Soviet Union had little choice but to encourage and support anti-imperialist movements and governments. Imperialism's goal would still have been to destroy socialism no matter what and, therefore, in its own self-defense, the USSR had to try to weaken its adversary in every way it could. The most 'risk-free' strategy would be one which avoided direct confrontation with the US while offering newly independent countries an alternative to being integrated into the world capitalist system.

But it is far from an absolute certainty that a more all-sided form of peaceful coexistence with the West would not have worked. After all, given a chance to intervene overtly in Hungary in 1956, the US backed off – a clear sign that it was not prepared to take the military and political risks involved in carrying out its announced policy of 'rolling back' communism in Eastern Europe. And even after Soviet support proved to be of decisive importance in enabling Vietnam to frustrate US intervention in that country, there were many signs indicating that Washington was prepared to reach a new accommodation with Moscow – especially since, by then, the Soviets had achieved a rough nuclear parity with their adversaries.

In any event, the policy actually followed, despite what appeared to be some signal initial successes, ultimately proved unavailing. This was not a failure of tactics. It was, in essence, the failure of a strategy which itself was based on a profound misassessment of the actual world balance of forces – most especially of the relative strengths of the 'two world systems'. In the final analysis, it was a failure which demonstrated that the theory of 'two world systems' was itself built on sand.

9 Conclusion:
Where to? What Next?

In the darkness with a great bundle of grief, the people march,
In the night, and overhead a shovel of stars for keeps,
  the people march:
'Where to? What next?'

Carl Sandburg, 'The People Yes'

While the collapse of 'actually existing socialism' deepened what was already a crisis of the left throughout the world, it also opened up an array of new opportunities for socialists. Certainly it is disappointing – and not only to its most avid adherents – that the social experiment begun with the Bolshevik Revolution in 1917 has failed. But to the extent that failure reflected fundamental conceptual flaws in the assessment of historical possibilities and a voluntarist/totalitarian vision of socialism, there is little point in mourning the system's demise.

If anything, the passing of 'actually existing socialism' and its attendant political organizations and ideological constructs is more likely to advance the broader socialist cause than to set it back. For if this system – despite some significant accomplishments over the course of three-quarters of a century – was ultimately no more than a historical derangement without a future, then its passing has removed an impediment to a process of reality-based social development.

Now the question confronting those of us still committed to the socialist cause is not so much Lenin's *What Is To Be Done?* as his earlier *Where To Begin?* Not only will our reflections on socialism's prospects unfold in the shadow of 'actually existing socialism's' demise; we start perforce at a moment when all the traditional ideological constructs of the socialist legacy have been called into question.

End of an Era

In a philosophical sense, modern socialism was born with Marx's famous comment that 'The philosophers have only *interpreted* the world .... The point, however, is to *change* it.' [1] Today, as the battered socialist movement seeks ways to revive its project, it would be well to remind ourselves that before we can even begin to think about changing the world, we must be sure that we understand it.

Consequently, the first step toward making socialism a historical force once again is a new assessment of the world we live in. For it is fairly clear as we approach the twenty-first century that ours is not the world which provided the raw material for the theories which heretofore have informed the socialist project. On the contrary: it is a world which, in many crucial ways, has confounded some of Marxism's most fundamental propositions.

To begin with, we must come to terms with the inescapable fact that the decomposition of 'actually existing socialism' has brought an era of world history to an end – an era shaped by the presumption that a functional socialist mode of production and a 'socialist camp' had come into existence and were contending with capitalism for world hegemony. As a result, the International Communist Movement and the political relationships and assessments which were based on those assumptions have been rendered obsolete.

Still, some – mostly the remnants of ineffectual Communist Parties – remain in denial, arguing in the face of all the evidence that 'actually existing socialism' remains alive and, in some cases, is doing well. As proof they point to the fact that Communist Parties continue to hold power in China, Vietnam, Cuba and North Korea; and they see in a handful of non-governing Communist Parties who continue to vow fealty to the old orthodoxies the foundations of a still viable International Communist Movement. But closer scrutiny shows that such a reading of the world is out of touch with reality. The remaining 'socialist' countries may choose to keep that appellation, but – except for North Korea – they are all in the process of departing dramatically from those 'laws' which Marxist-Leninists had declared to be 'actually existing socialism's' indispensable characteristics.

China has already opened its economic system to a broad array of capitalist enterprise and private property that would have been unthinkable in the days when 'actually existing socialism' actually existed. And since, on the strength of this changeover, it seems to be well on the way to becoming one of the world's more important economic powers, the likelihood of it stepping back into the old administrative-command economy recedes with each passing day. On the other hand, the old communist political system remains in place. Unchecked power, with its attendant means and willingness for suppressing every expression of political opposition, is still concentrated in the hands of the Communist Party. But if China is at last trying to carry out the bourgeois-democratic revolution it needed when the communists first came to power in 1949, it will not be able indefinitely to adopt bourgeois economics without likewise instituting some form of bourgeois democracy.

Vietnam is clearly seeking a similar trajectory for its future development.

Cuban socialism, bereft of the massive Soviet economic assistance it received for almost 30 years, faces grim economic prospects. The US embargo, of course, has had a devastating impact on the Cuban economy. But that is the precise point. The underlying assumption of 'actually existing socialism' was that Third World countries like Cuba could be independent of the world capitalist economy by becoming part of a completely self-sufficient Soviet-dominated world socialist system. Today, however, Cuba is clamoring to be allowed back into the world capitalist economy and has started to permit a (so far) limited range of activity not controled by the centralized economic apparatus.

(North Korea, on the other hand, while trying to maintain the basic elements of the old Stalinist system, is apparently headed for a nepotistic political dynasty – a development, one would think, socialists would more likely see as a grim reminder of what 'actually existing socialism' was like than a cause for celebration.)

The people of these countries fought heroic battles in their respective struggles for national independence. But now that they are moving, in varying degrees and by various means, toward completing the bourgeois-democratic revolutions which were their natural trajectories, it would be a disservice to them – and a source of confusion for the socialist movement – to impose on them the unbearable ideological burden of upholding the tattered flag of a failed system. Whatever these countries may have in common, it is clearly not the basis for a revived 'socialist camp', let alone the foundations of an alternative 'world socialist system'. At home, their future lies with mixed economies and political systems reflecting them, not with centralized command economics and its attendant one-party dictatorship; internationally, it rests with integration into the world capitalist economy.

On the other hand, capitalism today is a more dominant and potent force than it ever has been – both on a world scale and in those countries Marxism has long considered the most ripe for socialism. It continues to revolutionize society's productive forces in ways that are, perhaps, even more transforming than the wonders of that earlier nineteenth century industrial revolution which first revealed the awesome power resident in the capitalist order. It has engendered revolutions in energy (nuclear power), production (computerized automation), communications (television, satellite systems), information processing and retrieval (computers) and the physical sciences more broadly. It has brought into being whole new technologies, harnessing not only physics and chemistry but even biology to its economic development. And because scientific discoveries and technological innovations of the last 50 years have obsolesced labor-intensive production as the chief engine of economic growth, the role of the industrial proletariat in the production process has been declining – a development which, at the very least, forces us to reconsider the role Marx forecast for that section of the working class in the revolutionary process. The information revolution is likewise altering the old methods of ideological control, thereby posing vast new challenges not only to capital but to movements of social change as well.

Contemporary capitalism is also markedly different from what it was in the pre-World War II years in terms of its global sweep. A qualitatively new level of internationalization has wrought major changes in all the relationships through which the world capitalist economy now functions. Although the threat posed by what turned out to be the ill-fated socialist experiment was undoubtedly a factor in restraining the intense inter-imperialist rivalries which led to two world wars, equally important has been the growing role of giant transnational banks and corporations and new state-supported regulating institutions through which all aspects of world capitalism are now increasingly mediated. Most important, though, is the fact that capital itself, in losing its particular national character, is undermining the compulsions which once drove rival capitalist states (and blocs of states) to war with each other.

One of the most significant alterations has been in the economic relationships between the Third World and the main centers of world capitalism. In the past, these were based principally on the former's role as the source of natural resources – both agricultural and mineral – to feed the industry of the developed capitalist countries. Virtually all of Africa and much of Asia was dominated by colonialism, while the nominally independent countries of the world's south were locked into a semi-colonial status.

Nor did the collapse of the colonial system, contrary to Marxist-Leninist predictions, significantly weaken or undermine the world capitalist economy. If anything, capitalist expansion in the Third World has accelerated since the mid-1970s. Assisted in no small measure by the revolutions in computerization, transportation, information and communications, international capital has begun to shift an increasingly significant part of its industrial capacity to this part of the world, a process which is undermining the vestiges of feudal and semi-feudal relations there and markedly altering the mode of production in the capitalist heartland.

Some Third World countries – Brazil, South Korea, China, Singapore and Thailand, among others – are on their way to being economic powerhouses. Not only are they becoming new centers of industrial production; their rapidly growing consumer markets have likewise become increasingly significant factors in world trade. And as the industrialized sector of the working class shrinks in the centers of the world capitalist economy, it is swelling in these newly industrialized countries.

To a certain extent, most socialists acknowledge the fact that capitalism has undergone major change. But there is little agreement as to its significance. While some have warned that prevailing socialist theory is out of date, the socialist movement has given little thought so far to the *political* implications of confronting a system so markedly different from the one identified by Lenin as capitalism in its final and 'moribund' stage.

Therefore, one of the first places to begin for those who would breathe new life into the socialist movement is with a new study of contemporary capitalism, one which goes beyond the tendency to equate analysis with denunciation. In particular, we should attempt to understand the modern production process and the functions performed by the new institutions capitalism has devised in order to rationalize itself. In doing so we must adopt a completely open-minded attitude which is prepared to reevaluate the assessments, laws, concepts and categories which Marxism developed to describe the old system.

For the fact is that Marxism-Leninism's central premise – that capitalism was in its final, 'moribund' stage and that proletarian revolution was a timely and objective prospect – has crumbled. If anything, in the last decade of the twentieth century world capitalism, for all its readily evident problems, is more stable than it was in 1916 when Lenin declared that it was on the ropes awaiting the proletariat's knockout punch. As we approach the end of the millennium, therefore, it is not so much Lenin's vision of proletarian revolution as Kautsky's concept of a new 'ultra-imperialist' stage of capitalism which history seems to be in the process of verifying.

Nevertheless, as they have for the past 75 years, Marxist-Leninists continue to base their perception of the world on an imminent capitalist collapse, citing every blip on capitalism's economic radar screen as new proof that 'the general crisis of capitalism is getting deeper'. Even today we can still hear echoes of that pathetically myopic view which sees any acknowledgment of capitalism's staying power as a 'betrayal' of the socialist cause in the angry protestations of those who seem to think that socialism's current anguish is more the consequence of glasnost than the system whose misrepresentations glasnost helped expose.

Both in substance and method, we cannot go on this way. The premise that world capitalism has played itself out and the long-awaited 'final conflict' for socialism is close at hand flies in the face of reality. It has propelled us down the path of apocalyptic fantasies and pseudo-revolutionary posturing and has been a major factor in our political marginalization. If we are to develop a relevant politics, we must come to terms with the fact that the material conditions for a proletarian-based socialist revolution have not appeared in any capitalist country in all the years when Marxist-Leninists were proclaiming its imminence – nor do they prevail anywhere in the world today.

It is time to acknowledge that Lenin was wrong. For if capitalism retains its capacity to revolutionize the forces of production and if it likewise continues to generate an economic surplus which it is willing to use – however sparingly and under protest – to curb potential revolutionary impulses among the workers, how imminent are the prospects for the emergence of an army of proletarians prepared to struggle to overturn the system? In other words, Lenin notwithstanding, the 'delay' in the world revolution was due not to subjective but objective factors.

Marxist-Leninists were never able to face up to this reality. Instead they comforted themselves with what would become a perennial self-deluding strain – that the proletariat was on the verge of a breakthrough toward that revolutionary consciousness which would be ready for and eagerly seek the communists' vanguard leadership.

The Unquiet Passing of Marxism-Leninism

History has not only overtaken Marxism-Leninism's central thesis on the nature of our present epoch – one of a moribund capitalism and impending world proletarian revolution – it has undermined Marxism-Leninism in general. Its particular conceptions of class struggle, the vanguard party, the transition to socialism, the dictatorship of the proletariat and the nature of socialism itself have little to offer a resuscitated socialist movement trying to develop a strategic outlook based on today's realities.

Class Struggle

'The history of all hitherto existing society is the history of class struggles', declare Marx and Engels at the beginning of their famous Manifesto.

While this broad concept is undoubtedly enlightening as a historical abstraction, its usefulness as a guide to socialist politics has been undermined over the decades by the dolorous legacy of dogmatic absolutism and economic reductionism in which Marxism-Leninism has encased it. Not only did the theorists of 'actually existing socialism' and the International Communist Movement become quite adept at wrapping themselves and their policies in the mantle of class struggle; their actual analyses tended to be highly simplistic and self-serving.

In this connection, it would be well to take another look at Gorbachev's 'new thinking' which provided the basis for his belated attempt to rescue Soviet socialism from itself – in particular the concept that ours is an age in which the struggle for certain common 'human interests' takes precedence over class struggle. More than any other, this provocative idea has been denounced by Gorbachev's opponents on the left as proof of an 'ideological surrender' to capitalism. Nevertheless, there is important food for thought here, in particular Gorbachev's assertion that there is 'an objective limit for class confrontation in the international arena: the threat of universal destruction'. This may sound like heresy, but the more trenchant question is whether or not it is true.

Any political movement – of whatever persuasion – which disregards or underestimates the dangers of 'universal destruction' currently embedded in society's military and economic norms is dangerously out of touch with reality. The most obvious 'objective limit' on class struggle is the possibility of nuclear war. For the internal logic of the traditional Marxist-Leninist view of class struggle has built into it the likelihood of armed confrontations which – if they occur at the level of state-to-state contention – open up the very real possibility that nuclear arms would be employed. We know how close the world came to such a turn of events during the Cold War.

Nor is it particularly helpful to hold – as some did then and some do now – that only the capitalist side was likely to employ nuclear weapons in a showdown. First of all, that assumption is highly dubious. (At most, the Soviets said they wouldn't be the 'first' to use nuclear weapons.) More important, the problem posed by nuclear war is not who to blame if it should come but how to prevent it. (Who will be left to hear protestations of innocence once the nuclear button is pushed?)

Nor is nuclear war the only source of potential catastrophe for humankind as a whole. Various forms of environmental destruction are making the world increasingly vulnerable to disasters which could make the planet unlivable while, for the first time ever, humanity confronts the limitations imposed on economic activity as a consequence of finite resources. The old Marxist-Leninist response to these concerns – that the only way to defend the common 'human interest' is by hastening the overthrow of capitalism – is both unacceptable and irresponsible. And yet it still echoes today among the orthodox. For instance, Sam Webb – a leading figure in the CPUSA – still argues:

> It is said that class interests should be subsumed and subordinated to universal human interests. But life shows that universal human interests can finally prevail only by the elimination of the system of capitalist exploitation for private profit – in other words, by the victory of the class struggle of all who labor. There is a conflict between universal human interests and the class struggle only if the former is used to obscure and expunge the latter. There is an alliance and infinity between the two when the primacy of the class struggle is recognized as crucial to the realization and eventual triumph of universal human interests.[2]

A socialist movement unprepared to challenge such obfuscation from those who are nominally in its ranks is destined to be intellectually barren and politically ambiguous. First we must be prepared to dispense with the more obvious demagogy of such comments. After all, the Soviet Union's abysmal record in protecting the environment – high-

lighted by Chernobyl but widely evident in the cavalier approach which
ignored the ecological consequences of much of its economic activity –
certainly should have demonstrated that the record of 'actually existing
socialism' when it came to protecting universal human interests was no
better than capitalism's.

Even more irresponsible is Webb's blithe assertion that the only way
to overcome these perils is by eliminating capitalism – an approach
which completely side-steps the issue at hand: what policies should
socialists pursue in dealing with fundamental threats to human survival
today when the possibilities for eliminating capitalism are slight or when
the direct and unqualified pursuit of class struggle goals might actually
heighten such threats?

A new, reality-based socialist movement cannot be satisfied with the
old view that the only way to overcome these dangers is by the triumph
of socialism. That may be true in the abstract. But the dangers are ready
to hand and could well develop to breaking point before socialism
arrives.

It is likewise obfuscating to pose this question as though it deals
with class struggle in general when its main point, as Gorbachev notes,
is 'class confrontation in the international arena'. In fact, a reexamination of the concept of 'international class struggle' itself is in order.

In the Marxist-Leninist framework this was seen as the struggle
between the two world systems – 'actually existing socialism' purportedly
representing the proletariat and world capitalism representing the bourgeoisie. As a practical matter this conflict took place principally in the
arena of state-to-state relations – thus making the Cold War the most
concentrated expression of class struggle. But if state-to-state relations
between socialist countries and capitalist countries are to be guided by
the principles of class struggle, and if class struggle is a principle taking
precedence over all others, where is the basis for a socialist foreign
policy based on peaceful coexistence? (It is to be hoped that this
question will become a real one in the future.) The fact is that, in
practice, 'international class struggle' turned out to be a euphemism, first
for the infamous Brezhnev Doctrine justifying Soviet military intervention in other socialist countries, and second for adventures in exporting
revolution – or, to be more precise, close alliance with the Soviet Union
– to other countries.

But if reality imposes 'objective limits' on one side in the class
struggle, does it not also impose limits on the other? One may say, of
course, that the callous capitalists don't care and can hardly be relied
upon to show restraint in pursuit of their class interests. And it would
be foolish to deny the possibility that a particularly zealous or unduly
optimistic ruling group on either side might even venture a roll of the
nuclear dice. Nevertheless, both sides in the class struggle really have
little choice but to assume that compromise and reason might prevail
and a way can be found to avert what would truly be the final conflict.

This is not simply optimistic speculation. The history of the Cold War shows that there was more than one occasion when each side pulled back from the nuclear brink even when the logic of the 'class struggle' might have suggested another course of action.

Nor can we go on looking at the movements for national liberation in the Third World as another expression of 'international class struggle'. For whatever illusions may have been advanced suggesting liberated countries might traverse some path of 'non-capitalist development', the objective content of those undertakings was, in essence, the struggle for national democracy. The challenge facing countries which have won their political independence is not how to build socialism but how to enter the world capitalist economy on the most favorable terms.

A new socialist movement must also undertake to divest the concept of class struggle from the narrow economism which, all too often, has dominated socialist thinking. For contrary to dogmatic prejudice, the battle between workers and capitalists over the terms of labor is only one aspect – and not necessarily the most important – of the class struggle. Time and again we have seen how so-called 'non-class' issues – racism, the Vietnam War, gender subordination, issues of democracy, environmental questions – have come to the fore as the cutting edge of politics for a moment or even an era; and we have also seen how some on the left have given these issues short shrift in the name of the primacy of the 'class struggle'. Not only does such an approach fly in the face of Marx's highly sophisticated understanding of class struggle; it rarely makes sense politically.

The Industrial Proletariat

In that context, we need to reassess the notion that the leading force in the class struggle will be the industrial proletariat. This Marxist proposition, which once seemed so eminently logical, clearly has to be rethought in the light of contemporary conditions. At the least, we have to recognize that there never was anything preordained or magical about the industrial proletariat.

Marx saw that section of the workers as the most likely to be in the van of the class struggle because of their numbers, their position in the production process and their greater receptivity to organization.

Certainly the numbers of those who work solely for wages has continued to grow to the point where they easily comprise the vast majority of society in the developed capitalist countries. But the labor-intensive production of pre-World War II industry has given way to high-tech processes of modern manufacture which easily surpass the old outputs while employing far fewer workers. As a result, the percentage of the working class employed in traditional mass-production industries today is much smaller than it was in Marx's – or even Lenin's – time. In the US, this has had a devastating impact on those unions which traditionally were the most militant and left-leaning. Today the vast majority of workers are employed in the service sector – a more difficult sector to organize.

The role of the industrial proletariat has also been altered significantly by the changing demography of the working class. Today women comprise almost half the public workforce. There has also been a spectacular growth in immigrant workers – largely from Third World countries. Fifty years ago in the US, the majority of African-Americans were employed in rural labor in the south. Today most are in urban areas where their presence has changed the racial composition of both the work force and virtually every major city.

While some number of women, immigrants and African-Americans have found employment in unionized heavy industry, the overwhelming majority of these 'new' workers have wound up in other areas of the workforce – service sectors, government employment, non-union industry and, for many, conditions of long-term unemployment. As a result, the traditional core of the industrial proletariat has tended to be more conservative than the rest of the working class on a wide range of political issues.

At the same time, these newly expanded sectors of the working class have not only brought issues of gender, race, nationality, legal status and democratic rights to the heart of the class struggle; they have broadened the entire notion of class struggle. As a result, the old economist hierarchy of issues is being dramatically undermined, so that today these 'non-economic' questions have become the magnets bringing large numbers of workers into the arena of politics. This shift has also broadened the locus of the class struggle away from the workplace and into social institutions and localities where electoral politics are played out.

In short, while the conflict between opposing classes rises spontaneously out of antagonistic property relations, it is a conflict which embraces every aspect of social life and no one can ordain a general hierarchy of significance to one arena over any other. Indeed, in its most mature stage – and I am not here trying to predict the particular form this will take – the focus of this contention is the struggle for political power.

The Vanguard Party

The mystique of Lenin's 'party of a new type' has lasted far too long and bequeathed the socialist movement too checkered a legacy to allow us simply to accept either its form or its underlying assumptions. However appropriate its principles of organization may have been in an autocratic Russia preparing for revolution at the turn of the century, its usefulness to a socialist movement trying to regenerate itself almost 100 years later is dubious at best.

Lenin's conception of the vanguard party can hardly be separated from the conditions out of which it arose: a working class itself only a decade or two removed from the countryside and constituting a small percentage of the population in a predominantly peasant country; czarist repression; the illegality of most socialist organizations; a rotting political structure holding back the country's economic development; and a people clearly readying for revolution.

If nothing else, a new socialist movement must determine the organizational structures appropriate to its own time, place, circumstance, condition and political mission. But there is also a considerable body of experience which should make us extremely wary of reproducing the dogmatic, sectarian and undemocratic tendencies which seem to be inherent in the models of the vanguard party we have encountered.

Rationalized by the proposition that the task of the vanguard was to prepare for proletarian revolution and, as a consequence, to expect the fierce repression of the ruling class, these parties – I am referring now to those in the developed capitalist countries – did little to justify their military-like discipline, centralization and hierarchical structure. Their view of themselves as the only legitimate revolutionary force was a fundamental source of sectarianism on the left, while their democratic centralism brought out the worst in their leaders and imposed a climate of intellectual conformity which became readily apparent to all but themselves.

Lenin's own broadmindedness may have checked many of these tendencies in his own time, but the whole experience of the communist movement demonstrates that an organization which depends on the enlightened outlook of those to whom it has ceded near-absolute power will quickly see the erosion of the democratic norms so central to its culture and its capacity for change.

The parallel with organized religion is telling. Just as the church hierarchy appointed itself the 'guardian of the faith' in order to defend its wealth and authority, so the vanguard party – or, more precisely, its central leadership – appointed itself the sole and ultimate defender and modifier of the only permissible doctrine informing 'actually existing socialism' and the International Communist Movement.

Nowhere was this more the case, of course, than in the Soviet Union and the other countries of the 'socialist camp'. During the glasnost years of critical retrospection, large numbers of Soviet scholars who had experienced the heavy hand of the party's ideological authority were finally able to speak of such things. The significance of these reflections rested in the fact that those who spoke up were neither dissidents nor defectors. Most were party members, Marxist-Leninists who had served and believed in the system. Three such – philosophy professors – offer this summation of the party's view of itself:

The Party apparat's conviction that it is universally competent has ideological roots. It substantiates its special position and rights by appeals to the communist idea and the Marxist-Leninist doctrine. With this aim in view, the doctrine as such has been raised to the degree of state ideology, having been preliminarily subjected to at least two barbaric operations. First, Marxism-Leninism was seen as the final dogma. It was believed that Marxism alone was quite enough to resolve successfully all fundamental issues – whether in machine-building, agrobiology, linguistics or any other sphere. Secondly, it was not enough simply to split the living doctrine into a number of dead formulae; there was also a need to stand guard over their purity and implant them in the mentality of citizens. It is the Party apparat that assumes the role of interpreter and guardian of the doctrine. It complements its function as supreme ruler with that of peculiar supreme priest.[3]

The Transition

I remain confident that capitalism does not mark the end point of social development and that it will be succeeded by a more equitable, efficient and socially responsible mode of production. But we clearly need a new perspective on what we mean by socialism and how the transition process might unfold. For it is doubtful to the point of near-certainty that either the process or the end result will look much like 'actually existing socialism'.

On the other hand, we should be extremely wary of the idea that we must formulate a new vision of how things would work and what life would be like in a future socialist society. For there is no surer way to throttle a revived socialist movement at birth than by engaging it in one more utopian exercise which, under present circumstances, no one could possibly take seriously.

The simple fact of the matter – which we should openly acknowledge – is that we do not know what socialism will look like. Nor should we expect to. In trying to imagine a future socialist society, all we can say with relative certainty is that it will seek to overcome the enormous discrepancies in wealth, power and quality of life characteristic of capitalism, as well as the inherent social irresponsibility which inevitably results from economic decision-making based principally on the drive for private profit. But what we can identify are the numerous ways in which Marxism-Leninism has inserted a totally skewed paradigm of the transition process into the socialist discourse.

Perhaps the chief point on which Marxist-Leninist theory corrupted Marx is the demarcation it made between the transition to socialism and socialism itself. Directly traceable to Stalin, this theoretical cornerstone of Marxism-Leninism simply overrode Marx's critical discovery that socialism would not be a completely new society based on negating all the economic, political and social relationships of capitalism, but rather was itself a lengthy process of transition from one mode of production to another. Marxism-Leninism, however, simply incorporated Stalin's proclamation that his 'revolution from above' in the Soviet Union had brought the 'transition' period to an end and that, under his leadership, socialism had been 'constructed' there.[4]

In accepting the Stalinist experience as a 'law' of socialism, Marxism-Leninism truncated into a period of less than 20 years what Marx had seen as taking an entire historical epoch. It also obscured Marx's distinction between socialism and communism, attributing to the former characteristics which Marx believed could only be realized in the latter.

In fact, and contrary to the Marxist-Leninist framework, the transition *process* actually begins under capitalism with the qualitative socialization of the work process, the emergence of a modern working class and the appearance of new collective forms of production and social management. Even before the overthrow of bourgeois political power, it is clearly possible to make significant modifications in the social arrangement, since capitalists themselves, alert to the signs of social unrest, can be forced to acquiesce in the establishment of extensive systems of social welfare. They have also recognized that a measure of state intervention into the economy is required to curb those irrationalities of capitalist production which jeopardize the stability of the system as a whole.

The bourgeoisie cannot prevent this development; indeed, against its own instincts and more often than not with great trepidation, it turns to these modifications in its ways of doing business both out of its own economic logic and in response to social pressure. These ameliorations do not, of course, alter the fundamental irrationality or property relations of a system in which the labor of the vast majority produces the wealth which winds up in the hands of a tiny handful. Nevertheless, they are the harbingers of a future society in which not only will the labor process be socialized, so will economic decision-making and distribution. How that will take place and to what extent are questions which cannot be answered in advance. It is to be hoped, in light of the Soviet experience, that those determinations will be made on economic rather than ideological grounds.

What seems most likely is that the transition to a new social and economic arrangement will be both lengthy and complex. And if the lessons flowing from the disintegration of 'actually existing socialism' are truly understood, then socialist society will emerge as the mixed economy which Marx anticipated. I believe this will be the case not because of some Marxist 'principle' mandating such a course, but because a new mode of production does not come into being fully formed on the basis of a prior grand design. Consequently, we will have to get used to the notion that socialism does not 'begin' at some historically demarcated point in time. Rather, it will unfold over the course of many decades and, as Marx noted, will constitute an 'entire historical epoch' in its own right.

In a sense, that process has already begun. Lenin's thesis that capitalism had exhausted its historical possibilities was clearly premature. Nevertheless, he was on to something real. As a result of the industrial revolution and the consequent expansion of socialization in the labor process, new structures and systems which were the very antithesis of capitalism *as the world had known it until then* were coming into being. At the same time, the very scale of capitalist production and the growing significance of international economic activity enhanced the role of the state as a significant actor in the system. But, contrary to Lenin who believed these were heralds of decay, these alterations actually ushered in an era of vast capitalist expansion.

Propelled by an array of new productive forces, these trends have accelerated since Lenin's time, resulting in one of those paradoxes which underscore the dialectics of history: the very tendencies which enabled capitalism to continue expanding also brought into being forms and methods suggestive of socialism.

Today, every capitalist country is based on a mixed economy of sorts, with a sizeable state-owned and operated structure existing alongside and, in many ways, orchestrating the vast 'private' sector. Such an arrangement is hardly 'socialist' in the sense that there is little element of genuine popular control over economic activity in either sector. On the other hand, when and if bourgeois political power is broken the transformation of the present state sector of the capitalist economy is likely to occur with far less disruption than would otherwise be the case.

The tendency toward a mix of economic forms is not limited to the most developed capitalist countries. In the developing countries there is growing recognition – even by revolutionary forces – that while unbridled capitalism is unacceptable, the conditions for socialism do not yet exist. And despite all the bravura proclamations on restoring capitalism to the former socialist countries, it is becoming increasingly apparent that a mixture of capitalist and socialist forms and property relations will prevail there as well. 'Actually existing socialism' may have been an unworkable system, but the countries in which it held sway will not be able to go back to capitalism's square one. For one thing, the old system provided a significant measure of economic protections and social welfare, which the masses of people now expect and which any government will have to take into account if it is to assure political stability. At the same time, the opportunities for primitive accumulation which launched modern capitalism in Western Europe and North America – the expropriation of the peasantry, the conquest of 'virgin' lands and the establishment of a colonial system – are no longer available.

One irony of the political processes now underway in the former Soviet Union, Eastern Europe and countries like China and Vietnam is that Gorbachev may yet be vindicated. For the essence of his perestroika was to transform the rigid Soviet administrative-command system into a mixed economy – but one with a nominally firmer ideological commitment to social protections for the people than seems to be the case in present-day Russia and the other former Soviet republics.

In this sense, it strikes me that those irate Marxist-Leninists presently denouncing the pull of the market and trends toward privatization in the Soviet Union are engaged in a futile exercise. The fact that virtually every socialist country is turning toward some level of privatization and market economics should tell us something. Some objective force, far more powerful than any theory, seems to be at work here.

Still, it seems highly unlikely that capitalism will simply 'grow' into socialism. For in order fully to impose the social will on production and society as a whole, the basic class relationships of capitalism will have to be overturned. And that is a process in which it would be unrealistic to expect the capitalists to cooperate. At that point, society's collision with the bourgeoisie will move beyond the struggle for reform and become a struggle for power.

No one can now predict what form that struggle will take. The successful 'seizures' of power in the past are clearly irrelevant. In the main cases – Russia in 1917, China, Vietnam and Cuba – the changeover took place in the context of a bourgeois-democratic revolution in which the revolutionary struggle was directed against either an outmoded feudal political structure, foreign (imperialist) domination or a combination of the two. In the countries which – in conjunction with the USSR – became the 'socialist camp', the transfer of power was conditioned by the Soviet Union's role in the liberation of Eastern Europe. But there is no precedent for the overthrow of bourgeois power in any developed capitalist country. The most we can say is that the ultimate contest for power will be addressed by the class and political forces bound to be thrown up by the circumstances of the time.

'Actually Existing Socialism'

It goes almost without saying that a new movement for socialism must develop a perspective on the 'actually existing socialism' of the Soviet Union and the countries of the 'socialist camp' which followed that model. We cannot avoid this question for, in light of the Soviet experience, everyone will want to know what kind of socialism we have in mind. Nor can we simply say 'our' socialism will be different and better.

This does not mean, as I have already pointed out, devising an alternative to the Soviet model. But we have an obligation, both to ourselves and those we hope to win to the socialist cause, to probe and understand the source of the Soviet system's failure. Simplistic answers blaming it all on Stalin, Gorbachev or the machinations of the CIA will not do. Neither is it enough to attribute the system's collapse to the absence of democracy – although its authoritarian political structure was certainly one of its most unsavory features.

But this was a system which failed even by its own standards. By resisting and proving impervious to the practical applications of the scientific and technological revolution – thereby widening the gap with capitalism in such crucial indices as labor productivity, the efficient use of resources and the proportional development of an all-sided economy – it failed the primary test of a new mode of production. Similarly with its political system, which was not only totalitarian but less flexible than the 'bourgeois democracy' Marxist-Leninists so cavalierly dismissed. (Even socialism's much-vaunted advantages in areas such as healthcare, unemployment and education have proven to be considerably less than claimed.)

At the heart of the problem is the administrative-command economy which Marxist-Leninists exalted as embodying the 'fundamental principles' of socialism. Although it seemingly worked for a while, a system which thumbs its nose at basic economic concepts and attempts to function on the basis of the subjectively derived 'science' of its wielders of power cannot take root. True, it enjoyed some initial successes in overcoming the backwardness of pre-revolutionary Russia; but it never came close to rivaling capitalism as an engine of economic efficiency, productivity and innovation. If anything, the gap between the two systems was growing. As a result, its claims to 'social justice' became increasingly difficult to sustain. And its failure to establish and enforce a system of accountability for its leaders stifled those possibilities for change which are essential to a society's ability to adapt to new circumstances.

The most fundamental structural weakness of 'actually existing socialism' was that while its leaders had the capacity to reproduce their hold over society, the system – unlike capitalism – never became a self-reproducing mode of production. Making matters worse, instead of heeding this fateful warning Marxism-Leninism celebrated it, proclaiming that 'the laws of socialism do not operate automatically.' [5] Of course, this supposed attribute of 'actually existing socialism' was nothing more than a convenient justification of the Communist Party's permanent claim to power.

Consequently, it was a system which was no better than its leaders – hardly a stable basis for a new mode of production which, in Marxist terms at least, was supposed to function independently of human consciousness. (If capitalism had been dependent on the quality of its principal political and economic leaders it would have long since passed into history.) But the very nature of a powerful bureaucratic establishment without a material stake in the system's efficient functioning tended to elevate mediocrities to leadership.

In the end, the ultimate irony of the system was that its most powerful and privileged institution – the ruling vanguard party – proved more a hindrance than a help in defending it. For decades of unchecked and unchallenged power had so locked the party into the status quo that it could not find the will to address the crying need to reform the outmoded structures and to discard – or significantly alter – either the institutions or the anachronistic theory on which its version of socialism had been founded.

The Dictatorship of the Proletariat

There are many good reasons for a new socialist movement to discard this principle which Lenin called 'a touchstone' of Marxism. For one thing, as we have previously noted, the changing character of the working class has called into question the vanguard role of its industrial proletariat. And in an age when the working class itself has come to encompass such a large percentage of the total social population, genuine majority rule would, perforce, be the same as working-class rule. (This was not yet the case in Marx's time or in Lenin's Russia.)

Further, the very concept of proletarian dictatorship was itself the embodiment of a nineteenth century view which saw the overthrow of capitalism and the establishment of socialism as the outcome of a simplistic class-versus-class political struggle. In Marx's framework, 'Society as a whole is more and more splitting up into two great hostile camps, into two great classes directly facing each other: Bourgeoisie and Proletariat.' [6] But the shrinking size and significance of the traditional industrial proletariat within a considerably variegated working class and the likely nature of a broad anti-capitalist coalition based both on class and various social sectors suggests that the old formula does not correspond to contemporary realities.

The most important reason for discarding the concept, however, is that as the result of concrete historical experience the dictatorship of the proletariat has come to mean a totalitarian system in which power is concentrated in the hands of a single, politically unaccountable vanguard party. In fact, the administrative-command economy required such a political system and Marxism-Leninism heralded it as the realization of the 'Leninist concept of the dictatorship of the proletariat'. It is a system with which we have become familiar.

In the name of stamping out the political organizations of the overthrown bourgeois class, the party suppressed all alternatives to itself, its policies, its conceptions and stewardship of its 'socialist' economy, and its ideology. Ordaining itself as the only legal and legitimate political force in a constitutionally mandated single-party system, the party even ruled out the possibility of an alternative *socialist* party. But the party controled more than 'actually existing socialism's' political structure. It also exercised absolute control over the state, the economy and every institution of ideology and culture.

Consequently, except in so far as the party might delegate some portion of its power, decision-making did not take place in the institutions of government or non-governmental institutions such as the trade unions, factory managements and professional organizations. (Even where these bodies exercised their limited authority, virtually all decision-makers were party members subject to party discipline.) The real seat of power in the country – not only ultimate, but day-to-day – was the Communist Party, an organization not subject to popular control even by way of the specious forms used in the election process.

Justifying this entire construct is the view of a single working-class ideology as the sole repository of objective truth. Not only does this concept defy empirical verification; more to the point, in actual social practice it ordains the proletariat's 'vanguard party' as the sole force capable of determining that truth. On this basis, the communists asserted that their party was the only possible instrument through which the proletariat could exercise its dictatorship. But while it might legitimately be argued that the party was the vehicle which focused working-class politics at the time of the Bolshevik Revolution, the idea that it continued to have such a mandate and play such a role for the next 70 years requires a leap of faith that few outside the Marxist-Leninist orthodoxy would make. And considering that the overtly repressive years of Stalin's terror and the numbing years of the Brezhnev stagnation comprised most of that period, even the orthodox must have wondered occasionally about the quality of the party's working-class halo.

In time, totalitarianism was elevated to the level of a socialist principle. The word itself, of course, was never used. The preferred term was 'proletarian democracy'. (The system obviously was neither proletarian nor democratic.) But self-description – the more so when it is self-congratulatory – is hardly a sound basis for forming a judgment of an individual, a political organization or a social system. At best, the adherents of this kind of 'proletarian democracy' are reminiscent of those 'condescending saviours' of the working class so ironically celebrated in the words of 'The Internationale'.

A totalitarian outlook and practice likewise became the norm in the International Communist Movement. While parties not holding state power clearly could not exercise the same degree of authority that their governing counterparts did, their top-down, totally centralized commandist structure was also seen as a 'proletarian' organizational principle because it reflected the realities of the production process – although why industrial regimentation should be treated as a proletarian virtue and be seen as applicable to the political process as well remains a mystery. Following that same logic, demands for greater democratic control over leadership were incessantly dismissed as the agonizing of petty-bourgeois individualism.

In part, the communist movement was vulnerable to totalitarianism because of its idealization of the Soviet Union. For if that paragon of 'real' flesh-and-blood socialism could make a proletarian virtue out of a single-party system, unlimited authority in the hands of the party leadership, censorship and the suppression of dissent, who were they to suggest other ways of functioning – especially if the party's subservient relationship with Moscow was the basis for an exalted view of itself as an agent of history and a condition for Soviet largesse? Needless to say, it was an outlook celebrated by party leaders who found its consecration of (their) authority both convenient and reassuring.

But while party functionaries might have narrowly self-serving reasons for upholding an outlook and a system which sanctified their near-absolute authority, they too – along with the party's lower echelon and rank-and-file members – were ideologically motivated. For when you boil it all down, the communist movement was attracted to and embraced totalitarianism because revolutionary zealots have what can only be characterized as an overpowering natural affinity for totalitarian methods of organization and absolutist modes of thought. Believing that their perspective was rooted in an all-embracing truth to which others were not privy, the communist movement saw itself as the bearer of the world's historical destiny – a privileged status permitting the regulation of others but not itself. It was an outlook which state power could only enhance – and did.

In the final analysis, it all comes down to this: Marx may have seen the dictatorship of the proletariat as the socialist counterpart to capitalism's dictatorship of the bourgeoisie; Lenin may have seen it as the instrument for suppressing the ousted bourgeois class; but the real substance of the dictatorship of the proletariat as demonstrated in life is the system which emerged under 'actually existing socialism.'

The Communist Paradigm

If socialism is best understood as a society in transition to communism, what then is the nature of a communist society? For good reason, Marx and Engels did not write extensively on this subject. (Their early writings contain some youthful idylls best treated as exercises in fantasy literature.) But they did advance two important ideas about communism which are most relevant to a socialist movement. One was the concept of socialism as the 'lower stage' of communism. The other was that where previous modes of production had reflected a condition of economic scarcity, communism – thanks to anticipated advances in scientific knowledge and the forces of production – would be based on an economy of abundance. As Engels put it:

> Large-scale industry will develop on a scale that will make its present level of development seem paltry ... [and] will provide society with a sufficient quantity of products to satisfy the needs of all. Similarly

agriculture ... will be given a quite new impulse, and place at society's disposal an ample quantity of products.[7]

These theorems were critical in establishing a materialist foundation for the socialist movement and effectively distinguished Marxism from both utopian socialism and anarchism. By relegating discussion on the specific features of communist society to future generations, they brought socialism out of the realm of speculation and into the world of politics. And their reminder that new social relations require a material foundation and cannot be brought into being by devising idealist schemes became a check – although never completely successful – on utopian tendencies in socialist ranks.

To the extent they did speculate on the features of communist society, Marx and Engels believed it would operate on the principle: from each according to ability; to each according to need. Such a society, they said, would have no need for 'special bodies of armed men' and other institutions of repression. Therefore the state as a repressive apparatus for keeping one class subject to another would 'wither away', leaving in place only its 'administrative' function. Lenin further amplified on this idea in his classic work, *State and Revolution*, declaring:

> When people have become so accustomed to observing the fundamental rules of social intercourse and when their labor has become so productive that they will voluntarily work *according to their ability* ... there will then be no need for society, in distributing products, to regulate the quantity to be received by each; each will take freely 'according to his needs'.[8]

Despite these attempts to put the discussion of a future communist society on a materialist basis, a new socialist movement would be well advised to steer clear of this topic completely. For one thing, it has always been one of the least convincing aspects of Marxist theory – one which inevitably encourages idealist tendencies in other areas. Individuals may wish to fantasize the nature of future societies, but a political movement which indulges such speculation perpetuates the dangerous notion of socialism as a 'wonder-drug' – a kind of social cure-all bound to sow illusions or invite justifiable ridicule.

Even more to the point, perhaps, the materialist considerations Marx and Engels brought to this discussion have themselves become somewhat dubious. Today the notion of unlimited growth in production has been called into question by aggravated problems of industrial pollution, toxic wastes, nuclear perils, ecological despoliation, looming environmental catastrophe and finite resources. Consequently, problems of unbridled population growth can no longer be dismissed as they once were by Marx and Engels. Rather than an idyllic world based on super-abundance, humanity's future is at least as likely to be shaped by the need to ensure justice and equity in a society characterized by limits.

Of course, science may well discover new boundless sources of energy. It may learn how to make the use of nuclear power safe and find benign ways of disposing of toxic wastes. It may develop new materials that will compensate for decimated natural resources and restore the planet's ozone layer. But until that happens, the idea of a communist society based on an unlimited economy of abundance had best be tabled.

Voluntarism and Dogmatism in the Socialist Project

Beyond its necessary critique of traditional Marxist and Marxist-Leninist doctrine, a resuscitated socialist movement must also examine certain tendencies which became identifying characteristics of its forbears: in particular, impulses toward voluntarism and dogmatism. Such inclinations seem to appear with regularity in ideologically motivated movements and so we can expect to encounter them again. But a socialist movement which can identify and see the negative consequences of such tendencies in its own legacy may be better prepared to curb them when they reappear in the future.

Even before the collapse of the 'socialist camp' made the question moot, the exaggerated claims and promethean promises of Marxism-Leninism had foundered on the forbidding reefs of realities it had obscured and, all too often, willfully distorted. Rarely has there been a supposedly scientific school of thought so prone to misassessments, wishful thinking, political obliviousness and a marked inclination to believe its own hyperbole.

In retrospect, one can see how these tendencies reflected a fundamentally idealist – that is, non-materialist – world outlook. Since human beings have the capacity to conceptualize their goals, idealist inclinations are, to a certain extent, ever-present in all social activity. But when a 'vanguard' immunizes itself against political accountability and treats its opinions as a theory so rooted in 'scientific law' that they take precedence over directly encountered realities, this valuable attribute of human cognition turns into its opposite – a roadmap for sectarianism, political arrogance and totalitarianism.

Voluntarism

At the center of Marx's historical materialist outlook is the following proposition: 'Human beings make their own history, but they do not make it just as they please; they do not make it under circumstances chosen by themselves, but under circumstances directly encountered, given and transmitted from the past.' [9]

Contrary to the above, however, the socialist movement has reflected a consistent tendency to overassess the capacity of the subjective factor in politics and to believe that resolute human consciousness alone can change social circumstances. Or, as Mao – surely one of the great voluntarists of communist history – was fond of saying: 'Political line determines everything.' Perhaps the most striking expression of this phenomenon in Marxism-Leninism is the belief that the vanguard party enjoys a seemingly unlimited capacity to order (and reorder) history on the basis of its own political principles.

Of course, a tendency toward voluntarism is almost inevitable in any revolutionary movement since a revolution is, by definition, an extraordinary attempt to change history by human activity. But while the subjective factor may well be the crucial one for success at the revolutionary moment, its capacity to change social relations is strictly limited by 'circumstances directly encountered, given and transmitted from the past'. The mark of a mature revolutionary movement is its ability to recognize those limitations and to readjust perspectives and even abandon goals considered as 'principles' when these prove to be unworkable or out of reach due to objective circumstance.

Movements and parties which fail to make those adjustments inevitably founder and come to naught. (Trotskyism, with its stubborn insistence that world proletarian revolution remains a timely and practical question, is a prime example.)

While a persistent pattern of voluntarism by a revolutionary movement invariably leads to a failure of the revolutionary project, its negative consequences are magnified a thousand-fold when put into practice by a party holding power. For with the full economic and military resources of state power at its command, a voluntarist-oriented ruling party can implement its policies by using arbitrary authority to bully its way past the checks social reality otherwise imposes. Thus the Soviet Union's administrative-command economy was, for a considerable time, immunized from the consequences of its economically unsound practices by state subsidies and deficit financing which covered over its gross inefficiency and waste.

An even more voluntarist approach to socialist construction was embodied in both the theory and practice of the 'Great Proletarian Cultural Revolution' in China. There Mao's desire to make a great leap into the future proposed to go further and faster than Stalin's 'Great Turn' did – and with even less of a material foundation.

In both cases, we can see the close and inevitable connection between a utopian conception of socialism and a voluntarist outlook on how to bring it about. It may be difficult for some to think of Stalin – the individual who more than any other made terror and a contempt for individual rights a central instrument of communist rule

– as a 'utopian', a term suggestive of high ideals and benevolence. (For some reason, the idea of Mao as a utopian doesn't seem as incongruous.) But even as the outlook of well-intentioned altruists, utopianism has a certain atmosphere of intellectual arrogance and condescension about it, implying a belief in one's own capacity not only to conceptualize ideal social arrangements but to direct history so as to realize them.

Stalin was a particular kind of utopian. He was an ideological zealot who had staked his prestige – to say nothing of his power – on an *a priori* certainty of the new social system's characteristic features. As a result, Stalinism attributed all opposition to this vision and all failures in carrying it out to subjective failings. For if the system was based on a 'scientific' conception of socialism, then opposition could only stem from a 'bourgeois world outlook' and failure could only reflect incompetence, 'opportunism' or deliberate 'treason'.

Although Marx's 'scientific socialism' was designed to put socialism on a historically rooted foundation, the Marxist legacy never completely freed itself from its utopian forbears. To some degree that was inevitable as Marx, Engels and other socialists speculated on the properties and characteristics of the coming social order. So long as such conjecture remained outside the realm of practical application, however, it was relatively harmless. (Less benign was the subsequent citation of these speculative thoughts as part of Marxist 'science', a practice which encouraged the dogmatic reification of Marxism.)

But as Communist Parties came to power first in Russia and then elsewhere, a persistent ultra-left current – invariably the political expression of voluntarism – swept through the communist movement. It is surely not without significance that the nominal 'socialist' transformations of the twentieth century have taken place everywhere *except* in those countries with presumably the most favorable objective conditions for socialism. It is likewise suggestive that it is precisely in those capitalist countries where communist parties have had a mass working-class following that tendencies toward 'revisionism' have been the most pronounced – an indication perhaps that in the countries of developed capitalism, the 'revolutionary spirit' is often strongest in those parties with the least degree of accountability to a mass social base.

In retrospect, however, we can see that the Soviet Union's own 'actually existing socialism' and its official Marxism-Leninism were the greatest purveyors of voluntarism and utopianism in the history of communism. Others were, of course, more extreme. (There always seems to be someone or some force to the left of the most virulent leftist.) But no other attempt to make history 'just as they please' had such a profound and longterm effect on both the communist movement and world history as did Stalin's 'revolution from above' in the early 1930s and the subsequent 'socialist' system which emerged from it.

Dogmatism

Just as 'actually existing socialism' bore little resemblance to Marx's notion that socialism was a transitional form linking capitalism and communism, so too was there little more than a formal relationship between Marxism-Leninism and the philosophical spirit and assumptions which illuminated Marx's work. Marxism-Leninism dutifully repeated certain propositions about class struggle, surplus value, world revolution, the dictatorship of the proletariat and so on. But the very act of treating these propositions as the 'essence' of Marxism was itself an expression of that same spirit of dogmatism which became such a glaring and characteristic disease of the International Communist Movement.

For those propositions were themselves the result of historical reflection and what Lenin called 'the concrete analysis of concrete conditions'. The tendency to elevate them to eternal principles, thereby removing them from their historical specificity, was perhaps the greatest disservice that Marxism-Leninism rendered the socialist movement, not least because it established an absolutist view of every assertion made in the name of Marxism. Historical 'laws', after all, are not subject to those essential dialectical qualifiers of scientific analysis – time, place and circumstance. As one high-ranking defender of the faith puts it:

> There is only one truth. The law of gravity does not apply exclusively to England simply because Newton was an Englishman. If there is a truth that applies only to Russia, or only to the United States, or to France, or to any other country, it means there is no truth at all.[10]

Unfortunately, such statements were not the inventions of unscrupulous anti-communists trying to demonstrate the absurdities of Marxism's claims on science. And yet Marxist-Leninist literature is replete with references to the 'purity' of its doctrine, the 'sacred' character of its principles and unscrupulous analogies between the physical sciences and the self-serving proclamations of its own high priests. How can any thinking person maintain respect for an ideological tendency which encourages its adherents to indulge in such blatant nonsense and actually rewards them for doing so?

But dogmatism is more than an embarrassing feature of 'actually existing socialism' and the movement built around it. Nor is it merely the result of shoddy thinking – although it clearly fosters modes of analysis which are simplistic to the point of puerility. In all doctrine-based movements – whether religious or secular – dogmatism is an infection which appears at the intersection of ideology and power. And by reifying the former in order to reinforce the latter, dogmatism functions as an instrument in the codification of existing authority.

In the communist movement, the principal repository of dogmatism has been Marxism-Leninism. By holding political analysis and critical thinking hostage to eternal principles and sacred texts, it became the agency for suppressing heresy, calumniating opponents and fostering a climate of ideological conformity and intellectual paralysis. Reinforcing the most dubious aspects of communist practice, Marxism-Leninism was a powerful barrier to unwelcome criticism and all attempts at internal reform except for those 'authorized' by communism's various ecclesiastic institutions.

It is a telling commentary on Marxism-Leninism's claim to science that its most damning charge against heretics within the ranks is revisionism – that is, the attempt to alter, reject or depart from 'basic principles'. The term crops up again and again in communism's checkered history and invariably on the same basis: abandonment of the notion that capitalism is on its last legs and that proletarian revolution is an imminent prospect on which the communist movement must base its political strategy. From Bernstein and Browder to Khrushchev and the Eurocommunists of the 1970s, this has been the basis for ideological and, in most cases, organizational excommunication.

One of the chief expressions of dogmatism in the communist movement – and a particular characteristic of Marxism-Leninism – was a marked penchant for universalizing the Soviet experience. Even Lenin – whose great materialist virtue was to address all questions not principally on the basis of doctrine but in light of concrete realities – occasionally fell into such a mode. Thus, while criticizing the dogmatism of 'infantile leftists', he was not above suggesting a 'repetition' of the Bolshevik Revolution's course of development as a 'historical inevitability':

> Certain fundamental features of our revolution have a significance that is not local, or peculiarly national, or Russian alone, but international .... I am speaking here of [international] in the narrowest sense of the word, taking international significance to mean the international validity or the historical inevitability of a repetition, on an international scale, of what has taken place in our country. It must be admitted that certain fundamental features of our revolution do possess this significance.[11]

Although Lenin's canonization of the Soviet experience statement is clearly cautious and somewhat reluctant ('It must be admitted, etc.'), no such hesitations are to be found in the subsequent certainty with which Marxism-Leninism promulgated its 'universal laws' of proletarian revolution, transition to socialism and the essential characteristics of socialist society. But as Rosa Luxemburg, a revolutionary thinker and leader generally excluded from the Marxist-Leninist pantheon, pointed out long before intellectual toadies had formulated such absolutes, 'Nothing is more contrary to the historic-dialectic method of Marxist thought than to separate social phenomena from their historic soil and to present these phenomena as abstract formulas having an absolute, general application.' 12

A new Socialist Movement

Where does all this leave those of us who, coming out of the Leninist legacy, still believe in socialism? Uncertain? Yes, but that's not necessarily a bad thing. Of course, it will take some getting used to. Ours has been a tradition steeped in a self-assurance which all too often was not only grating and uncalled-for; it was based, in good measure, on heatedly denying realities which others – not privy to our 'science' – kept calling to our attention. If an unaccustomed uncertainty is the price we have to pay for our emancipation from atrophied thought and cliché-ridden 'truths', it will be well worth it.

In the US today, most socialists – aside from those still locked into outmoded certainties – find themselves participating in a process of unaccustomed dialogue and collective reexamination with the goal of a regrouped and reoriented socialist movement. The following observations are offered in the spirit of that dialogue.

To begin with, I believe that we must face up to the fact that for us, the crisis of socialism did not begin with the collapse of the Soviet Union. Socialism in the US has been in crisis for more than 40 years, as demonstrated by the fact that during this period it has not had anything remotely resembling a mass social base. Members of socialist and communist organizations have been active in various mass movements which themselves have played a most important role in politics – in particular, the anti-war and anti-racist movements of the 1960s. But by no stretch of the imagination could it be said that these movements were influenced by a socialist perspective.

Consequently, US socialism resides in a world of its own, fundamentally an ideological rather than political space traditionally characterized by fierce but basically irrelevant debates. This condition should serve to remind us that socialism is primarily a concept in the minds of socialists. For most people, the point of political activity is to change ready-to-hand conditions of deprivation, injustice and oppression. What this means is that we must get back to the notion – which in the past we occasionally remembered to uphold in words – that genuinely popular movements for economic and social justice rather than inherited paradigms will determine our political agenda. The other way was not only arrogant. It was a prescription for perpetuating political futility and isolation.

As a result, the issues which are most likely to command the attention of a new socialist movement will focus on concrete questions of people's welfare, democracy and survival. I am not suggesting that we surrender a socialist perspective. But we must recognize that it is only as the existing system proves unwilling and incapable of responding to demands for reform that the popular movements will begin to raise their sights and address more fundamental questions of power and political realignment.

At the same time, there is no point in pretending that all popular struggles represent an equally significant challenge to capitalism. Elementary political sense shows that they do not. Certainly a new socialist movement must support and be active in all movements which attempt to expand democracy and improve the conditions of life for working people. But I strongly believe that the principal locus for building a movement for revolutionary political change in the US will be found in the intersection of class, race, nationality and gender: class because it is the property system and its basis in the exploitation of labor which is the cornerstone of capitalism, thereby making the working class the only viable mass social base for bringing that system to an end; race because historically this has been and continues to be the great divide in American social life which, in turn, has given rise to an advanced political consciousness in communities of color; nationality because immigration from Latin America and other parts of the Third World is rapidly changing the demographics of the US in general, but most especially of the working class; and gender because this is the area of US life in which the most dramatic social revolution of our time is taking place.

We will also have to come to terms with the fact that the era of the 'heroic guerilla' has come to an end. This is no small matter since, from Vietnam to El Salvador, support for and solidarity with national liberation struggles has been a driving force on the left – especially in the most developed capitalist countries – from the early 1960s to the mid-1980s. Of course, struggles for economic justice and national democracy in the Third World will continue to be central to world politics and it is incumbent on socialists in the capitalist heartland to support such movements. But we should also keep in mind that armed guerillas do not necessarily represent the most advanced or enlightened sectors of those struggles; nor should we perpetuate the illusion – so fashionable for a while in the recent past – that Third World national liberation movements will be world capitalism's gravediggers.

We must also be prepared to make a thorough and uncompromising reevaluation of the whole socialist ideological heritage. Clearly any attempt to perpetuate Marxism-Leninism – the sacred text of twentieth century communism – as our underlying framework will leave us mired in the failed constructs of the past. But a new socialist movement will have to go further and recognize that the exercise in iconography which appended an 'ism' to Marx's name has turned out to be a greater disservice to Karl Marx's ideas than all the attacks leveled at him in his own lifetime and since by the ideological representatives of capital.

Although idealist tendencies are to be found in the work of Marx and Engels – it would be surprising if they weren't – the negative consequences of those departures from materialist analysis do not rest primarily with them. Rather they rest principally with Marx and Engels' successors who lumped together a body of work informed by genuinely scientific investigation with a considerable amount of speculative extrapolation which, however provocative, can hardly be accorded similar standing.

Now it is long past time for socialists to divest themselves of that tail of an 'ism' which inevitably tended to transform the truly signal accomplishments of socialism's insightful pioneers into systems of intellectual suffocation. The very process of undertaking such a critique will serve a useful purpose if – all questions of substance aside – it frees socialism from that dolorous tendency to deify Marxist doctrine and to worship at its shrine which has plagued the socialist movement for the better part of 150 years.

I have no doubt that future generations will continue to view Marx and Engels as seminal figures in placing the search for social knowledge on a more scientific footing. In particular, I believe that Marx's historical materialist construct will be seen as a major turning point in that quest. But, as Roy Medvedev has pointed out, no science is characterized by the name of its founders. Many religions are – witness Christianity, Buddhism, Confucianism, for example. Astronomy, on the other hand, is not called Copernicanism, evolution is not Darwinism and Freudianism is only one school in the science of psychology. Surely this is why Marx declared he was not a Marxist.

Finally, following Marx, we have prided ourselves on the notion that our task was not simply to understand the world, but to change it. (In our vanity we ignored the fact that virtually all scientific advances have been closely linked to the active solution of practical questions.) All too often, however, this admirable standard led us to explain every phenomenon in accordance with received wisdom and our own preconceptions of change.

We need to get back to the idea that the real world is the only repository of truth; and that changing it depends on understanding it – not as something fixed in previous texts, but as a constantly developing, living organism in all its complexity, possibilities, limitations and richness.

Certainly it is hard to get used to the idea that the socialist epoch, which many of us thought had dawned in 1917, has not yet arrived. But accepting that fact and learning from this false start in the attempt to develop an alternative to capitalism can be an important first step in regaining the ideological momentum that will help put the socialist project back on history's agenda.

Notes and References

ABBREVIATIONS:

DIG: *Current Digest of the Soviet Press*
Fund: *Fundamentals of Marxist-Leninist Theory and Tactics of Revolution-*
  ary Parties
History CPSU: *The History of the CPSU (Short Course)*
IA: *International Affairs*
LCW: Lenin, *Collected Works*
LSW: Lenin, *Selected Works*
ME: Marx and Engels, *Complete Works*
MESW: Marx and Engels, *Selected Works in One Volume*
MGW: *Manchester Guardian Weekly*
MN: *Moscow News*
PA: *Political Affairs*
Polemic: *Polemic on the General Line of the International Communist*
  Movement
Preface: Marx, Preface to *The Critique of Political Economy*
Reader: *Reader in Marxist Philosophy*
STP: *Socialism: Theory and Practice*
WMR: *World Marxist Review*

Introduction

1. WMR, February 1990, p. 10.
2. PA, January, August 1992.
3. Boris Ponomarev, *Marxism-Leninism, A Flourishing Science* (New York: International, 1979).

Chapter 1 Marxism, Leninism and Marxism-Leninism

1. Leonid Brezhnev, cited by Mikhail Zimyanin, secretary of the CPSU Central Committee, in his opening address to a conference on 'Marxism–Leninism and the Present Epoch', Moscow, April 1980.
2. *Capital*, Vol. 1, 'Afterword to the Second German Edition', pp. 19–20 in the International Publishers Edition (New York: 1967).

3. *The Communist Manifesto*, in MESW, pp. 37–40.

4. *Socialism: Utopian and Scientific*, in MESW, p. 417.

5. Tom Bottomore, et. al., *A Dictionary of Marxist Thought*, (Cambridge, Mass.: Harvard University Press, 1987), p. 505.

6. Boris Ponomarev, *Marxism-Leninism, A Flourishing Science* (New York: International, 1979), p. 118.

7. *Fund.*, p. 36

8. *The Communist Manifesto*, in MESW, p. 63.

9. 'Two Tactics', in LCW, Vol. 9, p. 50.

10. Ironically, credit for first use of the telling hyphenation appears to rest with another old Bolshevik, Gregori Zinoviev, who coined the term 'Marxo–Leninism' in 1925. (Zinoviev was among those shot in the purges of the 1930s.) *See* Roy Medvedev, *Leninism and Western Socialism*, (London: Verso, 1981) p. 18.

11. Bruce Franklin, *The Essential Stalin*, (New York: Doubleday, 1972) p. 89.

12. Stalin, *Works*, 13 vols (Moscow: Foreign Language Publishing House, 1954–55), Vol. 9, p. 15.

13. 'The Roots of Stalinism', in *Science and Life*, November 1988, cited in DIG, 5 April 1989, p. 4.

14. *History CPSU*, pp. 105, 114. *The History of the CPSU (Short Course)* was the single most widely used text in the internal education work of the various Communist Parties throughout the 1940s and 1950s. It was first issued in the US in 1939 by International Publishers, the publishing house of the CPUSA. In 1940 International published the section on Marxist philosophy as a separate pamphlet, *Dialectical and Historical Materialism*. After Khrushchev's denunciation of Stalin in 1956, a new version of the CPSU History was produced. While following the outline of the original *Short Course*, this edition significantly altered the text in many places. It also completely rewrote the section on Marxist philosophy, eliminating the passages cited here. In 1975, International Publishers brought out a new edition of the pamphlet.

15. Bottomore et al., *Dictionary*, pp. 310–11.

16. *History CPSU*, p. 114.

17. LCW, Vol. 1, pp. 192, 194.

18. Trofim Lysenko, a young agronomist, created a sensation in the mid-1930s with his theory of 'progressive biology', whose fundamental thesis was the inheritance of acquired characteristics. Lysenko's charge that those who upheld traditional genetic theory were infected by 'bourgeois ideology' was hailed by Stalin, who incorporated it into his broader ideological purge of the period.

Large numbers of biologists and agricultural specialists who disagreed with Lysenko (and, therefore, Stalin) were arrested and a number were executed. Meanwhile Lysenko won two Stalin prizes, and in 1938 was appointed president of the Lenin Academy of Agricultural Sciences. In 1948 he undertook what Roy Medvedev would call 'the total pogrom of genetics' (*Let History Judge*, New York: Columbia University Press p. 561). The attempt to implement Lysenko's approach resulted in major setbacks in agriculture, but they remained official policy until some time after Stalin's death.

19. Stalin, *Economic Problems of Socialism in the USSR* (Moscow, 1952), p. 30.
20. Ibid., p. 31.
21. Ibid., p. 34.
22. Robert V. Daniels, *A Documentary History of Communism*, 2 vols (New York: Random House, 1960) p. 7 (translation by Daniels).
23. *Kommunist*, No. 18, 1979, noting the hundredth anniversary of Stalin's birth. The full text of this remarkable document was reprinted in *Political Affairs*, the theoretical journal of the US Communist Party, in July 1980.
24. Boris Ponomarev, *Communism in a Changing World* (New York: Sphinx, 1983), pp. 25–26.
25. *World Marxist Review*, the 'theoretical and information journal of Communist and Workers Parties', was perhaps the principle vehicle for thundering proclamations concerning the 'purity of Marxist theory' and assertions that socialist politics can be advanced 'only on the basis of this universally significant scientific doctrine'. See in particular the following issues: March 1983, pp. 1–5; May 1983, pp. 1–8; February 1984, pp. 1–7.
26. Speech at an International Conference on the Future of Socialism, 12 October 1990, in New York City, printed in *Crossroads*, December 1990, p. 2.
27. From 'The New Course' (1943) cited in Albert Fried and Ronald Sanders, *Socialist Thought, A Documentary History* (New York: Doubleday, 1964), p. 497.
28. Trotsky, *Basic Writings*, ed. Irving Howe (New York: Schocken Books, 1976), p. 127.
29. Cited in Isaac Deutscher, *The Prophet Armed: Trotsky 1879–1921* (New York: Knopf, 1965), pp. 158–9.
30. In Medvedev, *Leninism and Western Socialism*, p. 175. Medvedev notes that this quotation comes from the stenographic record of a speech made by Lenin before the Petrograd Soviet and that the

same statement as it appears in the *Collected Works* (edited under Stalinist supervision) contains language not in the original.

31. Ibid.
32. LCW, Vol. 21, p. 342; cited by Stalin in 'Concerning Questions of Leninism' (1926), in *Works*, Vol. 8, p. 73.
33. LCW, Vol. 33, p. 474.
34. Ibid.
35. Lin Piao, 1966 speech celebrating the Cultural Revolution, in *Important Documents of the Great Proletarian Cultural Revolution in China*, (Beijing: Foreign Language Press, 1970), p. 245.
36. Jean Daubier, *A History of the Chinese Cultural Revolution* (New York: Random House, 1974), p. 13.
37. *Polemic*, (Beijing: Foreign Language Press, 1965), p. 244.
38. Mao, *On the Correct Handling of Contradictions Among the People*, (New York: New Century, 1957) p. 29. A number of these propositions – particularly on the new, favorable world balance of forces, but also some tendencies to underestimate the consequences of a nuclear war – were subsequently adopted by the CPSU during the Brezhnev years.
39. *Polemic*, pp. 201–2.
40. Speech at the Supreme State Conference, 28 January 1958, cited in Stuart Schram, *Chairman Mao Talks to the People* (New York: Pantheon, 1974) p. 93.
41. Ibid., p. 94.
42. Mao, *A Critique of Soviet Economics* (New York: Monthly Review, 1977), p. 66.
43. Ibid., p. 54.
44. Ibid., pp. 84–5.
45. *Important Documents of the Cultural Revolution*, p. 130.
46. Comments by Mao as cited in Lin Piao's Report to the Ninth National Congress of the CCP, 1 April 1969, in Ibid., pp. 23, 31. The chief target of this diatribe was Liu Shao–chi, still head of state in 1966.
47. Mao, *Critique*, p. 48.
48. 'The Poverty of Philosophy', in *Reader*, p. 188.
49. Cited in Daubier, *History of the Chinese Cultural Revolution*, p. 312.

Chapter 2 Capitalism on the Rocks

1. *Communist Manifesto*, in MESW, p. 44.
2. Ibid., p. 63.
3. *Imperialism*, in MESW, p. 180.

4. Ibid., p. 233.
5. Ibid., p. 241.
6. Ibid., p. 260.
7. 'Imperialism and the Split in Socialism', in LCW, Vol. 23, pp. 105–7.
8. LCW, Vol. 27, p. 131.
9. G.A. Kozlov, *Political Economy: Capitalism* (Moscow: Progress, 1977), p. 375.
10. 'Foundations of Leninism', in LCW, Vol. 6, p. 99.
11. Cited in Stephen F. Cohen, *Bukharin and the Bolshevik Revolution* (New York: Oxford University Press, 1971), pp. 255–6.
12. Stalin, *Economic Problems of Socialism in the USSR* (Moscow: 1952) p. 30.
13. Ibid. pp. 31–2.
14. Ibid.
15. V. Trepelkov, *The General Crisis of Capitalism* (Moscow: Progress, 1983), p. 26.
16. *Documents of the International Conference of Communist and Workers Parties* (Moscow: Novosti, 1969) p. 13.
17. G. Chernikov, *The Crisis of Capitalism and the Condition of the Working People* (Moscow: Progress, 1980) p. 180.
18. Konstantin Zaradov, editor of WMR, cited in PA, January 1984, p.40.
19. Boris Ponomarev, *Lenin and the World Revolutionary Process*, (Moscow: Progress, 1980) pp. 233–4.
20. P. Novoselov, ed., *Problems of the Communist Movement* (Moscow: Progress, 1975) pp. 41–2.
21. 'The Triple-Tiered Crisis of Capitalism', PA, January 1984, p. 3.
22. *Fund.*, p. 221.
23. Greg Tarpinian, 'Labor and the Global Economy', *Crossroads*, February 1991.
24. Ivan Antonovich, vice-rector of the CPSU Central Committee's Academy of Social Sciences 'Dialectics of an Integral World', IA, Vol. 5, 1988, pp. 48–9.
25. *Fundamentals of Marxism–Leninism, a Manual* (Moscow: Foreign Languages, 1963) p. 294.
26. *Imperialism*, in MESW, p. 184.
27. Ibid., p. 224.
28. Ibid., p. 240.
29. While the US did not enter the war until 1941, after it was attacked by Japan, it was the main supplier and reserve for the French and British and Washington's policy at the time was clearly based on the notion that a Nazi–dominated Europe posed a grave threat to US national interests.

30. *Die Neue Zeit*, No. 5, 30 April 1915, cited by Lenin in 'The Collapse of the Second International', in LCW, Vol. 21, p. 223.
31. 'Imperialism', in MESW, p. 241.
32. Victor Sheinis, 'Structural Shifts in the Capitalist Economy and the Developing Nations' Prospects', *Asia and Africa Today*, No. 6, 1988.
33. 'Imperialism', in MESW, p. 262.
34. 'Preface' in MESW, p. 183.

Chapter 3 The Vanguard Party

1. 'An Urgent Question', in LCW, Vol. 4, p. 475.
2. *History CPSU*, p. 48.
3. 'An Urgent Question', in LCW, Vol. 4, pp. 221–2.
4. 'A Retrograde Trend in Russian Social–Democracy', in LCW, Vol. 4, p. 257.
5. *What Is to be Done?* in LCW, Vol. 5, p. 367.
6. LCW, Vol. 4, pp. 211–12.
7. Ibid., pp. 221–2.
8. Ibid., pp. 479–80.
9. LCW, Vol. 6, p. 503.
10. LCW, Vol. 9, p. 166. (Lenin includes here a number of topical, parenthetical asides which have been edited out.)
11. *Fund*, p. 339.
12. LCW, Vol. 10, p. 314.
13. Cited in Roy Medvedev, *On Socialist Democracy* (New York: Norton, 1975) p. 63, from the fifth Russian language edition of LCW, Vol. 41, p. 108.
14. Ibid., p. 63.
15. *History CPSU* (1960 edition) p. 357.
16. *What Is to be Done?* in LCW, Vol. 5, p. 440.
17. 'Terms of Admission into the Communist International', in LCW, Vol. 31, p. 210.
18. *Communist Manifesto*, in MESW, p. 46.
19. WMR, March 1988, p. 29.
20. Ibid.
21. *Fund*, pp. 336–40.
22. LCW, Vol. 10, pp. 442–3.
23. Pyotr Fedoseyev, vice-president of the USSR Academy of Sciences, in WMR, March 1983, p. 12–13.
24. Ibid.
25. Rosa Luxemburg, *The Russian Revolution and Leninism or Marxism?* (Ann Arbor, Mich.: University of Michigan Press, 1961) p. 102.

Chapter 4 The Transition

1. Fyodor Burlatsky, 'What Kind of Socialism Do We Need?' *Literary Gazette*, 3 June 1988, p. 35.
2. MESW, p. 52.
3. 'Two Tactics', in LCW, Vol. 9, p. 52.
4. Ibid., p. 50.
5. Ibid., p. 98.
6. Gennadi Lisichkin, 'Myths and Reality', in *Social Sciences*, quarterly journal of the USSR Academy of Sciences, No. 1, 1990, pp. 70–1.
7. 'Russian Communist Party Draft Program', in LCW, Vol., 29, pp. 112, 115. Since the text appears in Lenin's *Collected Works*, the assumption is that it was largely written by him.
8. Ibid., p. 116.
9. Trotsky, *Basic Writings*, ed. Irving Howe (New York: Schocken, 1976) p. 161.
10. Ibid., p. 162.
11. Leaders of the armies trying to oust the Bolsheviks in the civil war.
12. LCW, Vol. 33, p. 63.
13. *History CPSU*, p. 249.
14. LCW, Vol. 33, p. 61.
15. Ibid., p. 64.
16. LCW, Vol. 32, p. 326.
17. LCW, Vol. 33, p. 70.
18. All figures taken from Alec Nove, *An Economic History of the USSR*, (Harmondsworth: Penguin, 1969), Chapter 4.
19. 'On Cooperation', in LCW, Vol. 33, p. 467.
20. Ibid., p. 468.
21. Ibid., p. 474.
22. Ibid., pp. 470–1.
23. The text of Preobrazhensky's paper, delivered to the Communist Academy in 1924, appears in E.H. Carr's *Socialism in One Country: 1924–1926* (New York: Macmillan, 1958), Vol. 1, pp. 202–8; a later version, published in 1926, appears in Preobrazhensky's *The New Economics*.
24. N. Bukharin and E. Preobrazhensky, *The ABC of Communism*, ed. E.H. Carr, (Harmondsworth: Penguin, 1969, p. 28.
25. *History CPSU*, p. 288.
26. Ibid., p. 303.
27. Ibid., p. 288.
28. Medvedev, *Let History Judge*, p. 225.
29. Pravda, 6 January 1989, from DIG, 1 February 1989, p. 14.

30. Cited in Medvedev, *History*, pp. 240–1.
31. SCW, Vol. 12, pp. 22–3.
32. Ibid.
33. Trotsky, *Basic Writings*, p. 138.
34. Ibid., p. 182.
35. Ibid., p. 185.
36. Ibid., p. 183.
37. Cited in Roy Medvedev, *Leninism and Western Socialism* (London: Verso, 1981), p. 180.
38. *Fund*, p. 130.
39. Stalin, *Dialectical and Historical Materialism* (New York: International, 1940) p. 14.
40. *History CPSU*, p. 305.
41. *Fund*, pp. 129–30.
42. LCW, Vol. 23, p. 371.
43. Vladimir Stanis, *The Socialist Transformation of Agriculture*, (Moscow: Progress, 1976) p. 11.
44. *Fund*, p. 132
45. 'Imperialism', in LCW, Vol. 22, p. 205.
46. LCW, Vol. 25, p. 358.
47. 'State and Revolution', in LCW, Vol. 25, p. 426.
48. 'Critique of Gotha Program', in MESW, p. 323.
49. SCW, Vol. 11, p. 263.
50. Ibid.
51. 'Principles of Communism', in ME, Vol. 6, p. 350.
52. Grigory Vodolazov, 'A Philosophical and Sociological Commentary on V. Grossman's Novella, *Everything Flows*', reprinted in DIG, No. 37, 1989, p. 8.
53. LCW, Vol. 26, p, 52.
54. *History CPSU* (1939 edition), p. 180.
55. *History CPSU* (1960 edition), p. 211.
56. LCW, Vol. 24, p. 22.
57. Interview with Gabriel Popov, *Izvestia*, 28 June 1990, in DIG, No. 26, 1990.

Chapter 5 'Actually Existing Socialism'

1. Peter Fedoseyev, member of the CPSU Central Committee, vice-president of the USSR Academy of Sciences. WMR, March 1983, pp. 10–11.
2. Speech at Extraordinary Congress of Soviets, 1936, cited by Lisichkin in 'Myths and Reality', *Social Sciences*, 1990, No. 2, p. 144.

3. Ibid.
4. Anatoli Butenko, *Theory & Practice of Real Socialism* (Moscow: Novosti, 1983), pp. 17–18.
5. V. Afanasyev, *Socialism and Communism* (Moscow: Novosti, 1972), p. 71.
6. MESW, p. 52.
7. *Marx, Engels, Lenin on Scientific Communism* (Moscow: Progress, 1967) p. 327.
8. MESW, p. 52.
9. ME, Vol. 6, pp. 351–7.
10. LCW, Vol. 42, p. 96, cited in Richard Kosolapov, *Problems of Socialist Theory* (Moscow: Progress, 1974).
11. LCW, Vol. 33, p. 63.
12. Marx, *Capital* (New York: International, 1967), Vol. 1, p. 763.
13. *New York Review of Books*, 19 November 1992, p. 22.
14. Speech on the Agrarian Question, 4 June 1917, at the First Congress of Peasants' Deputies, in LCW, Vol. 24, pp. 502–3.
15. Stalin, *Economic Problems of Socialism in the USSR* (Moscow, 1952), p. 15.
16. Boris Bolotin, *Moscow News* No. 34, 1987, p. 11.
17. Report to CPSU Central Committee meeting, 15 March 1989, in DIG, 12 April 1989, pp. 4–5.
18. Report to the 18th Congress of the CPSU, 10 March 1939, in Stalin, *Problems of Leninism* (Moscow: Foreign Languages, 1958), pp. 765–6.
19. CPSU Report, 15 March 1989, pp. 3–4.
20. Medvedev, *History*, p. 248.
21. Ibid., p. 249.
22. For detailed facts and figures, *see* Ibid., pp. 248–54.
23. Ibid., p. 251.
24. Cited in Stephen F. Cohen and Katrina vanden Heuvel, *Voices of Glasnost* (New York: Norton, 1989), p. 146.
25. Cited in Stephen F. Cohen, *An End to Silence* (New York: Norton, 1982), pp. 223–6.
26. *Washington Post*, reprinted in MGW, 14 August 1983.
27. *Kommunist*, No. 3, in Robert V. Daniels, *A Documentary History of Communism*, 2 vols (New York: Random House, 1960), pp. 420, 422.
28. See Gorbachev's Report to the CPSU Central Committee Meeting of 27–8 January 1987.
29. Ibid., p. 14.
30. Abraham Brumberg, ed., *Chronicle of a Revolution* (New York: Pantheon, 1990), p. 54.

31. STP, September 1989, pp. 22–3.
32. *Communist Manifesto*, in MESW, p. 47.
33. Calculations drawn from reports of the State Committee on Statistics; see *The Economist*, 11 August 1990, p. 67.
34. *New York Times*, 15 November 1992.
35. See *Moscow News*, No. 14, 1988, p. 13.
36. See Marx, *Wages, Price and Profit*, in MESW, p. 202.
37. Stalin, *Economic Problems*, pp. 19, 23.
38. See Abraham Bergson, *Planning and Productivity Under Soviet Socialism* (New York: Columbia University Press, 1968) and *Productivity and the Social System – the USSR and the West* (Cambridge, Mass.: Harvard University Press, 1977).
39. Anders Aslund, *Gorbachev's Struggle for Economic Reform* (Ithaca, NY: Cornell University Press, 1989), p. 16.
40. Abel Aganbegyan, *The Economic Challenge of Perestroika* (Bloomington, Ind.: Indiana University Press, 1988) p. 36.
41. Figures provided by first deputy chairman of Gosstandart (State Committee for Standards), Boris Sokolov, *Izvestia*, 16 December 1987, cited in Aslund, *Gorbachev's Struggle*, p. 79.
42. *Ogonyok*, No. 29, 1987, cited in Aslund, *Gorbachev's Struggle*, p. 17.
43. Aganbegyan, *Economic Challenge*, p. 36.
44. Aslund, *Gorbachev's Struggle*, p. 77.
45. Brumberg, *Chronicle*, p. 53.
46. Mao, *A Critique of Soviet Economics* (New York: Monthly Review, 1977), p. 48.
47. Ibid., p. 51.
48. Ibid., pp. 88–9.
49. Usevolod Kulikov, 'Economic Laws of Socialism' *Social Sciences*, No. 4, 1990, p. 72.
50. 'Critique of the Gotha Program', in MESW, p. 325.
51. Kulikov, 'Economic Laws', p. 73.
52. 'Critique of the Gotha Program', in MESW, p. 322.
53. Ibid., p. 324.
54. Aslund, *Gorbachev's Struggle*, p. 19.
55. See *US News & World Report* (3 April 1989, pp. 43–4). Figures taken from both Soviet and western sources.
56. *Izvestia*, 26 May 1990, in DIG, Vol. 42, No. 21.
57. *New York Times*, 22 January 1990, p. A8.
58. Aganbegyan, *Challenge*, p. 16.
59. *Izvestia*, 26 May 1990.
60. Interviewed by the author in Tashkent, November 1989.
61. Interviewed by the author in Tallinn, November 1989.

62. Vladimir Tikhonov, *Soviet Economy: Achievements, Problems, Prospects* (Moscow: Novosti, 1983), p. 83.
63. *Izvestia*, 4 November 1990, in DIG, 5 December 1990, p. 12.
64. Mikhail Gorbachev, 'Tasks of the Party in the Radical Restructuring of Economic Management', Report to the Plenary Meeting of the CPSU Central Committee, 25–6 June 1987, p. 37.
65. See Marx, Preface, in MESW, pp. 182–3.
66. Report to the Congress of People's Deputies, 7 June 1989.
67. R. Bakhtamov and P. Volin. Cited in Roy Medvedev, On Socialist Democracy (New York: Norton, 1975), p. 393.
68. *25th Congress of the CPSU Documents & Resolutions*, (Moscow: Novosti, 1976), p. 47, 52.
69. *26th Congress of the CPSU Documents & Resolutions*, (Moscow: Novosti, 1981), pp. 42, 56.
70. WMR, May 1982, p. 48.
71. Medvedev, *Socialist Democracy*, p. 393.
72. *Literary Gazette*, July 1990.
73. Aganbegyan, *Economic Challenge*, p. 20.
74. Ibid., p. 85.
75. Ibid., p. 93.
76. Medvedev, *Socialist Democracy*, pp. 242–3.
77. 'A Historic Stage on the Road to Communism', WMR, December 1977, p. 7.
78. Tikhonov, *Soviet Economy*, p. 200.
79. A. Yegorov, director of the CPSU Institute of Marxism–Leninism, at a 1980 Conference on 'Marxism–Leninism and the Present Epoch', Moscow, STP Supplement V, 1980, p. 15.
80. Boris Ponomarev, *Communism in a Changing World* (New York: Sphinx, 1983), p. 65.
81. Program of the CPSU, adopted at its 22nd Congress, 31 October 1961; cited in Daniels, *Documentary History*, p. 337.
82. Nikolay Iribadjakov, 'Developed Socialist Society', PA, June 1974, p. 23.
83. Fedoseyev, WMR, March 1983, p. 15.
84. *Fund*, p. 197.

Chapter 6   Dictatorship of the Proletariat

1. *State and Revolution*, in LCW, Vol. 25, p. 411.
2. *Critique of the Gotha Program*, in MESW, p. 331. Marx's first known reference to the dictatorship of the proletariat is in his *Class Struggles in France, 1848–1850*, written in 1850. But according to

Lenin, Marx himself credited French workers who had come up with the slogan, 'Overthrow of the bourgeoisie! Dictatorship of the Working Class!' (See Roy Medvedev, *Leninism and Western Socialism* (London: Verso, 1981), p. 29.)

3. 'The Civil War in France', in MESW, p. 294.
4. Ibid., and introduction to the 1891 edition, in MESW, p. 262.
5. Ibid., p. 294.
6. *The Immediate Tasks of the Soviet Government*, in LSW, p. 424.
7. Cited by Medvedev, *Leninism and Western Socialism*, p. 49. (LCW, Vol. 10, p. 246, has a slightly different translation, but the substance is the same.)
8. *Renegade Kautsky*, in LCW, Vol. 28, p. 236.
9. Cited in Medvedev *Leninism and Western Socialism*, p. 52. See also *Left Wing Communism*, LCW, Vol. 31, pp. 44–5.
10. See Marx, 'Letter to J. Wedemeyer', 5 March 1852, in Marx and Engels, *Selected Correspondence*, p. 86.
11. Rosa Luxemburg, *The Russian Revolution and Leninism or Marxism?* (Ann Arbor, Mich.: University of Michigan Press, 1961), p. 79.
12. *State and Revolution*, in LCW, p. 337
13. Preface in MESW, p. 182.
14. P. Novoselov, ed., *Problems of the Communist Movement* (Moscow: Progress, 1975), p. 11.
15. Cited in Stalin, *Problems of Leninism* (Moscow: Foreign Languages, 1958), p. 169.
16. Ibid., p. 168.
17. G.A. Kozlov, *Political Economy: Socialism* (Moscow: Progress, 1977) p. 25.
18. Arvid Pelshe, CPSU Politburo member, WMR, January 1983, pp. 6–10.
19. Abdulsalam Guseinov, Vadim Mezhuyev and Valentin Tolstykh, 'The Apparat, the Party and Power', *Moscow News*, No. 5, 1990, p. 7.
20. Cited in Leonid Radzikhovsky, 'The 'Inner' Party', MN, No. 4, 1990, p. 6.
21. *Izvestia*, 2 November 1988, in DIG, 30 November 1988.
22. Ibid.
23. Mikhail Gorbachev, 'Reorganization and the Party's Personnel Policy', report to a Plenary Meeting of the CPSU Central Committee, 27 January 1987 (Moscow: Novosti, 1987) p. 16.
24. *Izvestia*, 30 June 1990, in DIG, Vol. 42, No. 26.
25. Roy Medvedev, *On Socialist Democracy* (New York: Norton, 1975) p. 111. See especially the whole of Chapter 6 on 'Inner–Party Democracy'.

26. *Renegade Kautsky*, in LCW, Vol. 28, p. 243.
27. *Immediate Tasks*, in LSW, p. 424.
28. *State and Revolution*, in LSW, p. 272.
29. LCW, Vol. 30, p. 421.
30. *Immediate Tasks* in LSW, pp. 421–2.
31. *Civil War in France*, in MESW, p. 297.
32. K. Zarodov, *The Political Economy of Revolution* (Moscow: Progress, 1981) p. 126. (Zarodov was at the time editor of the *World Marxist Review*.)
33. Cited in Michael Waller, *Democratic Centralism* (Manchester University Press, 1981), p. 53.
34. Ibid., p. 53.
35. See Robert Sharlet, 'De–Stalinization and Soviet Constitutionalism', in Stephen F. Cohen, et al. eds, *Soviet Union Since Stalin*, (Bloomington, Ind.: Indiana University Press), pp. 102–3.
36. Vladimir Alekseyevich Boldyrev, director of the Administration for the Protection of State Secrets in the Press under the USSR Council of Ministers. *Izvestia*, 3 November 1988; reprinted in DIG, 30 November 1988, p. 1.
37. Cited in Roy Medvedev, *On Socialist Democracy* p. 44.
38. *Soviet Life*.
39. *Renegade Kautsky*, in LCW, Vol. 28, p. 249.
40. *Pravda*, 20 February 1976. Reprinted in its entirety in PA, December 1976. The citations appear on p. 44.
41. *New Times*, No. 40, 1989, p. 32.
42. MN, 28 May 1989. See also DIG (No. 20, 1987, pp. 8–9) for articles detailing various Soviet court practices. For reports of treating political opponents as mental health cases, see especially an article by Soviet psychiatrist Mikhail Buyanov in *Uchitelskaya Gazeta*, 19 November 1988, excerpts from which appear in the *New York Times* of 22 November 1988; see also Vyacheslav Bakhmin, 'Looking into Psychiatric Wards', *New Times*, No. 37, 1990; and Natalya Gevorkyan, 'In the Madhouse', MN, No. 49, 1991.
43. Dmitri I. Plushkov, interviewed in Moscow by reporter Steven Erlanger, *New York Times*, 11 May 1992.
44. Cited in Abraham Brumberg, *Chronicle of a Revolution* (New York: Pantheon, 1990), p. 244 (fn). Vishinsky's comments are from his book, *The Theory of Legal Evidence in Soviet Law*.
45. Ibid., p. 86.
46. *Izvestia*, 13 July 1990, from DIG, 15 August 1990.
47. *Renegade Kautsky*, in LCW, Vol. 28, p. 108.

48. *26th Congress of the CPSU Documents & Resolutions* (Moscow: Novosti, 1981), p. 97.
49. Ibid., p. 98.
50. Medvedev, *On Socialist Democracy*, p. 169.
51. Ibid., p. 174.
52. Ibid., p. 188.
53. Roy Medvedev, *Let History Judge* (New York: Columbia University Press, 1989), p. 832.
54. *Socialist Realism in Literature and Art* (Moscow: Progress, 1971) p. 162.
55. From the statutes of the Union of Writers, cited in Medvedev, *On Socialist Democracy*, p. 175.
56. *Socialist Realism*, p. 13.
57. Report to the Leningrad branch of the Union of Soviet Writers and the Leningrad City Committee of the Communist Party, 21 August 1946. Cited in Robert V. Daniels, *A Documentary History of Communism*, 2 vols (New York: Random House, 1960) p. 299.
58. *Socialist Realism*, pp. 72–4. The inclusion of Tvardovsky's remarks in this collection of articles published in 1971 is rather remarkable. It was clearly out of step with the rest of the book and may have been 'smuggled' into it by a sympathetic editor.
59. Medvedev, *History*, p. 5.
60. Stephen F. Cohen, *An End To Silence* (New York: Norton, 1982) p. 139.
61. Medvedev, *On Socialist Democracy*, p. 193.

Chapter 7 World Revolution I

1. *Principles of Communism*, in ME, Vol. 6, p. 351.
2. *Communist Manifesto*, in MESW, p. 40.
3. Ibid., p. 63.
4. 'Letter to Engels', 8 October 1858, *Selected Correspondence*, p. 134.
5. Ibid., p. 6.
6. *Critique of Gotha Program*, in MESW, p. 327.
7. LCW, Vol. 8, p. 303.
8. *What Is To Be Done?* in LCW, Vol. 5, p. 386.
9. *Marxism and Revisionism*, in LCW, Vol. 15, p. 39.
10. F. Engels, Preface to *The Condition of the Working Class in England*, in MESW, Vol. 3, p. 450.
11. Ibid.
12. LCW, Vol. 15, p. 237.
13. LCW, Vol. 17, p. 95.

14. LCW, Vol. 18, p. 335.
15. LCW, Vol. 21, p. 126.
16. Ibid., p. 216.
17. Ibid.
18. *Collapse of Second International*, in LCW, Vol. 21, p. 242.
19. *Imperialism*, in LCW, Vol. 22, p. 301.
20. LCW, Vol. 21, pp. 242–3.
21. Ibid., p. 343.
22. *Imperialism and the Split in Socialism*, in LCW, Vol. 23, p. 105.
23. Cited by Lenin in *The Right of Nations to Self-Determination*, in LCW, Vol. 20, p. 430.
24. A resolution to this effect was proposed to the 1907 Congress of the Second International in Stuttgart by its Colonial Commission. The resolution was finally voted down by a vote of 127 to 108. [Cited in Tom Bottomore, et al., *A Dictionary of Marxist Thought* (Cambridge, Mass.: Harvard University Press, 1987), p. 235.]
25. LCW, Vol. 20, p. 404, from her article, 'The National Question and Autonomy' (1908–9).
26. Ibid., pp. 405–6, 411–12.
27. LCW, Vol. 23, p. 67.
28. LCW, Vol. 22, pp. 151–2.
29. Ibid.
30. LCW, Vol. 30, p. 159.
31. *The Path Which Led Me To Leninism*, in *Ho Chi Minh on Revolution*, pp. 64–5.
32. LCW, p. 244.
33. *Ho Chi Minh*, p. 23.
34. '7th Congress of the Russian Communist Party', March 1918, in LCW, Vol. 27, p. 119.
35. LCW, Vol. 21, p. 200.
36. Ibid., pp. 40–1.
37. LCW, Vol. 28, p. 113.
38. Cited in Fernando Claudin, *The Communist Movement from Comintern to Cominform* (New York: Monthly Review, 1975), Vol. 1, p. 104.
39. LCW, Vol. 31, p. 382.
40. *Fund*, p. 44.
41. Adopted at the 2nd Congress of the Comintern, August 1920, cited in Boris Leibson, *International Unity of Communists* (Moscow: Novosti, 1981) p. 17.
42. LCW, Vol. 30, p. 33.
43. Cited in Claudin, *Communist Movement*, Vol. 1, p. 71.

44. 'Report on the Tactics of the Russian Communist Party' to the Third Congress of the Communist International, 5 July 1921, in LCW, Vol. 32, p. 480.
45. Stalin, 'Foundations of Leninism', in Problems of Leninism (Moscow: Foreign Languages, 1958), p. 44.
46. Ibid., p. 197.
47. 'Stalinism and Bolshevism' in Trotsky, Basic Writings, ed. Irving Howe (New York: Schocken, 1976) p. 362.
48. Stalin, Problems of Leninism, p. 195.
49. LCW, Vol. 32, p. 492.
50. LCW, Vol. 33, p. 474.
51. Cited in Roy Medvedev, On Socialist Democracy, p. 186.
52. Stalin, Problems of Leninism, p. 199.
53. Mikhail Suslov, Leninism and the Revolutionary Transformation of the World (Moscow: Progress, 1971), p. 34.
54. See Outline History of the Communist International (Moscow: Institute of Marxism-Leninism of the CPSU, 1971), pp. 350–70.
55. Cited in Claudin, Communist Movement, Vol. 1, p. 171.
56. 'Preface', in MESW, p. 183.
57. Fund, p. 36.

Chapter 8   World Revolution II

1. V. Trepelkov, The General Crisis of Capitalism (Moscow: Progress, 1983), p. 21.
2. Engels, Principles of Communism, in ME, Vol. 6, p. 351.
3. Roy Medvedev, On Socialist Democracy (New York: Norton, 1975), p. 190. Medvedev points out that this statement was not openly cited in the Soviet Union until 1947.
4. LCW, Vol. 30, p. 293.
5. Trepelkov, General Crisis of Capitalism, p. 39.
6. Interview with Professor I. Krivoguz (April 1989), cited in Jonathan Eisen, The Glasnost Reader (New York: New American Library, 1990), p. 315.
7. Fund, p. 14.
8. Stalin, Economic Problems of Socialism in the USSR (Moscow: 1952), pp. 33, 35.
9. Ibid., p. 32.
10. Speech at Sixth Congress of the Socialist Unity Party of (East) Germany, 16 January 1963, cited in Polemic, p. 243.
11. Polemic, p. 63.
12. Fund, p. 92.

13. From the Statement of the Meeting of Representatives of the Communist and Workers' Parties (1960), in *Fund*, p. 68.
14. Brezhnev, Report to the 25th Congress of the CPSU, p. 12.
15. Andranik Migranyan, *Moscow News*, No. 34, 1989, p. 6.
16. Alexander Dubcek, *Hope Dies Last*, (New York: Kodanska International, 1993), p. 212.
17. Richard Kosolapov, *Problems of Socialist Theory* (Moscow: Progress, 1974), p. 19.
18. 1960 Statement, *Fund*, p. 78.
19. Ibid., pp. 82–3.
20. Kosolapov, *Problems of Socialist Theory*, p. 19.
21. *Fund.*, p. 325.
22. V. Solodovnikov and V. Bogoslovsky, *Non–Capitalist Development: An Historical Outline* (Moscow: Progress, 1975), p. 102.
23. V. Chirkin and Yu Yudin, *A Socialist–Oriented State* (Moscow: Progress, 1983), pp. 59–60.
24. Solodovnikov and Bogoslovsky, *Non-Capitalist Development*, p. 102.
25. *Fund*, pp. 357–9.
26. Solodovnikov and Bogoslovsky, *Non-Capitalist Development*, pp. 88–9.
27. Andrei Kolosov, 'Reappraisal of USSR Third World Policy', IA, No.5, 1990, pp. 35-6.
28. P. Novoselov, ed., *Problems of the Communist Movement* (Moscow: Progress, 1980) p. 42.
29. Trepelkov, *General Crisis of Capitalism*, p. 16.
30. *Fund*, p. 221.
31. Brezhnev, Report to the 25th Congress of the CPSU, p. 34.
32. *Fund*, p. 83.
33. Boris Ponomarev, *Lenin and the World Revolutionary Process* (Moscow: Progress, 1980) p. 73.
34. Cited in *Fund*, p. 78.
35. Trepelkov, *General Crisis of Capitalism*, p. 89.
36. Igor Andreyev, *The Non–Capitalist Way*, (Moscow: Progress, 1977), p. 19.
37. MESW, Vol. 2, p. 405.
38. LCW, Vol. 31, p. 244.
39. Kosolapov, *Problems of Socialist Theory*, p. 19.
40. *Fund*, p. 346.
41. Ibid., p. 97.
42. Karen Brutents, *National Liberation Revolutions Today* (Moscow: Progress, 1977), Vol. 2, p. 57.

43. Julius Nyerere, *The Basis of African Socialism*, cited in ibid., Vol. 2, p. 58.
44. See Brutents, *National Liberation*, Vol. 1, pp. 74–7.
45. 'Socialist Orientation: Reality and Illusions', IA, No. 7 1988, p. 84.
46. Ibid.
47. *New York Times*, 6 September 1993.
48. Interview, *The Guardian*, 2 May 1990.
49. 'Communist Manifesto', in MESW p. 39.
50. 'Developing Countries, Socialism, Capitalism', IA, March 1989, pp. 61–2.
51. 'National and International in Foreign Policy', IA, June 1989.

Chapter 9 Conclusion

1. 'Theses on Feuerbach', in MESW, p. 30.
2. 'The Class Struggle Today', PA, September–October 1993, p. 7.
3. Abdusalam Guseinov, Vadim Mezhuyev and Valentin Tolstykh, 'The Apparat, The Party and Power', MN, No. 5, 1990.
4. This point is discussed at some length in Chapter 4 above.
5. P. Novoselov, (ed.) ,*Problems of the Communist Movement* (Moscow: Progress, 1975) p. 11. Cited in Chapter 7 above.
6. *Communist Manifesto*, in MESW, p. 36.
7. *Principles of Communism*, in ME, Vol. 6, pp. 352–3.
8. *State and Revolution*, in LCW, Vol. 25, p. 469.
9. *Eighteenth Brumaire of Louis Bonaparte*, in MESW, p. 97.
10. Boris Leibson, *International Unity of Communists* (Moscow: Novosti, 1981), p. 61.
11. *Left–Wing Communism*, in MESW, p. 516.
12. Rosa Luxemburg, 'Organizational Questions of the Russian Social-Democracy', (1904), in *The Russian Revolution and Leninism or Marxism?* (Ann Arbor, Mich.: University of Michigan Press, 1961,) p. 96.

Bibliography

Books

Developed Socialism: Theory and Practice, Moscow: Progress, 1980.

Documents of the International Conference of Communist and Workers' Parties (Moscow, 5–17 June 1969). Moscow: Novosti, 1969, p.14.

Fundamentals of Marxism-Leninism, a Manual, Moscow: Foreign Languages, 1963.

Fundamentals of Marxist-Leninist Theory and Tactics of Revolutionary Parties, Moscow: Progress Institute of Social Sciences, 1985.

The History of the CPSU (Short Course), New York: International Publishers, 1939; Moscow: Foreign Languages, 1960.

Important Documents of the Great Proletarian Cultural Revolution in China, Beijing: Foreign Language Press, 1970.

Marxism-Leninism and the Present Epoch (Documents of an International Conference), special supplement of the journal, *Socialism: Theory and Practice,* Moscow: Novosti, 1980.

Marxist-Leninist Aesthetics and the Arts, Moscow: Progress, 1980.

Polemic on the General Line of the International Communist Movement, Beijing: Foreign Language Press, 1965.

Principles of Party Organization, Adopted at the Third Congress of the Communist International, 1921, Calcutta: Books & Periodicals, 1977.

Programme and Theses Adopted by the Sixth World Congress, 1928, reprinted Montreal: International Correspondence.

Socialist Realism in Literature and Art, anthology of articles, Moscow: Progress, 1971.

Strange Death of Soviet Communism, Special Issue of *The National Interest,* Washington, DC., 1993.

Twenty-Fifth Congress of the CPSU (Documents & Resolutions), Moscow: Novosti, 1976.

Twenty-Sixth Congress of the CPSU (Documents & Resolutions), Moscow: Novosti, 1981.

Twenty-Seventh Congress of the CPSU (Documents & Resolutions), Moscow: Novosti, 1986.

What Is Leninism? New York: International, 1936.

What Do You Have To Say? (Soviet comments on Perestroika). Moscow: Novosti, 1988.

Abalkin, Leonid: *The Strategy of Economic Development in the USSR*, Moscow: Progress, 1986.

Adoratsky, V.: *Dialectical Materialism*, New York: International, 1934.

Afanasyev, V.: *Socialism and Communism*, Moscow: Progress, 1972.

— *Fundamentals of Scientific Communism*, Moscow: Progress, 1977.

Aganbegyan, Abel: *The Economic Challenge of Perestroika*, Bloomington, Ind.: Indiana University Press, 1988.

— ed., *Perestroika 1989*, New York: Scribners, 1988.

— *Inside Perestroika*, New York: Harper & Row, 1989.

Ali, Tariq, ed.: *The Stalinist Legacy*, Boulder, Colo.: Lynne Rienner, 1985.

Almond, Gabriel: *The Appeals of Communism*, Princeton, NJ: Princeton University Press, 1954.

Amin, Samir: *Eurocentrism*, New York: Monthly Review, 1989.

Andreyev, Igor: *The Non-Capitalist Way*, Moscow: Progress, 1977

Aslund, Anders: *Gorbachev's Struggle for Economic Reform*, Ithaca, NY: Cornell University Press, 1989.

Balibar, Etienne: *On the Dictatorship of the Proletariat*, London: New Left Books, 1977.

Bernstein, Eduard: *Evolutionary Socialism*, New York: Schocken Books, 1961.

Blackburn, Robin: *After the Fall*, London: Verso, 1991.

Boffa, Giuseppe: *Inside the Khrushchev Era*, New York: Marzani & Munsell, 1959.

Bottomore, Tom, et al.: *A Dictionary of Marxist Thought*, Cambridge, Mass.: Harvard University Press, 1987.

Brumberg, Abraham, ed.: *Chronicle of a Revolution*, New York: Pantheon, 1990.

Brutents, Karen: *National Liberation Revolutions Today*, 2 vols., Moscow: Progress, 1977.

Bukharin, N. and Preobrazhensky, E.: *The ABC of Communism*, ed. E.H. Carr, Harmondsworth: Penguin, 1969.

Butenko, Anatoli: *Theory & Practice of Real Socialism*, Moscow: Novosti, 1983.

Byrnes, Robert F.: *After Brezhnev: Sources of Soviet Conduct in the 1980s*, Bloomington, Ind.: Indiana University Press, 1983.

Cameron, Kenneth Neill, *Stalin: Man of Contradiction*, Toronto: New Canada Publications, 1987.

Carr, E. H.: *The Bolshevik Revolution*, 3 vols., New York: Macmillan, 1950.

— *Socialism in One Country 1924–1926*, 3 vols. New York: Macmillan, 1958.

— and R. W. Davies: *Foundations of a Planned Economy*, Vols 1 and 2, New York: Macmillan, 1969, 1971.

— *Twilight of the Comintern, 1930–1935*, New York: Pantheon, 1982.

Charney, George: *A Long Journey*, Chicago: Quadrangle, 1968.

Chekharin, Evgeny: *The Soviet Political System under Developed Socialism*, Moscow: Progress, 1977.

Chernikov, G.: *The Crisis of Capitalism and the Condition of the Working People*, Moscow: Progress, 1980.

Chirkin, V., and Yudin, Yu.: *A Socialist Oriented State*, Moscow: Progress, 1983.

Claudin, Fernando: *The Communist Movement from Comintern to Cominform*, 2 vols., New York: Monthly Review, 1975

Cohen, Stephen F.: *Bukharin and the Bolshevik Revolution*, New York: Oxford University Press, 1971.

— ed., *An End to Silence*, New York: Norton, 1982.

— ed., *The Soviet Union Since Stalin*, Bloomington: Indiana University Press, 1980.

— and vanden Heuvel, Katrina: *Voices of Glasnost*, New York: Norton, 1989.

Cornforth, Maurice: *Materialism and the Dialectical Method*, New York: International, 1953.

— *Historical Materialism*, New York: International, 1954.

Corrigna, Philip, et. al.: *Socialist Construction and Marxist Theory*, New York: Monthly Review, 1978.

Dallin, David: *Soviet Foreign Policy after Stalin*, Philadelphia: J. R. Lippincott, 1961.

Daniels, Robert V.: *A Documentary History of Communism*, 2 vols., New York: Random House, 1960.

Daubier, Jean: *A History of the Chinese Cultural Revolution*, New York: Random House, 1974.

Davies, R.W.: *The Socialist Offensive (The Collectivization of Soviet Agriculture, 1929–30)*, Cambridge, Mass.: Harvard University Press, 1980.

— *Soviet History in the Gorbachev Revolution*, Bloomington: Indiana University Press, 1989.

Deutscher, Isaac: *The Prophet Unarmed, Trotsky: 1921–1929*, New York: Knopf, 1959.

— *The Prophet Outcast, Trotsky: 1929–1940*, New York: Knopf, 1963.

— *The Prophet Armed, Trotsky: 1879–1921*, New York: Knopf, 1965.

— *Stalin: A Political Biography*, Oxford: Oxford University Press, 1967.
— *Marxism in our Time*, Berkeley, Calif.: Ramparts Press, 1971.
Dimitrov, Georgi: *For the Unity of the Working Class Against Fascism (Report to the 7th Congress of the Communist International)*, London: Red Star Press, 1975.
Draper, Theodore: *American Communism and Soviet Russia*, Reprinted, New York: Octagon Books, 1977.
Dubcek, Alexander: *Hope Dies Last*, New York: Kodansha International, 1993.
Dyker, David A.: *The Soviet Economy*, New York: St. Martin's Press, 1976.

Edmonds, Robin: *Soviet Foreign Policy 1962–1973*, New York: Oxford University Press, 1975.
— *Soviet Foreign Policy: The Brezhnev Years*, New York: Oxford University Press, 1983.
Eisen, Jonathan: *The Glasnost Reader*, New York: New American Library, 1990.
Engels, Frederick: *Anti-Dühring*, New York: International, 1966.

Foster, William Z.: *Twilight of World Capitalism*, New York: International, 1949.
— *History of the Communist Party of the United States*, New York: International, 1952.
— *History of the Three Internationals*, New York: International, 1955.
Franklin, Bruce: *The Essential Stalin*, New York: Doubleday, 1972.
Fried, Albert and Sanders, Ronald: *Socialist Thought, a Documentary History*, New York: Doubleday, 1964.

Garthoff, Raymond L.: *Deterrence and the Revolution in Soviet Military Doctrine*, Washington, DC: Brookings Institution, 1990.
Gates, John: *The Story of an American Communist*, New York: Thomas Nelson, 1958.
Gelman, Harry: *The Brezhnev Politburo and the Decline of Detente*, Ithaca, NY: Cornell University Press, 1984.
Gill, Graeme: *Stalinism*, Atlantic Highlands, NJ: Humanities Press, 1990.
Gorbachev, Mikhail: *Political Report of the CPSU Central Committee to the 27th Party Congress*, Moscow: Novosti, 1986.
— *For a Nuclear-Free World*, Moscow: Novosti, 1987.
— *October and Perestroika*, Moscow: Novosti, 1987.

— On the Tasks of the Party in the Radical Restructuring of Economic
    Management, Report to the Plenary Meeting of the CPSU Central
    Committee, 25–6 June 1987.
— Perestroika, New York: Harper & Row, 1987.
— Reorganization and the Party's Personnel Policy, report to a Plenary
    Meeting of the CPSU Central Committee, 27 January 1987,
    Moscow: Novosti, 1987.
— On the Agrarian Policy of the CPSU in the Present Conditions,
    Moscow: Novosti, 1989.
— Report to the 19th All-Union Conference of the CPSU, Moscow:
    Novosti, 1989.
Guest, David: A Textbook of Dialectical Materialism, New York: Interna-
    tional, 1939.

Hanak, H.: Soviet Foreign Policy Since the Death of Stalin, London:
    Routledge & Kegan Paul, 1972.
Harrington, Michael: Socialism, New York: E.P. Dutton, 1972.
— The Twilight of Capitalism, New York: Simon & Schuster, 1976.
— The Next Left, New York: Henry Holt, 1986.
Healey, Dorothy: Dorothy Healey Remembers, New York: Oxford Univer-
    sity Press, 1990.
Heinman, S. A.: Scientific and Technical Revolution: Economic Aspects,
    Moscow: Progress, 1981.
Ho Chi Minh on Revolution: New York: Praeger, 1967.
Hosking, Geoffrey: The First Socialist Society, Cambridge, Mass.: Harvard
    University Press, 1985.
Howe, Irving and Coser, Lewis: The American Communist Party, New
    York: Praeger, 1962.

Inozemtsev, N.: Contemporary Capitalism: New Developments and Con-
    tradictions, Moscow: Progress, 1974.
Institute of Marxism-Leninism (CC/CPSU), Outline History of the
    Communist International, Moscow: Progress, 1971.

Kagarlitsky, Boris: The Thinking Reed, London: Verso, 1988.
Kaiser, Robert G.: Why Gorbachev Happened, New York: Simon &
    Schuster, 1992.
Kennan, George F.: Russia and the West Under Lenin and Stalin, Boston:
    Little, Brown, 1960.
— Soviet Foreign Policy 1917–1941, Princeton, NJ: Van Nostrand, 1960.
Khachaturov, T.: The Economy of the Soviet Union Today, Moscow:
    Progress, 1977.

Khrushchev, Nikita: *Khrushchev Remembers*, Boston: Little, Brown, 1970.
Khrushchev, Sergei: *Khrushchev on Khrushchev*, Boston: Little, Brown, 1990.
Kiselov, Victor: *Socialism: Crisis or Renewal*, Moscow: Progress, 1989.
Kolko, Gabriel: *Confronting the Third World, U.S. Foreign Policy 1945-1980*, New York: Pantheon, 1988.
Kosolapov, Richard: *Problems of Socialist Theory*, Moscow: Progress, 1974.
Kozlov, G.A., ed.: *Political Economy: Socialism*, Moscow: Progress, 1977.
Kuznetsov, B.G.: *Philosophy of Optimism*, Moscow: Progress, 1977.

Le Duan: *The Vietnamese Revolution: Fundamental Problems, Essential Tasks*, Hanoi: Foreign Languages, 1973.
Leibson, Boris: *International Unity of Communists*, Moscow: Novosti, 1981.
Lenin, V. I.: *Collected Works*, Moscow: Progress, 1966.
— *Selected Works in One Volume*, New York: International, 1971.
Leontiev, A.: *Political Economy*, New York: International, 1975.
Lewin, Moshe: *Political Undercurrents in Soviet Economic Debates*, Princeton, NJ: Princeton University Press, 1974.
Linden, Karl A.: *Khrushchev and the Soviet Leadership 1957–1964*, Baltimore, Md.: Johns Hopkins University Press, 1966.
Luxemburg, Rosa: *The Russian Revolution* and *Leninism or Marxism?*, Ann Arbor, Mich.: University of Michigan Press, 1961.
— *The Accumulation of Capital*, New York: Monthly Review, 1968.

Mao Zhedong: *On the Correct Handling of Contradictions Among the People*, New York: New Century Publishers, 1957.
— *A Critique of Soviet Economics*, New York: Monthly Review, 1977.
Marx, Karl: *Capital*, New York: International, 1967.
— and Engels Frederich: *Selected Correspondence*, Moscow: Foreign Languages, 1953.
— *Selected Works in One Volume*, New York: International, 1968.
— *Selected Works*, 3 vols Moscow: Progress, 1970.
— *Collected Works*, New York: International, 1975.
—, —, and Lenin, *On Scientific Communism*, Moscow: Progress, 1967.
— *On Historical Materialism*, Moscow: Progress, 1972.
— *On Dialectical Materialism*, Moscow: Progress, 1977.
Medvedev, Roy: *On Socialist Democracy*, New York: Norton, 1975.
— *Political Essays*, London: Bertrand Russell Peace Foundation, 1976.
— *Leninism and Western Socialism*, London: Verso, 1981.
— *Let History Judge*, New York: Columbia University Press, 1989.

— and Zhores A. Medvedev: *Khrushchev: The Years in Power*, New York: Norton, 1978.

Medvedev, Zhores A.: *Gorbachev*, New York: Norton, 1986.

Mehring, Franz: *Karl Marx*, Ann Arbor, Mich.: University of Michigan Press, 1962.

Meyer, Alfred G.: *Leninism*, New York: Praeger, 1967.

Nove, Alec: *An Economic History of the USSR*, Harmondsworth: Penguin 1969.

Novosolev, P., ed.: *Problems of the Communist Movement*, Moscow: Progress, 1975.

Ponomarev, Boris: *Marxism-Leninism, A Flourishing Science*, New York: International, 1979.

— *Lenin and the World Revolutionary Process*, Moscow: Progress, 1980.

— *Communism in a Changing World*, New York: Sphinx Press, 1983.

— et al., *A Short History of the CPSU*, Moscow: Progress, 1970.

Pozner, Vladimir: *Parting With Illusions*, New York: Atlantic, 1990.

Richmond, Al: *A Long View from the Left*, Boston, Mass.: Houghton Mifflin, 1973.

Rubinstein, Alvin Z.: *Moscow's Third World Strategy*, Princeton, NJ: Princeton University Press, 1988.

Rymalov, V.V.: *The World Capitalist Economy*, Moscow: Progress, 1978.

Schapiro, Leonard: *The Communist Party of the Soviet Union*, New York: Random House, 1960.

Schram, Stuart: *Chairman Mao Talks to the People*, New York: Pantheon, 1974.

Selsam, Howard, et. al., eds: *Reader in Marxist Philosophy*, New York: International, 1963.

— *Dynamics of Social Change (A Reader in Marxist Social Science)*, New York: International, 1970.

Shakhnazarov, Georgi: *The Destiny of the World*, Moscow: Progress, 1979.

— *The Coming World Order*, Moscow: Progress, 1981.

Shub, David: *Lenin*, Baltimore, Md: Pelican, 1967.

Slovo, Joe: *Has Socialism Failed?* London: Inkululeko, 1990.

Solodovnikov, V., and Bogoslovsky, V.: *Non-Capitalist Development: An Historical Outline*, Moscow: Progress, 1975.

Stalin, Josef: *Dialectical and Historical Materialism*, New York: International, 1940.
— *Marxism and the National Question*, New York: International, 1942.
— *The War of National Liberation*, New York: International, 1942.
— *The Great Patriotic War of the Soviet Union*, New York: International, 1945.
— *Mastering Bolshevism*, New York: New Century, 1946.
— *On Lenin*, Moscow: Foreign Languages, 1946.
— *Economic Problems of Socialism in the USSR*, Moscow, 1952; reprinted in Bruce Franklin, *The Essential Stalin*, New York: Doubleday, 1972.
— *Anarchism or Socialism?* New York: International, 1953.
— *Works*, 13 vols., Moscow: Foreign Languages, 1954–55.
— *Problems of Leninism*, Moscow: Foreign Languages, 1958.
— *Marxism and Problems of Linguistics*, Beijing: Foreign Languages, 1972.
— *On Organization*, Calcutta: New Book Center, 1975.
— *The National Question and Leninism*, Chicago: Liberator, n.d.
Stanis, Vladimir: *The Socialist Transformation of Agriculture*, Moscow: Progress, 1976.
Starobin, Joseph: *American Communism in Crisis, 1943–1957*, Berkeley, Calif.: University of California Press, 1973.
Strong, Anna Louise: *The Stalin Era*, New York: Mainstream, 1956.
Suslov, Mikhail: *Speech at the 20th Congress of the CPSU*, Moscow: Foreign Languages, 1956.
— *Leninism and the Revolutionary Transformation of the World*, Moscow: Progress, 1971.
Sweezy, Paul M.: *Post-Revolutionary Society*, New York: Monthly Review, 1980.
— and Bettelheim, Charles: *On The Transition to Socialism*, New York: Monthly Review, 1971.

Thomson, George: *From Marx to Mao Tse-Tung*, London: China Policy Study Group, 1971.
Tikhonov, Vladimir: *Soviet Economy: Achievements, Problems, Prospects*, Moscow: Novosti, 1983.
Trepelkov, V.: *The General Crisis of Capitalism*, Moscow: Progress, 1983.
Trotsky, Leon: *The Russian Revolution*, New York: Doubleday, 1959.
— *The Revolution Betrayed*, New York: Pathfinder, 1972.
— *Basic Writings*, edited by Irving Howe, New York: Schocken, 1976.
Tsipko, Alexander S.: *Is Stalinism Really Dead?* San Francisco: Harper Collins, 1990.

Tucker, Robert C.: *Stalin as Revolutionary*, New York: Norton, 1973.
— *Stalin in Power*, New York: Norton, 1990.

Ulam, Adam B.: *Expansion and Coexistence: The History of Soviet Foreign Policy 1917–1967*, New York: Praeger, 1968.
— *The Communists*, New York: Scribners, 1992.

Volkogonov, Dmitri: *Stalin: Triumph and Tragedy*, New York: Grove Weidenfeld, 1988.

Waller, Michael: *Democratic Centralism*, Manchester: Manchester University Press, 1981.
Werth, Alexander: *Russia Under Khrushchev*, New York: Hill & Wang, 1962.
Wolfe, Bertram D.: *Marxism: 100 Years in the Life of a Doctrine*, New York: Dial, 1965.
— *An Ideology in Power*, New York: Stein & Day, 1969.

Yevtushenko, Yevgeny: *Fatal Half Measures: The Culture of Democracy in the Soviet Union*, Boston: Little, Brown, 1991.

Zarodov, Konstantin: *The Political Economy of Revolution*, Moscow: Progress, 1981.
Zimmerman, William: *Soviet Perspectives on International Relations 1956–1967*, Princeton, NJ: Princeton University Press, 1967.

Periodicals

Asia and Africa Today, Moscow.
Crossroads (monthly) Oakland, California.
The Current Digest of the Soviet Press, Columbus, Ohio.
International Affairs (monthly), Moscow.
Kommunist, Theoretical Journal of the CPSU, Moscow.
Literary Gazette, Moscow.
Moscow News (weekly), Moscow
New Times (weekly), Moscow.
Political Affairs, theoretical journal of the US Communist Party, NY.
Social Sciences, USSR Academy of Sciences, Moscow.
Socialism: Theory and Practice (monthly), Moscow
Soviet Life (monthly), Moscow
World Marxist Review, Prague (through February, 1990)

Journal and Magazine Articles

Aleksandrov, Yevgeni, 'New Political Thinking: Genesis, Factors, Prospects', IA, December 1987.

Antonovich, Ivan, 'Dialectics of an Integral World', IA, May 1988.

Bovin, Alexander, 'Why the Afghan Revolution Failed', *Izvestia* 23 December 1988, in DIG, Vol. 50, No. 51.

Dansokho, Amath, 'Perestroika is for Everyone', WMR, February 1990.

Hall, Gus, 'Forging Unity through Struggle' PA, January 1992.

— Interview, PA, August 1992.

Kautsky, John H., 'Karl Kautsky and Eurocommunism', *Studies in Comparative Communism*, IA, March 1989.

— 'Developing Countries, Socialism, Capitalism' IA, March 1989.

Kiva, Aleksei, 'Socialist Orientation: Reality and Illusions' IA, July 1988.

Kommunist editors, 'J. V. Stalin and the Individual in History', PA, July 1980.

Kulikov, Vsevolod, 'Economic Laws of Socialism', *Social Sciences*, USSR Academy of Sciences, Vol. 4, 1990.

Lee, Vladimir and Mirsky, George: 'Socialist Orientation and New Political Thinking', *Asia & Africa Today*, April 1988.

Lisichkin, Gennadi, 'Myths and Reality', *Social Sciences*, Vols 1 and 2, 1990.

Mishkin, Alexander V., 'The Crisis of Marxism-Leninism', *New Outlook*, Fall 1990.

Popov, Gavriil, 'Evolution of Bureaucracy and Ways to Surmount It', STP, September 1989.

Sheinis, Victor, 'Structural Shifts in the Capitalist Economy and the Developing Nations' Prospects', *Asia & Africa Today*, No. 6, 1988.

Silber, Irwin, 'The Unquiet Passing of Marxism-Leninism', *Crossroads*, December 1990.

Symposium, 'Socialism: What Went Wrong?', *Crossroads*, November 1992.

Tarpinian, Gregory, 'Labor and the Global Economy', *Crossroads*, February 1991.

Tsipko, Alexander, 'The Roots of Stalinism, Science and Life', Moscow 1988 in DIG, 5, 12, 19, 26 April 1989.

Valkenier, Elizabeth Kridl: 'New Soviet Thinking About the Third World', *World Policy Journal*, Fall 1987.

Zaradov, Konstantin, 'Leninism and Some Questions of Internationalism', WMR, April 1982.

Index